Racism

Kevin Reilly, Series Editor

Racism

A GLOBAL
READER

Edited by
Kevin Reilly
Stephen Kaufman
Angela Bodino

M.E. Sharpe
Armonk, New York
London, England

Library of Congress Cataloging-in-Publication Data

Racism : a global reader / Kevin Reilly, Stephen Kaufman, and Angela Bodino, editors.
    p. cm. — (Sources and studies in world history)
Includes bibliographical references and index.
ISBN 0-7656-1059-0 (alk. paper) — ISBN 0-7656-1050-4 (pbk.: alk. paper)
  1. Racism. 2. Racism—History 3. Race relations—History. 4. Colonies. I. Reilly,
Kevin, 1941– II. Kaufman, Stephen, 1946– III. Bodino, Angela, 1940– IV. Series.

HT1521.R323 2003
305.8—dc21   2002066803

Printed in the United States of America

The paper used in this publication meets the minimum requirements of
American National Standard for Information Sciences
Permanence of Paper for Printed Library Materials,
ANSI Z 39.48-1984.

BM (c)   10   9   8   7   6   5   4   3   2   1
BM (p)   10   9   8   7   6   5   4   3   2   1

Contents

Foreword

When I began editing this series thirteen years ago, world history was a young field, with an uncertain future and infinite possibilities. Our title for the series, "Sources and Studies in World History" cast a wide net. Early volumes included a medieval Islamic primary source, an atlas of south Asia, a classic philosophy of history, and a short interpretive text in world history that was used in numerous introductory classes. Contemplating such diversity, a new editor at M.E. Sharpe asked if the series had any unifying theme beyond my desire to see each particular manuscript in print. I believed then, and now, that the variety of titles was neither capricious nor subjective. I felt a need for a wide range of materials to enable world history to grow as a teaching and research field, but I also wanted the series to point numerous roads to world history.

In the intervening years the first goal has been largely met. There are now abundant sources, primary and secondary, for students and teachers of world history. But the second need—to keep world history young, varied, experimental, and ever open to new approaches—requires even more resolute effort today.

Like an American teenager, world history has matured very rapidly. Under the aegis of university priorities, it has chosen a major and prepared for graduate school. Eschewing both grand visions and the entrenched specialties of other historians, the "new world history" has won academic respect by setting its sights on global themes like cultural encounters, biotic transfers, trade and technological diffusion, environment and climate, and migrations and diasporas. As a model for original research and graduate school education it would be hard to imagine a more fruitful strategy. However, undergraduates and the general public have traditionally looked to world history for something more: an ability to address the world's problems. Early in the twentieth century, the proponents of an older "new history" argued that a general history course ought to help people read the daily newspaper.

While faculty at many universities are pressed to view undergraduate education through the prism of the graduate school, we who teach at community colleges are still able to begin with the needs and interests of our introductory students, who reflect the range and diversity of our entire society. We can train citizens, rather than graduate students, by helping our students think more independently, critically, and historically about the problems that confront them and their world.

Racism is one of the most critical problems of the modern world. Yet, because of academic specialization and provincial perspectives, it is often approached piecemeal. Historians and social scientists in the United States have long studied racism as a "white/black" issue in temperate, mainland, middle North America, where "global diversity" means studying the range of immigrants to "America." Students of anti-Semitism or the Holocaust rarely compare notes with those who study caste or communal tensions in South Asia. Case studies and theoretical constructs are rarely passed across disciplines or area studies.

Racism: A Global Reader is intended to stimulate a more global and more interdisciplinary discussion about racism. The book is an outgrowth of a course called "Global Patterns of Racism: Literary, Anthropological, and Historical Perspectives," which we have been teaching at Raritan Valley College for almost ten years. The response from students, including alumni of an Internet version for secondary school teachers, public servants, and professionals, has encouraged us to seek a wider audience.

I thank my co-editors, Angela Bodino, professor of English literature, and Steve Kaufman, professor of anthropology, for generously allowing me to include our *Reader* in a series on world history, thus indulging my desire to demand the largest tent for history. It is my way of continuing the argument that history is too important to be left only to the historians, and that world history is not only a new sub-field of an ancient discipline; it is also a useful tool for our survival.

Kevin Reilly
Series Editor

Introduction and Acknowledgments

We recognized that we needed a college course and a book of readings on racism at our college when a Sunday afternoon lecture on the Holocaust by Elie Wiesel was interrupted by young men wearing Nazi armbands and shouting antiblack and anti-Semitic epithets. While there was something bizarre about this theatrical display of bigotry on a quiet suburban campus in one of the wealthiest counties in the country over fifty years after the end of World War II, there was also something ominous and foreboding in the anger and ignorance of those who would be our students. We decided something had to be done.

Thanks to a rich tradition of interdisciplinary teaching at Raritan Valley College, and with the help of a grant from Princeton University, the three of us—professors of history, anthropology, and literature—were able to meet regularly over the course of two years to plan and refine a series of lessons on racism that transcended the usual limits of discipline and field.

From the start, we knew that we had to help our students understand racism as a global problem. We wanted to overcome the tendency in our political culture to see problems only in the light of personal reflection: "If it's about me, I care; otherwise I can't be bothered." And we wanted to break away from the bias of our academic culture to channel all questions into the deepest grooves. We knew there was neither a course nor a book to do what we felt was necessary—to approach racism throughout the world and throughout history without reducing everything to an abstract universal (e.g., hate or human nature) that explained nothing because it covered everything. We wanted to survey a wide range of human behavior in its variety and concreteness, and still define patterns that would provide meaning and explanation. We wanted to understand the global patterns of racism.

We would like to thank the administration at Raritan Valley College, especially President G. Jeremiah Ryan and Vice President Marie Gnage, and their predecessors, Cary Israel and Charlotte Ravitz, for supporting the course and encouraging our work with the generous grant of release time and sabbatical leaves. In mounting the course for Internet instruction, Vice President Chuck Chulvick, Executive Director Mike Machnik, and Instructional Designer Holly Smythe provided invaluable assistance.

Throughout the development of the text and the course, colleagues in the college community helped us broaden the base of the conversation. Board member Evelyn Field, who participated in our first offering of the course, and English Department chair Carroll Wilson were early champions. Holocaust survivors Henry Sattler and Margit Feldman inspired us. Professors Siham Alfred and Glenn Ricketts helped us refine reading selections. Librarians Mary Ann Ryer and Debbie Dulepski and Instructional Designer Lonny Buinis helped us track down selections and illustrations.

Colleagues at Rutgers University provided both support and important perspectives: Michael Adas of the History Department, Len Bethel of the Department of Africana Studies, Dorothy Strickland of the Graduate School of Education at Rutgers University, and Michael Smith, chair of the Literacy Cluster of the Graduate School of Education and director of the National Writing Project site at Rutgers in partnership with Raritan Valley College.

National awards from Princeton University's Title VI program and the Instructional Administrators of the Association of Community Colleges provided moral as well as financial support. We are grateful for the encouragement and expertise of our editor Andrew Gyory, himself a historian of racism, and for Esther Clark's painstaking attention to the details of publication. We thank our inspired and inspiring students, not least Jackie Faigenbaum, Tony Kansagor, Debbie Bonanni, Patricia Brock, and Dan Teodoru, who have given us a renewed sense of energy and optimism even as the tensions engendered by racism become ever more present and perilous across the globe. Most important, we are grateful for the faith of our spouses Pearl, Phyllis, and Bud who inspired us when hope faltered and who remind us that love of humanity is the norm and racism the anomaly.

Racism

Part 1

Race: Definitions and Problems

The tools of "scientific racism" included calipers to measure the nose, beads to fill a skull, and the new invention of photography: in short, anything that would mark and measure human differences. *(Courtesy of United States Holocaust Memorial Museum Photo Archives)*

A book about racism must begin with some definitions. It would seem that, at the very least, we need to know what "race" is if we are to understand racism. In this section, we suggest the contrary, that a definition of "race" is not easy, and that many experts dispute even the need for such a definition. Further, we argue that we do not have to know what race is (or even whether there is such a thing as race) in order to recognize racism.

There is little scholarly agreement on the meaning of the term "race." A considerable part of the academic and scientific community now believes there is no such thing as race. This is a surprise to most people who think in such categories, and to many people who act as if race is an important fact. In other words, while race might be what social scientists call a social construct (society's invention), it is one that many people take very seriously in their thoughts and actions.

What do those scientists mean when they say that there is no such thing as race? Actually, they may mean a number of things. If the emphasis is on "thing," they may mean that race does not exist like sunlight, the oceans, or elephants; it is not an unchanging reality, recognizable to every observer in a similar way. This is what is meant when one says that race is a social construct. It is a category that our society uses to organize its world. We decide that there are "x" races in the world and then attribute a particular racial identity to people we see. Other societies have not divided their worlds into races, or have constructed different racial orderings.

Another reason for questioning the reality of race is this recognition that people define themselves and each other in many different ways—even when they think they are using racial categories. Steven A. Holmes' "You're Smart If You Know What Race You Are" makes this point. You may be even smarter if you do *not* "know what race you are."

Classifying people according to race is an exercise replete with problems. Race is intended as a category to be used for distinguishing different human groups on the basis of physical appearance. Skin color is most frequently used, but one could also use blood type, hair, eyes, noses and other facial features, or even, these days, DNA. One problem is that all of these characteristics exist in the real world in mixed bags. Not only does something like skin color change gradually from one locality to another (with variations even within a locality), but changes in skin color may not be related to changes in any of the other characteristics mentioned above. There is as much variation within a single race as there is between people of different races.

Yet, as Holmes notes, a larger percentage of anthropologists still think there is something that one could call race. Surely anyone can distinguish between a person whose ancestry is Scandinavian and one whose ancestors came from the Congo. The fact is that human populations have bred with neighbors (and local strangers) for longer and more continuous periods than they have migrated long distances for spouses.

Current scientific opinion about the meaning of race is summarized in Robert S. Boyd's "Color's Only Skin Deep: More Scientists Rejecting Race Concept, Saying It's a Social Idea with No Biological Reality." The question remains that even if we dismiss the traditional notion whether any sense can be made of the concept. Surely there has been some continuity of breeding populations in world history. What that continuity means is another question. We might feel fairly confident that we can see it in physical characteristics, and in some obvious cases we can. But if there are no necessary connections among physical characteristics, we would be hard pressed to find behavioral characteristics that parallel physical ones.

You're Smart If You Know What Race You Are

Steven A. Holmes

What difficulties does Holmes cite in classifying people according to race? Are there any scientific reasons for classifying people by race? Does race have any meaning? If so, what is it?

What do you make of the fact that only 50 percent of physical and cultural anthropologists agreed that there is such a thing as race while 41 percent disagreed?

Do you think there is such a thing as race?

Can you recognize the physical differences among people and still think there is no such thing as race?

As the conversation about race and racism swells to a cacophony of accusations, defenses and rationalizations, one question seems not to have been addressed: what do we mean by race, anyhow?

At first blush the answer seems self-evident. There are black people, and yellow people, and white people and red people, aren't there? Everyone knows that.

But in recent years there is a surprising lack of agreement among scientists over the popular notion of what constitutes a racial group. And even in their book, "The Bell Curve," which suggests that differences in intelligence between races are a matter of inheritance, Richard J. Herrnstein and Charles Murray duck the question. "The rule we follow here is a simple one," they write, "to classify people according to the way they classify themselves."

That might be a fine standard for measuring racial disparities in housing, income or employment. But when it's applied to biology, things get murky. Racial categories, especially in the United States, are often more poetry than science. American blacks almost invariably have some white ancestry, so their classification has more to do with politics and culture than with genes. . . .

Those looking to science to help clarify the issue may have to search elsewhere. In a 1985 survey of physical and cultural anthropologists, 50 percent agreed that there is such a thing as race, biologically speaking, and 41 percent disagreed.

"That's a revolution," said Leonard Lieberman, a professor of sociology and anthropology at Central Michigan University, who conducted the study. "Here is a concept around which this discipline had its beginnings. But now there is no longer a consensus."

Few scientists doubt that there are genetic differences between groups, but many say any diversion of Homo sapiens into four or five discrete groups is arbitrary. Take skin color, the most commonly cited racial trait. Does it help science distinguish among the sub-Saharan Africans, the people of the southern India and aboriginal people of Australia? All have dark skin. But the three are considered to be of different races.

Some of the other genetic similarities between peoples make for interesting groupings.

Jared Diamond, a professor of physiology at the U.C.L.A. School of Medicine, notes that only Eastern European Jews and French Canadians are genetically predisposed to Tay Sachs disease. Does that make them a racial group? Likewise, the gene that produces sickle cell anemia is relatively common among Africans, the people of the Arabian Peninsula and southern India. But it is rare among Northern Europeans and the Xhosa people of South Africa. Does that make Nelson Mandela and Bjorn Borg racial kin?

"We have information about far more similarities and differences among people based on traits other than skin color," Professor Diamond said. "But traditionally we have classified people by what we can actually see."

Anthropologists who defend the notion of race argue that while skin color may not be the best determinant, people who trace ancestry to the same geographic neighborhood and have similar inherited characteristics ought to be considered a single group.

"Races refer to geographically separated portions of species that are distinguishable by inherited characteristics," said Vincent Sarich, a professor of anthropology at the University of California at Berkeley, "That in no sense says that, therefore, all human variations need be explained racially."

It is hardly a wonder that some scientists feel the best way to approach the concept of race is not to.

"Historically, the word has been used in so many different ways that it's no longer useful in our science," Douglas Ubelaker, a physical anthropologist and a curator with the Smithsonian Institution's National Museum of Natural History, said recently in Discover magazine. "I choose not to define it at all. I leave the term alone."

Color's Only Skin Deep: More Scientists Rejecting Race Concept, Saying It's a Social Idea with No Biological Reality

Robert S. Boyd

What is the current state of science on race? In this selection, the author surveys a number of leading scientists and researchers in new fields such as molecular biology and genetics, as well as older fields such as anthropology. Their conclusions may surprise you.

How do you reconcile their dismissal of race with the commonsense recognition of human differences and even the practical applications of such specialists as forensic scientists?

If there were no such thing as race, and if people recognized that, would racism disappear?

Knight-Ridder Tribune News. As published in the *Houston Chronicle* on November 11, 1996, p. 8. Reprinted with permission of Knight Ridder/Tribune Information Services.

WASHINGTON—Thanks to spectacular advances in molecular biology and genetics, most scientists now reject the concept of race as a valid way to divide human beings into separate groups.

Contrary to public opinion, most researchers say they no longer believe races are distinct biological categories created by differences in the genes that people inherit from their parents. Genes vary, they say, but not in ways that correspond to the popular notion of black, white, yellow, red or brown races.

"Race has no basic biological reality," said Jonathan Marks, a Yale University biologist. "The human species simply doesn't come packaged that way."

A majority of biologists and anthropologists, drawing on evidence accumulated since the1970s, have concluded that race is a social, cultural and political concept based largely on superficial appearances.

"In the social sense, race is a reality; in the scientific sense, it is not," said Michael Omi, a specialist in ethnic studies at the University of California in Berkeley.

Luigi Cavalli-Sforza, a eminent professor of genetics at Stanford University, agreed. "The characteristics that we see with the naked eye that help us to distinguish individuals from different continents are, in reality, skin-deep," he said. "Whenever we look under the veneer, we find that the differences that seem so conspicuous to us are really trivial."

Scientists conceded that people do look different, primarily because of the varied environment in which their ancestors lived. And they agree as a social concept, race matters a great deal. The color of a person's skin, the texture of his hair, or the shape of her eyes can be sources of love, pride and partnership—or fear, hatred and injustice.

The idea that races are not the product of human genes may seem to contradict common sense.

"The average citizen reacts with frank disbelief when told that there is no such thing as race," said C. Loring Brace, an anthropologist at the University of Michigan.

The new understanding of race draws on work in many fields.

"Vast new data in human biology, prehistory and paleontology . . . have completely revamped the traditional notions," said Solomon Katz, an anthropologist at the University of Pennsylvania.

This is a switch from the prevailing scientific dogma of the 19th and much of the 20th century. Most scientists then believed humans could be sorted into inherited racial types distinguished primarily by skin color.

Government policies were based on alleged racial inequalities, including U.S. immigration laws designed to screen out "inferior" foreign stocks, bans on interracial marriage.

As recently as 1985, anthropologists split 50-50 when one of their number, Leonard Lieberman of Central Michigan University, asked in a survey if they believe in separate biological races.

A dwindling number of scholars still cling to notions of gene-based racial superiority. In his controversial 1994 book, "The Bell Curve," Charles Murray, a political scientist, asserted that African-Americans inherit lower intelligence than persons of Asian or European descent.

In response to "The Bell Curve," the American Anthropological Association adopted a statement declaring "differentiating species into biologically defined 'races' has proven meaningless and unscientific as a way of explaining variation, whether in intelligence or other traits."

As a sign of the change, Lieberman said most anthropology textbooks published in this decade have stopped teaching the concept of biological race.

In part, the new consensus is an effort by scientists to stop the misuse of race to justify the evils of racism.

"Misconceptions about race have led to forms of racism that have caused much social, psychological and physical harm," said Katz. "These misconceptions have their origin in various papers and books that depend heavily on old and outmoded biological concepts of race."

But the revised concept of race also reflects recent scientific work with DNA, the complex molecule that contains the genes in every living cell.

"The DNA support the concept that you can't draw boundaries around races," said a Yale geneticist, Kenneth Kidd, who studied minute variations in the genes of people from 42 different population groups around the globe.

Kidd said there is actually more genetic variation within a single African population than in all non-African peoples put together.

That is because those Africans that stayed in place gradually accumulated tiny variations in their DNA over thousands of generations. About 100,000 years ago, a few tribes emigrated to Europe, the Middle East and Asia, taking only a small subset of those genes with them. Since the migration, these travelers have not developed as many variations out of their smaller gene pool.

"Genetically, I am more similar to someone from China or the Amazon Basin than two Africans living in the same village are to each other," Kidd said. "This substantiates the point that there is no such thing biologically as race."

According to scientific consensus, physical traits such as skin color, eye shape and susceptibility to disease vary gradually between neighboring populations. Instead of abrupt changes, there are almost imperceptible shadings.

Only when people travel rapidly over great distances—as when slaves were brought from West Africa to America, or a Londoner jets to Tokyo—do the differences become distinct. This is especially true in the United States, which is occupied by immigrants from Europe, Africa and Asia, as well as Native Americans.

"When you sharply juxtapose populations that have been separated so long, of course they look different," said Moore. "But it doesn't last long. Soon they fall in love, marry, have kids, and everybody looks the same. Look at Puerto Rico."

Researchers say differences in skin color—the most common marker for race—arose from a combination of environmental pressures and random genetic mutations.

Most scientists have come to accept the evolutionary theory, based on DNA evidence, that modern humans (the species homo sapiens) originated in equatorial Africa about 200,000 years ago.

Our primitive ancestors' genes were programmed to produce dark skin. Their pigment protected them from the tropical sun's ultraviolet rays, which can cause cancer. The group of Africans who migrated north into Europe benefited from more sunlight, rather than less, because ultraviolet rays also make vitamin D, preventing rickets and other diseases.

By a flip of the genetic dice, some of the newcomers had a variant gene that gave them slightly lighter skin. These tended to get more vitamins, live longer and have more children, who in turn passed the trait on to their descendants.

The trend continued for generation after generation, eventually producing Anglo-Saxons, Swedes and other fair-skinned northern Europeans.

"Skin color genes are turned off and on very quickly in evolution," Moore explained. "People can go from black to white, or white to black, in 10,000 years."

Significantly, populations who live near the equator—in southern India, New Guinea or northern Australia—are just as dark as natives of West Africa, demonstrating that black skin depends more on environment than heredity.

Meanwhile, controversy continues over the possible link between race and intelligence.

Brace, who is writing a book on the subject, contended that intelligence is the only human trait that does not seem to vary from one population to another. Instead, he said basic intellectual capacity is distributed equally among all peoples, regardless of their skin color.

"We do get race differences in intelligence *tests*," Brace conceded, "but that is social, not biological in origin. Environmental and cultural factors—such as poor nutrition, poverty and bad schools—affect IQ scores, but not inherited intellectual capacity," he said.

"The word 'race' has many meanings and many uses, some reputable, some quite disreputable," said John Ladd, a Brown University philosophy professor, who chaired the panel. "We must try to sort out the difference."

Part 2

Toward a Definition of Racism: Some Test Cases

At his homemade stand in New Delhi, India, cobbler Suva Lal repairs shoes. Once known as "untouchables," Lal and other cobblers are known as Dalits. *(Associated Press Photo)*

Even if we cannot define race, we can define racism. That is because even if there is no such thing as race, people have behaved as if there were. Racism is prejudice or discrimination against other people because of their "race" or because of what is thought to be their race (their biology or ancestry or physical appearance). Racism involves the assumption that people's birth or biology determines who they are: that behavior is based on biology.

We will return to the issue of defining racism throughout this book, because it is not as easy as it might seem. You might think we could get a definition from a dictionary or a noted authority and then get on with it. But the reason we cannot is that the meaning of "racism" is not that scientific. Different scholars would give us different definitions. For example, in embracing something like our last definition—that racism is the identification of biology and behavior—we have left out the element of derision, disdain, or hatred. Does racism have to include a denigration of the other? Henry Lewis Gates argues in one of his many writings on the subject that even if no insult is intended, it would be racist for someone to ask him to sing Negro spirituals. Even if the person loved the music and meant no harm by the request, the assumption that because Gates is an African American he must know Negro spirituals would be a racist assumption that biology is behavior. According to this view, any form of stereotyping based on what is thought to be race is racist. This is a fairly strict definition of racism—yet one that does not depend on derision or an idea of inferiority.

Popular definitions of racism run an even wider gamut. For some people, any sign of derision expressed between people of different backgrounds is an expression of racism. But clearly, there can be derision, even hatred, between two people, even two people of different "races," without racism. An Orthodox Jewish rabbi, dressed in black and wearing earlocks, a beard, and a yarmulke, is berated at a traffic light by an incensed local driver in a pick-up truck who waves his middle finger in the air. This seems to be a clear case of racism, until they get to the next light and the rabbi notices the man is doing the same thing to everyone he sees.

Whether or not there is hatred, racism involves prejudice or discrimination. It may be personal or institutional, felt or unrecognized, but it is normally based on a stereotype that people of a particular genetic background all behave in some unappealing way; they *all* do, they have no choice, it is in the genes.

What causes racism? There are religious and philosophical answers that speak of "man's inhumanity to man," the force of evil, original sin, the devil within or without. There are also psychological answers that postulate aggressive drives, displaced frustrations, inner conflicts, problems of adjustment, self-esteem, abuse, and so on.

The problem with these sorts of answers is that they fail to take into consideration social context and historical change. While various sorts of inhumanity may have always existed, there is no reason to assume that racism has existed in all societies and in all time periods.

Some people argue that racism is, in fact, a phenomenon unique in modern society, in the last four or five hundred years. They point out that the word "race" is modern and that ideas of racial inferiority were first produced systematically in European and North American thought in the nineteenth century. The problem with this point of view is that many societies did not use the word "race," but discriminated against people for reasons of birth, blood, or biology, which amounts to the same thing. In this section we will look at some examples of such discrimination in societies that we are not used to thinking of as racist.

We begin by looking at the institution of caste in India, not necessarily to argue that caste is racist but to measure what racism is by asking how caste is similar and different. Next we look at a clear case of racism (and genocide) in Tasmania in the nineteenth century. We do this in a kind of pendulum swing back to racism (again in an unfamiliar context). Finally, in this section, we look at certain aspects of Japanese society, all of which make interesting comparisons with what we know of racism in the United States. None of this is done to place blame, but rather to get a better grip on how people of different societies throughout the world have treated "the Other," so that we can gain a clearer understanding of what racism was and is.

From *Caste and Race in India*

G.S. Ghurye

This selection is from a classic book by G.S. Ghurye (1893–1983), often called "the father of Indian sociology." First published in 1932, this excerpt from the fifth edition (1969) details certain "Features of the Caste System," specifically "Restrictions on Feeding and Social Intercourse." The other subsection of "Features of the Caste System" (not included here) are "Civil and Religious Disabilities and Privileges of Different Sections," "Segmental Di-

G.S. Ghurye. *Caste and Race in India,* 5th ed. (Bombay: Popular Prakashan, 1969), pp. 7–10.

vision of Society," "Hierarchy," "Lack of Unrestricted Choice Occupa-
tion," and "Restrictions on Marriage." Thus, the range of examples listed
here are limited to caste discrimination regarding food and some aspects
of social intercourse.

This brief description of some caste behavior in India in the twentieth
century offers a context for understanding both racism and the Western
experience with racism. We are not arguing that cases of caste discrimi-
nation are—or are not—examples of racism. In fact, Ghurye wrote this book
partly to counter the claim of H.H. Risley's The People of India *(1908) that*
caste differences had racial origins. Ghurye suggests that ideas of caste
had been given undue importance by British colonial officials like Risley,
who was in charge of the Indian census in 1901. Recently Nicholas B. Dirks
has argued in Castes of Mind *(2001) that British colonial policy was largely*
responsible for making caste the important social category it became in
India. But even if Indian castes were not based on physical differences, and
even if caste differences were encouraged by the needs of British coloni-
alism, Indians may have learned to think of castes as Europeans thought
of race.

These examples, then, are not to be interpreted as ancient or traditional.
Nor are they all current; many aspects of caste discrimination are now
illegal. But in the period in which this sort of behavior was practiced, was
caste like race? In what ways was this behavior "racist?" In what ways
was it not?

There are many rules as to what sort of food or drink can be accepted by a
person and from what castes. But there is very great diversity in this matter.
The practices in the matter of food and social intercourse divide India into two
broad belts. In Hindustan proper, castes can be divided into five groups; first,
the twice-born castes; second, those castes at whose hands the twice-born can
take "Pakka" food; third, those castes at whose hands the twice-born cannot
accept any kind of food but may take water; fourth, castes that are not untouchable yet are such that water from them cannot be used by the twice-born;
last come all those castes whose touch defiles not only the twice-born but any
orthodox Hindu. All food is divided into two classes, "Kachcha" and "Pakka,"
the former being any food in the cooking of which water has been used, and
the latter all food cooked in "ghee" without the addition of water. "As a rule
a man will never eat 'Kachcha' food unless it is prepared by a fellow caste-
man, which in actual practice means a member of his own endogamous group,
whether it be caste or sub-caste, or else by his Brahmin 'Guru' or spiritual
guide." But in practice most castes seem to take no objection to "Kachcha"
food from a Brahmin. A Brahmin can accept "Kachcha" food at the hands of
no other caste; nay, some of them, like the Kanaujia Brahmins, are so punc-
tilious about these restrictions that, as a proverb has it, three Kanaujifis require

no less than thirteen hearths. As for the "Pakka" food, it may be taken by a Brahmin at the hands of some of the castes only. On the whole, however, as E. A. Blunt has made out, there is "no relation between a caste's social position and the severity of its cooking taboo"; as many as thirty-six out of seventy-six castes of U.P. [the state of Uttar Pradesh] take "Kachcha" cooked food from only their own members and none others.

The ideas about the power of certain castes to convey pollution by touch are not so highly developed in Northern India as in the South. The idea that impurity can be transmitted by the mere shadow of an untouchable or by his approaching within a certain distance does not seem to prevail in Hindustan. No Hindu of decent caste would touch a Chamar, or a Dom; and some of the very low castes themselves are quite strict about contact. Thus "The Bansphor and Basor, themselves branches of the Dom caste, will touch neither a Dom, nor a Dhobi, whilst the Basor, with all the intolerance of the parvenu, extends his objections to the Musahar, Chamar, Dharkar and Bhangi."

In Bengal [Northwestern India] the castes are divided into two main groups: (1) the Brahmins, and (2) the Shudras. The second class is further divided into four sub-classes, indicating their status as regards food and water: (a) the Sat-Shudra group includes such castes as the Kayastha and Nabashakh; (b) then come the Jalacharaniya-Shudras, "being those castes, not technically belonging to the Nabashakh group, from whom Brahmins and members of the higher castes can take water"; then follow the Jalabyabaharya-Shudras, castes from whose hands a Brahmin cannot take water; last stand the Asprishya-Shudras, castes whose touch is so impure as to pollute even the Ganges water, and hence their contact must be avoided. They are thus the untouchables. In the matter of food Western Bengal resembles Hindustan except in this that in Bengal there are some people who will not accept any "Kachcha" food even from the hands of a Brahmin. "Pakka" food can be ordinarily taken not only from one's own or any higher caste, but also from the confectioner class, the Myras and Halwais. As regards the position of the untouchables the following observation will give a clear idea. "Even wells are polluted if a low caste man draws water from them, but a great deal depends on the character of the vessel used and of the well from which water is drawn. A masonry well is not so easily defiled as one constructed with clap pipes, and if it exceeds three and a half cubits in width so that a cow may turn round in it, it can be used even by the lowest castes without defilement. . . ." Certain low castes are looked down upon as so unclean that they may not enter the courtyard of the great temples. These castes are compelled to live by themselves on the outskirts of villages.

In Eastern and Southern Bengal and in Gujarat [Western India] and the whole of Southern India there is no distinction of food as "Kachcha" for the purposes of its acceptance or otherwise from anyone but a member of one's own caste. In Gujarat and Southern India, generally speaking, a Brahmin never thinks of accepting water, much less any cooked food, from any caste but that of the Brahmins, and all the other castes or groups of castes more or less follow the principle of accepting no cooked food from any caste that stands lower than itself in the social scale. This rule does not apply with the same strictness to accepting water. Again as a rule, a lower caste has no scruples in accepting cooked food from any higher caste. Thus all the castes will take cooked food from the Brahmin.

The theory of pollution being communicated by some castes to members of the higher ones is also more developed in Gujarat. Theoretically, the touch of a member of any caste lower than one's own defiles a person of the higher caste; but in actual practice this rule is not strictly observed. In the Maratha country the shadow of an untouchable is sufficient, if it falls on a member of a higher caste, to pollute him. In Madras, and especially in Malabar, this doctrine is still further elaborated, so that certain castes have always to keep a stated distance between themselves and the Brahmin and other higher castes so as not to defile the latter. Thus the Shanar, toddy-tapper of Tamilnad, contaminates a Brahmin if he approaches the latter within twenty-four paces. Among the people of Kerala, a Nayar may approach a Nambudiri Brahmin but must not touch him; while a Tiyan must keep himself at the distance of thirty-six steps from the Brahmin, and a Pulayan may not approach him within ninety-six paces. A Tiyan must keep away from a Nayar at twelve paces, while some castes may approach the Tiyan, though they must not touch him. A Pulayan must not come near any of the Hindu castes. So rigid are the rules about defilement which is supposed to be carried with them by all except the Brahmins, that the latter will not perform even their ablutions within the precincts of a Shudra's habitation. Generally the washerman and the barber that serve the general body of villagers, will not render their services to the unclean and untouchable castes. "Even a modern Brahmin doctor, when feeling the pulse of a Shudra, first wraps up the patient's wrist with a small piece of silk so that he may not be defiled by touching his skin."

Caste May Be India's Moral Achilles' Heel

Barbara Crossette

The consideration of Indian caste as a modern "human rights" issue may, according to this article, soon be on the United Nations agenda. But the author seems to accept the judgment that Indian caste is unique and that "racial discrimination" is "not the strongest ground" for challenging caste. Do you agree with these judgements? How might "Indian scholars and diplomats argue persuasively that caste is not based on race"? Could caste be based on something equivalent to race? Could caste simply be India's word for race?

Does the debate about caste in India remind you of debates about race in the United States? Is India now pursuing a policy of "affirmative action" for outcastes?

The United Nations has tackled apartheid, established tribunals to try war criminals in Bosnia and Rwanda, set up truth commissions in Central America and, most recently, warned Islamic zealots in Afghanistan not to suppress the rights of women. But is it ready to take on caste?

Nearly a quarter of a billion human beings in Hindu-dominated South Asia—most of them in India and Nepal—are born and die as untouchables, inheritors of an ancient system that divided people according to tasks they performed: literate Brahmins for intellectual and ritual functions Kshatriyas as warriors, Vaishyas to farm and conduct business and Shudras to swell the ranks of servants. Outside all of this were literally, the out-castes, the untouchables who still sweep the floors, wash the latrines and haul away buckets of human excrement. For a traditional Hindu of the upper castes, untouchables pollute everything they touch. Most live out their lives in terrible poverty and humiliation.

For more than a decade a few Indians have tried to get the United Nations to discuss the caste system as an effort to human rights, and this year one seems to be making some small progress. He is Yogesh Varhade, an Indian-born untouchable who leads a rights campaign from his base in Toronto where he has lived for 26 years.

"After the battle against apartheid," he says, "this is the biggest challenge to the United Nations system and civil society in general. The protests have to grow bigger to force the Indian Government to respect its own Constitution and International human rights laws. Otherwise India should be made an outcast in the International community—and learn how it feels."

Mr. Varhade this year succeeded in getting a committee in Geneva that monitors racial discrimination to make room for him on its agenda. It is not the strongest legal ground—Indian diplomats and scholars argue persuasively that caste is not based on race—but any ground will do for Mr. Varhade.

"A sick society," he argues, "needs to dismantle the thinking that assigns superiority and inferiority on the basis of birth, which has been taught by the Hindu religion for the last 3,000 years."

A Unique System

The issue of caste, however, is fraught with problems for international organizations and foreign governments. First the system is unique, and therefore it is hard to slot abuses of it into standard categories of human rights violations. And while it is also deeply rooted in India's history and traditions, modern India has taken steps to alter the system, giving untouchables constitutionally protected rights, as Mr. Varhade acknowledges. So on paper this is not apartheid. In fact, untouchables as well as tribal people and members of the lowest castes in the Hindu hierarchy benefit from broad affirmative action programs and are enjoying growing political power. Indians often feel justified in asking: What right does the outside world have to intervene?

Nonetheless, as India approaches its 50th anniversary of independence next year, it may be growing more vulnerable to scrutiny on this issue. The Committee on the Elimination of Racial Discrimination has asked India to report back next year on what it is doing to educate Indians about their rights and to guarantee constitutional protections. Last week, in addition, Human Rights Watch noted a "tenacious and widespread" belief in the inherent inferiority of lower castes and untouchables in a new study on India titled "Children in Bondage." The report says that 115 million school-age children work in India, more than 15 million in the virtual slavery of bonded labor.

The caste system is reinforced in many subtle ways, from advertisements for arranged marriage that specify caste or sub-caste to the columns and news reports written by journalists in a profession that is still "very Brahminical" said Ainslee Embree, a historian of Indian tradition now retired from Columbia University. He added that the growth of militant Hindu political parties has also enhanced caste divisions.

"Some old industrial families and business people are Hindu nationalists,"

Mr. Embree said, remembering a study that friends of his conducted in a bicycle factory that claimed to hire workers on merit. "All the managers were Brahmins and all the cleaners were sweepers," or low-caste, he said.

In India, some scholars say the system is evolving rapidly, producing anomalies. As some castes use politics to better their lot, there is some gains trickle down. But there are also growing tensions between and among castes. Romila Thapar, an Indian historian at Jawaharlal Nehru University, says that the growth of regional caste-based political parties, while promoting the interests of rising, often middle-level castes, does not necessarily lead to greater social integration or help improve the lives of the truly dispossessed.

Unexpected Changes

On the positive side, she said, the "reservations" or quotas that are set aside for untouchables or lower castes in government jobs, schools and universities have had an effect, even an excessive one at times. In some areas two thirds or more of such places are held in reserve for members of specified castes. That leads to claims on those places even by grandchildren of those who have made it through this route and prospered. And some former Hindus who converted to Christianity, Buddhism or even Islam to escape caste are now renouncing their conversions or insisting that they have not lost their old designations, in order to win a reserved job.

Ashis Nandy, director of the Center for the Study of Developing Societies in Delhi, says that the political and economic growth of the middle and lower castes has changed politics "beyond recognition." For the first time India has a Prime Minster, H. D. Dive Gouda, drawn from a lower caste.

Caste, said Mr. Nandy, "is now a principle of political mobilization rather than a matter of ritual distance." In the countryside, where caste clashes pit landlords against landless untouchables, fear among the upper castes is growing. The privileged use all sorts of powers—dispossession, police excesses, denial of jobs or water—to intimidate their inferiors.

Mr. Nandy said the upper castes, less than 10 or 15 percent of India's nearly a billion people, have long harbored a visceral fear of majority rule. He noted that all three attempts on the life of Mahatma Gandhi—who promoted caste integration—were by Brahmins, including the shooting in 1948 that killed him. "I do not believe it was because of their love for Mother India, or their devotion to her," he said. "It was because they were getting displaced."

In Black and White

Jared Diamond

This is a small section of a chapter on racial genocide from a recent book by a noted naturalist and anthropologist. It deals with the annihilation of the Aboriginal population of Tasmania and the massacres of mainland Australian Aborigines by Australian settlers in the nineteenth century. The author writes in the introduction, which we have omitted, that he is not interested in singling out Australians, that in fact he believes that the Australians were just one among many perpetrators of genocide.

What seem to be the causes of the annihilation of the Tasmanians? Were the same factors at work in the massacres of the mainland Aborigines? How was it possible for the European settlers to be so insensitive to the plight of the Aborigines?

Tasmania is a mountainous island similar in area to Ireland and lying two hundred miles off Australia's southeast coast. When discovered by Europeans in 1642, it supported about five thousand hunter-gatherers related to the Aborigines of the Australian mainland and with perhaps the simplest technology of any modern people. Tasmanians made only a few types of simple stone and wooden tools. Like the mainland Aborigines, they lacked metal tools, agriculture, livestock, pottery, and bows and arrows. Unlike the mainlanders, they also lacked boomerangs, dogs, nets, knowledge of sewing, and ability to start a fire.

Since the Tasmanians' sole boats were rafts capable of only short journeys, they had had no contact with any other humans since rising sea level cut off Tasmania from Australia ten thousand years ago. Confined to their private universe for hundreds of generations, they had survived the longest isolation in modern human history—an isolation otherwise depicted only in science fiction. When the white colonists of Australia finally ended that isolation, no two peoples on Earth were less equipped to understand each other than were Tasmanians and whites.

The tragic collision of these two peoples led to conflict almost as soon as British sealers and settlers arrived around 1800. Whites kidnapped Tasmanian children as laborers, kidnapped women as consorts, mutilated or killed men, trespassed on hunting grounds, and tried to clear Tasmanians off their land. Thus, the conflict quickly focused on lebensraum, which throughout human history has been among the commonest causes of genocide. As a result of the kidnappings, the native population of northeast Tasmania in November 1830 was reduced to seventy-two adult men, three adult women, and children. One shepherd shot nineteen Tasmanians with a swivel gun loaded with nails. Four other shepherds ambushed a group of natives, killed thirty, and threw their bodies over a cliff remembered today as Victory Hill.

Naturally, Tasmanians retaliated, and whites counterretaliated in turn. To end the escalation, Governor Arthur in April 1828 ordered all Tasmanians to leave the part of their island already settled by Europeans. To enforce this order, government-sponsored groups called "roving parties," consisting of convicts led by police, hunted down and killed Tasmanians. With the declaration of martial law in November 1828, soldiers were authorized to kill on sight any Tasmanian in the settled areas. Next, a bounty was declared on the natives: five British pounds for each adult, two pounds for each child, caught alive. "Black catching," as it was called because of the Tasmanians' dark skins, became big business pursued by private as well official roving parties. At the same time a commission headed by William Broughton, the Anglican archdeacon of Australia, was set to recommend an overall policy toward the natives. After considering proposals to capture them for sale as slaves, poison or trap them, or hunt them with dogs, the commission settled on continued bounties and the use of mounted police.

In 1830 a remarkable missionary, George Augustus Robinson, was hired to round up the remaining Tasmanians and take them to Flinders Island, thirty miles away. Robinson was convinced that he was acting for the good of the Tasmanians. He was paid £300 in advance, £700 on completing the job. Undergoing real dangers and hardship, and aided by a courageous native woman named Truganini, he succeeded in bringing in the remaining natives—initially, by persuading them that a worse fate awaited them if they did not surrender, but later at gunpoint. Many of Robinson's captives died en route to Flinders, but about two hundred reached there, the last survivors of the former population of five thousand.

On Flinders Island Robinson was determined to civilize and Christianize the survivors. His settlement was run like a jail, at a windy site with little fresh water. Children were separated from parents to facilitate the work of civilizing them. The regimented daily schedule included Bible reading, hymn singing, and inspection of beds and dishes for cleanness and neatness. However, the jail diet caused malnutrition, which combined with illness to make the natives die. Few infants survived more than a few weeks. The government reduced expenditures in the hope that the natives would die out. By 1869 only Truganini, one other woman, and one man remained alive.

These last three Tasmanians attracted the interest of scientists who believed them to be a missing link between human and apes. Hence, when the last man, one William Lanner, died in 1869, competing teams of physicians, led by Dr. George Stokell from the Royal Society of Tasmania and Dr. W.L. Crowther from the Royal College of Surgeons, alternately dug up and reburied Lanner's body, cutting off parts of it and stealing them back and forth from each other. Dr. Crowther cut off the head, Dr. Stokell the hands and feet, and someone else the ears and nose, as souvenirs. Dr. Stokell made a tobacco pouch out of Lanner's skin.

Before Truganini, the last woman, died in 1876, she was terrified of similar post-mortem mutilation and asked in vain to be buried at sea. As she had feared, the Royal Society dug up her skeleton and put it on public display in the Tasmanian Museum, where it remained until 1947. In that year the Museum finally yielded to complaints of poor taste and transferred Truganini's skeleton to a room where only scientists could view it. That too stimulated complaints of poor taste. Finally, in 1976—the centenary year of Truganini's death—her skeleton was cremated over the museum's objections, and her ashes were scattered at sea as she had requested.

While the Tasmanians were few in number, their extermination was disproportionately influential in Australian history, because Tasmania was the first Australian colony to solve its native problem and achieved the most nearly final solution. It had done so by apparently succeeding in getting rid of all its natives. (Actually, some children of Tasmanian women by white sealers survived, and their descendants today constitute an embarrassment to the Tasmanian government, which has not figured out what to do about them.) Many whites on the Australian mainland envied the thoroughness of the Tasmanian solution and wanted to imitate it, but they also learned a lesson from it. The extermination of the Tasmanians had been carried out in settled areas in full view of the urban press, and had attracted some negative comment. Hence the extermination of the much more numerous mainland Aborigines was instead effected at or beyond the frontier, far from urban centers.

The mainland governments' instrument of this policy, modeled on the Tasmanian government's roving parties, was a branch of mounted police termed "Native Police," who used search-and-destroy tactics to kill or drive out Aborigines. A typical strategy was to surround a camp at night and to shoot the inhabitants in an attack at dawn. White settlers also made widespread use of poisoned food to kill Aborigines. Another common practice was roundups in which captured Aborigines were kept chained together at the neck while being marched to jail and held there. The British novelist Anthony Trollope expressed the prevailing nineteenth-century British attitude toward Aborigines when he wrote, "Of the Australian black man we may certainly say that he has to go. That he should perish without unnecessary suffering should be the aim of all who are concerned in the matter."

These tactics continued in Australia long into the twentieth century. In an incident at Alice Springs in 1928, police massacred thirty-one Aborigines. The Australian Parliament refused to accept a report on the massacre, and two Aboriginal survivors (rather than the police) were put on trial for murder. Neck chains were still in use and defended as humane in 1958, when the Commissioner of Police for the state of Western Australia explained to the Melbourne *Herald* that Aboriginal prisoners preferred being chained.

The mainland Aborigines were too numerous to exterminate completely in the manner of the Tasmanians. However, from the arrival of British colonists in 1788 until the 1921 census, the Aboriginal population declined from about 300,000 to 60,000.

Today, the attitudes of white Australians toward their murderous history vary widely. While government policy and many whites' private views have become increasingly sympathetic to the Aborigines, other whites deny responsibility for genocide. For instance, in 1982 one of Australia's leading news magazines, *The Bulletin*, published a letter by a lady named Patricia Cobern, who denied indignantly that white settlers had exterminated the Tasmanians. In fact, wrote Ms. Cobern, the settlers were peace-loving and of high moral character, while Tasmanians were treacherous, murderous, warlike, filthy, gluttonous, vermin-infested, and disfigured by syphilis. Moreover, they took poor care of their infants, never bathed, and had repulsive marriage customs. They died out because of all those poor health practices, plus a death wish and lack of religious beliefs. It was just a coincidence that, after thousands of years of existence, they happened to die out during a conflict with the settlers. The only massacres were of settlers by Tasmanians, not vice versa. Besides, the settlers only armed themselves in self-defense, were unfamiliar with guns, and never shot more than forty-one Tasmanians at one time.

The Social Perception of Skin Color in Japan

Hiroshi Wagatsuma

This is the first in a series of readings on Japan. We choose Japan because it is not weighed down in the minds of Americans (and probably others) with associations of racism (Nor do we wish to make that association.) Our intention is to explore aspects of a society relatively unfamiliar to most readers in order to see how applicable ideas of race and racism are in a very different setting from most discussions of the topic.

This selection describes a preference for white skin by Japanese women. Such a preference immediately raises the suspicions of any American, white or black, who recognizes the telltale signs of racism in American culture. That is because in the history of American culture, the preference for white skin has had clear and unambiguous racial meaning.

In Japan, however, this preference for white skin is an esthetic matter that has little, if anything, to do with race. There are no doubt intrinsic Japanese roots for this preference, having to do with social class, perhaps— women can have white skin if they need not work in the sun—and cultural values that may seem strange to many Americans, but there is nothing here that concerns race in the usual sense of the term.

Japan lacks a history that identified whiteness or blackness with any group of people judged inferior or superior. There is in Japan very little experience with Africans. There is no history of enslaving Africans. If the Japanese think of themselves as white, theirs is not a whiteness opposed to some other group's inferior blackness. The Eta, Japanese outcastes, for instance, are not black; they are not even recognizable by physical characteristics. Consequently, it is difficult to see this as racist behavior—despite the fact that it is the very hallmark of racist behavior in the United States.

Things began to change with the arrival in Japan of Europeans and Africans after 1500, but the Japanese initially attributed African blackness to environmental factors. At this point the Africans (most of whom came with the lowly status of servants or slaves to Europeans) fit a preexistent negative esthetic norm. But even at this stage, it would be difficult to char-

"The Social Perception of Skin Color in Japan," reprinted by permission of *Dædalus*, Journal of the American Academy of Arts and Sciences, from the issue entitled, "Color and Race," Spring 1967, vol. 96, no. 2, pp. 129–139.

acterize the Japanese dislike of Africans' appearance as racist. The Japanese just did not like their looks.

Nevertheless, there is, perhaps early on in their encounter with Africans, the beginning of an assumption that dark skin signifies certain negative behavioral characteristics: stupid, uncivilized, vicious. These are the beginnings of racism against Africans. Such ideas imply that the Japanese would engage in systematic treatment of Africans as inferiors (were the occasion to arise). Of course, it did not. There was never a significant population of Africans or other black people in Japan, so we have no evidence of Japanese racism against them here.

Long before any sustained contact with either Caucasoid Europeans or dark-skinned Africans or Indians, the Japanese valued "white" skin as beautiful and deprecated "black" skin as ugly. Their spontaneous responses to the white skin of Caucasoid Europeans and the black skin of Negroid people were an extension of values deeply embedded in Japanese concepts of beauty. From past to present, the Japanese have always associated skin color symbolically with other physical characteristics that signify degrees of spiritual refinement or primitiveness. Skin color has been related to a whole complex of attractive or objectionable social traits. It might strike some as curious that the Japanese have traditionally used the word white (*shiroi*) to describe lighter shades of their own skin color. The social perception of the West has been that the Chinese and Japanese belong to a so-called "yellow" race, while the Japanese themselves have rarely used the color yellow to describe their skin. . . .

"White" skin has been considered an essential characteristic of feminine beauty in Japan since recorded time. An old Japanese proverb states that "white skin makes up for seven defects"; a woman's light skin causes one to overlook the absence of other desired physical features.

During the Nara period (710–793), court ladies made ample use of cosmetics and liberally applied white powder to the face. Cheeks were rouged. Red beauty spots were painted on between the eyebrows and at the outer corners of both the eyes and the lips. Eyelids and lips were given a red tinge. Both men and women removed their natural eyebrows and penciled in long, thick lines emulating a Chinese style. The custom of blackening teeth spread among the aristocratic ladies. In the next period (794–1185), when the court was moved to the new capital of Heian (Kyoto), countless references were made in both illustration and writing to round-faced, plump women with white, smooth skin. Necessary to beauty was long, black, straight hair that draped over the back and shoulders without being tied. One can illustrate this conception of white skin as a mark of beauty from *The Tale of Genji* by Lady Murasaki, a romance of the first decade of the eleventh century:

Her color of skin was very white and she was plump with an attractive face. Her hair grew thick but was cut so as to hang on a level with her shoulders—very beautiful.

Her color was very white and although she was emaciated and looked noble, there still was a certain fulness in her cheek.

In her personal diary, the same author depicted portraits of several court ladies:

Lady Dainagon is very small but as she is white and beautifully round, she has a taller appearance. Her hair is three inches longer than her height.

Lady Senji is a small and slender person. The texture of her hair is fine, delicate and glossy and reaches a foot longer than her height.

Lady Naiji has beauty and purity, a fragrant white skin with which no one else can compete.

Writing about the year 1002 in essays called *The Pillow Book*, the court lady Sei Shonagon described how she despised "hair not smooth and straight" and envied "beautiful, very long hair." In *The Tale of Glory*, presumably written in 1120 by Akazome Emon, a court lady, two beautiful women of the prosperous Fujiwara family are depicted: one with "her hair seven or eight inches longer than her height," and the other with "her hair about two feet longer than her height and her skin white and beautiful." From the eighth to the twelfth century, the bearers of Japanese cultural refinement were the court nobility who idled their lives away in romantic love affairs, practicing the arts of music and poetry. The whiteness of untanned skin was the symbol of this privileged class which was spared any form of outdoor labor. From the eleventh century on, men of the aristocracy applied powder to their faces just as the court ladies did.

In 1184, the warriors took the reins of government away from the effete courtiers and abruptly ended the court's rather decadent era. To protect the samurai virtues of simplicity, frugality, and bravery, the warriors set up headquarters in the frontier town of Kamakura located far away from the capital. The warriors maintained Spartan standards, as is evidenced in the many portrait paintings showing rather florid or swarthy countenances. Women still continued, however, the practices of toiletry established previously in the court. In 1333 the warriors' government was moved from Kamakura back to Kyoto, where the Ashikaga Shogunate family emulated court life and re-established an atmosphere of luxury among the ruling class.

Standards of feminine beauty still emphasized corpulence of body, white skin and black hair, which in this period was worn in a chignon. Preference was voiced for a woman with a round face, broad forehead, and eyes slightly down-turned at the corners. By this time, the old court custom of penciling eyebrows and blackening teeth had become incorporated into the puberty rites practiced for both boys and girls. Such rites were principally held by the warrior class but were later adopted by commoners. The writing of Yoshida Kenko, a celebrated poet and court official who became a Buddhist monk in 1324, exemplifies the continuing preoccupation this period had with the white skin of women. Yoshida wrote the following in his *Essays of Idleness*:

> The magician of Kume (as the legend runs) lost his magic power through looking at the white leg of a maiden washing clothes in a river. This may well have been because the white limbs and skin of a woman cleanly plump and fatty are no mere external charms but true beauty and allure.

Following a chaotic political period, the Tokugawa feudal government was established in 1603. It was to last until the modern period of Japan, more than two hundred and fifty years. Changes occurred in the ideals of feminine beauty during this period of continuing peace. Gradually, slim and fragile women with slender faces and up-turned eyes began to be preferred to the plump, pear-shaped ideal that remained dominant until the middle of the eighteenth century. White skin, however, remained an imperative characteristic of feminine beauty. Ibara Saikaku (1642–1693), a novelist who wrote celebrated books about common life during the early Tokugawa period, had the following to say about the type of female beauty to be found in Kyoto and Osaka.

> A beautiful woman with a round face, skin with a faint pink color, eyes not too narrow, eyebrows thick, the bridge of her nose not too thin, her mouth small, teeth in excellent shape and shining white.

> A woman of twenty-one, white of color, hair beautiful, attired in gentleness.

> Thanks to the pure water of Kyoto, women remain attractive from early childhood but they further improve their beauty by steaming their faces, tightening their fingers with rings and wearing leather socks in sleep. They also comb their hair with the juice of the *sanekazura* root.

Another author, depicting the beauties of the middle Tokugawa period of the 1770s, wrote: "A pair of girls wearing red-lacquered thongs on their tender feet, white as snow, sashes around their waists, with forms as slender as willow trees." Tamenaga Shunsui (1789–1843), an author of the late Tokugawa period, never forgot to mention white skin when describing the beautiful women of Edo (Tokyo):

> Her hands and arms are whiter than snow.

> You are well-featured and your color is so white that you are popular among your audience.

> This courtesan had a neck whiter than snow. Her face was shining as she always polished it with powder.

The use of good water and the practice of steaming the face were thought to make skin white and smooth. Rings and socks were worn in sleep to stunt excessive growth of limbs since small hands and feet were valued attributes of feminine charm. The juice of the *sanekazura* root was used to straighten the hair. These practices all confirm the continuous concern with white skin and straight hair. They also suggest, however, the possibility that many women were lacking in such standards of feminine beauty. The following quotation describes what was considered ugly:

> Disagreeable features for a woman are a large face, the lack of any tufts of hair under the temple, a big, flat nose, thick lips, black skin, a too plump body, excessive tallness, heavy, strong limbs, brownish wavy hair and a loud, talkative voice.

These were the comments of Yanagi Rikyo, a high-ranking warrior of the Koriyama fief, who was also a poet, artist, and noted connoisseur of womanhood in the late-eighteenth century. He contrasted these objectionable features with "the amiable features of a woman, a small and well-shaped face, white skin, gentle manner, an innocent, charming and attentive character." One might speculate that the supposed Polynesian or Melanesian strains, sometimes thought to have entered the Japanese racial mixture, would be responsible for flat noses, thick lips, or brownish, wavy hair. Such features are certainly not rare among Japanese, although they run directly counter to the Japanese image of beauty.

Because Mongoloid skin shows a very quick tendency to tan and to produce "black" skin, the Japanese can maintain lightness of skin only by total avoidance of sunlight. Not surprisingly, Tokugawa women made constant use of parasols or face hoods to hide their skin from sunlight and assiduously applied powder to face, neck, throat, and upper chest. In order to increase the whiteness and smoothness of their skin, women "polished" it in their baths with a cloth bag containing rice bran or the droppings of the Japanese nightingale. Application of other grains such as millet, barley, Deccan grass, and beans was also considered to have some "bleaching" effect on the skin. Juices taken from various flowers were also used for the same purpose, and many medicines were sold that promised "to turn the skin as white as the snow found on the peaks of high mountains."

When a woman's constant care of her skin achieved desired results, she would enjoy such praise as "Her face is so smoothly shiny that it seems ready to reflect," and "Her face can compete with a mirror," or "Her face is so shiny as to make a well polished black lacquered dresser feel ashamed."

From the beginning of the nineteenth century, the Kabuki actors set the standards of men's beauty. A rather feminine type of male with a slender figure, well-formed face, white skin, black hair, and red lips became a favorite object of feminine desire. Men possessing these elements of attractiveness would enjoy such a flattering remark as "You should be a Kabuki actor." By the middle of the nineteenth century, these characteristics began to be considered effeminate. A man with a more dusky skin and a piquantly handsome face became the preferred type.

The word *white* repeatedly used in the quotations taken from these various sources is the same Japanese word *shiroi* that is used to describe snow or white paper. There was no intermediate word between *shiroi* ("white") and *kuroi* ("black") used to describe skin color. When distinctions were made, there would be recourse to such words as *asa guroi* ("light black"). . . .

Not long after the first globe-circling voyages of Magellan, Westerners appeared on the shores of Japan. Dutch, English, Portuguese, and Spanish traders came to ply their trade in Japanese ports. Both Spanish and Portuguese missionaries sought to establish Christianity in Japan. Before the Tokugawa government sealed off Japan from the West, the Japanese had ample opportunity to observe white men for the first time. In these early contacts, the Portuguese and Spaniards were called *nanban-jin* or *nanban* meaning "southern barbarians," words adopted from the Chinese who had names to designate all the "inferior savages" living to the north, south, east, and west of the Middle Kingdom. The Dutch were called *komo-jin* or *komo*, "red-haired people."

In several of the colored pictures of the day that included both Japanese and Europeans, the Japanese artists painted the faces of the Portuguese, Spanish, and Japanese men in a flesh color or light brown, but depicted the faces of Japanese women as white in hue. In a few other pictures, however, some Portuguese are given white faces like Japanese women, while other Portuguese are given darker faces. Seemingly, the Japanese artists were sensitive in some instances to some form of color differential among the foreigners. Many Portuguese and Spaniards were actually not so white-skinned as northern Europeans, and after the long sea voyage to Japan, they undoubtedly arrived with rather well-tanned skins. The Dutch in the pictures, on the other hand, seem to be given invariably either gray or white faces. When contrasted with the Japanese women near them, the Japanese feminine face is painted a whiter hue than that of the Dutch.

The differences between the Japanese and the Europeans in these old prints are clearly depicted in hair color and facial characteristics. The Portuguese, Spaniards, and Dutch are all taller than the Japanese and are given somewhat unrealistically large noses. Their double eye folds and their bushy eyebrows and mustaches seem slightly exaggerated. The Portuguese and Spanish hair is painted brown although a few are given black hair. The Dutch hair is usually depicted as either red or reddish-brown in color. Written and pictorial descriptions indicate that the Japanese were more impressed with the height, hair color, general hairiness, big noses and eyes of the foreigners than with their lighter skin color. Some pictures include portraits of the Negro servants of the Portuguese and Dutch. The faces of Negroes are painted in a leaden- or blackish-gray, and their hair is shown as extremely frizzled. The physiognomy of the Negroes is somewhat caricatured and in some instances closely resembles the devils and demons of Buddhist mythology.

Some Japanese scholars of Dutch science seem to have had a notion that the black skin and frizzled hair of Negro servants were the result of extreme exposure to heat and sunshine in the tropical countries in which they were born. In 1787, such a scholar wrote of what he had learned from his Dutch friends about their Negro servants:

> These black ones on the Dutch boats are the natives of countries in the South. As their countries are close to the sun, they are sun-scorched and become black. By nature they are stupid.

> The black ones are found with flat noses. They love a flat nose and they tie children's noses with leather bands to prevent their growth and to keep them flat.

> Africa is directly under the equator and the heat there is extreme. Therefore, the natives are black colored. They are uncivilized and vicious in nature.

Another scholar wrote:

> Black ones are impoverished Indians employed by the Dutch. As their country is in the South and the heat is extreme, their body is sunscorched and their color becomes black. Their hair is burned by the sun and becomes frizzled but they are humans and not monkeys as some mistakenly think.

After the closing of the country by the Tokugawa government in 1639, the only contact of Japanese with Westerners, aside from the Dutch traders, would occur when shipwrecked Japanese sailors would occasionally be picked up by Western ships and taken for a period to a Western country. The reports about the English, Russians, and Spaniards made by these Japanese sailors upon their return commented much more on the hair and eyes of the Occidentals than upon the color of skin.

In 1853 Commodore Perry of the United States Navy came to Japan with his "black ships" and forced Japan to reopen her ports to foreign vessels. When Perry visited Japan for the second time in 1854, there were two American women on board. It was reported in a Japanese document:

> On board is a woman named Shirles, 31 years old and her child Loretta, 5 years old. Their hair is red. They have high noses white faces and the pupils of their eyes are brown. They are medium in size and very beautiful.

The portraits of Commodore Perry and five principals of his staff drawn by a Japanese artist show the Americans with noses of exaggerated size, large eyes, and brownish hair. Their faces are painted in a washed-out, whitish-ash color. In other pictures, however, both American and Japanese faces are painted with an identical whitish-gray, although the Americans are given brown hair and bushy beards. In some pictures showing the American settlements in Yokohama and Tokyo of the 1860s, the faces of both American and Japanese women are painted whiter than those of American and Japanese men. It may well be possible that the American men's faces were more sun-tanned and exposed to the elements during the voyage than the faces of the women who, observing canons of beauty much like those held by Japanese women, may have kept themselves out of the sun. Also, the artists may have simply resorted to convention by which women's faces were painted white.

In 1860 the Tokugawa government sent an envoy with an entourage of eighty-three warriors to the United States to ratify a treaty of peace and commerce between the United States and Japan originally signed in 1854. Some of the members of the entourage kept careful diaries and noted their impressions of the United States during their trip to Washington. Upon meeting the President of the United States, one samurai wrote: "President Buchanan, about 52 or 53 years of age, is a tall person. His color is white, his hair is white." The samurai leaders were surprised to attend formal receptions at which women were included and to find that American men acted toward their women as obliging servants. They were impressed with the daring exposure afforded by the decolletage of the formal evening gowns worn by women at these balls and receptions. In their diaries they noted their appreciation of American beauty, although they continued to express their preference for black hair:

> The women's skin was white and they were charming in their gala dresses decorated with gold and silver but their hair was red and their eyes looked like dog eyes, which was quite disheartening.

> Occasionally I saw women with black hair and black eyes. They must have been of some Asian race. Naturally they looked more attractive and beautiful.

Another man expressed his admiration for the President's niece, Harriet Lane, in true samurai fashion by composing a Chinese poem:

> An American belle, her name is Lane,
> Jewels adorn her arms, jade her ears.
> Her rosy face needs no powder or rouge.
> Her exposed shoulders shine as white as snow.

This American belle and her friends had asked another samurai at a party which women he liked better, Japanese or American. The samurai wrote in his diary:

> I answered that the American women are better because their skin color is whiter than that of the Japanese women. Such a trifling comment of mine obviously pleased the girls. After all, women are women.

After seeing about a hundred American children aged five to nine gathered at a May festival ball, another warrior wrote of his admiration of their beauty:

> The girls did not need to have the help of powder and rouge. Their skin with its natural beauty was whiter than snow and purer than jewels. I

wondered if fairies in wonderland would not look something like these children.

On the way back from the United States, the boat carrying the Japanese envoy stopped at a harbor on the African coast, and the samurai had a chance to see the black-skinned Africans inhabiting the region. They noted with disapproval their impression of Negroid features:

The black ones look like devils depicted in pictures.

The faces are black as if painted with ink and their physiognomy reminds me of that of a monkey.

In the early Meiji period, the Japanese began their self-conscious imitation of the technology of the West. Less consciously, they also began to alter their perception of feminine beauty. In their writings, they referred with admiration to the white skin of Westerners, but noted with disapproval the hair color and the hairiness of Westerners. Wavy hair was not to the Japanese taste until the mid-1920s. Curly hair was considered to be an animal characteristic. Mrs. Sugimoto, the daughter of a samurai, writes in her autobiography that, as a child with curly hair, she had her hair dressed twice a week with a special treatment to straighten it properly. When she complained, her mother would scold her, saying, "Do you not know that curly hair is like that of animals? A samurai's daughter should not be willing to resemble a beast."

The body hair of Caucasian men suggested a somewhat beastly nature to Japanese women, and, probably for reasons of this kind, Japanese women of the late-nineteenth century refused or were reluctant in many instances to become mistresses to Western diplomats.

By the mid-1920s the Japanese had adopted Western customs and fashions, including the singing of American popular songs and dancing in dance halls. They watched motion pictures with delight and made great favorites of Clara Bow, Gloria Swanson, and Greta Garbo. Motion pictures seem to have had a very strong effect in finally changing habits of coiffure and attitudes toward desirable beauty. During this period many Japanese women had their hair cut and, in spite of the exhortations of proud samurai tradition, had it waved and curled. They took to wearing long skirts with large hats to emulate styles worn by Greta Garbo. The 1920s were a time of great imitation. Anything Western was considered "modern" and, therefore, superior. This trend lasted until the mid-1930s when, under the pressure of the ultra-nationalist, militarist regime, the ties with Western fads were systematically broken.

Already in 1924, Tanizaki Junichiro depicted a woman who represented a kind of femininity that was appealing to "modern" intellectuals of the time. She was Naomi in *The Love of an Idiot*, and her physical attractiveness had a heavy Western flavor. She was sought after by a man who "wished if ever possible to go to Europe and marry an Occidental woman." Since he could not do so, he decided to marry Naomi, who had such Occidental features. He helped her refine her beauty and educated her so that she would become "a real lady presentable even to the eyes of the Occidentals." She became, instead, a promiscuous, lust-driven woman who turned her mentor-husband into a slave chained to her by his uncontrollable passion. An important aspect of Tanizaki's depiction of this Occidental-looking girl is the whiteness of her skin:

> Against the red gown, her hands and feet stand out purely white like the core of a cabbage.

> Her skin was white to an astounding degree. . . . All the exposed parts of her voluptuous body were as white as the meat of an apple.

There is a most interesting passage in this book, however, in which Tanizaki, with a note of disappointment, compares Naomi with a real European woman, a Russian aristocrat living in exile in Japan.

> [The Russian woman's] skin color . . . was so extraordinarily white, an almost ghostly beauty of white skin under which the blood vessels of light violet color were faintly visible like the veining of marble. Compared with this skin, that of Naomi's lacked clearness and shine and was rather dull to the eye.

The subtle, not fully conscious, trend toward an idealization of Western physical features by the Japanese apparently became of increasing importance in the twenties. It remained a hidden sub-current throughout the last war while Japan, as the "champion of the colored nations," fought against the "whites." In spite of propaganda emphasizing the racial ties between Japanese and other Asians, the "yellowness" of the Japanese was never quite made a point of pride. The rapidity with which Western standards of beauty became idealized after the war attests to the continuous drift that was occurring in spite of ten years of antagonism and military hostilities.

A History of the Outcaste: Untouchability in Japan

John Price

We are concerned in this selection not with skin color, white or black, nor with the appearance of Europeans, Africans, or other foreigners in recent historical time. Rather, we return to the issue of outcastes, untouchables, and in Japan, the Eta.

Price initially compares untouchability in India, Burma, Tibet, Korea, and Japan. In all of these cases, he finds that the outcastes are thought to be members of "impure" or "polluting" occupations. In all of these societies the outcastes are believed to be both necessary and foreign. In some cases they were aboriginal peoples, thought to be foreigners who long ago migrated into the society, but who never became fully assimilated. In what ways is this like racism? In what ways is it not?

Are any of the explanations of Eta origins convincing, or do they just seem to be attempts to make them foreign? What evidence do you see that the Eta are not a different "race?" Is this an example of racism? Is it racism even if the Eta are the same race as other Japanese.

The caste phenomenon, principally that involving some sort of pariah group, has appeared throughout the Far East. . . . [One authority] distinguishes between caste as hierarchical social structure peculiar to India and the severely segregated outcaste status involving some form of literal untouchability found in various Asian cultures. . . .

[He] points up some interesting parallels in the reports extant on untouchability in India, Tibet, Korea, and Japan. In each of these four Asian cultures, to the outcaste group is attributed an origin other than that of the majority. Thus an expression of ethnocentrism toward foreigners or outside races may have initially set these peoples apart. In India the untouchables are considered to be descendants of aboriginal tribes conquered by the Aryan invaders. In Tibet the Ragyappa are held to be an alien wandering tribe that settled down in their present location. In Korea the outcastes are supposedly descendant from "Tartars," and in Japan they are popularly held to come from various separate "races," including Koreans. However, popular theories are often after-the-fact rationalizations and must be carefully reviewed in the light of other evidence. Passin wrote, "These popular attributions express the feeling that the outcastes are so different from oneself that they must be a different race." Whatever the popular attributions of their origins, all of these outcaste groups spoke the same language, had the same religion, and identified with the same culture as the surrounding majority population.

In each culture the untouchables were seen as inferior, and as so polluted that their very presence is a danger to normal people. Marriage, eating together, and social visiting between untouchables and members of normal society were disdained. In each culture they were rigidly isolated in ghettos, often actually outside the regular communities, with segregated cemeteries. In each culture evidences of luxury on the part of outcastes, such as expensive clothes, were illegal or severely frowned upon. This segregation from normal society was balanced by autonomy and solidarity within outcaste communities.

In each culture the outcastes were restricted to the despised and menial but essential occupations, usually centered around blood, death, and dirt. Occupation was a major method of distinguishing outcastes. Some outcastes in all the societies worked with dead animals, as in butchering, removing carcasses, or leather work. They are usually associated with removing dirt. And there were other relatively clean services that by analogy, accidental association, or monopoly came to belong to the outcastes, such as the making of willow baskets in Korea or sandals in Japan. There were, of course, some differences in occupation among the various cultures, Outcastes laundered for others in India, whereas they did not do so in the other cultures. In Burma the care of temples was an outcaste function, whereas in the other cultures they were generally kept away from temples. Also, there were distinctions between occupations of outcastes who live in their own settled communities and itinerant floaters in India (settled vs. beggars), Korea (Paekchong vs. Chiain), and Japan (Eta vs. Hinin).

Elaborate etiquette was developed for business contacts: in both India and Japan outcastes had to come to the back door and were not permitted to enter the homes of the majority people. Except in the processes of butchering, outcastes could not handle foods to be eaten by ordinary people. In all four cultures hereditary hierarchy was important. In India, Japan, and Korea there were four basic, rigid castes or classes. In India and Japan the outcastes were technically outside and below the lowest caste, and in Korea they were a special part of the lowest class. All held outcaste status to be inevitable, immutable, and in some way deserved. Also, the concept of pollution was common to these four cultures—the magical, mechanistic, and aspiritual pollution that is resident in certain persons at birth or in certain things by their nature and that may flow out and contaminate other persons or things. Passin therefore suggests that untouchability was lacking as a continuing social dynamic in China because hierarchy there was more dependent on merit and less on heredity, and status was not held to be inevitable. . . .

The principal outcaste groups of Korea are the Paekchong—slaughterers, butchers, and tanners; and the Chiain—petty criminals, prostitutes, diviners, beggars, itinerant peddlers, and those who practice similar "floating" occupations. Both of these groups are thought to be descended from a wandering alien group called the kolisiuchay of the Koryo Period (918–1329 A.D.). From the fifteenth century these outcastes were required to live in segregated communities. The Paekchong held monopolies in the despised occupations and were permitted to drive out non-outcaste competitors. They were not considered worthy of citizenship and thus were exempted from military service and military taxes. (In all four countries there seem to have been certain limited advantages to being an outcaste, and there were economic as well as ideological reasons for the maintenance of an outcaste group.)

The Hindu-Buddhist proscriptions against the killing of animals, in Korea as in other countries, apparently played a major role in setting off the Paekchong as untouchable. In the first of the Yi dynasty in 1392, the Paekchong, along with seven other "vile occupations," were designated as a special subdivision of the fourth or lowest class. The term "Paekchong" came to embrace both the Paekchong proper and the Chiain. In 1894 the outcastes were "liberated" by an official decree but, as in Japan and later in India, discrimination continued as before.

The Outcastes in Japan

The history of the outcaste in Japan, like that of low social classes generally, is poorly documented. The available descriptions were written primarily by an elite minority centered around the capital and the major towns; they do not faithfully record the culture of the countryside majority.

Since outcastes are ideologically outside normal society, they have either been systematically ignored or information concerning them has been distorted. During the Tokugawa period (1603–1868 A.D.) outcastes were often not listed in census tabulations, and when they were, they were often listed separately from "people." Some maps were made without outcaste settlements drawn in, and distances indicated or maps were even foreshortened to exclude these communities. After their emancipation in 1871, the outcastes were officially defined as commoners and then largely ignored for official purposes. It has been government policy to contend that there are no outcastes and hence no outcaste problem apart from that of general social welfare. Thus the outcastes, who in fact were maintained as outcastes, and who expanded in population and number of communities in the past century, are not distinguishable in most population data. It is only in the last fifty years, with the introduction of a scientific tradition, that Japanese outcaste culture has begun to receive full exploration and description. . . .

At least four theories have used the evidence of similar names to postulate the origin of the Eta [the Japanese outcastes]. One theory held that a Philippine Negrito people, also called Eta, are ancestral to the Japanese Eta. Another theory is that the Eta are descended from a Hindu tribe called Weda. Oe Taku over forty years ago [1919], postulated that the Eta were descendants of a lost tribe of Hebrews. . . .

A more popular racial view is that the Eta are descended from Koreans who came as early war captives or who were immigrants who practiced tanning and furriery. Often they are held to be descended from captives taken in a battle during the regency of the Empress Jingu (201–269 A.D.), but even the battle is not fully substantiated. Some slight credence could be given to a modified Korean descent theory for three reasons. First, over two thousand years ago southern Korea and western Japan were occupied by essentially the same race and culture. Distinctive variations of East Asian culture and the Mongoloid race have since emerged in Korea and Japan, but these differences today cannot be validly projected back much over 1,500 years. Second, Koreans did immigrate to Japan in the early historic periods as skilled tradesmen, although most of them were accorded high status, immunities, and privileges, and thus would not enter the lower classes. Third, with modern discrimination in housing, employment, and marriage in Japan against the Koreans, a few Koreans have married outcastes, moved into outcaste communities, and thus in social fact have become pariahs. However, the majority of Koreans who immigrated to Japan formed their own enclaves within the cities, and seem to have emerged as one of the new low class segments of Japanese society rather than a separate caste.

Taken as a whole, the outcastes are not descendant from Koreans, but are Japanese. In fact, the earliest outcaste communities are in the Kinki district, the very heartland of historic Japanese culture, rather than in the extreme west where we would expect to find more "Korean genes," or the extreme north, where more "Ainu genes" are present. The outcastes form a race only in the sense of an "invisible race," a race visible only to the eyes of members of a certain cultural tradition.

Japan's Forgotten People Try to Make Voices Heard

Nicholas D. Kristof

Unlike the "invisible" Eta, the "forgotten" Ainu are an entirely different group of people in Japan—aboriginal inhabitants of the northern island of Hokkaido and perhaps the rest of Japan as well. Whether they are considered a separate race depends on what one means by the word, but they are certainly a population that has lived and interbred with each other separately for thousands of years before Japanese conquest (and some assimilation). Unlike the Eta, some Ainu do look different from many Japanese (and many are indistinguishable). In what ways are the Ainu like American Indians? Do they seem to be objects of racism? If this is a case of racism, which of the cases in previous selections does it resemble?

Shigeru Kayano has a slightly different take on the history of northern Japan than the school textbooks.

"Japan illegally occupies the huge land called Hokkaido, which consists of almost one-quarter of all Japanese territory," said Mr. Kayano, a Member of Parliament from this town in Hokkaido, the northernmost island of Japan. Japanese came to the island like an avalanche, and destroyed nature while looting fish, coal and everything from the woods.

Mr. Kayano is a member of the Ainu, an indigenous people who were hunting and fishing in northern Japan for countless centuries before other Japanese arrived. The Ainu today have even less voice in Japan than American Indians do in the United States, but Mr. Kayano and his son have helped spark a campaign to preserve Ainu culture.

"Compared to 13 years ago, when we began classes to teach the Ainu language, the progress is as great as the distance from the ground to the clouds," said Mr Kayan's son, Shiro, who runs the local Ainu museum.

This village of Nibutani, nestled beside a river in the jutting forests and mountains of Hokkaido, is a center for renaissance of Ainu culture. People are studying the Ainu language, which had almost died out, as well as old traditions such as weaving bark cloth or making dugout canoes.

The Ainu lived in northern Japan for thousands of years before the migration of other Japanese to Hokkaido in the 19th century. Indeed, it is possible that the Ainu were the original inhabitants of central and southern parts of Japan as well as here in the north.

Some studies suggest that the Ainu may be more closely related than today's Japanese to the Jomon people who founded Japan's first major civilization some 12,000 years ago. Moreover, Ainu words seem to have formed the basis for place names throughout Japan—even for Mount Fuji, the symbol of the nation.

The question remains, however, whether the Ainu renaissance has not happened a half-century too late. "It is surely late, and it's true that the language is almost lost," said Koichi Katzawa, an Ainu farmer living on the outskirts of Nibutani. "But there's a lot of spirit still, so I don't think it's too late. We've lost a lot, but if we want to get it back I think we can."

One problem is numbers: across Japan, only 24,000 people identify themselves as Ainu and nearly all of these are of mixed race; fewer than 100 Ainu are said to be of pure blood

Mr. Kaizawa, for example, says that he has mixed blood on both sides, and he himself married a non-Ainu Japanese woman. He says he does not mind if his children marry regular Japanese.

Ironically, it is his wife, Miwako, who despite her lack of Ainu blood is pressing the children to marry Ainu.

"I'm telling them to marry Ainu, because Ainu blood is already too thin in this family," Mrs. Kaizawa said, laughing, as she sat in her living room. "But the kids won't listen to me."

The mixed marriages are arguably the result of a measure of acceptance in Japan toward the Ainu. In the 19th century, when American society frowned on marriages between whites and Indians, Japanese were often marrying Ainu.

Indeed, some scholars and social commentators say that one reason why Japanese men tend to have more facial hair than Koreans or Chinese is a history of intermarriage with Ainu. When Prime Minister Yasuhiro Nakasone was criticized a decade ago for insensitivity to the Ainu, he responded that with his bushy eyebrows and heavy beard, he himself probably had a good bit of Ainu blood.

Mr. Kaizawa argues that one of the main problems is that the Government seems to do its best to ignore the existence of the Ainu.

"I don't think they want to admit that there's another race in this country," Mr. Kaizawa said. "I believe that America admits that Indians were an indigenous people, and that funds are provided for Indian culture, and that some Indian history is taught in the schools. American Indians tell us we're 25 to 30 years behind them."

Mr. Kaizawa added that he does not regard the United States as a model for treatment of indigenous peoples. But he suggested that it would be nice if Japanese school textbooks taught about the Ainu, instead of virtually ignoring them as they do now.

One obstacle for the present cultural renaissance is that the Ainu traditions are not particularly practical in daily life. Last year, for example, a group of Ainu tried after a 120-year gap to revive the old method of hunting deer, without guns or even bows and arrows.

That method was to capture a deer by driving it into a river or over a cliff. Some hunters managed to spot and chase three deer, but the quarry escaped. Still, a good time was had by all, except possibly the deer.

One of those trying to promote Ainu traditions is Rumiko Fujiya, who for 30 years has been weaving clothing out of bark in the traditional way. She learned the practice from her mother, and now she demonstrates the methods in an Ainu museum run by the Kayano family here, in Nibutani.

"I learned this from my mother," Mrs. Fujiya said, as she carefully wove a rough but beautiful cloth from a cord made of bark. "I have daughters, but they won't do it. They see me do this work and they don't seem attracted to it now."

Part 3

A Model of Racism: Settler Expansion and the "Internal Other"

A BUSH CUT.

" *Faith! an' a noice gug Ned has made av yez, Paddy, wid that hair-cut. Shure, look at all yer timples bare there!*"

In the nineteenth century, Irish immigrants and Irish-Americans were often portrayed with ape-like features, as in this 1897 cartoon. *(Ross Woodrow and The University of Newcastle)*

We began the last section by looking at caste in India. From one perspective "caste" in India is certainly unique, but every society divides its members into more or less permanent groups and such groups are often organized (as in India) by family and function. The word *casta* was first used in India by the Portuguese, who saw a similarity between the Indian division of society into *varnas* [priests, warriors, producers, and serfs] and a similar division of Portuguese society into castes. Indeed, most European societies from the Middle Ages until at least the sixteenth century saw themselves divided into three castes or *estates* [clergy, aristocrats, and everyone else]. As late as 1789 the French Revolution was triggered when Louis XVI called into session the "Estates General," which had not been summoned since 1615. In the intervening 174 years, the so-called third estate had grown in power and self-consciousness to such a degree that it was no longer willing to be counted as one-third of the Estates General, inevitably outvoted by the first and second estates representing the clergy and aristocracy. In a sense, modern society began in 1789 when the Abbé Sieyès asked, "What is the Third Estate?" and answered: "The entire nation." All premodern societies might be seen as caste societies—societies in which one's function, status, place was determined at birth, as opposed to modern societies that assume legal equality, the opposite of defined place.

Caste is not race, but insofar as it is inherited, closed at birth, it is remarkably similar. The treatment of outcastes in India, Burma, Tibet, Korea, and Japan suggest even greater similarity to the ways in which some people have designated certain races as inferior. There is a similarity between Buddhist designations of certain occupational groups (tanners, leather workers, butchers, and others associated with death) and the medieval European Christian designation of Jews as impure because of their association with money. We might extend this correspondence to include Indian outcasts labeled polluted because of their association with sanitation. In all these cases, we have a society tabooing a particular group as an impure "Other" because of the work or the function they are made to perform. In all cases, it is work that has to be done and work that the dominant society has allowed or encouraged the sub-group in the society to do. But because there is such a religious, ideological, or emotional prohibition against doing that work, the taboo is strongly felt and rigidly applied. The internal "other" is kept eternally separate by proscriptions against intermarriage, by physical separation, separate clothing, sometimes touching phobias, all the more necessary precisely because these internal others are not recognizable as different. We call them "internal Others" because that phrase captures the dilemma and anxiety of the dominant society. Because they do not look different, because they are internal, not a recognizably foreign population, they can go unnoticed, and their pollution can poison others. Yet they cannot be made external, completely Other, because the dominant society requires their work.

In considering global patterns of racism we are seeking to understand not just individual historical causes, but the repeating patterns of behavior that might be called racist. We will call one of these patterns "the internal Other."

Another pattern emerges in the readings from the previous unit. The case of Japan is suggestive. While the Eta in Japan are treated like an internal Other, the Ainu are a recognizably different population, not responsible for any particular job or function, but exploited as cheap labor and treated as second-class citizens. As they themselves have indicated, their status in Japan is very much like that of the American Indian. They are an aboriginal population that has been conquered and controlled by a more powerful society. In this case, the Japanese were neighbors, but Japanese colonization and settlement of Hokkaido was similar to European settlement in the Americas, and in Australia and Tasmania. We call this pattern the racism of "settler societies."

When scholars speak of racism as a modern phenomenon, they are referring to the theorizing about race and the practice of racism in European settler societies after 1492. As Europeans settled in the Americas after 1492 they not only recognized a different race of people, but also practiced certain kinds of discriminatory behavior based on that recognition. They assumed that as Europeans or Christians they were superior and entitled to rule, convert, discipline, and punish those they perceived as inferior native populations. They let themselves assume—and this is, perhaps, a key to all cases of racism—that the indigenous people were invariably and inherently inferior, and that this inferior condition was a mark of their race.

Some of these cases of European settler racism were more benign than others. While the overall impact of the European settlement on Amerindian populations was devastating, one might distinguish between motives. Along a continuum of assistance, instruction, conversion, exploitation, domination, or annihilation, for instance, racism might be absent from the first two or three. Indeed, if racism necessitates a belief in inherent inferiority, then efforts at instruction or conversion might seem to rule racism out.

History is full of examples of people settling among other people. The grasslands of the Eurasian Steppe that stretches from Eastern Europe to north of China has pushed innumerable peoples to settle where others lived: Aryan settlers in India after 1500 B.C.E., Hittites in Egypt, Dorians in Greece, Eastern Huns in China, Western Huns pushing other peoples into Europe 2,500 to 1,500 years ago, and then the Mongols and Turks doing much the same. Ancient history is also full of examples of colonization: Phoenicians in Carthage, Greeks in Italy, Romans in North Africa, Chinese in Vietnam. There are also numerous examples of peoples conquering and converting another: Muslims in India, Aztecs in Guatemala, Russians in Siberia, Fulani in Nigeria, and Australians in Tasmania (to name a few). Are all of these cases racist? Probably not. Are some of them? Almost certainly. We will look at two of these examples—the Muslim conquests and the Chinese expansion into Vietnam in the seventh century—to get some comparative bearings.

What are the elements in settlement that invoke racism? Some sort of disparagement of the indigenous people, certainly. The conviction that they are inferior. But again racism need not be as broad as the "only good Indian is a dead Indian" view. Often settlers ignore, rather than disparage, the indigenous population. Sometimes settlement is easier on the conscience if the settlers can believe they are settling a virgin land.

Settler racism can be found in many forms in the initial European settlement of the Americas, North and South (though, again, perhaps not always and everywhere). Similar examples of settler racism can be found in European settlement in Asia. In general, Europeans did not settle in Asia in great numbers. Europeans in India, China, Japan, and Southeast Asia from 1500 to almost 1800 were predominantly merchants, soldiers, and priests who were relegated to small enclaves on the Asian coastline. There were, however, some settler colonies (in South Africa, Australia, New Zealand, and some Spice Islands) that developed a settler mentality about the native inhabitants. We have already looked at one of the more egregious of these cases in Tasmania.

Settler societies witnessed other forms of racism besides that directed against the original inhabitants. Settlement was often a continuous process in which new waves of settlers were introduced, often from different parts of the world and often to function in different niches or layers of society. Thus, the American settler society introduced African slaves to serve as plantation labor and, to a lesser extent, mine workers and household help, between 1500 and the nineteenth century. At the same time, European workers, farmers, and servants were introduced into American society, sometimes to work side by side with slaves, but more often to fill different niches in the colonial labor pool. The mixture of these elements led almost inevitably to white racism against black Africans, especially by European workers who, while free, lived only marginally better lives, sometimes did the same work, and often could imagine competing for the same work and standard of living, if and when slavery were ended. The idea that Africans were inherently destined for slavery developed easily among European settlers who were afraid they were not.

It is conceivable that European slave owners could have thought in nonracist ways about the African slaves on their plantations. There is some evidence that some did. But the existence of the additional European labor force (the

Irish actually worked on sugar plantations in Barbados before African labor was substituted in the mid-seventeenth century) made for volatile discrimination and competition.

Racism would not have developed out of the physical mix of different peoples in settler societies unless there was also the vocabulary of race to express it. We take the word "race" to be obvious and ancient, but it is not. The word "race" was not used in the modern sense until the eighteenth century. In the sixteenth and seventeenth centuries, the word was used to mean "the human race," a "race of poets," the "race of women," and a lot of other things. The modern use of the word, to designate one of the branches of humanity, developed in the scientific anthropology of eighteenth- and nineteenth-century Europe and America. That this philosophical and scientific interest arose in the period of European expansion and conquest was not coincidental. Ideas of the races of mankind were inevitably shaped by the goals of European expansion and domination.

The fifteenth-century Spanish who first settled in the Americas had, however, already started to use the word "race" in a different sense than the medieval or the modern. In the process of forcing Muslims and Jews out of the Iberian peninsula, they used the word "race" to refer to Christians and Jews. In some ways, this was not far from the later use of the word to mean "peoples descended from the same ancestors" since most people were born Christians or Jews. But because the Spanish Inquisition had already forced some Jews to convert to Catholicism, the Spanish discussion of race in the fifteenth century might include not only Jews but also Conversos, "new Christians" whose ancestors had been Jews.

The Christian conquest of the last Muslim fort in Spain, Granada, corresponded with the expulsion of the Jews, and Columbus's voyage—all in 1492. But the Spanish concern for racial purity in 1492 had more to do with the Jewish religious minority within Spain than with the inhabitants of new worlds. (The treasurer of Ferdinand and Isabella, Luis Santangel, was a Converso businessman who secured financing for Columbus's first voyage from a trust fund that he and an important Jewish merchant controlled.) The role of court Jews in pre-Inquisition Spanish society as important middlemen who loaned money at interest, provided financing for princes and kings, and could be trusted administrators was fairly common throughout Europe. Their special function was the result of Christian rules against money lending and on Jewish involvement in many other occupations. Nevertheless, the wealth and power that some court Jews and Jewish financiers accumulated sometimes made them easy prey for European monarchs. Why borrow when they could confiscate? And a few righteous remarks about racial purity added moral force to expediency.

The Jews were an internal Other in Christian society. They were often invited by princes and kings to live nearby, provide financing, expertise, or services that Christians did not perform. But their very specialness made them vulnerable to popular jealousy or resentment. The historical relationship of early Christian and Roman society to ancient Judaism also provided opportunity for Christian demagoguery that could direct violence against the Jews. In the eleventh and twelfth centuries, Christian crusades to the Holy Land were often preceded by massacres of European Jews.

The sort of racism that Christians practiced against Jews, culminating in the Nazi Holocaust, was unique in its scope and its cold-blooded execution. But there had been numerous earlier cases of pogroms and persecutions against Jews, and the Jews were not the only internal Other in European society. Gypsies, homosexuals, Muslims, and various immigrant groups had from time to time been persecuted for similar reasons.

Indeed, the internal Other need not be limited to these examples. All societies have used designated others to perform tasks that are not allowed or cannot be performed by the majority population. Turkish and other Muslim regimes from the fifteenth to nineteenth centuries used captured and converted Christians to staff their armies, special security guards, administrations, and sometimes highest government offices. As outsiders, these new converts had no ties to old feuding families, clans, or vested interests. Not all of these were cases of racism. Indeed, when the Muslims converted these Christian slaves to Islam the slaves were not thought to be inherently inferior—though they still remained slaves.

This distinction between racism that follows settlement and racism that responds to preexisting Otherness is, or course, purely formal. Often the Other is a descendant of previous settlers. The bloodletting that accompanied the breakup of Yugoslavia in the late 1990s was a product of much earlier settlement. The Serbian "ethnic cleansing" of Bosnian Muslims was an attempt to eradicate an inner Other Muslim population that Turks had established there hundreds of years ago.

Inner Others can also be products of recent settlement. In order to justify Israeli claims to West Bank settlement areas, conservative Israeli governments have placed Russian immigrants and religious nationalists in highly fortified enclaves in the midst of an overwhelming Palestinian population. Sometimes the introduction of a new Other is unintentional or driven by other pressures and forces. Turkish workers in Germany today, like Italian workers in the Americas a hundred years ago, are driven by market forces rather than political agendas, but the effect can be the same.

The rest of this book is based on this model of racism as the product of settler societies and confrontations with Inner Others. Any model is only good if it adds to our understanding. A good model should help us see things we might not have seen otherwise. It should enable us to make connections that would not otherwise have occurred to us. But any model is a simplification that obscures some things by clarifying others. As you read further, it might be useful to ask what this model brings into clearer focus, and what it obscures.

From *Race and Slavery in the Middle East: An Historical Enquiry*

Bernard Lewis

Have all societies which have expanded, conquered, colonized, or settled the territory of others been racist in their attitudes or behavior? In this and the following selection we will examine two important examples that occurred long before the expansion of Europe—in the seventh and eighth centuries.

The expansion of Islam was, by far, the most rapid and extensive expansion not only of this period but in most of human history. Between the conquests of Alexander the Great in the fourth century B.C.E. and those of the Mongols in the thirteenth century C.E., nothing compares to the speed and range of Muslim expansion from the death of the prophet Muhammad in 632 to the rout of the Chinese army at the Talas River in Central Asia in 751. In more than a hundred years a new religion from Arabia swept over North Africa to the Iberian Peninsula and through the Middle East to India and China. It was both a conquest of faith and a conquest of Arab armies, followed by genuine conversions, the creation of a hemispheric Muslim civilization, and the settlement of Arab governors and administrators. In all of this, was there also Arab or Muslim racism directed against the indigenous peoples? This is the question that Bernard Lewis, the historian of Islam, sets out to answer in this selection.

Lewis deals with Arab attitudes toward non-Arabs, slaves, and blacks. What are these different attitudes? Are any of them "racist?" What does this say about Islamic expansion and racism? Finally, Lewis suggests a gradual diminution of Arab prejudice against non-Arabs, but an increasing prejudice against blacks. When did this happen? Why?

Race

The advent of Islam created an entirely new situation in race relations. All the ancient civilizations of the Middle East and of Asia had been local, or at most regional. Even the Roman Empire, despite its relatively larger extent, was essentially a Mediterranean society. Islam for the first time created a truly universal civilization, extending from Southern Europe to Central Africa, from the Atlantic Ocean to India and China. By conquest and by conversion, the Muslims brought within the bounds of a single imperial system and a common religious culture peoples as diverse as the Chinese, the Indians, the peoples of the Middle East and North Africa, black Africans, and white Europeans. Nor was this coming together of races limited to a single rule and a single faith. The Muslim obligation of pilgrimage, which requires that every adult Muslim, at least once in his lifetime, must go on a journey to the holy places in Mecca and Medina, brought travelers from the remotest corners of the Muslim world, covering vast distances, to join with their fellow believers in common rites and rituals at the very center of the Islamic faith and world. The pilgrimage, probably the most important factor of individual, personal mobility in premodern history, combined with the better-known forces of conquest, commerce, and concubinage to bring about a great meeting and mixing of peoples from Asia, Europe, and Africa.

* * *

Islam in Arabia

The ultimate Islamic text is the Qur'an, and any enquiry into Islamic beliefs and laws must begin there. There are only two passages in the Qur'an which have a direct bearing on race and racial attitudes. The first of these occurs in chapter XXX, verse 22, and reads as follows:

> Among God's signs are the creation of the heavens and of the earth and the diversity of your languages and of your colors. In this indeed are signs for those who know.

This is part of a larger section enumerating the signs and wonders of God. The diversity of languages and colors is adduced as another example of God's power and versatility—no more.

The second quotation, chapter XLIX, verse 13, is rather more specific:

> O people! We have created you from a male and a female and we have made you into confederacies and tribes so that you may come to know

one another. The noblest among you in the eyes of God is the most pious, for God is omniscient and well-informed.

It will be clear that the Qur'an expresses no racial or color prejudice. What is perhaps most significant is that the Qur'an does not even reveal any awareness of such prejudice. The two passages quoted show a consciousness of difference; the second of them insists that piety is more important than birth. The point that is being made, however, is clearly social rather than racial— against tribal and aristocratic rather than against racial pride.

In the Qur'an, the question of race is obviously not a burning issue. It became a burning issue in later times, as can be seen from the elaboration on texts by subsequent commentators and by the collectors of tradition.

The evidence of the Qur'an on the lack of racial prejudice in pre-Islamic and the earliest Islamic times is borne out by such fully authenticated fragments of contemporary literature as survive. As in the Qur'an, so also in the ancient Arabian poetry, we find an awareness of difference—the sentiment of an Arab as against a Persian, Greek, or other identity. We do not, however, find any clear indication that this was felt in racial terms or went beyond normal feeling of distinctness which all human groups have about themselves in relation to others.

On the specific question of color, ancient Arabian literature is very instructive. The early poets used a number of different words to describe human colors, a much wider range than is customary at the present time. They do not correspond exactly to those that we use now and express a different sense of color—one more concerned with brightness, intensity, and shade than with hue. Human beings are frequently described by words which we might translate as black, white, red, olive, yellow, and two shades of brown, one lighter and one darker. These terms are usually used in a personal rather than a ethnic sense and would correspond to such words as "swarthy," "sallow, "blonde," or "ruddy" in our own modern usage more than to words like, "black" and "white." Sometimes they are used ethnically but even then in relative rather than an absolute sense. The Arabs, for example, sometimes describe themselves as black in contrast to Persians, who are red, but at other times as red or white in contrast to the Africans, who are black. The characteristic color of the Bedouin is variously stated as olive or brown.

In early Arabic poetry and historical narrative, the Persians are sometimes spoken of as "the red people," with a suggestion of ethnic hostility. This seems to date back to pre-Islamic times—to Arab resistance to Persian imperial penetration in Arabia and Arab reaction to the disdain which the civilized Persians showed for the semi-barbarous tribes on their desert frontier. After the Arab conquest of Iran, the roles were reversed; the Arabs were now the imperial masters, and the Persians their subjects. In this situation, the term "red people" acquired a connotation of inferiority and was used in particular reference to the non-Arab converts to Islam. Redness is similarly ascribed to the conquered natives of Spain, to the Greeks, and to other Mediterranean peoples of somewhat lighter skin than the Arabs.

As between Arabs and Africans the situation is more difficult to assess. There are verses, indeed many verses, attributed to pre-Islamic and early Islamic poets which would suggest very strongly a feeling of hatred and contempt directed against persons of African birth or origin. Most if not all of these, however, almost certainly belong to later periods and reflect later problems, attitudes, and preoccupations.

* * *

Prejudice and Piety

In ancient Arabia, as elsewhere in antiquity, racism—in the modern sense of the word—was unknown. The Islamic dispensation, far from encouraging it, condemns, even the universal tendency to ethnic and social arrogance and proclaims the equality of all Muslims before God. Yet, from the literature, it is clear that a new and sometimes vicious pattern of racial hostility and discrimination had emerged from within the Islamic world.

Conquest and Enslavement

This great change of attitude, within a few generations, can be attributed in the main to three major developments.

The first of these is the fact of conquest—the creation by the advancing Arabs of a vast empire in which the normal distinctions inevitably appeared between the conquerors and the conquered. At first, Arab and Muslim were virtually the same thing and the distinction could be perceived as religious. But as conversions to Islam proceeded very rapidly among the different conquered peoples, a new class came into existence—the non-Arab converts to Islam, whose position in some ways resembled that of the native Christians in the latter-day European empires. According to the doctrines of Islam—repeatedly reaffirmed by the pious exponents of the Faith—the non-Arab converts were the equals of the Arabs and could even outrank them by superior piety. But the Arabs, like all other conquerors before and since, were reluctant to concede equality to the conquered; and for as long as they could, they maintained their privileged position. Non-Arab Muslims were regarded as inferior and subjected to a whole series of fiscal, social, political, military, and other disabilities. They were known collectively as the *mawali* (sing. *mawla*), a term the primary meaning of which was "freedman." Many indeed were brought to Islam by way of capture, enslavement, and manumission—a process reflected in a famous if spurious *hadith*, according to which the Prophet said:

> Will you not ask me why I laugh? I have seen people of my community who are dragged to Paradise against their will. They asked, "O Prophet of God, who are they?" He said, "They are non-Arab people whom the warriors in the Holy War have captured and made to enter Islam"

Already in antiquity, some Greek philosophers had argued that slavery was beneficial to the barbarian slave, in that it initiated him to a better and more civilized way of life. The religious version of this—of slavery as a road to the blessings of Islam—later became a commonplace. But the earliest converts who came by this road encountered difficulties. . . .

A second factor of importance was the wider range of experience which conquest brought to the Arabs. Before Islam, their acquaintance with Africa was substantially limited to Ethiopia, a country with a level of moral and material civilization significantly higher than their own. During the lifetime of the Prophet, the good reputation of the Ethiopians was further increased by the kindly welcome accorded to Muslim refugees from Mecca. After the conquests, however, there were changes. Advancing on the one hand into Africa and on the other into Southwest Asia and Southern Europe, the Arabs encountered fairer-skinned peoples who were more developed and darker-skinned peoples who were less so. No doubt as a result of this they began to equate the two facts.

Coupled with this expansion was the third major development of the early Islamic centuries—slavery and the slave trade. The Arab Muslims were not the first to enslave black Africans. Even in Pharaonic times Egyptians had already begun to capture and use black African slaves, and some are indeed depicted on Egyptian monuments. There were black slaves in the Hellenistic and Roman worlds—but they seem to have been few and relatively unimportant, and regarded no differently from other slaves imported from remote places. The massive importation of black slaves and the growth of ethnic, even racial specialization in the slave population date from after the Arab expansion in Africa and were an indirect and unintended consequence of one of the most important humanitarian advances brought by the Islamic dispensation.

Inevitably, the large-scale importation of African slaves influenced Arab (and therefore Muslim) attitudes to the peoples of darker skin whom most Arabs and Muslims encountered only in this way.

This changing attitude affected even freemen of African ancestry—even descendants of the Companions of the Prophet. Thus 'Ubaydallah, the son of Abu Bakra, was appointed governor of Sistan in 671 and again in 697. Already by that time blackness had become a reproach; and a poet, in a satire against him, said:

> The blacks do not earn their pay
> by good deeds, and are not of good repute
> The children of a stinking Nubian black—
> God put no light in their complexions!

* * *

In Black and White

The Qur'an gives no countenance to the idea that there are superior and inferior races and that the latter are foredoomed to a subordinate status; the overwhelming majority of Muslim jurists and theologians share this rejection. There are some early traditions, and early juridical opinions and rulings citing them, which assign a privileged status to the Arabs, as against other peoples within the Islamic community. The Caliph 'Umar is even quoted, improbably, as saying that no Arab could be owned. Some pagan Arabs were in fact enslaved by the early caliphs and even by the Prophet himself, and the idea of Arab exemption from the normal rules regarding enslavement was not approved by later jurists.

Such an opinion did indeed reflect the social realities in the early centuries of the Islamic Empire, created by Arab conquests. By the ninth century, however, this privileged status had for all practical purposes ended. Some jurists, citing early traditions and the Qur'an itself, totally reject the idea of Arab or any other ethnic privilege. Even those who grant some limited acceptance to the idea, do so on the basis of kinship with the Prophet and reduce it to a kind of social prestige, of limited practical significance. At no time did Muslim theologians or jurists accept the idea that there may be races of mankind predisposed by nature or foredoomed by Providence to the condition of slavery.

Such ideas were, however, known from the heritage of antiquity and found echoes in Muslim writings, the more so when they began to correspond to the changing realities of Muslim society. Aristotle, in his discussion of slavery, had observed that while some are by nature free, others are by nature slaves. For such, the condition of slavery is both "beneficial and just," and a war undertaken to reduce them to that condition is a just war.

This idea, along with others from the same source, was taken up and echoed by a few Muslim Aristotelians. Thus the tenth-century philosopher al-Farabi lists, among the categories of just war, one the purpose of which is to subjugate and enslave those whose "best and most advantageous status in the world is to serve and be slaves" and who nevertheless refuse to accept slavery. The idea of natural slavery is mentioned, though not developed, by some other Aristotelian philosophers. Al-'Amiri, for example, follows Aristotle in comparing the natural superiority of master to slave with the equally natural superiority of man to woman.

Aristotle does not specify which races he has in mind, merely observing that barbarians are more slavish (doulikoteroi) than Greeks, and Asiatics more so than Europeans. That, according to Aristotle, is why they are willing to submit to despotic government—that is, one that rules them as a master (despotes) rules his slaves. By the tenth and eleventh centuries, some Muslim philosophers were more specific. The great physician and philosopher Avicenna (980–1037) notes as part of God's providential wisdom that he had placed, in regions of great heat or great cold, peoples who were by their very nature slaves, and incapable of higher things—"for there must be masters and slaves." Such were the Turks and their neighbors in the North and the blacks in Africa. Similar judgments were pronounced by his contemporary, the Ismaili theologian Hamid al-Din al-Kirmani (d. 1021), who was chief of missions of the Fatimid Caliphate in Cairo. In a philosophical work, he dismisses "the Turks, Zanj, Berbers, and their like" as "by their nature" without interest in the pursuit of intellectual knowledge and without desire to understand religious truth.

By this time, the great majority of Muslim slaves were either Turks or blacks, and Aristotle's doctrine of natural slavery, brought up to date, provided a convenient justification of their enslavement.

From *The Vermilion Bird: T'ang Images of the South*

Edward H. Schafer

This selection is excerpted from a book about the Chinese conquest of what is today southern China and Viet-Nam (together called Nam-Viet here) dur-

Edward H. Schafer. *The Vermilion Bird: T'ang Images of the South,* selections from pages 56–57, 58–59. Copyright © 1967 by The Regents of the University of California.

*ing the period of the Chinese T'ang dynasty (618–907). The Chinese called
themselves "the Hua people" and they called the various people of the south
"the Man people," Man being the general Chinese term for "southern heathen." In this selection, the author discusses Chinese (Hua) administration
of the southern lands and peoples.*

*Compare the Chinese conquest of the south with the Muslim expansion.
To what extent was the Chinese conquest "racist"? Was racism an inevitable aspect of conquest and settlement, or did it depend on the circumstances and people involved?*

Nam-Viet was notorious as a supplier of slaves, especially females: "Slave
girls of Viet, sleek of buttery flesh," wrote an appreciative Yuan Chen. Most
of these unfortunates were aborigines, sold to Chinese and sent to the great
cities of the north to tend the wants of the aristocracy. Neighboring Fukien
and Kweichow were also sources of human flesh, and in the ninth century
Fukien had the additional distinction of being the chief supplier of young
eunuchs to the capital. Even Szechwan, long since assimilated to the Middle
Kingdom [as China was called], was a source of native slaves, as Li Te-yu
attests, "a majority of the men of Shu sell their girls to become men's
concubines."

The chronicle of slavery in medieval China is not a pretty one, despite the
efforts of occasional benevolent rulers. The good acts of one did not bind his
successor. There were also local magistrates opposed to slavery. Examples
from both national and local levels follow. When Li Fu, a scion of the house
of T'ang, came to administer Jung in 783, he found that the captured "Western
Plain" rebels were being enslaved. He sought out their families, and eventually
gave them all their freedom. At about this same time, the sovereign Te Tsung
decreed a halt to the traffic in boys and girls in western Nam-Viet. In April
of 809 the new ruler Hsien Tsung, acting on the advice of Li Chiang and Po
Chu-i, who had pointed out to him the prevalence of selling persons of decent
families into slavery in Lingnan, Kweichow and Fukien, decreed the abolition
of the slave trade. There is no evidence that these royal acts had any permanent
effect. When Liu Tsung-yuan arrived at his humble magistracy in Liu-chou in
815, for instance, he found the custom there of persons pledging themselves
as security for loans. If principal and interest were not duly paid, the debtors
were enslaved. Liu abolished this hideous usury, partly at his own expense,
and his methods became models for other counties in which the practice prevailed. When the good governor K'ung K'uei came to rule over Nan-hai, he
received commissions from the magnates of Ch'ang-an to purchase southern
slaves, especially women, for them. Not only did he reject these requests, but
he forbade the sale of girls in Nam-Viet altogether.

Except for brief and local relief such as this, the non-Chinese peoples of
the south were systematically enslaved throughout the T'ang period, whether

"willingly" (as for debt) or unwillingly (as prisoners of war). The young women of the Thais and other ethnic communities were the chief sufferers. Not until the flourishing of the romantic *tz'u* style in poetry in the tenth century, especially at the hands of such masters of glamor as Ou-yang Chiung and Li Hsun, did the native girls of Nam-Viet achieve even so ambiguous a status as that of geisha or sing-song girl—to become the early sisters of the sweetly submissive congai of the French colonials of nineteenth-century Annam. We shall see them in this new role presently.

Both conscience and law permitted the enslavement of these subject peoples all the more readily because of two persistent views of them—an older one, that they were not really human, and a younger one, derived from the first, that they were not really civilized. The Man and the Lao and all the rest of them were animalian, and the graphs which represented their names almost invariably showed the recognizable symbol of a wild beast or a reptile. More specifically, the several tribesmen were said to be dragon men, or shark men, or dog men, or tiger men, or whatever—that is, they were semi-men who could convert themselves into animals and shared the attributes and mysterious powers of animals. In consequence, the Hua-men felt free to treat them as animals. Such treatment was given specious justification by the observation of such customs as totemic emblems and hunting taboos. A more "civilized" but accordingly more detestable variant of these notions (which had some basis in aboriginal belief), was the common one that the indigenes *resembled* animals in speech, thoughts, and habits. Even such an intelligent man as Han Yu did not hesitate to write of them as "like langurs or macaques," in short as apelike. . . .

In any case, the goodmen of the Hua race had a lively vocabulary to characterize these despised clowns, these bad replicas of themselves. When the victorious general Kao P'ien, after his successes in Nam-Viet, was sent to Szechwan in 875 to deal with the Yunnanese incursions, he spoke contemptuously of the "Southern Man" in an official report as "petty rogues, easily stood up to." His mature opinion was not much different from the puerile reaction of the pampered "boys"—stablehands and falconers—of the emperor Hsi Tsung: in 881 they preceded that unhappy monarch to Ch'eng-tu, fleeing from Ch'ang-an before the peasant armies of Huang Ch'ao; one of them, inspecting a temporary palace there, remarked, "Men say that Hsi-ch'uan is Man—but as I look at it today, it is not so bad after all." The arrogant youth was flogged to death for his impertinence. The fact remained, Szechwan was "Man country"—barbarous! Similarly, Te Tsung reviled his minister Lu Chih, a native of the civilized and only moderately southern town of Su-chou as "old Lao slave!" Lu Chih was no Lao, but as a southerner he could be called a Lao in a moment of passion, as he might be called an ape or a devil. If the snobbery of a northerner of the Yellow River valley could see a boor and a clodhopper (to say the least) in a native of the great lake and river system in the near south, it is easy to imagine his attitude toward the creoles—the Chinese born in Fukien, Lingnan, or Kweichow: they partook of the unpleasant character of the aborigines. This attitude was useful for the diffusion of northern culture. Local Chinese rulers did their best to surround themselves with noted scholars and politicians from the north. This was especially so in the little independent regimes which sprang up after the dissolution of the T'ang empire. Liu Yen, founder of the Han state in Lingnan, for instance, told visitors from the north that "he was ashamed to be the liege of savages and barbarians." Specifically: the natives, of whatever breed, were volatile, miserly, and cruel, "treacherous on the inside, simple on the outside." "They love swords and treat death lightly." But all alike, indigene or creole, lacked real moral standards, and had the avaricious souls of merchants: "South of the Five Mountain Passes men are commingled with the barbarian Lao, knowing nothing of education or public spirit—they take wealth to be manliness." This is the true northern aristocrat's way of ridiculing the upstart southern-born Chinese bourgeois, who, since late in the century, was privileged to rise to posts of importance through the examination system. But though the yokels were little better than the savages among whom they lived, the abuse they endured was not quite as severe as the humiliation and pain suffered by their aboriginal neighbors.

Yet more enlightened views existed, and on every level of quality. To begin at the greatest eminence: fearful for the safety of T'ai Tsung, who was devoted to hunting, an officer asked that prince to take thought for his subjects: "Heaven has commanded Your Enthroned Eminence to act as father and mother to both Hua and barbarian—how can you treat yourself so lightly?" All men were equal, then, under the divine parent. The sovereign's reply is not recorded. But it is known that his noble father took a humane attitude towards his non-Chinese subjects. "If only our Pastors and Protectors could embrace them with loyalty and good faith," said Kao Tsu, denying the petition of a Szechwanese governor who wished to lead a punitive expedition against the restless Lao tribes, "they would all come of themselves to submit. How may we lightly set buckler and battle axe in motion, fishing and hunting these folk, as if we compared them to birds and beasts? Surely that is not the aim of the Father and Mother of his people!" Occasionally (but rarely, I fear) this admirable attitude was shared by a responsible agent of the Son of Heaven on the frontier. It is told that in 703 P'ei Huai-ku, a well-disposed official in Kweichow, brought about the surrender of a triumphant rebel, the aborigine Ou-yang Ch'ien, and all of his hopeful hordes. Disagreeing with the idea that "the barbarian Lao are faithless," he got in direct touch with that chieftain, saying, "Loyalty and faith allow us to communicate even with divine intelligences—surely, then, with these men of the border!"

The Origins of Racism in England and Spain

Audrey Smedley

This selection is comprised of three excerpts from a recent book by a modern historian of racism. We begin with her historical investigation into the use of the word "race" in European languages. Why is this important? What does her investigation tell you about the roots of racism in Europe?

The second section deals with "English Ethnocentrism and the Idea of the Savage." What is the difference between ethnocentrism and racism? What do you make of the thesis that "it was the English experience with the Irish 'which was the root of English racial attitudes' "? Were these attitudes ethnocentric or racist? In what ways were the Irish the forerunners of a plantation slave class for the English, a model later forced upon Africans?

The third section, on Spain, suggests another route to racism. Why, according to the author, did some Spanish wish to make Judaism a matter of blood and heredity rather than faith and personal commitment? Why was the search for New Christians an important step in the development of racism?

What is the significance of Smedley's ideas about the origins of racism in England and Spain?

The Etymology of the Term "Race"

In the fifteenth century, western and northern Europeans ventured out from their geographic and historical isolation and discovered the rest of the world.

Within the next five hundred years, European exploration, expansion, colonial settlement, and exploitation changed the course of human history and generated complex new relationships among the peoples of the world.

In the process of exploration and penetration into what was terra incognita, European adventurers encountered other peoples totally unknown to them before that time. The sometimes awesome and exotic groups had material, religious, and social life-ways alien and unexpected to the peoples of Europe. The strangeness of the peoples and their habitats challenged the imaginations of the explorers, prompting a rash of speculations and novel interpretations of the new discoveries. In order to grapple both intellectually and practically with these alien societies, Europeans imposed upon them meanings and identities that fit within their own historical understandings, experiences, and preconceptions of what the world was all about. At some time in the process they began to use the term "race" to characterize differences among human groups. Because they left little record of the source of the term, we have only a hint of the specific meaning(s) attached to it. . . .

In fact, "race" did not appear in the English language as a technical term with reference to human groups until the seventeenth century, when it was apparently employed in several ways. One referred to the characteristics or common qualities of certain types of persons. Thus, for example, John Bunyan in *Pilgrim's Progress* referred to a race of "saints." Shakespeare, along with other writers, seemed to associate the term with the idea of the inherited disposition or temperament of individuals. Other writers conveyed the sense of a class or type of person when they spoke of a "race of bishops" or "the race of womankind." The second usage was more incipiently technical in that various learned men, in their attempts to describe and classify different human groups occasionally used the term interchangeably with "species" as a general mode of categorizing peoples. William Petty and a few other writers connected "races" with "generations," which we shall see was an apt reflection of its source.

The earliest Spanish dictionary, the *Tesoro de la Lengua Castellana o Espanola* of Coharruvias (1611), specifically identifies "raza" as referring to the "caste or quality of authentic horses," which are branded with an iron so as to be recognized. But two other meanings are given: One pertains to threads in the weave of a cloth, the other alone refers to humankind. Here, "raza" is taken in a negative sense to connote some Moorish or Jewish ancestors in one's lineage. During the period of the Inquisition in Spain, the term "raza" was sometimes applied to families suspected of heresy and to New Christians to distinguish them from the older peasant Christian community. By 1737, the *Diccionario de la Lengua Castellana* gives as the first and primary meaning "the caste or quality of origin or lineage" when speaking about "los hombres," noting only later in that same passage its earlier usage for animals and cloth weaves. . . .

The identification of race with a breeding line or stock of animals carries with it certain implications for how Europeans came to view human groups. One is that the question of species differentiation is really left moot. The line or stock is perceived as a variation of a larger entity or group within which all individuals can interbreed. The fact of the existence of a perceived capacity for members of one line to interbreed with another or others is in itself a recognition of the sameness, the oneness of the category, and it reflects adherence to biblical authority. Second, among farmers and herders, who were perhaps the first to invent and use this term, it is well known that certain behavioral propensities are inheritable in highly inbred lines of animals. This is cognitively associated with the unmistakable observation of the heritability of biophysical features.

Following from this, a third and related implication is that value judgments are critical to the identification of the breeding line, for it is specifically for some culturally valued quality or qualities that deliberate intervention in the reproductive process has occurred. That is, qualities that the human controller has deemed desirable are evoked by the deliberate breeding of certain animals within the same population. Thus, inherent within the term "race" is a potential and real ranking and evaluation of both physical and behavioral traits. To those using the term, such ranking and judgment are real because of the known centuries of human experimentation and breeding of domestic animals. These value judgments become potentials whenever the term "race" can be or is applied to other biological forms, including humans.

Finally, unlike other terms for classifying people (e.g., "nation," "people," "variety," "kind," etc.), the term "race" places emphasis on innateness, on the inbred nature of whatever is being judged. Whatever is inheritable is also permanent and unalterable (except through calculated breeding in future generations), whether it be body size, horn length, fur length or color, or aggressiveness, fearsomeness, docility dullness, intelligence, or any other states of being that humans attribute to their animals. The term "race" made possible an easy analogy of inheritable and unchangeable features from breeding animals to human beings.

Race, then, was not just a reasonably felicitous term that was applied arbitrarily and sporadically to indigenous peoples of other lands. This analysis shows that there were useful and important substantive aspects of its referential meaning that were already present when Europeans began to use the term as the prime mechanism for conveying human group differences. It was an eminently appropriate term for the world-view about all human differences that the English and other Europeans were beginning to evolve.

However, the English in North America were to develop and elaborate the implications of the term "race" to a much higher degree than either the Spanish, the Portuguese, or the French. The Spanish and Portuguese who settled Latin America evolved a very different perspective on human differences that did not result in the construction of rigidly exclusive "racial" groups, as occurred in North America and South Africa. . . .

English Ethnocentrism and the Idea of the Savage

Leonard Liggio, in exploring the race idea and raising a more general question about the comparative differences between the English colonization practices and those of other Europeans, asks, "How is it possible to explain the fact that the English developed the most racist attitudes toward the natives wherever they expanded or established overseas colonies?" He proposes an unexpected hypothesis, that it was the English experience with the Irish "which was the root of English racial attitudes." Perhaps because of the intractable and seemingly irreconcilable contemporary conflict between these two peoples, other historians have turned their attention to this long-standing belligerence for insights into the general English attitudes toward indigenous peoples and the nature of English colonial and imperial policies.

Throughout the sixteenth and seventeenth centuries, and especially during the reign of Elizabeth I, Englishmen focused their attention, and a great deal of hostility, toward Ireland and the Irish people. The era was punctuated by periodic attempts to finally conquer the Irish, on the one hand, and by several major Irish rebellions, on the other. The last of the sixteenth-century rebellions (1597), which brought forth the wrath of Queen Elizabeth and the final triumph of her forces over the native chieftain Hugh O'Neill, was the climax of four centuries of repeated invasions, implacable Irish resistance, and failed attempts to consolidate English power over the western island. A brief review of this history is very instructive.

The first invasion and attempt to settle Ireland occurred under Henry II in 1169 and 1171, as part of the expansion of Anglo-Norman civilization following the Norman invasion of England. By the end of the century, most of Ireland was under some semblance of English control in the form of Anglo-Norman barons who had been given titles to Irish lands, which they ruled as personal fiefdoms. But the scattered Irish clans, lacking a centralized government, proved impossible to vanquish and control. Within a short time they had regained most of their lands and had begun the first of several great revivals of

Gaelic culture that flourished from time to time throughout the thirteenth through the fifteenth centuries.

One development, however, was particularly upsetting and threatening to the nominal rulers of Ireland. Those Englishmen who had settled in Irish lands (called Old English), especially in remote areas away from the pale, intermingled with the Irish and increasingly "went native," that is, they assimilated Irish culture and language. To halt what the English saw as the erosion of civilized culture and the degeneracy of Englishmen in Ireland, the English Crown established legal restrictions forbidding Englishmen to wear Irish dress or hairstyles, to speak the Irish language, or to intermarry or trade with the Irish. These restrictions, the Statutes of Kilkenny, also outlawed Irish games, poetry, and music, apparently under the assumption that these cultural features were too seductive for young Englishmen to resist. Such prohibitions, and others, stayed in effect until the seventeenth century. But they had little consequence for the preservation of English culture, even though increasingly more Englishmen were encouraged to settle in Ireland throughout this period and to promote English culture.

The English were frustrated by their inability to establish complete suzerainty over Irish lands (some of which were in the control of Irish brigands) or to transform the natives and absorb them into English culture. Throughout the period of English attempts to subdue these lands and peoples, one ostensible objective was to spread English civilization. But the underlying reality and primary aim was the confiscation of Irish lands, the establishment of an agrarian economy, and the exploitation of native labor.

The English attitude toward the Irish, almost from the beginning of penetration into the western island, was one of contempt for Irish culture or lifestyles. This was matched by intense Irish hatred of all that was English. Thus extreme ethnocentrism ensued between these two peoples early in the contact period, which is a common result of situations in which one people attempt to conquer another. But the conflict was not only based on the ethnic chauvinism of two peoples competing for political supremacy, as in the case of the many other confrontations between the emerging nation-states of Europe. The hostility between the Irish and English went much deeper. It exemplified an age-old struggle, symbolized in biblical times in the conflict between Cain and Abel, and one that has resurged many times in many places throughout human history. It was the clash between a people who were nomadic or semi-nomadic pastoralists and those who settled on the land as farmers and cultivated a sedentary way of life. It was a fundamental conflict between two very different life-styles, two different views of the world, two different value systems, and two different sets of problems and solutions for them. . . .

The contempt and hatred that the English had for Irish culture were expressed by Giraldus Cambrensis as early as 1187. "They are a wild and inhospitable people," he claimed. "They live on beasts only, and live like beasts. . . . This people despises agriculture, has little use for the money-making of towns." He described their uncleanliness, their flowing hair and beards infested with lice, their barbarous dress and their laziness. "They think that the greatest pleasure is not to work and the greatest wealth is to enjoy liberty." James Myers asserts that it was this inordinate love of liberty to which Giraldus Cambrensis and his successors objected, and this critique of the Irish continued throughout succeeding centuries.

At the time that Columbus was exploring the New World, the English under Henry VII in 1494 began a new policy designed to settle the Irish problem once and for all through forced colonization. Henry VIII, however, was more benign in his approach, preferring to provide mechanisms by which the Irish would voluntarily submit to his rule. But it was he who built defensive forts and established the first standing army in Ireland with the intention of ridding the fertile areas of all those who refused to submit to English rule. The colonization policy was continued by Henry VIII's successors.

Irish resistance throughout the sixteenth century enraged many of the English, who persisted in viewing the Irish as "rude, beastly, ignorant, cruel and unruly infidels." According to William Thomas, writing in 1552, the "wild" Irish were unreasonable beasts who knew neither God nor good manners and who lived with their wives and children in filth along with their animals. Some Englishmen argued what was to become a familiar strain in European attitudes toward Indians and Africans in the New World during the coming centuries: that the Irish were better off as slaves of the English than they were retaining the brutish customs of their traditional culture. While confiscating Irish lands, many English military leaders, some of whom were later to be involved in the colonization of New England and the Virginia colonies, regularly killed women and children, which has prompted some historians to accuse the English of genocide. Humphrey Gilbert, whom David B. Quinn called a "bloodthirsty sadist," justified this barbaric treatment by arguing that the men who fought the war could not be maintained without the women who milked the cattle and provided them with food "and other necessaries." During the final years of the Nine Years' War, many of the Irish were driven off to western Ireland and their chief form of wealth, their cattle, was destroyed. Lands were taken over by the younger sons of English gentry, who subsequently set about to create an agricultural and commercial society. The Irish who remained were reduced to involuntary laborers. Under English law they were not allowed to own land, hold office, be apprenticed to any skill or craft, or serve on juries. Their principal identity was that of cheap labor.

Toward the middle of the seventeenth century, another more widespread rebellion by the Irish and by some of the Old English took place. This was followed by extremely repressive measures on the part of the English under Oliver Cromwell. According to Liggio:

> Cromwell's army in Ireland, often New England Puritan led or inspired, carried out the most complete devastation that Ireland experienced until that time. Extermination became a policy. Massacres were carried out. Prisoners of war were transported to servitude in the new English colonies in the West Indies. Ireland like New England was taken with the Bible in one hand, the sword in the other. Lord Clarendon observed that the Cromwellian policy was to act without "any humanity to the Irish nation, and more especially to those of the old native extraction, the whole race whereof they had upon the matter sworn an utter extirpation."

The significance of this brutal treatment and the transportation of large numbers of captive peoples of both sexes to the sugar plantations in the West Indies rested upon the growing image of the Irish as something less than human, as a people whose capacity for civilization was stunted. This view took form slowly but was perhaps common among some English elite by the early seventeenth century. . . .

Hereditary Social Identity: The Lesson of Catholic Spain

Because of the mutual influences that the Spanish and English had on one another during the early centuries of exploration and colonization, it is useful to consider those features of Spanish life and thought that may have influenced English ideologies about human differences. As already suggested, the Spanish had quite a different history and experience with human diversity from the English. Since the eighth century, the [Iberian] peninsula had been dominated by a civilization that was among the world's most tolerant, at least for a while. Under Muslim hegemony, Spain had experienced the formation of a heterogeneous, multi-cultural, multi-"racial" society. For a while, Muslims, Christians, and Jews led culturally productive lives together and had remarkably benign relationships among themselves, with some exceptions, even to the point of considerable intermarriage. However, with the rise to political power of some of the Christian kingdoms and with the thrust to regain Spanish territory for the Catholic Church ("the Reconquest"), beginning as early as the ninth century, Jews and Muslims came under pressure to convert. Conflict ensued, and the entire social system gradually became rigidified into three ethnic-religious "castes" whose relationships in the fifteenth and sixteenth centuries were often characterized by fear, mistrust, envy, and hatred.

Some 300,000 Jews became Christian by the end of the fifteenth century, a time when the marriage of Ferdinand and Isabella had become the political fulcrum symbolizing the rise of modern Catholic Spain. Known as "conversos," these former Jewish families were rich and urban; they also constituted the largest proportion of the educated. The Moors [Muslims], who tended to be concentrated in the southern regions of Spain in Valencia, Granada, and Castile, underwent forced baptisms early in the sixteenth century, but their customs, traditions, and language [Arabic] continued intact for a while. The Moors came to constitute an underclass of laboring people who remained somewhat culturally distinct from the Spanish. Eventually, the state expelled all of the Moriscos, as they were called; some 275,000 were shipped off to North Africa between 1609 and 1614.

Jealous of the wealth, power, and influence of the Jewish families who had converted, many of whom were using their new Christian identity to advance themselves in the civil or church hierarchies, some of the Christian leaders began to question the theological probity of some conversos. Many Christians in the countryside, of peasant backgrounds, emerged as antagonists, not only to the already declining Muslim influence but also to what they believed to be the Jewish domination of trade, commerce, banking, scholarship, and the arts. In a drama characterized by intrigues, petty jealousies, and varied political machinations, opponents began to charge that some of the conversos and their descendants (the New Christians) were secretly practicing Judaism. An inquisition directed at heretics was established in 1478, sanctioned by the Catholic kings and the church. It was designed to weed out recalcitrant converts or "secret" Jews by investigating personal behavior and genealogies for the taint of Jewishness. Some of the ideas that became basic ingredients of a racial world-view were set in motion during this period of rising Christian intolerance and rampant persecution of Jews and Moors.

A major contribution to Western thought was the belief engendered by the Inquisition in the hereditary nature of social status, a theme often carried through in the extreme. Family ties were closely scrutinized to discover the "hidden Jew" and a social stigma was attached to anyone or any family that had even a remote association with someone prosecuted by the Inquisition. Although lineal descent seemed to be the avenue of heritability of social standing (vis-a-vis the church) this was not consistently observed. The result was that many Spaniards, including some non-Jews, sought a certificate of "purity" that, for a fee, would be issued by the church. It constituted a guarantee of one's genealogical purity from "any admixture of Jew or Moor" or from condemnation by the Holy Office. These "certificates of Limpieza de Sangre" (purity of blood) were not only a major source of revenue for the church, but were also vital requirements for social mobility, as certain occupations and activities were closed by law to the families of converts.

The idea that social standing is inheritable is an ancient one associated with societies in which there are class divisions, occupational specializations, and private or lineage property. Spanish folk ideology and the practices of the Spanish church and state seemed to define Jewishness and Moorishness as something almost biological, using the idiom of "blood" ties. Elaborate tests for finding social genealogical connections were incipient mechanisms for establishing social placement. And the Spanish use of the term "race," along with "castas," for both Jews and Moors bespeaks a potentially new kind of image of what were essentially ethnic (religious) differences.

Americo Castro agrees that what was occurring in Spain under the Inquisition was a hardening of ethnic differences, rather than an appeal to some biogenetic reality. He says, "From the fifteenth century on, 'purity of blood' has meant consciousness of caste." It has nothing to do with physical traits or "racial physical type." Yet to equate sections of the society with breeding lines of animals, even symbolically, is to suggest a kind of permanency and immutability to their social qualities that are found only in biological transmission. This attests to the great degree to which Catholic political powers, both papal and secular, were anxious and willing to separate out these populations and to eliminate the Jewish and Moorish cultural influences among them. In this way, the Catholic leaders of Spain could extend and consolidate their power over a population that was essentially homogeneous in religion and culture and uniformly responsive to imposed laws and sanctions.

But any idea of biologically hereditary social positions was contradicted by the more massive uses of conversion, essentially baptism, to eliminate the presence of Jews and Moors in Spanish society. The vast majority of those converted remained Christian, and the acceptance of these former Jews and former Muslims and their descendants as legitimate members of the Catholic community and the state is in opposition to the tenets of modern race ideology, which precludes forever the possibility of such a transformation. The apparent contradiction between the reality of the alteration of social identity, under pressure, and the notion that social identity is a concomitant of unique biological features that are exclusive and unalterable was never resolved and probably never even recognized by the thinkers and philosophers of the Inquisition. . . .

Thus some of the major ingredients for the ideology and world-view of "race" were present in the thought patterns and understandings of both Spanish and English peoples during the critical period when European colonial settlements in the New World began. All of the European conquerors and colonizers turned to the use of the term "race" (raza, race, reazza). They all shared a common belief that their victims were some form of "savages," despite recognized diversity among the cultures of indigenous peoples and different conceptions of savagery in the European minds. And all of the Europeans initiated the practice of slavery, both with Indians and with imported Africans.

Part 4

European Settler Society: The Iberian Conquest of the New World

Indians accused of sodomy are thrown to the dogs on orders from Balboa. *(From DeBry's* Great Voyages *[1590-1634])*

The previous selections on T'ang China and Islamic expansion remind us that European expansion after 1492 was not an entirely new development in world history. There had been important precursors. Further, we see racist elements in these earlier conquests, though we see nonracist and perhaps antiracist sentiment as well; and we see change. Bernard Lewis is not the only commentator on Islam to point out that Muslims identified slavery with blacks only after the ninth century. Islam may have initially challenged Arab prejudices against blacks, but then later succumbed to them. Similarly in China, some travelers, administrators, and soldiers denied the humanity of southern peoples of Nam-Viet; others insisted on it. That these peoples were generally thought of as barbarians reveals prejudice; that some of these "barbarians" served as intermediaries and Chinese allies shows otherwise.

Can we draw any conclusions from these examples? Perhaps we can see how conquest or expansion can provide soil for prejudice to grow, though it is not universal among the conquerors. For prejudice, much less racism, to become a dominant view or enshrined practice, perhaps other conditions have to develop, such as an identification of a particular people with inferior or subject status—not just defeat, but "defeatedness," the assumption that a people are ordained for slavery or subjection.

This case was made by some of the Spanish conquerors of the Americas. In an important debate before the Spanish king Charles in 1550, Juan Gines de Sepulveda, a Spanish aristocrat, scholar and translator of Aristotle, argued that the defeat of the Indians in the Caribbean and Mexico was testament enough to their natural inferiority. He pointed, for instance, to the conquest of Mexico by Hernan Cortes and asked: "Could there be a better or clearer testimony of the superiority that some men have over others in talent, skill, strength of spirit, and virtue? Is it not proof that the Mexicans are slaves by nature?"

In that great debate at Valladolid, Spain, in 1550, Sepulveda was answered by Bartolomeo de Las Casas, who had come to the New World as a soldier but, horrified by the barbarity of the conquest, joined the Dominican clergy and devoted his life to improving the lives of the Indians. To counter Sepulveda, Las Casas quoted from an ancient Roman historian who praised Roman rule of Spain in the same way that Sepulveda spoke of Spanish rule of Mexico. Then he said: "I would like to hear Sepulveda in his cleverness, answer this question: Does he think that the war of the Romans against the Spanish was justified in order to free them from barbarism? And this question also: Did the Spanish wage an unjust war when they vigorously defended themselves against them?"[1]

The royal judges issued no decision, allowing the debate of the century to end in a draw and the policy of enslavement to continue. The success of Las

Casas might ironically be measured in his petition to the king in 1516 to import slaves from Spain (Europeans or Africans) in order to leave the Indians alone. In 1518 the crown accepted the recommendation for Africans and a Mediterranean plantation society spread to the Americas. Las Casas later objected to slavery in any form, but it was too late. The institutional interests of slave owners, the emerging plantation class, and the conquistadors won out.

As you read this section, ask yourself how some members of the conquest society become racist while others, like Las Casas, champion the oppressed. If conquest, expansion, or settler societies do not turn all of their members into racists, what accounts for the differences between those who do and those who do not? Do the racists come from a particular social class? Do they represent particular interests in the society? Is it possible for someone who grows up in a society like this to escape racism entirely, or is it only a matter of choosing one group over another, for example, Indians over Africans?

Reading Smedley in the previous section suggests another set of problems to consider here. In the United States, we are used to thinking of racism as a matter of skin color, black and white. Smedley's argument that European racism developed initially against the Irish and Jews is an interesting challenge to that preconception. If she is right, color or blackness was not a primary cause of white racism in Europe. This is an important issue in determining the roots of white racism in the Americas. This is a long debate among American historians. In Part 6 (Reilly, "Race and Racism") you will read a brief excerpt from Winthrop Jordan's *White Over Black* which makes a strong case for antiblack prejudice in European, especially English, thought *before* the introduction of African slavery. Others have argued (and Smedley supports this) that it was the exclusive enslavement of Africans that led to white racism (antiblack racism), not the other way around. Smedley makes much (perhaps too much) of Irish pastoralism as the essential difference with the English. (Conquest of the Other can always produce some rationale in the minds of the conquerors.) But the importance of religion in both English and Spanish expansion is interesting. In both cases the other—Irish Catholics and both Spanish Jews and Muslims—were demonized because of their religion. This was the age of the Protestant Reformation and Catholic Counter-Reformation when such matters were taken very seriously.

Even despite the rise of religious fundamentalism in the United States today, we abhor religious fanaticism and pride ourselves on our toleration. It is difficult to imagine Americans wanting to kill others because of their religion. Unfortunately it is somewhat easier for us to imagine Americans killing because of color, which we call race. But Smedley reminds us that in the sixteenth century religion meant race. The Irish were thought by the English to be a different race because they were Catholics. The Jews who looked like other Spaniards were not Christians, nor were the Moors (Muslims).

When you read these selections, notice the role that religion plays in the Spanish encounter with the Indians. Are the Indians more vulnerable to Spanish depredation because they are a different color, because they are weak, or because they are non-Christian?

There is an added element here. While the Spanish were conquering the Americas they were also engaged in the Inquisition against people not because of their own religion, but because of their parents', grandparents', or ancestors' religion. As Smedley points out, the Conversos were Catholics whose ancestors had been Jewish or Muslim. The implication is that despite their conversions, even that of the parents or grandparents, they were still not properly Catholic. Their Jewish or Muslim ancestry could not be removed. It was in the blood, a stain that could not be washed away, not even by baptism and the sacraments. While this was not orthodox Catholicism by any means, it is a model definition of racism.

Racism is at root a belief that the other's moral or behavioral inferiority is endemic and inherited. That European racism began over religious inheritance makes perfect sense when we recall the importance of religion at the time, the sixteenth century, when Europeans expanded throughout the world. Perhaps the real roots of modern racism are not in the European involvement in the Atlantic slave trade, but in the Protestant Reformation and the Spanish "Reconquest" of the Iberian Peninsula. In fact, since that reconquest was part of a crusading movement that went back to 1095, we might better see the roots of modern racism in Christian expansion against the Muslims. Even as tolerant a Christian as Las Casas believed that "neither the Greeks nor the Romans nor the Turks nor the Moors should be said to be exercising justice, since neither prudence nor justice can be found in a people that does not recognize Christ. . . ."[2]

Notes

1. Bartolomeo de Las Casas, *In Defense of the Indians*, trans. Stafford Poole, C.M. (DeKalb: Northern Illinois University Press, 1992), p. 43.
2. Ibid., p. 54.

Hispaniola

Bartolomeo de Las Casas

Bartolomeo de Las Casas (1474–1566) wrote the brief but important book from which this selection is drawn in order to convince King Charles V of Spain to end the enslavement of Indians. The book was widely translated by Spain's enemies and became the basis of the Black Legend according to which Protestant Europeans argued that Catholic Spanish colonialism in the Americas was the worst. In response one might note that the Spanish at least encouraged criticism of slavery, while other countries produced no Las Casas or Valladolid debate.

If Las Casas frames his account as an epic battle between the forces of goodness and the forces of evil, his anecdotes are based on events he witnessed himself or were the common currency of the time.

This selection from the book deals with the island of Hispaniola, the first one the Spanish settled. In fact, on Christmas Eve, 1492, Columbus ("the Admiral") settled the first colony in the New World on the northwest coast (modern Haiti) in a place he christened Navidad after his ship, the Santa Maria, *had broken up in the nearby waters. Later he planted the capital of the Spanish empire in the Americas at Santo Domingo (today the capital of the Dominican Republic, the eastern half of the island of Hispaniola).*

What seemed to motivate the conquistadors in committing such atrocities against the Indians? Was it racism?

Are all atrocities racist? Are all atrocities committed against people of another "race" racist?

This [Hispaniola] was the first land in the New World to be destroyed and depopulated by the Christians, and here they began their subjection of the women and children, taking them away from the Indians to use them and ill use them, eating the food they provided with their sweat and toil. The Spaniards did not content themselves with what the Indians gave them of their own free will, according to their ability, which was always too little to satisfy enormous appetites, for a Christian eats and consumes in one day an amount of food that would suffice to feed three houses inhabited by ten Indians for one month. And they committed other acts of force and violence and oppression which made the Indians realize that these men had not come from Heaven.

From *The Devastation of the Indies: A Brief Account*, trans. Herma Briffault (Baltimore: Johns Hopkins University Press, 1992), selections from pp. 32–35, 40–41.

And some of the Indians concealed their foods while others concealed their wives and children and still others fled to the mountains to avoid the terrible transactions of the Christians.

And the Christians attacked them with buffets and beatings, until finally they laid hands on the nobles of the villages. Then they behaved with such temerity and shamelessness that the most powerful ruler of the islands had to see his own wife raped by a Christian officer.

From that time onward the Indians began to seek ways to throw the Christians out of their lands. They took up arms, but their weapons were very weak and of little service in offense and still less in defense. (Because of this, the wars of the Indians against each other are little more than games played by children.) And the Christians, with their horses and swords and pikes began to carry out massacres and strange cruelties against them. They attacked the towns and spared neither the children nor the aged nor pregnant women nor women in childbed, not only stabbing them and dismembering them but cutting them to pieces as if dealing with sheep in the slaughter house. They laid bets as to who, with one stroke of the sword, could split a man in two or could cut off his head or spill out his entrails with a single stroke of the pike. They took infants from their mothers' breasts, snatching them by the legs and pitching them headfirst against the crags or snatched them by the arms and threw them into the rivers, roaring with laughter and saying as the babies fell into the water, "Boil there, you offspring of the devil!" Other infants they put to the sword along with their mothers and anyone else who happened to be nearby. They made some low wide gallows on which the hanged victim's feet almost touched the ground, stringing up their victims in lots of thirteen, in memory of Our Redeemer and His twelve Apostles, then set burning wood at their feet and thus burned them alive. To others they attached straw or wrapped their whole bodies in straw and set them afire. With still others, all those they wanted to capture alive, they cut off their hands and hung them round the victim's neck, saying, "Go now, carry the message," meaning, Take the news to the Indians who have fled to the mountains. They usually dealt with the chieftains and nobles in the following way: they made a grid of rods which they placed on forked sticks, then lashed the victims to the grid and lighted a smoldering fire underneath, so that little by little, as those captives screamed in despair and torment, their souls would leave them.

I once saw this, when there were four or five nobles lashed on grids and burning; I seem even to recall that there were two or three pairs of grids where others were burning, and because they uttered such loud screams that they disturbed the captain's sleep, he ordered them to be strangled. And the constable, who was worse than an executioner, did not want to obey that order (and I know the name of that constable and know his relatives in Seville), but instead put a stick over the victims' tongues, so they could not make a sound, and he stirred up the fire, but not too much, so that they roasted slowly, as he liked. I saw all these things I have described, and countless others.

And because all the people who could do so fled to the mountains to escape these inhuman, ruthless, and ferocious acts, the Spanish captains, enemies of the human race, pursued them with the fierce dogs they kept which attacked the Indians, tearing them to pieces and devouring them. And because on few and far between occasions, the Indians justifiably killed some Christians, the Spaniards made a rule among themselves that for every Christian slain by the Indians, they would slay a hundred Indians. . . .

Because the particulars that enter into these outrages are so numerous they could not be contained in the scope of much writing, for in truth I believe that in the great deal I have set down here I have not revealed the thousandth part of the sufferings endured by the Indians, I now want only to add that, in the matter of these unprovoked and destructive wars, and God is my witness, all these acts of wickedness I have described, as well as those I have omitted, were perpetrated against the Indians without cause, without any more cause than could give a community of good monks living together in a monastery. And still more strongly I affirm that until the multitude of people on this island of Hispaniola were killed and their lands devastated, they committed no sin against the Christians that would be punishable by man's laws, and as to those sins punishable by God's law, such as vengeful feelings against such powerful enemies as the Christians have been, those sins would be committed by the very few Indians who are hardhearted and impetuous. And I can say this from my great experience with them: their hardness and impetuosity would be that of children, of boys ten or twelve years old. I know by certain infallible signs that the wars waged by the Indians against the Christians have been justifiable wars and that all the wars waged by the Christians against the Indians have been unjust wars, more diabolical than any wars ever waged anywhere in the world. This I declare to be so of all the many wars they have waged against the peoples throughout the Indies.

After the wars and the killings had ended, when usually there survived only some boys, some women, and children, these survivors were distributed among the Christians to be slaves. The *repartimiento* or distribution was made according to the rank and importance of the Christian to whom the Indians were allocated, one of them being given thirty, another forty, still another, one or two hundred, and besides the rank of the Christian there was also to be considered in what favor he stood with the tyrant they called Governor. The pretext was that these allocated Indians were to be instructed in the articles of the Christian Faith. As if those Christians who were as a rule foolish and cruel and greedy and vicious could be caretakers of souls! And the care they took was to send the men to the mines to dig for gold, which is intolerable labor, and to send the women into the fields of the big ranches to hoe and till the land, work suitable for strong men. Nor to either the men or the women did they give any food except herbs and legumes, things of little substance. The milk in the breasts of the women with infants dried up and thus in a short while the infants perished.

From *Red Gold: The Conquest of the Brazilian Indians, 1500–1760*

John Hemming

While the Spanish conquered the Indians of the West Indies, Mexico, Central America, Peru, and western South America, the Portuguese colonized Brazil. Portuguese access to the eastern region of South America was sanctioned by the Pope in the Treaty of Tordesillas (1494), which divided the world between Spanish and Portuguese empires, giving the Portuguese the right to make conversions along the coasts of Africa and the sea routes to India traveled by Portuguese mariners, but also including the eastern bulge of South America which was "discovered" by the Portuguese Cabral in 1500. Since the line of Tordesillas ran through South America east of the Andes, the Portuguese and Spanish were frequently at odds along the boundary. These tensions were, of course mitigated by the papal decision, as well as negotiations between the Spanish and Portuguese monarchs, especially as the two crowns were united between 1580 and 1640 (when the events described in this selection took place).

In South America, as in the West Indies and Mexico, one of the forces most protective of Indian interests was the church. While settlers wanted labor to exploit, the church wanted to save souls. Not all churchmen championed the Indians as vigorously as Las Casas, a Dominican, but a similar role was played after 1549 by the newly founded Spanish Jesuit order in Brazil, led by Father Manoel da Nobrega. Other Jesuits came from Peru along with Spanish settlers. In this selection John Hemming first describes

Reprinted by permission of the publisher from *Red Gold* by John Hemming, Cambridge, MA: Harvard University Press. Copyright © 1978 by John Hemming, selections from pp. 243–246, 254, 273–274.

the Jesuit protection of the Guaraní Indians from bands of adventurers and
slave traders. Notice the different interests of European settlers. Compare
the interests of Spanish and Portuguese settlers. Are the interests of the
crown closer to those of the settlers or those of the church?

What is the interest of the church? One story not recounted here is told
in the film The Mission. *It reminds us that there is not even a single church*
position because it shows how the settlers were able to drive a wedge
between the Jesuit missionaries and the Pope.

What are the causes of this brutality? Is it racist? If so, what makes it
racist? If not, why not?

In the wake of the Spanish settlers came Spanish Jesuits, the founders of
the famous theocracy of the Paraguayan missions. The black-robed Fathers
marched across from Peru and found wonderfully apt converts in the Guaraní.
Of all the Brazilian Indians, the Guaraní were the most spiritual, believing in
a single creator god and easily led by messianic leaders. One of the first Jesuits
in Paraguay, Alonso de Barzana, wrote from Asuncion in 1594 that "all this
nation is very inclined to religion, whether true or false. Had the Christians
given them a good example, and had various sorcerers not deceived them, they
would not only be Christians, but devout Christians. They know all about the
immortality of the soul and greatly fear the anguera, which are souls that have
emerged from dead bodies: they say that these go about terrifying people and
causing harm. They have the greatest love and obedience for the Fathers if
these give them a good example—but the same or more for the sorcerers who
deceive them with false religion. . . . This propensity to serve anyone in the
name of religion has led many heathen Indians among them to claim to be
sons of god and prophets. Indians raised among Spaniards have also escaped
and joined hostile [tribes], some calling themselves popes, others Jesus Christ,
and for their sensuality they have formed convents of nuns whom they
abuse. . . . They have spread thousands of idolatries and superstitions and rites
of these shamans, whose chief doctrine is teaching them to dance day and
night until they die of hunger, having neglected their crops. These tribes are
great farmers: they have vast quantities of food, especially maize, various kinds
of manioc and other fine roots and a great amount of fish."

When Barzana wrote about the Guaraní in 1594 he reported that the greater
part of them had already died of epidemics, ill-treatment and wars, and many
more were following their shamans and refusing to admit Jesuits. But the field
was extremely fertile for missionaries. They could hardly fail to create flourishing missions among a people that was naturally devout and already settled
as skilled farmers.

Barzana wrote that in Guairá alone there were said to be a hundred thousand
Guaraní and also the great and valiant tribe of Ibirajara. Two Jesuits, the Por-

tuguese Manoel de Ortega and the Irishman Thomas Fields, opened up the Guairá mission at the end of the sixteenth century. They operated "roving missions," moving from one village or nomadic group to another. By 1607 they were ready to found permanent mission settlements. These were known as reductions, because the Indians were congregated in them and "reduced" to a Christian and civilised way of life. Thirteen reductions were created among the Guairá Indians, in the vast, fertile plain east of the Paraná, between the Iguaçú to the south and Paranapanema to the north. They were formed in the face of opposition from the Spanish colonists, who wanted to use Indian labour, either in allotments known as encomiendas or as personal servants called by the Inca word yanacona.

During the years when Spanish Jesuits were crossing the Paraná into Guairá, the settlers of São Paulo, 400 miles to the east, were planning attacks on the Indians living to the south and west of their frontier town. The townsmen of São Paulo—known as Paulistas—called the Guaraní Indians Carijó. In European eyes, the Carijó were the best tribe on the coast of Brazil. "These are domestic and civilised, for men and women wear cotton sheaths like Moorish loincloths, live in houses, plant manioc and vegetables, have a good appearance and external grace, and some of them are as well proportioned as any Europeans." "They go half naked . . . wearing mantles, either of fine matting or skins or featherwork . . . with a form of smock tied above their haunches or falling down to the knees on the men and to mid-leg on the women. . . . The women and girls go bare-headed, with their hair agreeably bound with little ribbons of grasses dyed in lively shining colours." They were gentler and more apt for conversion than their Tupi enemies—even though the Guaraní and Tupi languages were very similar and the two groups clearly had a common origin.

Nóbrega himself wanted to lead a mission westwards from his new creation of Piratininga: "My heart always told me that I should send to the Carijó." Two Jesuits were sent south from São Paulo to the forests of the Carijó in August 1554. They were to make peace between the Carijó (Guaraní) and the Tupi of São Paulo, ensure a safe route from the coast of Santa Catarina to Paraguay, and try to found a great mission among the Carijó. Successful at first, they were soon killed by the Carijó—at the instigation of a Spaniard from Paraguay. These missionaries . . . thus became the first Jesuit martyrs in Brazil, and the first victims of the inevitable clash between Portuguese and Spanish colonists in southern Brazil.

The Paulistas initially had enough local Indians to live comfortably. Nóbrega complained that Paulistas "can think of nothing but living off the work of their slaves, who fish and collect food for them. Laziness has taken such hold of them, and they are so addicted to sensuality and other vices, that they are not even cured by being excommunicated for possessing these slaves. . . . All or most of the men in this land have consciences weighed down by the slaves they possess against all reason."

By the 1580s the Indians around São Paulo were becoming extinct and the colonists began to look hungrily towards the populous Carijó. Some sailed down the coast from São Vicente to raid the coastal Carijó of the Lagoon. In 1585 the town council of São Paulo made the first open reference to Indian slavery. It authorised a raid into the sertão in search of Indians. The justification was, quite blatantly, need for slave labour. "This land is in great danger of being depopulated because its inhabitants do not have [Indian] slaves as they used to, by whom they have always been served. This is the result of many illnesses . . . from which over 2000 head of slaves have died in this captaincy in the past six years. This land used to be ennobled by these slaves, and its settlers supported themselves honourably with them and made large incomes."

The Carijó reacted by a half-hearted move against the young settlement of São Paulo itself. They delivered no attack, but the colonists felt threatened by the Carijó in 1590 and again in 1593–94. Whether the threat was genuine or not, it was sufficient justification for the town council to beg the Captain-Major Jorge Correia to do something. He responded by leading another expedition against the Carijó and Tupina. Jerónimo Leitão attacked the Carijó on the coast as far as Paranaguá in 1595–96, and then spent six years assaulting villages along the Anhemby (Tietê) river. Spanish Jesuits claimed that he and his mameluco half-castes destroyed 300 villages, exterminating or enslaving their 30,000 inhabitants. Another official campaign marched north-westwards to the Paranaíba and spent the four years from 1596 to 1600 ravaging Indian tribes. It may have penetrated as far as the Goiás, deep in the heart of Brazil.

These expeditions were the start of an extraordinary movement of slaving, prospecting, raiding and exploring by the Paulistas. For a century and a half the tiny frontier town of São Paulo—which in 1600 had no more than 2000 inhabitants, and consisted of a hundred rustic houses clustered on a hilltop—sent groups of men plunging into the forests and rivers of central South America. The expeditions have come to be known as bandeiras, and the tough woodsmen who marched on them as bandeirantes. It was a movement that has stirred the imagination of Brazilian historians. There is now a formidable literature about the bandeirantes, inspired by pride at their endurance and achievements as explorers, and by disgust at their slaving and atrocities against the Indians.

The bandeirantes marched into the forests year after year throughout the seventeenth century. São Paulo was often empty, "evacuated by its inhabitants finding relief in the sertão"—the sertão was the jungle, the wilderness that stretched interminably across the plateaux to the west of São Paulo, and "relief" meant the riches to be gained from captive Indian slaves. For a Paulista's prestige lay in his Indian slaves. The farms around São Paulo were too poor and its frontier was too remote from the sea for the Paulistas to be able to afford many African slaves. The men of São Paulo therefore thrust inland to prey on the Indians. One governor said of them that "any man too poor to have anyone to serve him would rather submit to travelling for many years in the sertão in search of someone to work for him than to serve someone else for a single day." And the town council of São Paulo admitted to another governor: "Your Worship well knows that the Portuguese are not workers, especially when they are out of their own country."

The bandeirantes' treks through the forests and along the rivers were desperately tough. A Portuguese Jesuit marvelled at their misdirected endurance. "One is astounded by the boldness and impertinence with which, at such great cost, men allow themselves to enter that great sertão for two, three, four or more years. They go without God, without food, naked as the savages, and subject to all the persecutions and miseries in the world. Men venture for two or three hundred leagues into the sertão, serving the devil with such amazing martyrdom, in order to trade or steal slaves." And a Spanish Jesuit became almost humble when he compared the bandeirantes' hardships with his own. "These Portuguese do and suffer incomparably more to win the bodies of the Indians for their service than I do to win their souls for heaven. For they are always on journeys on foot that are long and difficult. They lack all necessities of this life, suffering hunger, exhaustion and nakedness, always on guard against a thousand ambushes, with bodies and souls constantly in danger—all to catch four Indians, who run off or die on them next day. . . ."

The Spanish Jesuits' reductions full of thousands of Guaraní were an irresistible temptation to the bandeirantes. The Paulistas were devout Christians after their fashion. They liked to claim that the slaves they brought back were entering the bosom of the Church and were being saved spiritually—even if they suffered and died physically. The bandeirantes were also patriotic, but their nationalism was Portuguese and directed against the Spaniards. They conveniently ignored the fact that the King of Portugal was also King of Spain, just as they ignored Jesuit censure of their slaving. Their patriotism and religion were showy and reactionary, and wholly subordinate to their selfish interests.

It was thus not long before the Paulistas turned against the Spanish Jesuit missions. It was so much easier to attack these great settlements than to chase through the forests after isolated villages or roaming bands of wild Indians. The mission Indians were already disciplined and acculturated. The Jesuits had taught them to obey Christian masters and to labour in the mission plantations. They spoke a language akin to Tupi, one that all Paulistas understood. They were hard workers and good woodsmen; and their women were among the most beautiful in Brazil. . . .

The Kings of both Spain and Portugal had always justified their American conquests by proclaiming that these colonies brought Christian civilisation to the natives—whether they wanted it or not. Both countries issued a torrent of legislation condemning illegal enslavement of Indians.

Of all the Brazilian tribes, the Guaraní responded to Christianity with most fervour and understanding. The Jesuits were the most determined and intelligent of the missionary orders. Their Paraguayan missions were the most successful attempt at conversion or acculturation of any South American Indians. Amid all the hypocritical claptrap about the benefits of Christianity, these missions demonstrated that in the right circumstances something could be done. And yet it was against these model missions that the bandeirantes launched their armed raids, and led off thousands of loyal, peaceful, Christian Indians into illegal slavery.

The Jesuits had great influence in Spain and Portugal, and eloquent propagandists in men llike Ruiz de Montoya, the "Apostle of Guairá." He bombarded the King with memorials about the Paulistas' iniquity, and his *Spiritual Conquest Made by the Missionaries of the Society of Jesus in the Provinces of Paraguay, Parana, Uruguay and Tape* was a brilliant manifesto. It contained enough exaggeration and embellishment to arouse a reader's full sympathy and indignation, and yet remained essentially accurate. The Jesuits even had it translated into Guaraní to stimulate their native converts.

Other authorities confirmed the Jesuits' outrage. Don Pedro Estevan Davila, Governor of Buenos Aires, told the King that in Rio de Janeiro "before my very eyes they were selling Indians brought to that city by the citizens of São Paulo, as if they were slaves and considered as such by Your Majesty. I made enquiries, and ascertained verbally that between 1628 and 1630 the citizens of São Paulo brought over 70,000 souls from the reductions of the Fathers of the Society of the [Guairá] district of this province of Paraguay. In doing this, those settlers of Sao Paulo practised such incredible cruelties and inhumanity that by their actions they ceased to be Christian Catholics."

The Jesuits cleverly introduced a political element into their campaign against the bandeirantes. There was growing unrest among the Portuguese subjects of the King of Spain. Ruiz de Montoya warned the King that the Portuguese planned to rebel and seize much of the Indies for their country. This was why they were so determined to destroy Spanish Jesuit reductions.

King Philip IV issued a furious denunciation of the bandeirantes on 16 September 1639 and an edict on 31 March 1640. He accused the Paulistas of destroying, "according to various authentic reports, over 300,000 souls including captives and dead. With this all those provinces, once so spacious and full of Indians, came to an end." By 1650 the Jesuits had only twenty-two out of their original forty-eight missions in the provinces of Paraná, Guairá, Uruguay and Itatín. These contained 40,000 souls, whereas the baptism books showed that 150,000 had been baptised in these provinces. . . .

Part 5

European Settler Colonialism: North America

Page from the first Bible translated into a Native American language, 1663.

The dynamic of settlement in someone else's land is complex. We have seen the obvious exploitation of Indian land and labor in South America. The grants of the Spanish crown to the conquistadors were like their feudal precedents, grants of labor on land. In some ways the labor was more important than the land. Cortes and others received enormous areas that included numerous villages, but because there were so few Spanish and because they had no intention of actually working the land, their grants were worthless without the Indian obligations to labor.

The English colonization of North America was different. Families came to settle towns and to farm. This made for a different response to the Native American population. Unlike the bandeirantes, who captured Indians to turn them into dependent laborers, the English sought to clear the land for themselves.

It is easier to exploit land with a minimum of guilt, fuss, or explanation, if the land is empty. The desire to believe the land was there for the taking contributed in North America to the myth of the Virgin Land. When live Indians made their presence and possession of the land obvious, the alternative was annihilation. But when, as in Brazil, the settlers wanted labor more than land, the Indian population was not as quickly removed, either in imagination or actual fact. This may be one reason why the Indian population of Brazil (and perhaps more generally of South and Central America) remained larger than that of North America. Perhaps the logic of true settler colonialism, as opposed to military conquest, is genocide.

From *Of Plymouth Plantation*

William Bradford

The following excerpt by William Bradford (1590–1657) describes the first encounter between English pilgrims and Native Americans (probably the

Of Plymouth Plantation 1620–1647 by William Bradford. A New Edition, The Complete Text, with Notes and an Introduction by Samuel Eliot Morison. Copyright © 1952 by Samuel Eliot Morison and renewed 1980 by Emily M. Beck (New York: Alfred A. Knopf, 1987), pp. 64–66, 68–70.

Nauset Indians) at Cape Cod in 1620. In what ways were the plans and expectations of these pilgrims similar to, and different from, those of the Spanish conquistadors? Was conflict with the Native Americans inevitable? Did the Pilgrims have the intention or capacity to live peacefully with the Indians? Do you see evidence of racism in this first encounter?

Although explicit and scientific racist ideology did not emerge until the nineteenth century, these early encounters, like those between the conquistadors and the Indians, lay some groundwork. What evidence is there that the Pilgrims saw the Indians as a different race or species, as an unredeemable Other? What evidence is there that they did not? What similarities do you see in the attitudes and advantages of the conquistadors and Pilgrims toward the Indians and why? What are the differences and why do they exist?

Book I, Chapter X. Showing How They Sought Out a Place of Habitation; and What Befell Them Thereabout

Being thus arrived at Cape Cod the 11th of November, and necessity calling them to look out a place for habitation (as well as the master's and mariners' importunity); they having brought a large shallop with them out of England, stowed in quarters in the ship, they now got her out and set their carpenters to work to trim her up; but being much bruised and shattered in the ship with foul weather, they saw she would be long in mending. Whereupon a few of them tendered themselves to go by land and discover those nearest places, whilst the shallop was in mending; and the rather because as they went into that harbor there seemed to be an opening some two or three leagues off, which the master judged to be a river. It was conceived there might be some danger in the attempt, yet seeing them resolute, they were permitted to go, being sixteen of them well armed under the conduct of Captain Standish, having such instructions given them as was thought meet.

They set forth the 15th of November; and when they had marched about the space of a mile by the seaside, they espied five or six persons with a dog coming towards them, who were savages; but they fled from them and ran up into the woods, and the English followed them, partly to see if they could speak with them, and partly to discover if there might not be more of them lying in ambush. But the Indians seeing themselves thus followed, they again forsook the woods and ran away on the sands as hard as they could, so as they could not come near them but followed them by the track of their feet sundry miles and saw that they had come the same way. So, night coming on, they made their rendezvous and set out their sentinels, and rested in quiet that night; and the next morning followed their track till they had headed a great creek and so left the sands, and turned another way into the woods. But they still followed them by guess, hoping to find their dwellings; but they soon lost both them and themselves, falling into such thickets as were ready to tear their clothes and armor in pieces; but were most distressed for want of drink. But at length they found water and refreshed themselves, being the first New England water they drunk of, and was now in great thirst as pleasant unto them as wine or beer had been in foretimes.

Afterwards they directed their course to come to the other shore, for they knew it was a neck of land they were to cross over, and so at length got to the seaside and marched to this supposed river, and by the way found a pond of clear fresh water, and shortly after a good quantity of clear ground where the Indians had formerly set corn, and some of their graves. And proceeding further they saw new stubble where corn had been set the same year; also they found where lately a house had been, where some planks and a great kettle was remaining, and heaps of sand newly paddled with their hands. Which, they digging up, found in them divers fair Indian baskets filled with corn, and some in ears, fair and good, of divers colors, which seemed to them a very goodly sight (having never seen any such before). This was near the place of that supposed river they came to seek, unto which they went and found it to open itself into two arms with a high cliff of sand in the entrance but more like to be creeks of salt water than any fresh, for aught they saw; and that there was good harborage for their shallop, leaving it further to be discovered by their shallop, when she was ready. So, their time limited them being expired, they returned to the ship lest they should be in fear of their safety; and took with them part of the corn and buried up the rest. And so, like the men from Eshcol [Moses' scouts in Numbers 13.23–26], carried with them of the fruits of the land and showed their brethren; of which, and their return, they were marvelously glad and their hearts encouraged.

After this, the shallop being got ready, they set out again for the better discovery of this place, and the master of the ship desired to go himself. So there went some thirty men but found it to be no harbor for ships but only for boats. There was also found two of their houses covered with mats, and sundry of their implements in them, but the people were run away and could not be seen. Also there was found more of their corn and of their beans of various colors; the corn and beans they brought away, purposing to give them full satisfaction when they should meet with any of them as about some six months afterward they did, to their good content.

And here is to be noted a special providence of God, and a great mercy to this poor people, that here they got seed to plant them corn the next year, or else they might have starved, for they had none nor any likelihood to get any till the season had been past, as the sequel did manifest. Neither is it likely they had had this, if the first voyage had not been made, for the ground was now all covered with snow and hard frozen; but the Lord is never wanting unto His in their greatest needs; let His holy name have all the praise.

The month of November being spent in these affairs, and much foul weather falling in, the 6th of December they sent out their shallop again with ten of their principal men and some seamen, upon further discovery, intending to circulate that deep bay of Cape Cod. The weather was very cold and it froze so hard as the spray of the sea lighting on their coats, they were as if they had been glazed. Yet that night betimes they got down into the bottom of the bay, and as they drew near the shore they saw some ten or twelve Indians very busy about something. They landed about a league or two from them, and had much ado to put ashore anywhere it lay so full of flats. Being landed, it grew late and they made themselves a barricado with logs and boughs as well as they could in the time, and set out their sentinel and betook them to rest, and saw the smoke of the fire the savages made that night. When morning was come they divided their company, some to coast along the shore in the boat, and the rest marched through the woods to see the land, if any fit place might be for their dwelling. They came also to the place where they saw the Indians the night before, and found they had been cutting up a great fish like a grampus, being some two inches thick of fat like a hog, some pieces whereof they had left by the way. And the shallop found two more of these fishes dead on the sands, a thing usual after storms in that place, by reason of the great flats of sand that lie off.

So they ranged up and down all that day, but found no people, nor any place they liked. When the sun grew low, they hasted out of the woods to meet with their shallop, to whom they made signs to come to them into a creek hard by, the which they did at high water; of which they were very glad, for they had not seen each other all that day since the morning. So they made them a barricado as usually they did every night, with logs, stakes and thick pine boughs, the height of a man, leaving it open to leeward, partly to shelter them from the cold and wind (making their fire in the middle and lying round about it) and partly to defend them from any sudden assaults of the savages, if they should surround them; so being very weary, they betook them to rest. But about midnight they heard a hideous and great cry, and their sentinel called "Arm! arm!" So they bestirred them and stood to their arms and shot off a couple of muskets, and then the noise ceased. They concluded it was a company of wolves or such like wild beasts, for one of the seamen told them he had often heard such a noise in Newfoundland.

So they rested till about five of the clock in the morning; for the tide, and their purpose to go from thence, made them be stirring betimes. So after prayer they prepared for breakfast, and it being day dawning it was thought best to be carrying things down to the boat. But some said it was not best to carry the arms down, others said they would be the readier, for they had lapped them up in their coats from the dew; but some three or four would not carry theirs till they went themselves. Yet as it fell out, the water being not high enough, they laid them down on the bank side and came up to breakfast.

But presently, all on the sudden, they heard a great and strange cry, which they knew to be the same voices they heard in the night, though they varied their notes; and one of their company being abroad came running in and cried, "Men, Indians! Indians!" And withal, their arrows came flying amongst them. Their men ran with all speed to recover their arms, as by the good providence of God they did. In the meantime, of those that were there ready, two muskets were discharged at them, and two more stood ready in the entrance of their rendezvous but were commanded not to shoot till they could take full aim at them. And the other two charged again with all speed, for there were only four had arms there, and defended the barricado, which was first assaulted. The cry of the Indians was dreadful, especially when they saw the men run out of the rendezvous toward the shallop to recover their arms, the Indians wheeling about upon them. But some running out with coats of mail on, and cutlasses in their hands, they soon got their arms and let fly amongst them and quickly stopped their violence. Yet there was a lusty man, and no less valiant, stood behind a tree within half a musket shot, and let his arrows fly at them; he was seen [to] shoot three arrows, which were all avoided. He stood three shots of a musket, till one taking full aim at him and made the bark or splinters of the tree fly about his ears, after which he gave an extraordinary shriek and away they went, all of them. They [the English] left some to keep the shallop and followed them about a quarter of a mile and shouted once or twice, and shot off two or three pieces, and so returned. This they did that they might conceive that they were not afraid of them or any way discouraged.

Thus it pleased God to vanquish their enemies and give them deliverance; and by His special providence so to dispose that not any one of them were either hurt or hit, though their arrows came close by them and on every side [of] them; and sundry of their coats, which hung up in the barricado, were shot through and through. Afterwards they gave God solemn thanks and praise for their deliverance, and gathered up a bundle of their arrows and sent them into England afterward by the master of the ship, and called that place the First Encounter.

Narrative of the Captivity and Restoration

Mary Rowlandson

Mary Rowlandson (1636–1711), the wife of a minister in the Massachusetts Bay Colony, was kidnapped and held for ransom in the last months of King Philip's War (1675–76), the most important Indian war in New England. King Philip, son of the Native American leader Massasoit, was the chief of the Wampanoag Indians. Mary Rowlandson's popular narrative, published in 1682, describes the massacre of the colonists and members of her family, as well as her capture, her captivity, and eventual rescue. In this selection, we follow Mrs. Rowlandson with her Indian captives as they retreat. Each section of the "Narrative" is called a "remove," chronicling the constant retreat of the Indians before the English, from February until May of 1676, when the Indians were defeated. Notice how Mrs. Rowlandson's tragic removal from her family and community corresponds to the triumphant removal of the Indians by the English soldiers. Notice how Mrs. Rowlandson looks to the biblical accounts of exile and sacrifice to find hope in her own predicament.

How does Mary Rowlandson understand the Native Americans who have captured her? Would you characterize her attitude toward them as racist? Is racism an inevitable result of this conflict?

On the tenth of February 1675, came the Indians with great numbers upon Lancaster: their first coming was about sunrising; hearing the noise of some guns, we looked out; several houses were burning, and the smoke ascending

---

The text used is *Original Narratives of Early American History, Narratives of Indian Wars 1675–1699*, vol. 14, edited by C.H. Lincoln (1952). All copies of the first edition have been lost. Like most modern editors, Lincoln has chosen to reprint the second "addition," Cambridge, Massachusetts, by Samuel Green in 1682. The full title is *The sovereignty and goodness Of GOD, together with the faithfulness of his promises displayed; being a narrative of the captivity and restoration of Mrs. Mary Rowlandson, commended by her, to all that desires to know the Lord's doings to, and dealings with her. Especially to her dear children and relations. The second Addition Corrected and amended. Written by her own hand for her private use, and now made public at the earnest desire of some friends, and for the benefit of the afflicted. Deut. 32.39. See now that I, even I am he, and there is no god with me, I kill and I make alive, I wound and I heal, neither is there any can see deliver out of my hand.*

to heaven. There were five persons taken in one house; the father, and the mother and a sucking child, they knocked on the head; the other two they took and carried away alive. There were two others, who being out of their garrison upon some occasion were set upon; one was knocked on the head, the other escaped; another there was who running along was shot and wounded, and fell down; he begged of them his life, promising them money (as they told me) but they would not hearken to him but knocked him in head, and stripped him naked, and split open his bowels. Another, seeing many of the Indians about his barn, ventured and went out, but was quickly shot down. There were three others belonging to the same garrison who were killed; the Indians getting up upon the roof of the barn, had advantage to shoot down upon them over their fortification. Thus these murderous wretches went on, burning, and destroying before them.

At length they came and beset our own house, and quickly it was the dolefulest day that ever mine eyes saw. The house stood upon the edge of a hill; some of the Indians got behind the hill, others into the barn, and others behind anything that could shelter them; from all which places they shot against the house, so that the bullets seemed to fly like hail; and quickly they wounded one man among us, then another, and then a third. About two hours (according to my observation, in that amazing time) they had been about the house before they prevailed to fire it (which they did with flax and hemp, which they brought out of the barn, and there being no defense about the house, only two flankers at two opposite corners and one of them not finished); they fired it once and one ventured out and quenched it, but they quickly fired it again, and that took. Now is the dreadful hour come, that I have often heard of (in time of war, as it was the case of others), but now mine eyes see it. Some in our house were fighting for their lives, others wallowing in their blood, the house on fire over our heads, and the bloody heathen ready to knock us on the head, if we stirred out. Now might we hear mothers and children crying out for themselves, and one another, "Lord, what shall we do?" Then I took my children (and one of my sisters', hers) to go forth and leave the house: but as soon as we came to the door and appeared, the Indians shot so thick that the bullets rattled against the house, as if one had taken an handful of stones and threw them, so that we were fain to give back. We had six stout dogs belonging to our garrison, but none of them would stir, though another time, if any Indian had come to the door, they were ready to fly upon him and tear him down. The Lord hereby would make us the more acknowledge His hand, and to see that our help is always in Him. But out we must go, the fire increasing, and coming along behind us, roaring, and the Indians gaping before us with their guns, spears, and hatchets to devour us. No sooner were we out of the house, but my brother-in-law (being before wounded, in defending the house, in or near the throat) fell down dead, whereat the Indians scornfully shouted, and hallowed, and were presently upon him, stripping off his clothes, the bullets flying thick, one went through my side, and the same (as would seem) through the bowels and hand of my dear child in my arms. One of my elder sisters' children, named William, had then his leg broken, which the Indians perceiving, they knocked him on [his] head. Thus were we butchered by those merciless heathen, standing amazed, with the blood running down to our heels. My eldest sister being yet in the house, and seeing those woeful sights, the infidels hauling mothers one way, and children another, and some wallowing in their blood: and her elder son telling her that her son William was dead, and myself was wounded, she said, "And Lord, let me die with them," which was no sooner said, but she was struck with a bullet, and fell down dead over the threshold. I hope she is reaping the fruit of her good labors, being faithful to the service of God in her place. In her younger years she lay under much trouble upon spiritual accounts, till it pleased God to make that precious scripture take hold of her heart, "And he said unto me, my Grace is sufficient for thee" (2 Corinthians 12.9). More than twenty years after, I have heard her tell how sweet and comfortable that place was to her. But to return: the Indians laid hold of us, pulling me one way, and the children another, and said, "Come go along with us"; I told them they would kill me: they answered, if I were willing to go along with them, they would not hurt me.

Oh the doleful sight that now was to behold at this house! "Come, behold the works of the Lord, what desolations he has made in the earth." Of thirty-seven persons who were in this one house, none escaped either present death, or a bitter captivity, save only one, who might say as he, "And I only am escaped alone to tell the News" (Job 1.15). There were twelve killed, some shot, some stabbed with their spears, some knocked down with their hatchets. When we are in prosperity, Oh the little that we think of such dreadful sights, and to see our dear friends, and relations lie bleeding out their heart-blood upon the ground. There was one who was chopped into the head with a hatchet, and stripped naked, and yet was crawling up and down. It is a solemn sight to see so many Christians lying in their blood, some here, and some there, like a company of sheep torn by wolves, all of them stripped naked by a company of hell-hounds, roaring, singing, ranting, and insulting, as if they would have torn our very hearts out; yet the Lord by His almighty power preserved a number of us from death, for there were twenty-four of us taken alive and carried captive.

I had often before this said that if the Indians should come, I should choose rather to be killed by them than taken alive, but when it came to the trial my mind changed; their glittering weapons so daunted my spirit, that I chose rather to go along with those (as I may say) ravenous beasts, than that moment to end my days; and that I may the better declare what happened to me during that grievous captivity, I shall particularly speak of the several removes we had up and down the wilderness.

"The First Remove"

Now away we must go with those barbarous creatures, with our bodies wounded and bleeding, and our hearts no less than our bodies. About a mile we went that night, up upon a hill within sight of the town, where they intended to lodge. There was hard by a vacant house (deserted by the English before, for fear of the Indians). I asked them whether I might not lodge in the house that night, to which they answered, "What, will you love English men still?" This was the dolefulest night that ever my eyes saw. Oh the roaring, and singing and dancing, and yelling of those black creatures in the night, which made the place a lively resemblance of hell. And as miserable was the waste that was there made of horses, cattle, sheep, swine, calves, lambs, roasting pigs, and fowl (which they had plundered in the town), some roasting, some lying and burning, and some boiling to feed our merciless enemies; who were joyful enough, though we were disconsolate. To add to the dolefulness of the former day, and the dismalness of the present night, my thoughts ran upon my losses and sad bereaved condition. All was gone, my husband gone (at least separated from me, he being in the Bay; and to add to my grief, the Indians told me they would kill him as he came homeward), my children gone, my relations and friends gone, our house and home and all our comforts—within door and without—all was gone (except my life), and I knew not but the next moment that might go too. There remained nothing to me but one poor wounded babe, and it seemed at present worse than death that it was in such a pitiful condition, bespeaking compassion, and I had no refreshing for it, nor suitable things to revive it. Little do many think what is the savageness and brutishness of this barbarous enemy, Ay, even those that seem to profess more than others among them, when the English have fallen into their hands.

Those seven that were killed at Lancaster the summer before upon a Sabbath day, and the one that was afterward killed upon a weekday, were slain and mangled in a barbarous manner, by one-eyed John, and Marlborough's Praying Indians, which Capt. Mosely brought to Boston, as the Indians told me.

"The Second Remove"

But now, the next morning, I must turn my back upon the town, and travel with them into the vast and desolate wilderness, I knew not whither. It is not my tongue, or pen, can express the sorrows of my heart, and bitterness of my spirit that I had at this departure: but God was with me in a wonderful manner, carrying me along, and bearing up my spirit, that it did not quite fail. One of the Indians carried my poor wounded babe upon a horse; it went moaning all along, "I shall die, I shall die." I went on foot after it, with sorrow that cannot be expressed. At length I took it off the horse, and carried it in my arms till my strength failed, and I fell down with it. Then they set me upon a horse with my wounded child in my lap, and there being no furniture upon the horse's back, as we were going down a steep hill we both fell over the horse's head, at which they, like inhumane creatures, laughed, and rejoiced to see it, though I thought we should there have ended our days, as overcome with so many difficulties. But the Lord renewed my strength still, and carried me along, that I might see more of His power; yea, so much that I could never have thought of, had I not experienced it.

After this it quickly began to snow, and when night came on, they stopped, and now down I must sit in the snow, by a little fire, and a few boughs behind me, with my sick child in my lap; and calling much for water, being now (through the wound) fallen into a violent fever. My own wound also growing so stiff that I could scarce sit down or rise up; yet so it must be, that I must sit all this cold winter night upon the cold snowy ground, with my sick child in my arms, looking that every hour would be the last of its life; and having no Christian friend near me, either to comfort or help me. Oh, I may see the wonderful power of God, that my Spirit did not utterly sink under my afflic- tion: still the Lord upheld me with His gracious and merciful spirit, and we were both alive to see the light of the next morning.

"The Third Remove"

The morning being come, they prepared to go on their way. One of the Indians got up upon a horse, and they set me up behind him, with my poor sick babe in my lap. A very wearisome and tedious day I had of it; what with my own wound, and my child's being so exceeding sick, and in a lamentable condition with her wound. It may be easily judged what a poor feeble condition we were in, there being not the least crumb of refreshing that came within either of our mouths from Wednesday night to Saturday night, except only a little cold water. This day in the afternoon, about an hour by sun, we came to the place where they intended, viz. an Indian town, called Wenimesset, northward of Quabaug. When we were come, Oh the number of pagans (now merciless enemies) that there came about me, that I may say as David, "I had fainted, unless I had believed, etc." (Psalm 27.13). The next day was the Sabbath. I then remembered how careless I had been of God's holy time; how many Sabbaths I had lost and misspent, and how evilly I had walked in God's sight;

which lay so close unto my spirit, that it was easy for me to see how righteous it was with God to cut off the thread of my life and cast me out of His presence forever. Yet the Lord still showed mercy to me, and upheld me; and as He wounded me with one hand, so he healed me with the other. This day there came to me one Robert Pepper (a man belonging to Roxbury) who was taken in Captain Beers's fight, and had been now a considerable time with the Indians; and up with them almost as far as Albany, to see King Philip, as he told me, and was now very lately come into these parts. Hearing, I say, that I was in this Indian town, he obtained leave to come and see me. He told me he himself was wounded in the leg at Captain Beers's fight; and was not able some time to go, but as they carried him, and as he took oaken leaves and laid to his wound, and through the blessing, of God he was able to travel again. Then I took oaken leaves and laid to my side, and with the blessing of God it cured me also; yet before the cure was wrought, I may say, as it is in Psalm 38.5–6 "My wounds stink and are corrupt, I am troubled, I am bowed down greatly, I go mourning all the day long." I sat much alone with a poor wounded child in my lap, which moaned night and day, having nothing to revive the body, or cheer the spirits of her, but instead of that, sometimes one Indian would come and tell me one hour that "your master will knock your child in the head," and then a second, and then a third, "your master will quickly knock your child in the head."

This was the comfort I had from them, miserable comforters are ye all, as he said. Thus nine days I sat upon my knees, with my babe in my lap, till my flesh was raw again; my child being even ready to depart this sorrowful world, they bade me carry it out to another wigwam (I suppose because they would not be troubled with such spectacles) whither I went with a very heavy heart, and down I sat with the picture of death in my lap. About two hours in the night, my sweet babe like a lamb departed this life on Feb. 18, 1675. It being about six years, and five months old. It was nine days from the first wounding, in this miserable condition, without any refreshing of one nature or other, except a little cold water. I cannot but take notice how at another time I could not bear to be in the room where any dead person was, but now the case is changed; I must and could lie down by my dead babe, side by side all the night after. I have thought since of the wonderful goodness of God to me in preserving me in the use of my reason and senses in that distressed time, that I did not use wicked and violent means to end my own miserable life. In the morning, when they understood that my child was dead they sent for me home to my master's wigwam (by my master in this writing, must be understood Quinnapin, who was a Sagamore [Algonquin], and married King Philip's wife's sister; not that he first took me, but I was sold to him by another Narragansett Indian, who took me when first I came out of the garrison). I went to take up my dead child in my arms to carry it with me, but they bid me let it alone; there was no resisting, but go I must and leave it. When I had been at my master's wigwam, I took the first opportunity I could get to go look after my dead child. When I came I asked them what they had done with it; then they told me it was upon the hill. Then they went and showed me where it was, where I saw the ground was newly digged, and there they told me they had buried it. There I left that child in the wilderness, and must commit it, and myself also in this wilderness condition, to Him who is above all. God having taken away this dear child, I went to see my daughter Mary, who was at this same Indian town, at a wigwam not very far off, though we had little liberty or opportunity to, see one another. She was about ten years old, and taken from the door at first by a Praying Ind. and afterward sold for a gun. When I came in sight, she would fall aweeping; at which they were provoked, and would not let me come near her, but bade me be gone; which was a heart-cutting word to me. I had one child dead, another in the wilderness, I knew not where, the third they would not let me come near to: "Me (as he said) have ye bereaved of my Children, Joseph is not, and Simeon is not, and ye will take Benjamin also, all these things are against me." I could not sit still in this condition, but kept walking from one place to another. And as I was going along, my heart was even overwhelmed with the thoughts of my condition, and that I should have children, and a nation which I knew not, ruled over them. Whereupon I earnestly entreated the Lord, that He would consider my low estate, and show me a token for good, and if it were His blessed will, some sign and hope of some relief. And indeed quickly the Lord answered, in some measure, my poor prayers; for as I was going up and down mourning and lamenting my condition, my son came to me, and asked me how I did. I had not seen him before, since the destruction of the town, and I knew not where he was, till I was informed by himself, that he was amongst a smaller parcel of Indians, whose place was about six miles off. With tears in his eyes, he asked me whether his sister Sarah was dead; and told me he had seen his sister Mary; and prayed me, that I would not be troubled in reference to himself. The occasion of his coming to see me at this time, was this: there was, as I said, about six miles from us, a small plantation of Indians, where it seems he had been during his captivity; and at this time, there were some forces of the Ind. gathered out of our company, and some also from them (among whom was my son's master) to go to assault and burn Medfield. In this time of the absence of his master, his dame brought him to see me. I took this to be some gracious answer to my earnest and unfeigned desire. The next day, *viz.* to this, the Indians returned from Medfield, all the company, for those that belonged to the other small company, came through the town that now we were at. But before they came to us, Oh! the outrageous roaring and hooping that there was. They began their din about a mile before they came to us. By their noise and hooping they signified how many they had destroyed (which was at that time twenty-three). Those that were with us at home were gathered together as soon as they heard the hooping, and every time that the other went over their number, these at home gave a shout, that the very earth rung again. And thus they continued till those that had been upon the expedition were come up to the Sagamore's wigwam; and then, Oh, the hideous insulting and triumphing that there was over some Englishmen's scalps that they had taken (as their manner is) and brought with them. I cannot but take notice of the wonderful mercy of God to me in those afflictions, in sending me a Bible. One of the Indians that came from Medfield fight, had brought some plunder, came to me, and asked me, if I would have a Bible, he had got one in his basket. I was glad of it, and asked him, whether he thought the Indians would let me read? He answered, yes. So I took the Bible, and in that melancholy time, it came into my mind to read first the 28th chapter of Deuteronomy, which I did, and when I had read it, my dark heart wrought on this manner: that there was no mercy for me, that the blessings were gone, and the curses come in their room, and that I had lost my opportunity. But the Lord helped me still to go on reading till I came to Chap. 30, the seven first verses, where I found, there was mercy promised again, if we would return to Him by repentance; and though we were scattered from one end of the earth to the other, yet the Lord would gather us together, and turn all those curses upon our enemies. I do not desire to live to forget this Scripture, and what comfort it was to me.

Now the Ind. began to talk of removing from this place, some one way, and some another. There were now besides myself nine English captives in this place (all of them children, except one woman). I got an opportunity to go and take my leave of them. They being to go one way, and I another, I asked them whether they were earnest with God for deliverance. They told me they did as they were able, and it was some comfort to me, that the Lord stirred up children to look to Him. The woman, viz. goodwife Joslin, told me she should never see me again, and that she could find in her heart to run away. I wished her not to run away by any means, for we were near thirty miles from any English town, and she very big with child, and had but one week to reckon, and another child in her arms, two years old, and bad rivers there were to go over, and we were feeble, with our poor and coarse entertainment. I had my Bible with me, I pulled it out, and asked her whether she would read. We opened the Bible and lighted on Psalm 27, in which Psalm we especially took notice of that, ver. ult., "Wait on the Lord, Be of good courage, and he shall strengthen thine Heart, wait I say on the Lord."

"The Fourth Remove"

And now I must part with that little company I had. Here I parted from my daughter Mary (whom I never saw again till I saw her in Dorchester, returned from captivity), and from four little cousins and neighbors, some of which I never saw afterward: the Lord only knows the end of them. Amongst them also was that poor woman before mentioned, who came to a sad end, as some of the company told me in my travel: she having much grief upon her spirit about her miserable condition, being so near her time, she would be often asking the Indians to let her go home; they not being willing to that, and yet vexed with her importunity, gathered a great company together about her and stripped her naked, and set her in the midst of them, and when they had sung and danced about her (in their hellish manner) as long as they pleased they knocked her on head, and the child in her arms with her. When they had done that they made a fire and put them both into it, and told the other children that were with them that if they attempted to go home, they would serve them in like manner. The children said she did not shed one tear, but prayed all the while. But to return to my own journey, we traveled about half a day or little more, and came to a desolate place in the wilderness, where there were no wigwams or inhabitants before; we came about the middle of the afternoon to this place, cold and wet, and snowy, and hungry, and weary, and no refreshing for man but the cold ground to sit on, and our poor Indian cheer.

Heart-aching thoughts here I had about my poor children, who were scattered up and down among the wild beasts of the forest. My head was light and dizzy (either through hunger or hard lodging, or trouble or all together), my knees feeble, my body raw by sitting double night and day, that I cannot express to man the affliction that lay upon my spirit, but the Lord helped me at that time to express it to Himself. I opened my Bible to read, and the Lord brought that precious Scripture to me. "Thus saith the Lord, refrain thy voice from weeping, and thine eyes from tears, for thy work shall be rewarded, and they shall come again from the land of the enemy" (Jeremiah 31.16). This was a sweet cordial to me when I was ready to faint; many and many a time have I sat down and wept sweetly over this Scripture. At this place we continued about four days.

"The Fifth Remove"

The occasion (as I thought) of their moving at this time was the English army, it being near and following them. For they went as if they had gone for their lives, for some considerable way, and then they made a stop, and chose some of their stoutest men, and sent them back to hold the English army in play whilst the rest escaped. And then, like Jehu, they marched on furiously, with their old and with their young: some carried their old decrepit mothers, some carried one, and some another. Four of them carried a great Indian upon a bier; but going through a thick wood with him, they were hindered, and could make no haste, whereupon they took him upon their backs, and carried him, one at a time, till they came to Banquaug river. Upon a Friday, a little after noon, we came to this river. When all the company was come up, and were gathered together, I thought to count the number of them, but they were so many, and being somewhat in motion, it was beyond my skill. In this travel, because of my wound, I was somewhat favored in my load; I carried only my knitting work and two quarts of parched meal. Being very faint I asked my mistress to give me one spoonful of the meal, but she would not give me a taste. They quickly fell to cutting dry trees, to make rafts to carry them over the river: and soon my turn came to go over. By the advantage of some brush which they had laid upon the raft to sit upon, I did not wet my foot (which many of themselves at the other end were mid-leg deep) which cannot but be acknowledged as a favor of God to my weakened body, it being a very cold time. I was not before acquainted with such kind of doings or dangers. "When thou passeth through the waters I will be with thee, and through the rivers they shall not overflow thee" (Isaiah 43.2). A certain number of us got over the river that night, but it was the night after the Sabbath before all the company was got over. On the Saturday they boiled an old horse's leg which they had got, and so we drank of the broth, as soon as they thought it was ready, and when it was almost all gone, they filled it up again.

The first week of my being among them I hardly ate any thing; the second week I found my stomach grow very faint for want of something; and yet it was very hard to get down their filthy trash; but the third week, though I could think how formerly my stomach would turn against this or that, and I could starve and die before I could eat such things, yet they were sweet and savory to my taste. I was at this time knitting a pair of white cotton stockings for my mistress; and had not yet wrought upon a Sabbath day. When the Sabbath came they bade me go to work. I told them it was the Sabbath day, and desired them to let me rest, and told them I would do as much more tomorrow; to which they answered me they would break my face. And here I cannot but take notice of the strange providence of God in preserving the heathen. They were many hundreds, old and young, some sick, and some lame; many had papooses at their backs. The greatest number at this time with us were squaws, and they traveled with all they had, bag and baggage, and yet they got over this river aforesaid; and on Monday they set their wigwams on fire, and away they went. On that very day came the English army after them to this river, and saw the smoke of their wigwams, and yet this river put a stop to them. God did not give them courage or activity to go over after us. We were not ready for so great a mercy as victory and deliverance. If we had been God would have found out a way for the English to have passed this river, as well as for the Indians with their squaws and children, and all their luggage. "Oh that my people had hearkened to me, and Israel had walked in my ways, I should soon have subdued their enemies, and turned my hand against their adversaries" (Psalm 81.13–14).

Remarks Concerning the Savages of North America

Benjamin Franklin

Much has been made of the contradictions inherent in the foundations of the American Dream. On the one hand there is the Enlightenment faith in reason and temporal progress that supplanted the Puritan emphasis on Original Sin and hope for spiritual salvation. Thomas Jefferson (1743–1826) articulates this faith when he writes in the Declaration of Independence of the equality of all men and their inalienable right to "life, liberty, and the pursuit of happiness."

On the other hand, the eighteenth century also saw an increasing reliance on slavery as economic necessity, the institution Jefferson attempted to criticize in his original draft of the Declaration, even while slavery provided the basis for his wealth. There are contradictory perspectives on the Indians as well, who were being decimated through settlement, disease, and armed conflict, even while they were admired by these founders of the new government, Jefferson and Benjamin Franklin (1706–1790).

This excerpt from Franklin's "Remarks Concerning the Savages of North America" (1784), offers an admiring profile of Indian life. It is, however, as much a satire of Puritan righteousness as it is appreciation for Indian survival skills, pragmatism, and common sense so suitable for a life in the woods or even an eighteenth-century frontier town.

What is Franklin's attitude toward the Indians? How does it differ from

From *The Writings of Ben Franklin*, vol. X, ed. Albert Henry Smyth (New York: Macmillan, 1907).

that of William Bradford? What is his attitude toward religion? How do you account for the changed depiction of Indians from the seventeenth century to the eighteenth century? How do you account for the continuing oppression in spite of this apparently changing ideology?

Savages we call them, because their manners differ from ours, which we think the perfection of civility; they think the same of theirs.

Perhaps, if we could examine the manners of different nations with impartiality, we should find no people so rude, as to be without any rules of politeness; nor any so polite, as not to have some remains of rudeness.

The Indian men, when young, are hunters and warriors; when old, counselors; for all their government is by counsel of the sages; there is no force, there are no prisons, no officers to compel obedience, or inflict punishment. Hence they generally study oratory, the best speaker having the most influence. The Indian women till the ground, dress the food, nurse and bring up the children, and preserve and hand down to posterity the memory of public transactions. These employments of men and women are accounted natural and honorable. Having few artificial wants, they have abundance of leisure for improvement by conversation. Our laborious manner of life, compared with theirs, they esteem slavish and base; and the learning, on which we value ourselves, they regard as frivolous and useless. An instance of this occurred at the Treaty of Lancaster, in Pennsylvania, anno 1744, between the government of Virginia and the Six Nations. After the principal business was settled, the commissioners from Virginia acquainted the Indians by a speech, that there was at Williamsburg a college, with a fund for educating Indian youth; and that, if the Six Nations would send down half a dozen of their young lads to that college, the government would take care that they should be well provided for, and instructed in all the learning of the white people. It is one of the Indian rules of politeness not to answer a public proposition the same day that it is made; they think it would be treating it as a light matter, and that they show it respect by taking time to consider it, as of a matter important. They therefore deferred their answer till the day following; when their speaker began, by expressing their deep sense of the kindness of the Virginia government, in making them that offer; "for we know," says he, "that you highly esteem the kind of learning taught in those Colleges, and that the maintenance of our young men, while with you, would be very expensive to you. We are convinced, therefore, that you mean to do us good by your proposal; and we thank you heartily. But you, who are wise, must know that different nations have different conceptions of things; and you will therefore not take it amiss, if our ideas of this kind of education happen not to be the same with yours. We have had some experience of it; several of our young people were formerly brought up at the colleges of the northern provinces; they were instructed in all your sciences; but, when they came back to us, they were bad runners, ignorant of every means of living in the woods, unable to bear either cold or hunger, knew neither how to build a cabin, take a deer, or kill an enemy, spoke our language imperfectly, were therefore neither fit for hunters, warriors, nor counselors; they were totally good for nothing. We are however not the less obliged by your kind offer, though we decline accepting it; and, to show our grateful sense of it, if the gentlemen of Virginia will send us a dozen of their sons, we will take great care of their education, instruct them in all we know, and make men of them."

Having frequent occasions to hold public councils, they have acquired great order and decency in conducting them. The old men sit in the foremost ranks, the warriors in the next, and the women and children in the hindmost. The business of the women is to take exact notice of what passes, imprint it in their memories (for they have no writing), and communicate it to their children. They are the records of the council, and they preserve traditions of the stipulations in treaties 100 years back; which, when we compare with our writings, we always find exact. He that would speak, rises. The rest observe a profound silence. When he has finished and sits down, they leave him 5 or 6 minutes to recollect, that, if he has omitted anything he intended to say, or has anything to add, he may rise again and deliver it. To interrupt another, even in common conversation, is reckoned highly indecent. How different this from the conduct of a polite British House of Commons, where scarce a day passes without some confusion, that makes the speaker hoarse in calling to order; and how different from the mode of conversation in many polite companies of Europe, where, if you do not deliver your sentence with great rapidity, you are cut off in the middle of it by the impatient loquacity of those you converse with, and never suffered to finish it!

The politeness of these savages in conversation is indeed carried to excess, since it does not permit them to contradict or deny the truth of what is asserted in their presence. By this means they indeed avoid disputes; but then it becomes difficult to know their minds, or what impression you make upon them. The missionaries who have attempted to convert them to Christianity, all complain of this as one of the great difficulties of their mission. The Indians hear with patience the truths of the Gospel explained to them, and give their usual tokens of assent and approbation; you would think they were convinced. No such matter. It is mere civility.

A Swedish minister, having assembled the chiefs of the Susquehanah Indians, made a sermon to them, acquainting them with the principal historical facts on which our religion is founded; such as the fall of our first parents by eating an apple, the coming of Christ to repair the mischief, His miracles and suffering, &c. When he had finished, an Indian orator stood up to thank him. "What you have told us," says he, "is all very good. It is indeed bad to eat apples. It is better to make them all into cider. We are much obliged by your kindness in coming so far, to tell us these things which you have heard from your mothers. In return, I will tell you some of those we have heard from ours. In the beginning, our fathers had only the flesh of animals to subsist on, and if their hunting was unsuccessful, these were starving. Two of our young hunters, having killed a deer, made a fire in the woods to broil some part of it. When they were about to satisfy their hunger, they beheld a beautiful young woman descend from the clouds, and seat herself on that hill, which you see yonder among the blue mountains. They said to each other, it is a spirit that has smelled our broiling venison, and wishes to eat of it; let us offer some to her. They presented her with the tongue; she was pleased with the taste of it, and said, 'Your kindness shall be rewarded; come to this place after thirteen moons, and you shall find something that will be of great benefit in nourishing you and Your children to the latest generations.' They did so, and, to their surprise, found plants they had never seen before; but which, from that ancient time, have been constantly cultivated among us, to our great advantage. Where her right hand had touched the ground, they found maize, where her left hand had touch it, they found kidney-beans, and where her backside had sat on it, they found tobacco." The good missionary, disgusted with this idle tale, said, "What I delivered to you were sacred truths, but what you tell me is mere fable, fiction, and falsehood." The Indian, offended, replied, "My brother, it seems your friends have not done you justice in your education; they have not well instructed you in the rules of common civility. You saw that we, who understand and practice those rules, believed all your stories; why do you refuse to believe ours?"

When any of them come into our towns, our people are apt to crowd round them, gaze upon them, and incommode them, where they desire to be private; this they esteem great rudeness, and the effect of the want of instruction in the rules of civility and good manners. "We have," say they, "as much curiosity as you, and when you come into our towns, we wish for opportunities of looking at you; but for this purpose we hide ourselves behind bushes, where you are to pass, and never intrude ourselves into your company."

Their manner of entering one another's village has likewise its rules. It is reckoned uncivil in traveling strangers to enter a village abruptly, without giving notice of their approach. Therefore, as soon as they arrive within hearing, they stop and hollow [holler], remaining there till invited to enter. Two old men usually come out to them, and lead them in. There is in every village a vacant dwelling, called the strangers' house. Here they are placed, while the old men go round from hut to hut, acquainting the inhabitants, that strangers are arrived, who are probably hungry and weary; and every one sends them what he can spare of victuals, and skins to repose on. When the strangers are refreshed, pipes and tobacco are brought; and then, but not before, conversation begins, with inquiries who they are, whither bound, what news, &c.; and it usually ends with offers of service, if the strangers have occasion of guides, or any necessaries for continuing their journey; and nothing is exacted for the entertainment.

The same hospitality, esteemed among them as a principal virtue, is practiced by private persons; of which Conrad Weiser, our interpreter, gave me the following instances. He had been naturalized among the Six Nations, and spoke well the Mohawk language. In going through the Indian country, to carry a message from our Governor to the Council at Onondaga, he called at the habitation of Canassatego, an old acquaintance, who embraced him, spread furs for him to sit on, placed before him some boiled beans and venison, and mixed some rum and water for his drink. When he was well refreshed, and had lit his pipe, Canassatego began to converse with him; asked how he had fared the many years since they had seen each other; whence he then came; what occasioned the journey, &c. Conrad answered all his questions; and when the discourse began to flag, the Indian, to continue it, said, "Conrad, you have lived long among the white people, and know something of their customs; I have been sometimes at Albany, and have observed, that once in seven days they shut up their shops, and assemble all in the great house; tell me what it is for? What do they do there?" "They meet there," says Conrad, "to hear and learn good things." "I do not doubt," says the Indian, "that they tell you so; they have told me the same; but I doubt the truth of what they say, and I will tell you my reasons. I went lately to Albany to sell my skins and buy blankets, knives, powder, rum, &c. You know I used generally to deal with Hans Hanson; but I was a little inclined this time to try some other merchant. However, I called first upon Hans, and asked him what he would give for beaver. He said he could not give any more than four shillings a pound; 'but,' says he, 'I cannot talk on business now; this is the day when we meet together to learn good things, and I am going to the meeting.' So I thought to myself, 'Since we cannot do any business today, I may as well go to the meeting too,' and I went with him. There stood up a man in black, and began to talk to the people very angrily. I did not understand what he said; but, perceiving that he looked much at me and at Hanson, I imagined he was angry at seeing me there; so I went out, sat down near the house, struck fire, and lit my pipe, waiting till the meeting should break up. I thought too, that the man had mentioned something of beaver, and I suspected it might be the subject of their meeting. So, when they came out, I accosted my merchant. 'Well, Hans,' says I, 'I hope you have agreed to give more than four shillings a pound.' 'No,' says he, 'I cannot give so much; I cannot give more than three shillings and sixpence.' I then spoke to several other dealers, but they all sung the same song, -three and sixpence, -three and sixpence. This made it clear to me, that my suspicion was right; and, that whatever they pretended of meeting to learn good things, the real purpose was to consult how to cheat Indians in the price of beaver. Consider but a little, Conrad, and you must be of my opinion. If they met so often to learn good things, they would certainly have learned some before this time. But they are still ignorant. You know our practice. If a white man, in traveling through our country, enters one of our cabins, we all treat him as I treat you; we dry him if he is wet, we warm him if he is cold, we give him meat and drink, that he may allay his thirst and hunger; and we spread soft furs for him to rest and sleep on; we demand nothing in return. But, if I go into a white man's house at Albany, and ask for victuals and drink, they say, 'Where is your money?' and if I have none, they say, 'Get out, you Indian dog.' You see they have not yet learned those little good things, that we need no meetings to be instructed in, because our mothers taught them to us when we were children; and therefore it is impossible their meetings should be, as they say, for any such purpose, or have any such effect; they are only to contrive *the cheating of Indians in the price of beaver.*"

National Expansion from the Indian Perspective

R. David Edmunds

This article by a modern historian offers an interpretation of the idea of manifest destiny or the peopling of America at odds with the traditional settler-centered view. How does Edmunds counter the traditional view of U.S. expansion? Why does he argue that the Indians were not a barrier to American expansion?

In what ways were the North American frontiersmen like the bandeirantes of Brazil (see Hemming's Red Gold, *in Part 4)? Were the North American frontiersmen more interested in land than labor? If so, why? What effect*

Edmunds, R. David. "National Expansion from the Indian Perspective" in *Indians in American History*, ed. Frederick E. Hoxie. © 1988 by Harlan Davidson, Inc. Reprinted by permission of Harlan Davidson, Inc. All Rights Reserved. pp. 159–165.

did that difference have? Did the British government play a protective role
for the Indians? Were the British analogous to the Portuguese monarchy
or to the Catholic church in Brazil? Did these different circumstances lead
to different forms of Indian resistance to white settlement? Is there a similar
history of so-called mixed bloods in North and South America?

This selection is not only about a different culture than the Brazilian, it
also concerns a later period. Compare it not only to the selection from Red
Gold *but also to the selections from Bradford, Rowlandson, and Franklin.*
Did the settlers become more tolerant, or less? Did they become more or
less racist from the sixteenth to the nineteenth century?

Most Americans have readily accepted the conventional view that the westward expansion of the American frontier marked a similar advance of "civilization" over "savagery." Imbued with an ethnocentric bias, textbooks throughout the late nineteenth and much of the twentieth centuries described Indian people as part of a wilderness habitat to be altered, eradicated, or pushed further west. Indeed, in all editions published prior to the late 1960s, the most widely adopted college textbook focusing upon the history of the American westward movement discussed Indian-white relations in a chapter entitled "The Indian Barrier," while popular accounts of the American West as portrayed in movies and television emphasized the Indians' armed, if futile, resistance to the march of American "progress."

Such an interpretation is markedly simplistic and reflects an ignorance of the interaction of Indian and non-Indian peoples on the American frontier. Of course Indians sometimes resisted white expansion, but more often they interacted peacefully with white frontiersmen, shaping the region's social and economic institutions and modifying their own society to better accommodate both to a changing environment. Moreover, this interaction provides some valuable insights into the attitudes and assumptions of American society. Americans' opinions about Indians not only reflect their beliefs regarding minority groups but also illustrate their appraisal of themselves. For many nineteenth-century Americans, a preconceived and often erroneous conception of Indian or "savage" life provided a welcome contrast to what they envisioned as the "progress of American civilization."

During the first quarter of the nineteenth century, attitudes toward Indians probably differed between American frontiersmen and political leaders in Washington. Most of the Founding Fathers were the products of Enlightenment philosophy; and although they viewed Indian people as lesser beings, they still had been influenced by Rousseau's conceptions of the "noble savage." More ethnocentric than racist, they believed that the Indians could be converted into small yeomen farmers and eventually assimilated into American society. Since most Indians already had been forced from the eastern seaboard, politicians in

Washington, D.C. did not view them as a threat. Thomas Jefferson may have encouraged the proprietors of government-sponsored Indian factories (or trading posts) to lure the tribes-people into debt so they would be forced to cede their surplus lands, but he also supported a systematic program to provide the Indians with agents and farm implements so they could learn to be farmers.

American frontiersmen were less willing to assimilate the Indians. Although American historians continue to argue over the reasons frontiersmen moved west, most scholars agree that economic opportunity was of primary importance. Many frontiersmen were economic opportunists, eager to better their lot, and they had no qualms about seizing every advantage that furthered their aspirations. If some of those advantages came at the expense of the Indian people, it caused little concern to frontier entrepreneurs willing to ride roughshod over any group denying them access to riches. To many frontiersmen, the lands and the resources controlled by Indians were "plums ripe for the plucking." At worst, Indians were a threat; at best, they were a nuisance.

Conflicts over Indian policy spurred considerable disagreement between local, state, and federal governments. Many of these disputes reflect a theme familiar to most American historians: the federal government's inability to maintain effective control over its western citizens. Between 1795 and 1809, federal officials signed seventeen treaties with the tribes of Ohio, Indiana, Illinois, and Michigan, but the agreements were honored more in their violation than in their adherence. Imbued with a sense of their own self-righteousness, American frontiersmen ignored the treaty regulations and regularly crossed over onto National Indian lands to hunt, trap, or establish homesteads. Although federal officials in Ohio and Indiana made desultory attempts to protect Indian interests, they could not stop the tide of American aggrandizement. White trespass upon Indian lands reached such proportions that in 1808 William Henry Harrison, the governor of Indiana Territory, complained:

> The people of Kentucky . . . make a constant practice of crossing over onto Indian lands . . . to kill deer, bear, and buffaloe [*sic*]. . . . One hunter will destroy more game than five of the common Indians.

And in response to a more serious problem, Harrison added, "A great many of the Inhabitants of the Fronteers [*sic*] consider the murdering of the Indians in the highest degree meritorious." Federal lawmakers in Washington might be willing to differentiate between Indian and white lands, but for many frontiersmen the western territories were a vast cornucopia to be exploited. They disregarded Indian claims to the land and its resources.

American aggression caused considerable problems for the Indian people of Ohio, Indiana, and Illinois. Not only were their homelands overrun by frontiersmen, but the invaders severely depleted the game animals. Moreover, Indian attempts to seek justice brought little recourse since white juries systematically freed most Americans accused of crimes against the tribesmen. Not surprisingly, resentment swelled and the tribes struck back at the Americans. Unwilling to admit that they were the authors of their own misfortune, American frontiersmen in the first decade of the nineteenth century blamed the British, whom they charged with inciting the Indians against the settlements. Although the British did exercise considerable influence among the tribes, a close examination of these events indicates Indian resistance to American expansion was a natural, indigenous act. The British did attempt to manipulate Indian resentment of the Americans for their own purposes; however, in most instances the tribesmen were more militant than the Crown, and British Indian agents often attempted to restrain the warriors rather than precipitate a general conflict with the United States. In these instances, the Indians welcomed the technical and logistical support of the Crown, but their decision to resist the Americans was their own.

Traditionally, historians have championed Tecumseh, the Shawnee war chief, as the architect of the Indian resistance that coalesced prior to the War of 1812. Both British and American authors have been eager to point out that from 1809 through 1811, the Shawnee statesman traveled among the western tribes attempting to enlist the warriors into a pan-Indian political and military organization designed to defend the remaining Indian land base east of the Mississippi. In contrast, Tecumseh's brother, Tenskwatawa, known as the Prophet, usually has been portrayed as a religious charlatan who rode Tecumseh's coattails to a position of minor prominence. Yet throughout American history, during periods of significant stress, Indian people traditionally have turned to religious leaders or revitalization movements for their deliverance. Spiritual spokesmen such as Neolin, the Delaware prophet who emerged prior to Pontiac's rebellion; Handsome Lake of the Senecas, a contemporary of Tenskwatawa; and the Paiute Wovoka and his Ghost Dance are good examples of holy men who arose to meet their people's needs.

It appears from recent scholarship that Tenskwatawa was more instrumental than Tecumseh in forging the Indian coalition in the years preceding the War of 1812. Upon examination of all the primary materials focusing on these events, it is clear that for four years, from 1805 until 1809, the religious teachings of the Prophet were the magnet that attracted thousands of Indians, first to Greenville, in Ohio, then to Prophetstown. Although there are extensive references to the Prophet and his movements in documents from this period, there is no mention of Tecumseh prior to April 1808, when British officials in Canada mention that "the Prophet's brother" visited Amherstburg. William Henry Harrison, Tecumseh's primary antagonist, does not mention the Shaw-

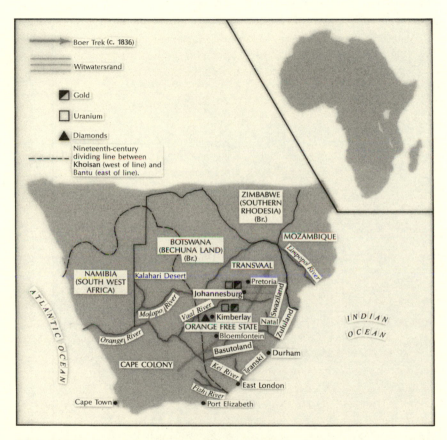

Southern Africa in the nineteenth century. *(Kevin Reilly)*

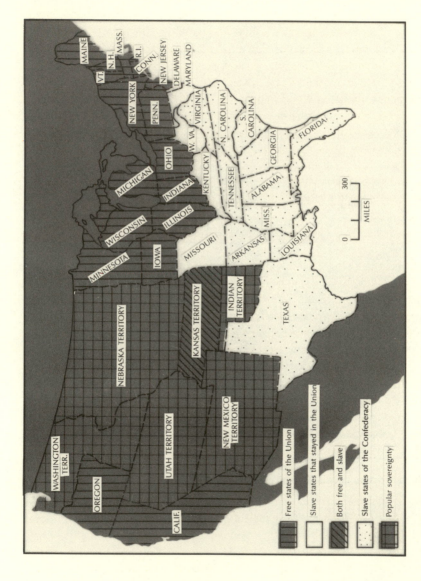

The United States during the Civil War. (*Kevin Reilly*)

nee chief until August 1810, and then Harrison also refers to him only as "the Prophet's brother," since he evidently had not yet learned Tecumseh's name. Indeed, Tecumseh did not challenge his brother for leadership until after the Treaty of Fort Wayne (1809), which transferred extensive Indian landholdings in Indiana to the United States. The Shawnee war chief then used his brother's religious movement as the base for his ill-fated, political-military confederacy.

White historians have probably championed Tecumseh as the author of the Indian resistance movement since his concepts of political and military unity seemed more logical (by white standards) than the Prophet's religious revitalization. In retrospect, white historians had little understanding of Indian religious doctrines, but they believed that if they had been Indians, they also would have attempted to forge the tribes into a multitribal confederacy. Yet the Prophet's doctrines had more appeal to the Indians. Americans have idolized Tecumseh because they believe that he fits their concept of the "noble savage"; since his death both folklorists and historians have enshrouded the Shawnee chief with extensive apocrypha.

Recent inquiry has also illustrated that different socioeconomic groups on the frontier reacted to the Indians in different ways. Historians have indicated, for example, that much of the violence between Indians and whites that occurred in the Far West during the middle decades of the nineteenth century was triggered by miners and other more transient workers, not farmers. Many white farmers who saw themselves as permanent residents of a region were interested in promoting peace and stability between the white and Indian populations. In contrast, miners were eager for the maximum exploitation of mineral resources and had little interest in the long-term development of a region. Preferring to make their "stake" and then retire to more comfortable surroundings, miners and other transients viewed Indians as impediments to their success and were quite willing to eliminate them. In addition, since many miners and other transient laborers often were unemployed, they sometimes welcomed the opportunity to draw rations and wages for service in militia or paramilitary units that were formed to suppress "Indian uprisings." Such earnings hardly matched the riches of a bonanza strike in the gold fields but, for destitute laborers, payment for military services offered ready cash.

The notion that frontier transients formed the backbone of frontier militias suggests an explanation for other Indian-white confrontations. In 1774 Lord Dunmore's War was precipitated when frontier riffraff murdered innocent Shawnees and Delawares along the Ohio. Almost sixty years later, on May 14, 1832, the Black Hawk War probably would have terminated without bloodshed if the drunken militia partially composed of miners from Wisconsin's Fever River District and commanded by Major Isaiah Stillman had not attacked Black Hawk's envoys as the old Sauk war chief prepared to surrender. The resulting Battle of Stillman's Run ended any chance for the hapless Sauks and Foxes to withdraw peacefully to Iowa. On November 28, 1864, illtrained and drunken militia were also responsible for the slaughter of more than 150 Cheyennes and Arapahos at Sand Creek in Colorado. Many of the volunteers making up this force were unemployed miners lured west by the Colorado gold rush of the late 1850s. Illegal trespass by miners onto Indian lands in the Black Hills also triggered the last of the Sioux wars, culminating in Custer's defeat at the Battle of the Little Big Horn. Other miners organized the mob who murdered 144 Apaches at Camp Grant, near Tucson, Arizona, in April 1871.

In retrospect, if Indian lands held valuable resources, those treasures were exploited. Although the federal government might promise to protect the inviolability of Indian real estate, such promises often were broken. The consequences of this repeating cycle should have a profound message for tribal communities holding valuable mineral or water resources in the twentieth century.

Disputes between Indians and whites over Indian lands in the Southeast also offer some interesting insights into the conflict between frontiersmen and federal officials while illustrating the entrepreneurial values of the Jacksonians. By the 1820s, many Americans were dissatisfied with the established organic economic system that emphasized careful centralized planning (a national bank, tariffs, federal support for internal improvements, etc.), and new entrepreneurs emerged who argued that "the powdered wig set" (the federal government) controlled the nation's resources for their own benefit. After the adoption of the cotton gin spread cotton production across the Gulf plains, Indian lands in the region became the focus of local land speculators. Their complaint was not that the federal government had failed to purchase Indian land holdings (indeed, by the 1820s much of the former tribal holdings already were in the public domain) but that the government did not immediately buy all Indian lands remaining within their respective states and send the tribes packing across the Mississippi.

In contrast, many officials in Washington, as exemplified by President John Quincy Adams, still gave at least lip service to the civilization programs that had been in force since the beginning of the century. In theory, the Indians were to adopt white values and be assimilated into American society. In actuality, Adams also may have favored some type of removal program, but he championed carefully planned and legalistic procedures through which the changing status of the Indians and their tenure of tribal lands could be delineated.

Any delays necessitated by long-term planning were unacceptable to local expansionists. In Georgia a group of these expansionists, led by Governor George M. Troup, negotiated the Treaty of Indian Springs with a faction representing a minority of the Creek Confederacy treaty was signed by federal officials, but these men were clearly acting on behalf of Troup. After the treaty was ratified by the Senate in March 1825, the Creeks executed William Mc-Intosh, the leader of the treaty faction. In response, Troup threatened to overrun Creek lands with the Georgia militia. Federal officials interceded, nullifying the Treaty of Indian Springs, but signed the Treaty of Washington with the Creeks one year later. The new treaty also called for the cession of Creek lands in Georgia (already a fait accompli, since settlers had moved into the region); but the terms were more favorable for the Indians, and the federal government promised to guarantee the remaining Creek lands in Alabama. In theory at least, federal officials had interceded to partially protect Indian interests from expansionists at the state and local levels of government.

Whether the Adams regime would (or could) have honored its promises remains doubtful, but in 1828 Andrew Jackson was elected to the presidency and a spokesman for the frontier entrepreneurs was in the White House. Jackson's election also marked an increase in federal pressure to remove the tribespeople to the trans-Mississippi west. Although previous administrations had counseled the Indians to remove, they had appraised the problem from an ethnocentric rather than a racial perspective. Presidents such as John Quincy Adams believed the Indians to be inferior, but from Adams' viewpoint they were inferior because they had not attained the socioeconomic-political level of Europeans or Americans. If Indians would adopt white ways and become civilized, they could be assimilated into American society.

The Jacksonians had no intention of assimilating the Indians into American society. Regardless of the tribespeople's adoption of American institutions, frontier entrepreneurs wanted them removed from their lands and forced beyond the frontier. The Cherokee's "civilization" program, for example, afforded them little protection from white Georgians. After gold was discovered on Cherokee lands, white Americans ignored the tribe's constitution, newspaper, and pious Protestant congregations. Tribal lands were overrun. Regardless of how "civilized" the Cherokees had become, other Americans still saw them as "Indians" and, therefore, not encompassed in the protection that the Constitution extended to white men.

Part 6

Settler Racism and Slavery

Between 1882 and 1927, at least 5,000 black men were lynched in the United States, mostly by vigilante mobs. But some official executions were equally grotesque. Here, the opera house of Livermore, Kentucky, was the site of a public execution of a black man by the audience. Holders of orchestra tickets were allowed six shots; balcony tickets got one. *(Le Petit Journal, May 11, 1911)*

In this part, we turn from settler racism directed against the indigenous inhabitants whom the settlers displaced (Indians in the Americas) to settler racism by the dominant settlers against another "foreign" population, but in this case a population imported as slaves.

We have mentioned that the settlers of North America were more interested in land than labor, those in South America more desirous of labor. Despite these differences, the demographic losses of Native Americans in both North and South America were enormous. So, when sugar plantations were transferred to the Caribbean and Brazil, a new source of laborers had to be imported to be exploited. In Barbados, Irish laborers sufficed for the first few decades, but increasingly after 1640, Africans were used, and, unlike the Irish, they were imported as slaves.

As we will see in the following readings, this importation of a people who looked physically different from the Europeans, almost solely as slaves, re-created the tendency we saw in post ninth-century Islamic expansion to identify black skin and subservience. If not at first, at least eventually this association provided the fuel for ideas of "race" and "theories" of racial inferiority and superiority that rationalized the social and economic privilege of whites.

Race and Racism

Kevin Reilly

This selection explores two issues worth considering. The first is whether racism is universal and ancient or a development of modern, especially European, settlement. "Race" appears to be a modern word. The identification of slavery and race is mainly modern, as are explicit theories of race and expressions of racist (i.e., hereditary) inferiority. We have already explored this question even if we have not answered it.

Next, we look at the argument for cultural causes of white racism before European enslavement of Africans. Did white racism originate in ideas of whiteness or in the social and economic exploitation of African slavery? "The Burden of Slavery" argues for the latter.

From *The West and the World* (New York: HarperCollins, 1989), pp. 44–70. Copyright © 1989 by Kevin Reilly. All rights reserved.

Nevertheless, slavery did not impose the same racism everywhere. Indeed, slavery was different in North and South America. What are some of these differences? What do differences in miscegenation or manumission rates indicate about Latin and English attitudes toward race? Was one tradition more racist than others? Do North Americans have a more black-and-white idea of race? Is that more racist?

Is Racism Universal or Recent?

Have all people been "racist" in one way or another? Have all people assumed that their way of doing things was naturally, inevitably superior to that of other people? Anthropologists who have studied the enormous variety of human experience do not agree on the answer to this question. One anthropologist, Claude Levi-Strauss, argues that all people have believed themselves superior. In fact, he says, it was common for preliterate peoples to imagine themselves as the only real human beings, calling themselves "the men" and others "the ghosts."

The myths of tribal and traditional societies have sometimes denied a common human origin. Eskimos, for instance, tell a story about the Great Being creating a colorless people called "white men" before getting the ingredients right for the perfect in-nu, the ancestors of the Eskimos. A similar North American legend recounts how the Great Spirit had to create man three times. The first time the creation was not baked long enough and came out white. The second time the oven was too hot, and man came out burnt black. Finally, the Great Spirit created the perfect golden human being. Myths like this, according to Levi-Strauss, suggest that racism is virtually universal.

A different view is offered by another anthropologist, Michel Leiris:

> The first point which emerges from any examination of the data of ethnography and history is that race prejudice is not universal and is of recent origin. Many of the societies investigated by anthropologists do indeed display group pride, but while the group regards itself as privileged compared with other groups, it makes no "racist" claims and, for instance, is not above entering into temporary alliances with other groups or providing itself with women from them.

Any generalization about primitive, tribal, or traditional societies is difficult, if not impossible. What we can do briefly is look at some of the ancient societies we know for evidence of racism. If we turn to the ancient Mediterranean world, where there was a considerable amount of contact with lighter-skinned people in the North and darker people to the South, racism is difficult to find.

Black people, especially, were viewed favorably by the ancient Egyptians, Hebrews, Greeks, and Romans. The Africans from Nubia and Ethiopia were frequently praised for their beauty, fighting ability, and civilization. Moses married a Kushite woman (from Nubia), and "the anger of the Lord was roused" against those who objected. For the Nubian was to live with the Egyptian, Babylonian, Philistine, and Tyrian, and Zion was to "be called a mother in whom men of every race are born."

The ancient Egyptians also both praised and condemned the people of Kush. But even those Kushites who were their enemies were not racially stereotyped by the Egyptians. Some Kushites fought in Egyptian legions, married Egyptian women, and helped shape a racially diverse society.

From the time that the Greek poet Homer spoke of the "blameless Ethiopians" the attitude of the Greco-Roman world toward Africans and Asians was tolerant and respectful. The ancient Greeks called some of their neighbors "barbarians," but this meant only that they could not speak Greek. Greeks accepted foreigners who seemed to be cultured (which is to say, foreigners who learned Greek language and customs). When the Greek troops under Alexander the Great conquered Persia and India, ten thousand Greek soldiers married Hindu Indian women, and Alexander himself married two Persian princesses. Since Alexander and his soldiers imagined that they brought the benefits of Greek culture and civilization, they knew that their sons and daughters would be raised like other Greeks. They had no fear of producing offspring less than human or of corrupting a Greek "race" or "blood." They were concerned about culture, not biology, and they did not assume that culture had anything to do with biology.

In relation to blacks, a recent study concludes as follows:

> It is important to emphasize that the overall, but especially more detailed Greco-Roman, view of blacks was highly positive. Initial, favorable impressions were not altered, in spite of later accounts of wild tribes in the far south and even after encounters with blacks had become more frequent. There was clear-cut respect among Mediterranean peoples for Ethiopians, and their way of life. And, above all, the ancients did not stereotype all blacks as primitives defective in religion and culture.[1]

The Color of Slaves

In the Roman Empire, Roman slaves came from captured peoples of Africa, Asia, and Europe. Since slaves could not be identified as a single physical type, the Romans did not develop racist ideas about slavery. But in periods when the Romans enslaved a particular ethnic group in large numbers, they did tend to stereotype that group as slaves. Thus, after the Romans conquered and enslaved many of the light-skinned Scythians from Thrace (north of Greece), they thought of Thracians as slaves. Then a Roman actor would wear a red wig to play a slave because Thracians had red hair. Similarly, the Thracian name Rufus came to be regarded as a typical slave's name. Thracians were even depicted as lazy, called "boy," and considered inferior.

Ethnic stereotypes changed as the Romans drew their slaves from different ethnic groups. With the Roman conquest of Gaul (France) and Britain in the first century B.C.E., the Roman stereotype of slaves more closely resembled the light-skinned, blond Gauls and Britains.

After the collapse of Roman power, one of the main sources of slaves for the Byzantine Empire and the emerging European states was the Caucasus Mountains (an area the size of California between the Black Sea and the Caspian Sea south of modern Russia).

Caucasia was a prime source of slaves throughout the Middle Ages because it remained politically fragmented and highly populated. It also was an easy area in which to play one ethnic group against another and was easily accessible from the Black Sea.

Thus, the Caucasians (who ironically came to define "whiteness" after 1800) were the stereotypic slaves of the Middle Ages. "Chastity is unknown and theft is rampant among them," wrote one eleventh-century observer.

> Coarse is their nature and coarse is their speech. . . . He only works under the threat of the cane or the stress of fear. When you find him lazy—it is simply because he delights in laziness and not because he does not feel equal to work. You must then take to the cane, chastise him and make him do what you want.[2]

In the later Middle Ages, European slaves were taken increasingly from areas north and west of the Caucasus. The Slavic peoples of the Balkans and Southern Russia were pressed into slavery by Italian traders, while the Slavs of Central Europe fell victims to the German expansion eastward. Ever since, the word "Slav" has been synonymous with "slave" in European languages.

Where then did the identification of slavery with black Africans arise? It probably originated in the Muslim world of the Middle East and North Africa. The Koran is free of color prejudice, even of Arab ethnocentrism, seeing the racial differences of mankind as a divine miracle. But despite the Muslim idea of brotherhood and the writings of the Prophet, the logic of Islamic expansion meant that slaves had increasingly to be drawn from the periphery of the Muslim world. Islamic law held that no freeborn Muslim could be sold into slavery. Nor could a Jew or Christian who remained under the protection of the Muslim peace, the Dar al-Islam. Thus, slaves had to be taken from captives outside the expanding borders of the Muslim world. In the early history of Islamic expansion that area included Europe, and Muslims first made no distinction between European and African slaves. However, as European armies became better able to defend their territories, the supply of European slaves diminished. Increasingly after the tenth century, Muslim slaves were drawn from the more politically fragmented areas of tropical Africa.

The strong centralized states of Sudanic Africa were usually converted to Islam, rather than conquered militarily, but that conversion put the Muslims within the reach of the stateless, more vulnerable black peoples further south.

As the proportion of black slaves increased in the Islamic world, slavery became increasingly identified with blackness. As early as the ninth century, the traditional Arabic word for slave (abid) was being limited to black slaves. White slaves were called mamluks. Soon abid was used to refer to blacks whether slave or free. While there were examples of important blacks in Muslim society (a ruler of Egypt in the tenth century, for instance), blacks increasingly found themselves at the bottom of the social pyramid and the butt of racist generalizations. By the fourteenth century even the great historian of Islam, Ibn Khaldun, could write that "the only people who accept slavery are the Negroes, owing to their low degree of humanity and their proximity to the animal stage."[3]

And like the Thracians, the Caucasians, the Slavs, and so many before them, blacks were described in Muslim accounts of the thirteenth and fourteenth centuries, as lazy, lecherous, dishonest, thieving, lying, careless, stupid, and "the most stinking of mankind in the armpits and sweat."[4]

Fourteenth-century Europeans still knew slaves as "Slavs," but a series of developments—especially sugar production and ocean navigation—introduced them to African slaveholding and the racist justifications that had already been developed.

Sugar, Sails, and Slaves

Sugar cultivation originated on the Bengal coast of India. It reached Egypt by the tenth century, and the Europeans discovered it in Syria during the First Crusade. Both Christian and Muslim planters spread the cultivation and refining of sugar throughout the Mediterranean from 1300 to 1500, and in about 1520 the Portuguese began production in Brazil.

Two factors made sugar a key stimulant to slavery. It was an extremely labor intensive crop, requiring vast numbers of unskilled laborers. And it became enormously popular. "What used to be a medicine is nowadays eaten as a food,"[5] one observer remarked in 1572. Virtually unknown beyond the pharmacy shelves in 1400, the new "food" became the main product of the slave plantations of the New World. By 1800 Parisians were consuming ten pounds per person per year.

The European sailing vessel was as important as the sugar plantation in the rise of African slavery. Indeed, without sailing ships that were able to negotiate the rough seas of the Atlantic, there would have been no New World slave plantations. The Portuguese, under Prince Henry (the Navigator, 1394–1460), were in the ideal position to combine the heavy construction and square sails of Northern European sailing ships with the maneuverability of the smaller lateen (triangular sail) craft, which had become common in calmer Mediterranean waters since the Arabs had brought them from the Sea of Oman. By using triangular sails, Portuguese caravels could sail against the wind along the coast of Africa, while square sails allowed them to make use of favorable winds. Portugal was especially well placed to secure its own supply of African slaves. The Mediterranean trade was increasingly controlled by the Italian city of Genoa in the early fifteenth century. Genoa was an aggressively commercial and egalitarian city that excluded nobles from public office but sold thousands of Christian slaves to the Muslims of Egypt and Syria along with anything else that would turn a profit. As the Ottoman Empire secured control of the sources of Christian slaves in the Black Sea area and the Balkans (and finally Constantinople in 1453), Europeans were forced to turn to African slaves for their households and Mediterranean sugar plantations. In the early 1400s, most of the slaves on the island of Crete were Greek. By the end of the century, most were African.

Portugal was able to benefit from the closing of the Eastern Mediterranean source of Christian slaves and to gain its own foothold along the Atlantic. Encouraged by a papal order to conquer and enslave the infidels, pagans, and unbelievers, King Dom Joao I (r. 1385–1433) and his son Prince Henry forced the Muslims out of Portugal a century before the Spanish forced the Muslims from Spain. In 1415 Henry conquered the city of Ceuta in Morocco, on the North Africa coast. In 1420 the Portuguese occupied Madeira (for wheat, and then sugar, cultivation). The Azores were integrated into the Portuguese Atlantic trading area in 1430.

Henry's goal in Africa was to convert the Muslims and obtain the gold of the Sudan. But it was a short step from conquering Muslims in Morocco to taking captives on the Mauritanian coast. In 1441 one of the prince's household knights led a landing party on a nighttime assault on coastal villages south of the Sahara and brought the captives to the prince. Henry "reflected with great pleasure upon the salvation of those souls that before were lost."[6] But his response to the enslavement of Africans may not have been typical.

On an August morning in 1444 the first cargo of West African slaves arrived at the Portuguese port of Lagos aboard a caravel. The Portuguese historian Zurara was there.

> What heart could be so hard not to be pierced with pity to see that company? For some kept their heads low and their faces bathed in tears, others stood groaning in sadness; others buried their faces in the palms of their hands and threw themselves on the ground. Though we could not understand the words of their language, the sound of it measured their grief. Then to increase their sufferings came the captors to divide their captives into fifths; to part fathers from sons, husbands from wives, brothers from brothers. . . . And what a difficult task! As soon as sons were parted from fathers they rushed over to join them; the mothers clasped their children in their arms, threw themselves on the ground, caring little for the beatings they received, if only they might not be torn from their children.[7]

Zurara evidently was not the only onlooker to be repelled by the sight. He suggests that the townspeople of Lagos and other spectators were so overcome that they intervened to prevent the distribution of slaves. As a consequence, some were freed. Women were adopted by Portuguese families. Men were taught trades and skills. Some men as well as women married Portuguese after accepting Christianity.

Not all Europeans were as "color-blind" as these Portuguese on the dock at Lagos in 1444. Indeed, not all Portuguese were. In Christian Europe as a whole, and possibly in northern Europe more particularly, a traditional religious symbolism of whiteness and blackness had become more significant in the centuries before the Portuguese overseas expansion.

The Problem of Whiteness

Christians thought of sin as the blackening of a white soul. They thought of God, virtue, purity, and redemption in terms of radiating light or whiteness. Angels and the holy were bathed in white light. Even the Middle Eastern Jesus was gradually whitened until he became a fair-skinned, blond, blue-eyed European in the paintings of the Middle Ages. In striking contrast, the devil was dressed in black; he was the "Prince of Darkness."

According to the Oxford English Dictionary, by the end of the fifteenth century the meaning of "black" had clearly negative implications:

> Deeply stained with dirt; soiled, dirty. . . . Having dark or deadly purposes, malignant; pertaining to or involving death, deadly; baneful, dis-

astrous, sinister. . . . Foul, iniquitous, atrocious, horrible, wicked. . . .
Indicating disgrace, censure, liability to punishment.[8]

Whiteness may have become more of a problem for northern Europeans
than it was for southern Europeans. Not only were the northerners more fearful
of the powers of darkness they believed to be taking over the world, they also
were physically whiter and blonder. Whiteness became a mark of beauty for
those whose skins were particularly pale. Queen Elizabeth, the Protestant
daughter of Henry VIII, was celebrated by the English (as were other women)
for the lily-whiteness of her skin:

Her cheek, her chin, her neck, her nose,
This was a lily, that was a rose;
Her handle so white as whales bone,
Her finger tipt with Cassidone;
Her bosom, sleek as Paris plaster
Held up two bowles of Alabaster.[9]

Dirty Words and White Lies

The problem of whiteness was examined indirectly by the great poet of Elizabeth's England, William Shakespeare. *Othello*, one of Shakespeare's greatest
plays, gives us a clear indication of the Elizabethan Christian responses to
whiteness and blackness. The play, which was probably written in 1604 (the
year after Elizabeth's death), is based on an earlier Italian story of a black
African general's marriage to a fair-skinned Venetian. Shakespeare contributes so much to the original story, though, that we can consider it his own.

Othello is the black Moor (or Muslim). Shakespeare pictures him as especially noble, generous, and loving. Desdemona, his wife, is completely devoted
to him. They love each other selflessly and without suspicion. But their love
is corrupted by the racism of those around them. For example, the Venetian
gentlemen, including Desdemona's father, continually refer to Othello as the
"lusty Moor" or the "lascivious Moor." Desdemona's father was dead set against
her marriage to the "damned" Moor, whose "sooty bosom" must, he feels, have
won his "fair" daughter's heart by "foul charms." Othello is "damned" because
he's black; even his name suggests he has come out of hell. His black skin
must be only the exterior of a "sooty bosom" inside. It seems unnatural to the
father that a daughter as fair or white as Desdemona could be attracted to
someone as black as Othello. Therefore, Othello must have used "foul charms"
(we would say "black magic") to trick her. All of the elements of white racism
are there.

The real force of a racism that identifies black skin with dirt, sex, and sin is displayed in the play by one of Othello's white assistants, Iago. Iago was passed up for a promotion. Perhaps that is why he suspects that Othello has seduced his wife:

> I hate the Moor;
> And it is thought abroad, that 'twixt my sheets
> He has done my office.

Iago is able to save himself from being poisoned by the absurd suspicion only by infecting others. He proceeds to attack Desdemona (whom he says he loves) in order to get at Othello (whom he has come to hate). He resolves to "turn her virtue into pitch"—in short, to "blacken" her image in the eyes of Othello.

Othello is himself so indoctrinated by the racist color scheme of his adopted culture that he easily believes that his loving wife would accept a white lover. Manipulated by Iago to suspect his wife, even Othello can see her sin only in racist terms:

> Her name, that was as fresh,
> As Dian's visage, is now begrim'd and black
> As mine own face.

Finally, the noble Moor is driven to kill the loving wife that he calls "the fair devil." It is white racism that really kills Desdemona. Iago uses "dirty" words, spoken from "dark shadows." But the noble Moor is the instrument, the victim, and the accused. After he "puts out the light" of his life, he is condemned by Desdemona's servant:

> O! the more angel she,
> And you the blacker devil. . . .
> She was too found of her most filthy bargain. . . .
> O gull! O dolt! As ignorant as dirt!"

Shakespeare's play is not racist, but it exposes the racial attitudes of Elizabethan society by playing upon the symbols for white and black. Othello was a long tradition in English theater that used the Moor to portray sexuality, evil, and the devil.

Negro y Blanco

It is interesting to compare the image of blacks in the plays of Elizabethan England and in those of Spain and Portugal, where there also was a literary renaissance in the sixteenth century.

The great Spanish dramatist Lope de Vega wrote dozens of plays that dealt with various aspects of Spanish life. One of his plays that offers us an insight into the Spanish understanding of race is *El Negro del Mejor Amor*.

The play is also the story of a Moor, a black North African Muslim, who visits Italy. Antiobo, the black prince, is the son of Duliman, king of Algeria, and the beautiful black Sofonisba. Antiobo, raised a Muslim, worries his father, we learn in the first act, because he displays an unusual concern for his father's Christian captives. To test his son, Duliman sends Antiobo on a fleet of Algerian warships to join the Turks in an attack on the Christian island of Sardinia. When the fleet arrives, Antiobo's true faith asserts itself and he joins the Sardinian Christians to defeat the combined Muslim forces he was supposed to lead. Victorious in the Christian cause, Antiobo spends the rest of his life a hero among the Sardinians. The play concludes after Antiobo's death, with another Turkish assault on Sardinia. This time the body of Antiobo rises from the grave to save the island for Christianity again. The differences between *Othello* and *El Negro del Mejor Amor* are striking. Antiobo is a Christian hero—not despite the fact he's black, but despite the fact he was raised as a Muslim. Religion, not race, is the important issue that Lope's play depends upon for its emotive power and meaning. Antiobo was part of a long tradition in Mediterranean literature that depicted the "good black," the Christian Ethiopian, who fought alongside the Christians against the Muslims.

Spanish Christians, who included converted Moors, acknowledged the Ethiopian Christian church as older than their own. Piety and legitimacy were often "black" for the Spanish. Don Juan Manuel (1282–1349) told the story in *El Conde Lucanor* of a king who was duped by three men who pretended to weave a garment so fine that only a legitimate son could see it. As the king rode through the streets naked, all of his fawning subjects complimented him on his "beautiful robe." Only a lowly black stable boy stepped forward to tell the king he had no clothes.

The Red and the Black

"In Spain it is a kind of title of nobility not to descend from Jews or Moors. In America, the skin, more or less white, is what dictates the class that an individual occupies in society."[10] So wrote Alexander von Humboldt of his visit to the Americas around 1800. While this was generally true, at least of Spanish America by 1800, racial distinctions developed gradually in America.

While the Spanish conquistadores brought some of their African (as well as European) slaves with them in their campaign of conquest of the Americas, the social position of these slaves was established by tradition. Native Americans had no defined place in the European social system. The very first European response to the Amerindians was Columbus's enslavement of some as specimens of scientific curiosity and a present for Ferdinand and Isabella. The first response of the conquistadores was to ally with some and to capture and kill many more of the Native Americans in the course of their conquest. As a result of war, and especially disease, it is likely that 70–90 percent of the Native American population was wiped out in the first century of European penetration, from 1492 to 1600. Any European toleration of racial differences must be put in that context.

The toleration deserves notice, however, if only because it contrasts markedly with what came later. In 1503 the governor of Santo Domingo was instructed by the Spanish crown to see to it that some Spanish Christians were married to Native Americans. While this order might have been a limited experiment, it was also a reflection of the crown's overriding concern for Christian marriages. (At the same time white female slaves were sent to Santo Domingo.) By 1514, 171 of 689 Spaniards in Santo Domingo were married, 64 to Indian women.

The half-Spanish, half-Indian "mestizos" of the early colonial period often found themselves at the top of the social hierarchy. If they constituted a new aristocracy, it may have been, in part, because of the social background of later Spanish immigrants. Miguel de Cervantes described Spanish America in 1613 as follows:

> The refuge and haven of all the poor devils of Spain, the sanctuary of the bankrupt, the safeguard of murderers, the way out for gamblers, the promised land for ladies of easy virtue, and a lure and disillusionment for the many, and a personal remedy for the few.[11]

Indians were protected from the more exploitative colonists by the crown and the church in the sixteenth century. Bartolomeo de Las Casas and other Spanish theologians even argued (before a change of heart in the 1520s) that Africans ought to be enslaved so that Indians could be protected. On 9 June 1537, Pope Paul III declared that Indians were true men and not beasts and, thus, should not be reduced to slavery. But while Spanish kings, including Charles I and Philip II, eliminated slavery among the Indians of Mexico and the Andes out of a concern for their own souls as well as those of the natives,

King Joao III and other Portuguese monarchs contented themselves with guidelines. Instructions of 1548, for instance, declared that the purpose of the Portuguese in colonizing Brazil was the conversion of the natives and that this could best be achieved by protecting them and preventing slavery, but that slave licenses could be issued in times of need, and captives of "just wars" on hostile tribes could be enslaved. By 1574 the notion of "just war" was broad enough to include almost any slave raiding, and even when the Spanish king Philip II took the Portuguese crown in 1580 the laws remained the same.

Indian slavery in the Americas was to prove short-lived, however. Of the three forces of European conquest—church, crown, and colonists—only the colonists benefited from Indian slavery. The church thrived on free souls, the crown on subjects. A continent of slaves would benefit the landowners. A continent of free souls could be shepherded by the church and governed by the crown.

The initial grants of land and power to the conquistadores had the effect of setting up a new feudal class in competition with the crown. Initially Hernan Cortes (1485–1547), the conqueror of Mexico, received a grant, called an encomienda, of twenty-two towns in Mexico that gave him control over 115,000 people. By 1600 the Spanish crown was able to replace the encomienda system with one of crown administration and labor control, called the repartimiento. The royal repartimiento did not turn out to be less brutal than the feudal servitude of the encomienda. The Indians' masters merely changed from local colonists to the distant monarchy as administered by local colonists. While Indians lived in villages rather than plantations, their lives were dominated increasingly by the local hacienda and labor market.

Nevertheless, it might seem odd that the church and crown discouraged Indian slavery while encouraging African slavery. But on reflection, the reason for this disparity is apparent. Neither the church nor the crown could control or influence Africans in Africa. Aside from occasional explorers, European forces did not penetrate the coast of Africa until the late nineteenth century. Prior to that, Africans could be exploited, mobilized, or converted only after they were taken to the New World as slaves.

The Burden of Slavery

Sometimes the exception proves the rule. Listen to the master of a slave ship, Captain Thomas Phillips, in 1694. The good captain complained of the developing racism of his fellow English, and found it odd that Africans were despised simply because they were black. The good slaver said that he could not imagine why they should be despised for

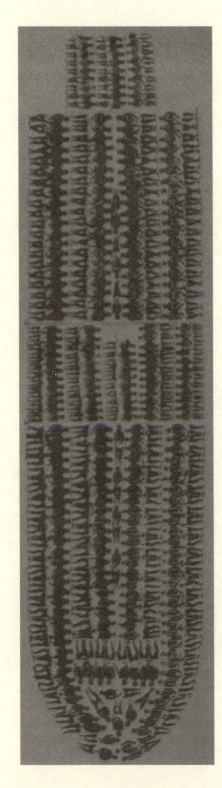

To attain maximum profit, slave ships packed human "cargo" as tightly as possible for the two- to three-month passage from Africa to the Americas.

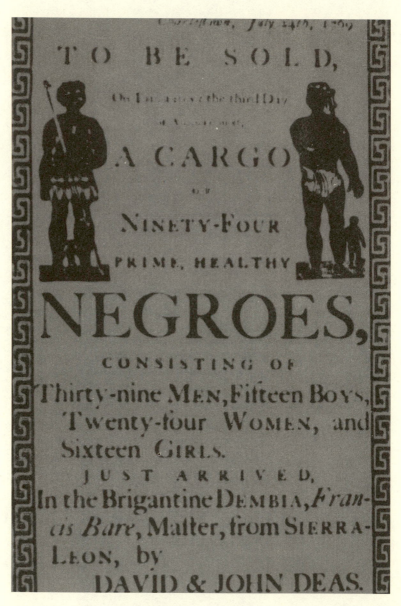

A notice advertising the sale of 94 "prime, healthy Negroes" from West Africa in 1769, a tiny fraction of the 10 to 20 million Africans brought to the Americas from the fifteenth to the nineteenth centuries.

their color, being what they cannot help, and the effect of the climate it has pleased God to appoint them. I can't think there is any intrinsic value in one color more than another, nor that white is better than black; only we think it so because we are so, and are prone to judge favorable in our own case, as well as the blacks, who, in odium of the color, say the devil is white, and so paint him.[12]

Statements like that could not have been made by many slave ship captains, nor by many other people who profited directly from the capture, sale, or use of African slaves. The fact that this captain could be so open suggests that there could be good men operating cruelly in a brutal system. But the fact that his statement was unusual also shows that most people were molded by the system, however noble their feelings initially were. It was not possible for many slavers to maintain such views very long and still go about their business. It was almost inevitable that a society that made slavery a way of life would normally think in racist terms, at least when all those slaves were black. Certainly Europeans were better able to tolerate their brutal exploitation of Africans by imagining that these Africans were an inferior race or, better still, not even human. In this sense, slavery encouraged European racism. C. R. Boxer has observed, "One race cannot systematically enslave members of another on a large scale for over three centuries without acquiring a conscious or unconscious feeling of racial superiority."[13]

Slavery was not a single system, however, not even on the plantations and mines of the Americas. It developed at different times and at different paces (earlier and, in general, more quickly in Latin America than British America). It also developed in the context of different European social systems. Latin American slavery from 1500 to 1800 developed in a traditional society where feudal law, ideas, and habits were still important. Spaniards were born into a particular estate or caste and accepted that. Virtually no one believed in equality. They took the Church, the sacraments, and salvation very seriously. Members of the nobility really cared about their honor. Soldiers were motivated by fear and plunder. Religious fanaticism was considered virtuous. Life was a trial, usually brutal and bloody, offering only rare moments of passion. English society, on the other hand, was becoming increasingly capitalist and middle-class between 1600 and 1800. The English paid more attention to money and profit. Society was more fluid, less fixed. Science was beginning to take the place of religion, and the idea of equality was beginning to replace that of caste.

This is not to say that English society was opposed to slavery. Some Englishmen were. Others were defensive about their involvement in slavery, or aggressive about pursuing their own profits.

English slavery was neither more humane (out of a greater sense of equality) nor more brutal (out of a freer profit motive) than Spanish slavery. Some English societies could be among the worst in the Americas. Jamaica certainly was.

> This was a society in which clergymen were "the most finished debauchers" in the land; in which the institution of marriage was officially condemned among both masters and slaves; in which the family was unthinkable to the vast majority of the population and promiscuity the norm; in which education was seen as an absolute waste of time and teachers shunned like the plague; in which the legal system was quite deliberately a travesty of anything that could be called justice; and in which all forms of refinements, or art, or folkways, were either absent or in a state of total disintegration.[14]

Perhaps Jamaica represented one side of capitalism. Absentee landlords organized the entire island into plantations for the single purpose of producing sugar and making them rich. Perhaps the other side of capitalism was represented by the colonies that became the northern United States and Canada—legislating against slavery. preferring free or wage labor. In between, areas like the southern United States blunted both the exploitation and equalitarianism of emerging capitalism in creating plantations "at home."

In general, the slave systems of the Latin America may have been harder on the slaves than those of British North America. Since the Iberians imported more slaves and continued the slave trade longer, the lives of slaves were often cheaper. The slaves of the southern United States were among the few to reproduce themselves; they were often able to maintain families; and to a certain degree they shared in the higher standard of living of the United States by 1800.

Two qualifications must be kept in mind, however. The first is that slavery was always coercive and demoralizing. If there were fewer slave revolts in the United States than in the Caribbean and South America, it was because greater white power in the United States made revolt suicidal.

The second qualification, more important for the purpose of this chapter, is that the worst slave systems might not have the most racist. While there is clearly a correlation between slavery and racism in general, there may not be a correlation between the brutality of the slave system and the highest degrees of racism. In short, it is possible that Latin American slavery was worse than British, but that British racism was worse than Latin American. We will look at two indicators for this judgement—manumission (or the act of freeing slaves) and miscegenation (or racial interbreeding) in both Latin and British societies in order to evaluate this possibility.

British vs. Latin American Slavery: Racism and Manumission

Let us take a look at some of the evidence. For one thing, it seems pretty clear that bondage was a more permanent condition for the slave in the United States and British Caribbean islands than it was in Latin America. A much higher proportion of slaves in the Spanish and Portuguese colonies were given their freedom than in the British colonies. This attitude toward giving the slave freedom (manumission) is very important because it shows that the white colonizers need not view the Africans as permanently and incurably inferior. In Brazil (settled by the Portuguese) and in Spanish America the law did not declare that a slave was necessarily a slave for his whole life or that his children were necessarily slaves—as was legally the case in the United States after the 1660s.

In Latin America there were a number of ways that slaves might attain freedom. They might purchase it by hiring themselves out on Sundays or one of the 85 holidays on the Catholic calendar. In Cuba or Mexico they had the right to have their purchase price declared, and could pay it in gradual installments. This became a widespread custom, especially in Cuba. A slave who was worth $600 could purchase freedom in 24 installments of $25 each. Each installment purchased one twenty-fourth of freedom, and the first payment allowed the slave to move from the master's house. Though the cost may have been considerably higher than the price of passage from Africa, slaves who were able to work for their freedom were not different in principle from the white debtors of Europe who were forced to work as servants for a stated period. The relationship between master and slave was almost contractual, based on a legal agreement (though usually unwritten) between two parties (though not entered freely). There were at least some cases of slaves paying everything but the last installment in order to *avoid* complete freedom and the taxes and military service that went along with it.

There were other ways for a Latin American slave to be freed. Thousands of slaves in Venezuela and Colombia were freed by Simon Bolivar when they enlisted in the army for the wars of independence. Similarly, many of the slaves who joined the armies of Brazil and Argentina were freed. Cuba periodically issued a degree that automatically freed slaves who escaped to its shores and embraced Christianity. In most Latin American societies a slave who was unjustly punished could be freed by the judge. A Brazilian slave who had ten children could demand freedom legally. Other legal routes to freedom included denunciation of a brutal master, purchase by an African brotherhood, providing information in a criminal case, or discovering an especially large diamond or gold vein in the mines. The existence of quilombos (colonies of runaways) also offered the possibility of illegal escape from the slave system.

The legal roads to manumission, however, were probably not as important as the social approval that custom and the church gave to the act of freeing a slave. Even the culture of the slave owners held that manumission was a noble and generous act, a good thing to do. Happy occasions—the birth of a son, the marriage of a daughter, religious and national holidays, and family cele-brations—were considered opportunities to ceremonially free one or a number of slaves in Latin America. It was considered appropriate and commendable for a slave child to be freed at baptism with the payment of a small fee ($25 in Cuba), and many slaves chose a godfather for their children with this hope in mind. While there were objections to manumission on everything from se-curity to morality grounds (it encouraged theft and prostitution, some said), in general Latin Americans were far more favorably disposed to manumission than North Americans.

In the British colonies manumission was frequently viewed with alarm. Most of the British islands placed heavy taxes (often more than the value of the slave) on those slave owners who attempted it. In all cases a slave could not be freed without the owner's consent, and sometimes the consent of others was also required. In most of the British colonies (including the United States) a black or dark-skinned person of African descent was automatically assumed to be a slave. In some cases the slave was allowed to prove that he had been freed (whereas he was presumed free in Latin American courts, and had to be proved a slave). Laws in Georgia, Mississippi, and South Carolina did not even allow the slave to establish a claim to freedom. According to the South Carolina law of 1740 "all negroes . . . mulattoes, or mestizos, who are or shall hereafter be in the province, and all their issue and offspring, born or to be born, shall be and they are hereby declared to be and remain forever hereafter absolute slaves." Thus, when William Sanders, recently freed in Virginia, re-turned to South Carolina in 1756, he was arrested. "For evidence of his being a freeman," the warden of the workhouse wrote in the *South Carolina Gazette*,

> he produces a pass, signed David Stuard, August County, Va., August the 18th, 1755, for William Sanders, a freeman, to pass and repass, which is indorsed by several other magistrates in North Carolina which name of William Sanders he now assumes, and pretends he is the same iden-tical person, and a freeman. But as there is great reason to suppose he is a slave, and escaped from some person in Virginia or thereabouts, any

person that can claim their property in him within six months, may have him upon payment of charges to the warden of the workhouse.[15]

One wonders what proof would have been sufficient.

Even those few freed slaves in the United States were often forced back into slavery. Virginia required a freed slave to leave the state in a year or be sold "for the benefit of the Literary Fund." In many states of the southern United States, a freed slave could be sold back into slavery for the failure to pay a debt or a fine. The laws of the British West Indies and of the United States offered no hope for the slave to purchase his or her freedom, and these laws assumed that slavery was perpetual. The only hope was manumission by the slave's owner, and though this occasionally occurred there were too many obstacles for it ever to become a widespread practice.

In the slave states of the United States by 1860 only about 6 percent of the black population was free. [If we include the equal number of free African Americans who lived in the northern states,] only 10 percent of the black population . . . was free. In startling comparison, at the time of Brazilian emancipation in 1888, about 75 percent of the black population was already free. This was largely the result of different attitudes toward manumission.

These different attitudes toward manumission are significant in two ways. They show that South Americans were more willing to allow black people freedom and independence, and also that South American societies became so populated with free blacks that it was impossible to identify the cultural condition of slavery with the biological condition of black skin. Spanish and Portuguese settlers often spoke of slavery as an unfortunate condition to which anyone might fall prey. They saw slavery as the mark of social, not racial inferiority. They were able to distinguish between a person's color and culture. In that sense, Iberian slavery was the result of less racist attitudes, and it created a society where racism was less pronounced.

Again, we are speaking only of racism, not the brutality of slavery. It is quite possible that South American societies treated their slaves more brutally than North American societies did. The Iberian willingness to manumit slaves only tells us about their attitudes toward black people; it says nothing about their treatment of the slaves who were not freed. Some historians have argued, for instance, that the Spanish and Portuguese slaveholders frequently freed the sick and elderly slaves because they had become too expensive to keep. North American slaveholders were rarely that cruel—or that willing to have a free African population in their midst.

The popularity of manumission in Latin American slave society may not always have been a tribute to their kindness. Since the slave trade continued well into the nineteenth century in Latin America, slaves were considerably cheaper than in the United States, which suspended the slave trade in 1808. That meant that Latin American slave owners could afford to work their slaves to death, buy more, and still free some of them. Even if that occurred, however, Latin American slavery still created a less racist society.

Let us return to the evidence. Perhaps the most striking feature for northern visitors to Latin American slave society was that black people were found everywhere. One English visitor to Brazil in the middle of the nineteenth century expressed his surprise this way:

> I have passed black ladies in silks and jewelry, with male slaves in livery behind them. Today one rode past in her carriage, accompanied by a liveried footman and a coachman, Several have white husbands. The first doctor of the city is a colored man; so is the President of the Province.[16]

Another visitor said that the African Brazilian

> seemed to be the most intelligent person he met because every occupation, skilled and unskilled, was in the Negroes' hands. Even in Buenos Aires theirs was the hand that built the best churches. They were the field hands, and in many places the miners; they were the cooks, laundresses, the mammies, the concubine of the whites, the nurses about the houses, the coachmen, and the laborers on the wharves. But they were also the skilled artisans who built the houses, carved the saints in the churches, constructed the carriages, forged the beautiful ironwork one sees in Brazil, and played in the orchestras.[17]

Free Brazilians of African descent achieved positions of considerable prestige, and were recognized in their time and by the Brazilian history books since. Two of the leading political figures of the seventeenth century were mulattoes. João Fernandes Vieira (d. 1681) was a guerilla leader, military commander of a mulatto regiment that defeated the Dutch, and a provincial governor. Antonio Viera (1608–97) was one of the Portuguese Empire's most gifted scholars and preachers, a Jesuit advisor to King João IV, and persuasive spokesmen for human rights. Brazilian mulattoes also included the country's first portrait painter (Manuel da Cunha, 1737–1809), the leading architect and sculptor (Antonio Francisco Lisboa, c. 1735–1814), and a number of important Brazilian writers, composers, and musicians. Such men were exceptions, especially in politics. One is reminded of the visitor who was told that wealth rather than color was the basis for political office. "But isn't the governor a mulatto?" the visitor asked. "He was; but he isn't anymore," was the reply.

"How can a governor be a mulatto?"[18] But Brazilian culture was a richer blend of the African and Portuguese than was Brazilian politics. Brazilian religion, music, and dance retained distinct ties to Africa. Brazilian literature, as well, has always been written by descendants of Africa and Portugal, and many of the most heroic and human of Brazilian heroes and heroines (in fiction and history) are African.

The *United States Magazine and Democratic Review* in 1844 recognized the gap between the treatment of Africans in the United States and Latin America. In Mexico "and in Central America, and in the vast regions still further south," the *Review* observed, "the negro is already a freeman—socially as well as politically, the equal of the white. Nine-tenths of the population there is made up of the colored races; the Generals, the Congressmen, the Presidents are men of mixed blood."[19]

Many North Americans recognized that their own prejudices against black people were greater in the United States than south of the border. Some like George Bancroft echoed the above quoted sentiments of the *Review* by arguing that the acquisition of Texas would allow black people "to pass to social and political equality in the central regions of America, where the prejudices of race do not exist."

It was not true in 1844 that all South American blacks were free; some were still slaves. And it would be an exaggeration to say that no racial prejudice existed in the Iberian colonies: almost no whites were enslaved, and it was much more difficult for an African or Indian to become prosperous and accepted. With that qualification, however, the contrast holds. South American society was much more open for the descendants of Africans. Freedom was easier to attain, and it meant more once it was won. Prejudice was less, as was the discrimination (in neighborhoods, schools, hotels, and public accommodations) that became such a hallmark of racial experience in the United States. The lynch law and anti-Negro riots that became such a standard feature of the history of the United States in the nineteenth and twentieth centuries were absent from South American experience. In Latin American struggles for independence, blacks (free and slave) were recruited without prejudice. White dockworkers in Brazil worked for the abolition of slavery by refusing to work on slave ships at the same time that North American white workers rioted against Lincoln's draft law by attacking black families instead of Southern troops.

British vs. Latin American Slavery: Racism and Miscegenation

Why the difference? What accounts for the virulence of British, North American racism compared with the relatively mild prejudice in Latin America? The answers are many, and they have been hotly debated. We have already suggested a few. Perhaps the simple fact that British and other northern Europeans were so white skinned (compared to the more olive-skinned Spanish and Portuguese) was a factor. The patterns of settlement were also different. The Spanish and Portuguese conquerors came to the New World without their wives. Many, in fact, were not married. From the earliest years of the settlement they developed a permissive attitude toward interracial sex (miscegenation). The British settlers of North America, on the other hand, generally came with their wives and families. British wives were also often independent enough to insist that their slave-owning husbands keep their racial affairs private. Even when Iberian women came to the Americas to raise families, they came from a European culture where men and male values (machismo) were more clearly dominant. Iberian men in the Americas flaunted their black mistresses, recognized their black children, and often moved all of their families into the same large patriarchal home. While most states in the United States passed stiff laws against interracial sex (forcing men to be discreet), Latin American societies openly encouraged miscegenation as a proof of male potency and a way of life.

Miscegenation, like manumission, may have been popular in Latin America for less than noble reasons. But both practices created a population and a set of values which made race almost meaningless. How could one talk of "pure" races or even of race when the vast majority of the population was neither black nor white, but shades of olive and brown? How could one speak of the natural abilities (or inabilities) of the Negro when they were neither slave nor free, but both, and when they were planters, writers, masons, and bureaucrats?

By at least the nineteenth century, the majority of Afro-Americans in most countries south of the United States were neither black nor slaves. It became impossible to make generalizations even about the Negro. That was the very least that a racist had to be able to do. In the United States before the Civil War "Negro" meant slave. Neither the northern nor southern states wanted a population of free Africans. Southerners saw free blacks as deadly threats to the slave system: they believed that freed slaves incited slave rebellions, and the mere existence of prosperous or free blacks challenged the official racist doctrine that Africans were inherently inferior. Again, the Brazilian situation offers an interesting contrast. Brazilians not only used free blacks to capture runaway slaves, but Brazilian slave holders never developed the official North American doctrine of inherent African inferiority. Free blacks were banned from northern territories in the United States as well as from the southern slave states. Even the northern abolitionists (who worked for the end of slavery) often sought the disappearance of Negroes as well. They toyed with schemes to resettle the freed slaves in Africa, or (like George Bancroft) they sought black emigration to Mexico or South America. The United States, North and South, was largely a society of two groups: black slaves and free whites. The North American hostility to miscegenation and manumission kept the descendants of Africans as black (or visible) as possible, and blacks were assumed to be slaves. This insistence on a two-caste society was so strong that even today North Americans classify any light-skinned person with a touch of African ancestry as a Negro. Even today in the United States people must be white or black and they are white only if their ancestry is all white. Blacks include (in common language and official census reports) not only "pure" Africans but anyone who is not "pure" white.

South American whites never insisted that there were only two races (excluding Indians); they did not relegate all people of mixed ancestry to the status of "the other" as if they were mongrel dogs. North Americans persisted in the belief (despite the evidence of their eyes) that there were only two racial types: pure whites and the others. South Americans recognized that there were many, and they encouraged the miscegenation which created many different racial categories between lily white and jet black.

Brazil, again, offers an interesting contrast to our way of thinking of race. In Brazil people are *pretos* (blacks) or *preto retino* (dark black) or *cabra* (dark) or *cabo verde* (dark with straight hair) or *escuro* (less dark) or *mulato escuro* (rich brown) or *mulato claro* (light brown) or *pardo* (lighter still) or *sarara* (light skinned with kinky hair) or *moreno* (light skin and straight hair) or *branco da Bahia* (native whites with slight African ancestry) or brunet whites or blond whites. Spanish Americans think in equally rich racial terms. To the extent that Spanish Americans think of *negro* at all (or Portuguese of *nego*) it means black. No Latin American would think of calling an *escuro* or *pardo* a *negro*; *escuros* and *pardos* are obviously lighter.

This complex racial vocabulary south of the Rio Grande shows that Latin Americans are not color blind. Instead, they see much greater racial variety than North Americans do. Actually, their extreme sensitivity to racial differences enables them to be less racist than the North American black versus white vision permits. White racism still exists in Mexico and Latin America, but many frankly recognize that most people are "mixed," and they find value in continuing the mixing. The Mexicans express this goal by calling themselves proudly "a bronze nation." They enthusiastically proclaim the destiny of Mexico to be the miscegenation of Africans, Europeans, and Indians—the "bronzing" of all peoples. Try to imagine the "bronze nation" as a cultural idea in the United States, despite all the talk of melting pots.

Latin Americans have broken down racial barriers through miscegenation. Partly because they came as soldiers or conquerors without families, but also partly because they took so many Africans as slaves, they almost inevitably established societies which paid scant attention to race. It was never possible for people, the majority of whom considered themselves shades of brown, to work up fears of being overwhelmed by Africans. All but one of the slave states of the United States ended the slave trade before the federal prohibition in 1808. Brazilians continued the slave trade until 1851. By that time over half the Brazilians were black or brown. In the United States never more than 19 percent of the population was classified as Negro, and the percentage declined steadily from that high point of 1790. Brazilians may have been more committed to slavery, but the whites of the United States were more committed to racial separation.

Notes

1. Frank M. Snowden, Jr., *Before Color Prejudice: The Ancient View of Blacks* (Cambridge, Mass.: Harvard University Press, 1983), pp. 55–58

2. Ibn Botlan, "Introduction to the Art of Making Good Purchases of Slaves" as quoted in William McKee Evans, "From the Land of Canaan to the Land of Guinea: The Strange Odyssey of the 'Sons of Han,' " *American Historical Review* 85:1 (1980), p. 24.

3. Ibn Khaldun, *An Arab Philosophy of History: Selections from the Prolegomena of Ibn Khaldun of Tunis (1332–1406)*, trans. Charles Issawi (London, 1955), p. 98. Quoted in William McKee Evans, *op. cit.*, p. 32.

4. William McKee Evans, *op. cit.*, p. 32.

5. Fernand Braudel, *The Structure of Everyday Life*, trans. Sian Reynolds (New York: Harper & Row, 1981), p. 224.

6. A.J.R. Russell-Wood, "Iberian Expansion and the Issue of Black Slavery: Changing Portuguese Attitudes, 1440–1770," *American Historical Review* 83 (1978), p. 28.

7. Zurara, *Chronique de Guinee*. Adapted from the English translation of Beazley and Prestage, *Chronicle of the Discovery and Conquest of Guinea*, 1:ch.25. Quoted in A.J.R. Russell-Wood, "Iberian Expansion and the Issue of Black Slavery," *American Historical Review* 83:1 (1978), p. 30.

8. Winthrop Jordan, *White Over Black* (Baltimore: Penguin Books, 1968), p. 7.

9. [George Puttenham?], *Partheniades*, quoted in Winthrop Jordan, *op. cit.*, p. 8.

10. Magnus Morner, *Race Mixture in the History of Latin America* (New York: Little Brown, 1967).

11. Opening lines of "Celoso extremeno" (1613). Quoted in C. R. Boxer, *Race Relations in the Portuguese Colonial Empire 1415–1825* (Oxford, U.K.: Clarendon Press, 1963).

12. Winthrop Jordan, *White Over Black* (Baltimore: Penguin Books, 1968), p. 11. Spelling and punctuation are modernized.

13. C.R. Boxer, *Race Relations in the Portuguese Colonial Empire, 1415–1825* (Oxford, U.K.: Oxford University Press, 1963), p. 56.

14. Orlando Patterson, *The Sociology of Slavery: An Analysis of the Origins, Development, and Structure of Negro Slave Society in Jamaica* (Rutherford, N.J.: Fairleigh Dickinson University Press, 1969), p. 9.

15. Daniel C. Littlefield, *Rice and Slaves: Ethnicity and the Slave Trade in Colonial South Carolina* (Baton Rouge: Louisiana State University Press, 1981), pp. 167–168.

16. Thomas Ewbank, *Life in Brazil, or the Land of the Cocoa and the Palm* (New York: Harper and Brothers, 1856), p. 266.

17. Frank Tannenbaum, *Slave and Citizen* (New York: Random House, 1946), p. 39.

18. A.J.R. Russell-Wood, *The Black Man in Slavery and Freedom in Colonial Brazil* (London: The Macmillan Press), 1982. This quotation is adapted from that on p. 72.

19. Quoted in Carl N. Degler, *Neither Black Nor White* (New York: Macmillan, 1971), p. 16.

Life of an American Slave

Frederick Douglass

Frederick Douglass (1818–1895) published his Narrative *in 1845, about midway between the Nat Turner Rebellion in 1831 and the start of the Civil War in 1861. The autobiography describes in stark and eloquent terms his enslavement, his indomitable belief in his right to be free, and his struggle and successful flight to the North when he was twenty years old.*

A contemporary of Emerson and Thoreau, Douglass became a heroic personification of their transcendentalism, the model of New England idealism. Explaining a philosophy of "Self-Reliance" and his faith in the spark of divinity within each individual, Emerson wrote in 1841, "Be it known unto you that henceforward I obey no law less than the eternal law." And Thoreau on July 4, 1854, said at an abolitionist rally, "The law will never make men free; it is men who have got to make the law free."

The following passages describe Douglass's ability to teach himself to read, his spontaneous resistance to the beatings of the man hired to break his spirit, and the promise of freedom he attributed to the sailing of ships away from Baltimore's harbor. Later, in 1859, although he was a respected writer, lecturer, and abolitionist newspaper publisher, Douglass was forced to flee to England to avoid capture and forced return to Virginia for alleged support of John Brown's raid on Harper's Ferry. In 1860 he returned to the United States and led the drive to abolish slavery. After the Civil War, Douglass continued his opposition to discrimination during Reconstruction.

From *Narrative of the Life of Frederick Douglass, an American Slave, Written by Himself*, 1845, chapters 6–10.

He increasingly came to believe that blacks must ultimately work indepen-
dently from whites to wrest enough power to become truly free.
    Consider the effects of racism on both slaves and slave holders. Consider,
too, the role of religion in the narratives of Douglass and seventeenth- and
eighteenth-century writers. How does Douglass's experience compare to
that of other victims of slavery?

My new mistress proved to be all she appeared when I first met her at the door,—a woman of the kindest heart and finest feelings. She had never had a slave under her control previously to myself, and prior to her marriage she had been dependent upon her own industry for a living. She was by trade a weaver; and by constant application to her business, she had been in a good degree preserved from the blighting and dehumanizing effects of slavery. I was utterly astonished at her goodness. I scarcely knew how to behave towards her. She was entirely unlike any other white woman I had ever seen. I could not approach her as I was accustomed to approach other white ladies. My early instruction was all out of place. The crouching servility, usually so acceptable a qualities in a slave, did not answer when manifested toward her. Her favor was not gained by it; she seemed to be disturbed by it. She did not deem it impudent or unmannerly for a slave to look her in the face. The meanest slave was put fully at ease in her presence, and none left without feeling better for having seen her. Her face was made of heavenly smiles, and her voice of tranquil music.

But, alas! this kind heart had but a short time to remain such. The fatal poison of irresponsible power was already in her hands, and soon commenced its infernal work. That cheerful eye, under the influence of slavery, soon became red with rage; that voice, made all of sweet accord, changed to one of harsh and horrid discord; and that angelic face gave place to that of a demon.

Very soon after I went to live with Mr. and Mrs. Auld, she was kindly commenced to teach me the A, B, C. After I had learned this, she assisted me in learning to spell words of three or four letters. Just at this point of my progress, Mr. Auld found out what was going on, and at once forbade Mrs. Auld to instruct me further, telling her, among other things, that it was unlawful, as well as unsafe, to teach a slave to read. To use his own words, further, he said, "If you give a nigger an inch, he will take an ell. A nigger should know nothing but to obey his master—to do as he is told to do. Learning would spoil the best nigger in the world. Now," said he, "if you teach that nigger (speaking of myself) how to read, there would be no keeping him. It would forever unfit him to be a slave. He would at once become unmanageable, and of no value to his master. As to himself, it could do him no good, but a great deal of harm. It would make him discontented and unhappy." These words sank deep into my heart, stirred up sentiments within that lay slumbering, and called into existence an entirely new train of thought. It was a new and special revelation, explaining dark and mysterious things, with which my youthful understanding had struggled, but struggled in vain. I now understood what had been to me a most perplexing difficulty—to wit, the white man's power to enslave the black man. It was a grand achievement, and I prized it highly. From that moment, I understood the pathway from slavery to freedom. It was just what I wanted, and I got it at a time when I the least expected it. Whilst I was saddened by the thought of losing the aid of my kind mistress, I was gladdened by the invaluable instruction which, by the merest accident, I had gained from my master. Though conscious of the difficulty of learning without a teacher, I set out with high hope, and a fixed purpose, at whatever cost of trouble, to learn how to read. The very decided manner with which he spoke, and strove to impress his wife with the evil consequences of giving me instruction, served to convince me that he was deeply sensible of the truths he was uttering. It gave me the best assurance that I might rely with the utmost confidence on the results which, he said, would flow from teaching me to read. What he most dreaded, that I most desired. What he most loved, that I most hated. That which to him was a great evil, to be carefully shunned, was to me a great good, to be diligently sought; and the argument which he so warmly urged, against my learning to read, only served to inspire me with a desire and determination to learn. In learning to read, I owe almost as much to the bitter opposition of my master, as to the kindly aid of my mistress. I acknowledge the benefit of both.

I had resided but a short time in Baltimore before I observed a marked difference, in the treatment of slaves, from that which I had witnessed in the country. A city slave is almost a freeman, compared with a slave on the plantation. He is much better fed and clothed, and enjoys privileges altogether unknown to the slave upon the plantation. There is a vestige of decency, a sense of shame, that does much to curb and check those outbreaks of atrocious cruelty so commonly enacted upon the plantation. He is a desperate slaveholder, who will shock the humanity of his non-slaveholding neighbors with the cries of his lacerated slave. Few are willing to incur the odium attaching to the reputation of being a cruel master; and above all things, they would not be known as not giving a slave enough to eat. Every city slaveholder is anxious to have it known of him, that he feeds his slaves well; and it is due to them to say, that most of them do give their slaves enough to eat. There are, however, some painful exceptions to this rule. Directly opposite to us on Philpot Street, lived Mr. Thomas Hamilton. He owned two slaves. Their names were Henrietta and Mary. Henrietta was about twenty-two years of age, Mary was about fourteen; and of all the mangled and emaciated creatures I ever looked upon, these two were the most so. His heart must be harder than stone, that could look upon these unmoved. The head, neck, and shoulders of Mary were literally cut to pieces. I have frequently felt her head, and found it nearly covered with festering sores, caused by the lash of her cruel mistress. I do not know that her master ever whipped her, but I have been an eye-witness to the cruelty of Mrs. Hamilton. I used to be in Mr. Hamilton's house nearly every day. Mrs. Hamilton used to sit in a large chair in the middle of the room, with a heavy cowskin always by her side, and scarce an hour passed during the day but was marked by the blood of one of these slaves. The girls seldom passed her without her saying, "Move faster, you black gip!" at the same time giving them a blow with the cowskin over the head or shoulders, often drawing the blood. She would then say, "Take that, you black gip!"—continuing, "If you don't move faster, I'll move you!" Added to the cruel lashings, to which these slaves were subjected, they were kept nearly half-starved. Mary seldom knew what it was to eat a full meal. I have seen Mary contending with the pigs for the offal thrown into the street. So much was Mary kicked and cut to pieces, that she was oftener called "pecked" than by her name.

I lived in Master Hugh's family about seven years. During this time, I succeeded in learning to read and write. In accomplishing this, I was compelled to resort to various stratagems. I had no regular teacher. My mistress, who had kindly commenced to instruct me, had, in compliance with the advice and direction of her husband, not only ceased to instruct, but had set her face against my being instructed by any one else. It is due, however, to my mistress to say of her, that she did not adopt this course of treatment immediately. She at first lacked the depravity indispensable to shutting me up in mental darkness. It was at least necessary for her to have some training in the exercise of irresponsible power, to make her equal to the task of treating me as though I were a brute.

My mistress was, as I have said, a kind and tender-hearted woman and in the simplicity of her soul she commenced, when I first went to live with her, to treat me as she supposed one human being ought to treat another. In entering upon the duties of a slaveholder, she did not seem to perceive that I sustained to her the relation of a mere chattel, and that for her to treat me as a human being was not only wrong, but dangerously so. Slavery proved as injurious to her as it did to me. When I went there, she was a pious, warm, and tender-hearted woman. There was no sorrow or suffering for which she had not a tear. She had bread for the hungry, clothes for the naked, and comfort for every mourner that came within her reach. Slavery soon proved its ability to divest her of these heavenly qualities. Under its influence, the tender heart became stone, and the lamblike disposition gave way to one of tigerlike fierceness. The first step in her downward course was in her ceasing to instruct me.

Frederick Douglass (1818–1895), an undated photograph. *(Associated Press Photo)*

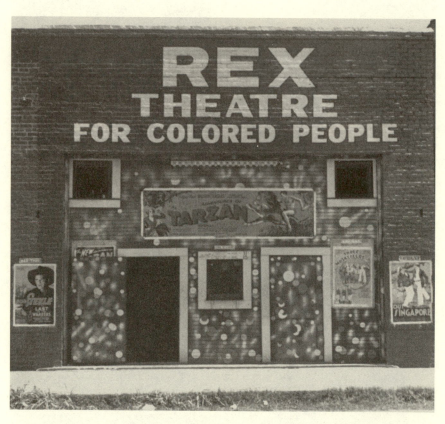

A segregated movie house in Washington, D.C., June 1937. *(Library of Congress, courtesy of United States Holocaust Memorial Museum Photo Archives)*

She now commenced to practice her husband's precepts. She finally became even more violent in her opposition than her husband himself. She was not satisfied with simply doing as well as he had commanded; she seemed anxious to do better. Nothing seemed to make her more angry than to see me with a newspaper. She seemed to think that here lay the danger. I have had her rush at me with a face made all up of fury, and snatch from me a newspaper, in a manner that fully revealed her apprehension. She was an apt woman; and a little experience soon demonstrated, to her satisfaction, that education and slavery were incompatible with each other.

From this time I was most narrowly watched. If I was in a separate room any considerable length of time, I was sure to be suspected of having a book, and was at once called to give an account of myself. All this, however, was too late. The first step had been taken. Mistress, in teaching me the alphabet, had given me the inch, and no precaution could prevent me from taking the ell.

The plan which I adopted, and the one by which I was most successful, was that of making friends of all the little white boys whom I met in the street. As many of these as I could, I converted into teachers. With their kindly aid, obtained at different times and in different places, I finally succeeded in learning to read. When I was sent on errands, I always took my book with me, and by going one part of my errand quickly, I found time to get a lesson before my return. I used also to carry bread with me, enough of which was always in the house, and to which I was always welcome; for I was much better off in this regard than many of the poor white children in our neighborhood. This bread I used to bestow upon the hungry little urchins, who, in return, would give me that more valuable bread of knowledge. I am strongly tempted to give the names of two or three of those little boys, as a testimonial of the gratitude and affection I bear them; but prudence forbids;—not that it would injure me, but it might embarrass them; for it is almost an unpardonable offence to teach slaves to read in this Christian country. It is enough to say of the dear little fellows that they lived on Philpot Street, very near Durgin and Bailey's shipyard. I used to talk this matter of slavery over with them. I would sometimes say to them, I wished I could be as free as they would be when they got to be men. "You will be free as soon as you are twenty-one, but I am a slave for life! Have not I as good a right to be free as you have?" These words used to trouble them, they would express for me the liveliest sympathy, and console me with the hope that something would occur by which I might be free.

I was now about twelve years old, and the thought of being a slave for life began to bear heavily upon my heart. Just about this time, I got hold of a book entitled "The Columbian Orator." Every opportunity I got, I used to read this book. Among much of other interesting matter, I found in it a dialogue between a master and his slave. The slave was represented as having run away from his master three times. The dialogue represented the conversation which took place between them, when the slave was retaken the third time. In this dialogue, the whole argument in behalf of slavery was brought forward by the master, all of which was disposed of by the slave. The slave was made to say some very smart as well as impressive things in reply to his master—things which had the desired though unexpected effect; for the conversation resulted in the voluntary emancipation of the slave on the part of the master.

In the same book, I met with one of Sheridan's mighty speeches on and in behalf of Catholic emancipation. These were choice documents to me. I read them over and over again with unabated interest. They gave tongue to interesting thoughts of my own soul, which had frequently flashed through my mind, and died away for want of utterance. The moral which I gained from the dialogue was the power of truth over the conscience of even a slaveholder. What I got from Sheridan was a bold denunciation of slavery, and a powerful vindication of human rights. The reading of these documents enabled me to utter my thoughts, and to meet the arguments brought forward to sustain slavery; but while they relieved me of one difficulty, they brought on another even more painful than the one of which I was relieved. The more I read, the more I was led to abhor and detest my enslavers. I could regard them in no other light than a band of successful robbers, who had left their homes, and gone to Africa, and stolen us from our homes, and in a strange land reduced us to slavery. I loathed them as being the meanest as well as the most wicked of men. As I read and contemplated the subject, behold! that very discontentment which Master Hugh had predicted would follow my learning to read had already me to torment and sting my soul to unutterable anguish. As I writhed under it, I would at times feel that learning to read had been a curse rather than a blessing. It had given me a view of my wretched condition, without the remedy. It opened my eyes to the horrible pit, but to no ladder upon which to get out. In moments of agony, I envied my fellow-slaves for their stupidity. I have often wished myself a beast. I preferred the condition of the meanest reptile to my own. Any thing, no matter what, to get rid of thinking! It was this everlasting thinking of my condition that tormented me. There was no getting rid of it. It was pressed upon me by every object within sight or hearing, animate or inanimate. The silver trump of freedom had roused my soul to eternal wakefulness. Freedom now appeared, to disappear no more forever. It was heard in every sound, and seen in every thing. It was ever present to torment me with a sense of my wretched condition. I saw nothing without seeing it, I heard nothing without hearing it, and felt nothing without feeling. It looked from every star, it smiled in every calm, breathed in every wind, and moved in every storm.

I often found myself regretting my own existence, and wishing myself dead, and but for the hope of being free, I have no doubt but that I should have killed myself, or done something for which I should have been killed. While in this state of mind, I was eager to hear any one speak of slavery. I was a ready listener. Every little while, I could hear something about the abolitionists. It was some time before I found what the word meant. It was always used in such connections as to make it an interesting word to me. If a slave ran away and succeeded in getting clear, or if a slave killed his master, set fire to a barn, or did any thing very wrong in the mind of a slaveholder, it was spoken of as the fruit of abolition. Hearing the word in this connection very often, I set about learning what it meant. The dictionary afforded me little or no help. I found it was "the act of abolishing"; but then I did not know what was to be abolished. Here I was perplexed. I did not dare to ask any one about its meaning, for I was satisfied that it was something they wanted me to know very little about. After a patient waiting, I got one of our city papers, containing an account of the number of petitions from the north, praying for the abolition of slavery in the District of Columbia, and of the slave trade between the States. From this time I understood the words abolition and abolitionist, and always drew near when that word was spoken, expecting to hear something of importance to myself and fellow-slaves. The light broke in upon me by degrees. I went one day down on the wharf of Mr. Waters; and seeing two Irishmen unloading a scow of stone, I went, unasked, and helped them. When we had finished, one of them came to me and asked me if I were a slave. I told him I was He asked, "Are we a slave for life?" I told him that I was. The good Irishman seemed to be deeply affected by the statement. He said to the other that it was a pity so fine a little fellow as myself should a slave for life. He said it was a shame to hold me. They both advised me to run away to the north; that I should find friends there, and that I should be free. I pretended not to be interested in what they said, and treated them as if I did not understand them. I feared they might be treacherous. White men have been known to encourage slaves to escape, and then, to get the reward, catch them and return them to their masters. I was afraid that these seemingly good men might use me so; but I nevertheless remembered their advice, and from that time I resolved to run away. I looked forward to a time at which it would be safe for me to escape. I was too young to think of doing so immediately; besides, I wished to learn how to write, as I might have occasion to write my own pass. I consoled myself with the hope that I should one day find a good chance. Meanwhile, I would learn to write.

The idea as to how I might learn to write was suggested to me being in Durgin and Bailey's ship-yard, and frequently seeing the ship carpenters, after hewing, and getting a piece of timber ready for use, write on the timber the name of that part of the ship for which it was intended. When a piece of timber was intended for the larboard side, it would be marked—"L." When a piece was for the starboard side, it would be marked thus—"S." A piece for the larboard side forward, would be marked thus—"L. F." When a piece was for starboard side forward, it would be marked thus—"S. F." For larboard aft, it would be marked thus—"L. A." For starboard aft, it would be marked thus— "S. A." I soon learned the names of these letters, and for what they were intended when placed on a piece of timber in the ship-yard. I immediately commenced copying them, and in a short time was able to make the four letters named. After that, when I met with any boy who I knew could write, I would tell him I could write as well as he. The next word would be, "I don't believe you. Let me see you try it." I would then make the letters which I had been so fortunate as to learn, and ask to beat that. In this way I got a good many lessons in writing, which it is quite possible I should never have gotten in any other. During this time, my copy-book was the board fence, brick wall, and pavement; my pen and ink was a lump of chalk. With these, I learned mainly how to write. I then commenced and continued copying the Italics in Webster's Spelling Book, until I could make them all without looking on the book. By this time, my little Master Thomas had gone to school, and learned how to write, and written over a number of copy-books. These had been brought home, and shown to some of our near neighbors, and then laid aside. My mistress used to go to class meeting at the Wilk Street meetinghouse every Monday afternoon, and leave me to take care of the house. When left thus, I used to spend the time in writing in spaces left in Master Thomas's copy-book, copying what he had written. I continued to do this until I could write a hand very similar to that of Master Thomas. Thus, after a long, tedious effort for years, I finally succeeded in learning how to write.

In a very short time after I went to live at Baltimore, my old master's youngest son Richard died; and in about three years and six months after his death, my old master, Captain Anthony, died, leaving only his son, Andrew, and daughter, Lucretia, to share his estate. He died while on a visit to see his daughter at Hillsborough. Cut off thus unexpectedly, he left no will as to the disposal of his property. It was therefore necessary to have a valuation of the property, that it might be equally divided between Mrs. Lucretia and Master Andrew. I was immediately sent for, to be valued with the other property. Here again my feelings rose up in detestation of slavery. I had now a new conception of my degraded condition. Prior to this, I had become, if not insensible to my lot, at least partly so. I left Baltimore with a young heart overborne with sadness, and a soul full of apprehension. I took passage with Captain Rowe, in the schooner Wild Cat, and, after a sail of about twenty-four hours, I found myself near the place of my birth. I had now been absent from it almost, if not quite, five years. I, however, remembered the place very well. I was only about five years old when I left it, to go and live with my old master on Colonel Lloyd's plantation; so that I was now between ten and eleven years old.

We were all ranked together at the valuation. Men and women. Old and young, married and single, were ranked with horses, sheep, and swine. There were horses and men, cattle and women, pigs and children, all holding the same rank in the scale of being, and were all subjected to the same narrow examination. Silvery-headed age and sprightly youth, maids and matrons, had to undergo the same indelicate inspection. At this moment, I saw more clearly than ever the brutalizing effects of slavery upon both slave and slaveholder.

After the valuation, then came the division. I have no language to express the high excitement and deep anxiety which were felt among us poor slaves during this time. Our fate for life was now to be decided. We had no more voice in that decision than the brutes among whom we were ranked. A single word from the white men was enough—against all our wishes, prayers, and entreaties—to sunder forever the dearest friends, dearest kindred, and strongest ties known to human beings. In addition to the pain of separation, there was the horrid dread of falling into the hands of Master Andrew. He was known to us all as being a most cruel wretch,—a common drunkard, who had, by his reckless mismanagement and profligate dissipation, already wasted a large portion of his father's property. We all felt that we might as well be sold at once to the Georgia traders, as to pass into his hands; for we knew that that would be horror and dread.

I suffered more anxiety than most of my fellow slaves. I had known what it was to be kindly treated; they had known nothing of the kind. They had seen little or nothing of the world. They were in very deed men and women of sorrow, and acquainted with grief. Their back had been made familiar with the bloody lash, so that they had become callous; mine was yet tender; for while at Baltimore I got few whippings, and few slaves could boast of a kinder master and mistress than myself; and the thought of passing out of their hands into those of Master Andrew—a man who, but a few days before, to give me a sample of his bloody disposition, took my little brother by the throat, threw him on the ground, and with the heel of his boot stamped upon his head till the blood gushed from his nose and ears—was well calculated to make me anxious as to my fate. After he had committed this savage outrage upon my brother, he turned to me, and said that was the way he meant to serve me one of these days,—meaning, I suppose, when I came into his possession.

Thanks to a kind Providence, I fell to the portion of Mrs. Lucretia, and was sent immediately back to Baltimore, to live again in the family of Master Hugh. Their joy at my return equaled their sorrow at my departure. It was a glad day to me. I had escaped a [fate] worse than lion's jaws. I was absent from Baltimore, for the purpose of valuation and division, just about one month, and it seemed to have been six.

Very soon after my return to Baltimore, my mistress, Lucretia, died, leaving her husband and one child, Amanda; and in a very short time after her death, Master Andrew died. Now all the property of my old master, slaves included, was in the hands of strangers,—strangers who had had nothing to do with accumulating it. Not a slave was left free. All remained slaves, from the youngest to the oldest. If any one thing in my experience, more than another, served to deepen my conviction of the infernal character of slavery, and to fill me with unutterable loathing of slave holders, it was their base ingratitude to my poor old grandmother. She had served my old master faithfully from youth to old age. She had been the source of all his wealth; she had peopled his plantation with slaves; she had become a great grandmother in his service. She had rocked him in infancy, attended him in childhood, served him through life, and at his death wiped from his icy brow the cold death-sweat, and closed his eyes forever. She was nevertheless left a slave—a slave for life—a slave in the hands of strangers; and in their hands she saw her children, her grandchildren, and her great-grandchildren, divided, like so many sheep, without being gratified with the small privilege of a single word, as to their or her own destiny. And, to cap the climax of their base ingratitude and fiendish barbarity, my grandmother, who was now very old, having outlived my old master and all his children, having seen the beginning and end of all of them, and her present owners finding she was of but little value, her frame already racked with the pains of old age, and complete helplessness fast stealing over her once active limbs, they took her to the woods, built her a little hut, put up a little mud-chimney, and then made her welcome to the privilege of supporting herself there in perfect loneliness; thus virtually turning her out to die! If my poor old grandmother now lives, she lives to suffer in utter loneliness; she lives to remember and mourn over the loss of children, the loss of grandchildren, and the loss of great-grandchildren. They are, in the language of the slave's poet, Whittier, "Gone, gone, sold and gone To the rice swamp dank and lone Where the slave-whip ceaseless swings, Where the noisome insect stings, Where the fever-demon strews Poison with the falling dews, Where the sickly sunbeams glare Through the hot and misty air:—Gone, gone, sold and gone To the rice swamp dank and lone, From Virginia hills and waters—Woe is me, my stolen daughters!"

The hearth is desolate. The children, the unconscious children, who once sang and danced in her presence, are gone. She gropes her way, in the darkness of age, for a drink of water. Instead of the voices of her children, she hears by day the moans of the dove, and by night the screams of the hideous owl.

All is gloom. The grave is at the door. And now, when weighed down by the pains and aches of old age, when the head inclines to the feet, when the beginning and ending of human existence meet, and helpless infancy and painful old age combine together—at this time, this most needful time, the time for the exercise of that tenderness and affection which children only can exercise toward a declining parent—my poor old grandmother, the devoted mother of twelve children, is left all alone, in yonder little hut, before a few dim embers. She stands—she sits—she staggers—she falls—she groans—she dies and there are none of her children or grandchildren present, wipe from her wrinkled brow the cold sweat of death, or to place beneath the sod her fallen remains. Will not a righteous God vie for these things?

In about two years after the death of Mrs. Lucretia, Master Thomas married his second wife. Her name was Rowena Hamilton. She was the eldest daughter of Mr. William Hamilton. Master now lived in St. Michael's. Not long after his marriage, a misunderstanding took place between himself and Master Hugh; and as a means of punishing his brother, he took me from him to live with himself at St. Michael's. Here I underwent another most painful separation. It, however, was not so severe as the one I dreaded at the division of property; for, during this interval, a great change had taken place in Master Hugh and his once kind and affectionate wife. The influence of brandy upon him, and of slavery upon her, had effected a disastrous change in the characters of both; so that, as far as they were concerned, I thought I had little to lose by the change. But it was not to them that I was attached. It was to those little Baltimore boys that I felt the strongest attachment. I had received many good lessons from them, and was still receiving them, and the thought of leaving them was painful indeed. I was leaving, too, without the hope of ever being allowed to return. Master Thomas had said he would never let me return again. The barrier betwixt himself and brother he considered impassable.

I then had to regret that I did not at least make the attempt to carry out my resolution to run away; for the chances of success are tenfold greater from the city than from the country.

I sailed from Baltimore for St. Michael's in the sloop Amanda, Captain Edward Dodson. On my passage, I paid particular attention to the direction which the steamboats took to go to Philadelphia. I found, instead of going down, on reaching North Point they went up the bay, in a north-easterly direction. I deemed this knowledge of the utmost importance. My determination to run away was again revived. I resolved to wait only so long as the offering of a favorable opportunity. When that came, I was determined to be off.

I have now reached a period of my life when I can give dates. I left Baltimore, and went to live with Master Thomas Auld, at St. Michael's, in March 1832. It was now more than seven years since I lived with him in the family of my old master, on Colonel Lloyd's plantation. We of course were now almost entire strangers to each other. He was to me a new master, and I to him a new slave. I was ignorant of his temper and disposition; he was equally so of mine. A very short time, however, brought us into full acquaintance with each other. I was made acquainted with his wife not less than with himself. They were well matched, being equally mean and cruel. I was now, for the first time during a space of more than seven years, made to feel the painful gnawings of hunger—a something which I had not experienced before since I left Colonel Lloyd's plantation. It went hard enough with me then, when I could look back to no period at which I had enjoyed a sufficiency. It was tenfold harder after living in Master Hugh's family, where I had always had enough to eat, and of that which was good. I have said Master Thomas was a mean man. He was so. Not to give a slave enough to eat, is regarded as the most aggravated development of meanness even among slave holders. The rule is, no matter how coarse the food, only let there be enough of it. This is the theory; and in the part of Maryland from which I came, it is the general practice,—though there are many exceptions. Master Thomas gave us enough of neither coarse nor fine food. There were four slaves of us in the kitchen— my sister Eliza, my aunt Priscilla, Henny, and myself; and we were allowed less than half of a bushel of cornmeal per week, and very little else, either in the shape of meat or vegetables. It was not enough for us to subsist upon. We were therefore reduced to the wretched necessity of living at the expense of our neighbors. This we did by begging and stealing, whichever came handy in the time of need, the one being considered as legitimate as the other. A great many times have we poor creatures been nearly perishing with hunger, when food in abundance lay mouldering in the safe and smoke-house, and our pious mistress was aware of the fact; and yet that mistress and her husband would kneel every morning, and pray that God would bless them in basket and store!

Bad as all slaveholders are, we seldom meet one destitute of every element of character commanding respect. My master was one of this rare sort. I do not know of one single noble act ever performed by him. The leading trait in his character was meanness and if there were any other element in his nature, it was made subject to this. He was mean; and, like most other mean men, he lacked the ability to conceal his meanness. Captain Auld was not born a slave-holder. He had been a poor man, master only of a Bay craft. He came into possession of all his slaves by marriage; and of all men, adopted slaveholders are the worst. He was cruel, but cowardly. He commanded without firmness. In the enforcement of rules, he was at times rigid, and at times lax. At times, he spoke his slaves with the firmness of Napoleon and the fury of a demon; at other times, he might well be mistaken for an inquirer who lost his way.

He did nothing of himself. He might have passed as a lion, but for his ears. In all things noble which he attempted, his own meanness shone most conspicuous. His airs, words, and actions, were the airs, words, and actions of born slaveholders, being assumed, were awkward enough. It was not even a good imitator. He possessed all the disposition to deceive, but wanted the power. Having no resources within himself, he was compelled to be the copyist of many, and being such, he was forever the victim of inconsistency; and of consequence he was an object of contempt, and I was held as such even by his slaves. The luxury of having slaves of his own to wait upon him was something new and unprepared for. He was a slaveholder without the ability to hold slaves. He found himself incapable of managing his slaves either by force, fear, or fraud. We seldom called him "master"; we generally called him "Captain Auld," and were hardly disposed to title him at all. I doubt not that our conduct had much to do with making him appear awkward, and of consequence fretful. Our want of reverence for him must have perplexed him greatly. He wished to have us call him master, but lacked the firmness necessary to command us to do so. His wife used to insist upon our calling him so, but to no purpose. In August 1832, my master attended a Methodist camp meeting held in the Bay-side, Talbot county, and there experienced religion. I indulged a faint hope that his conversion would lead him to emancipate his slaves, and that, if he did not do this, it would at any rate, make him more kind and humane. I was disappointed in both these respects. It neither made him to be humane to his slaves, nor to emancipate them. If it had any effect on his character, it made him more cruel and hateful in all his ways for I believe him to have been a much worse man after his conversion than before. Prior to his conversion, he relied upon his own depravity to shield and sustain him in his savage barbarity; but after his conversion, he found religious sanction and support for his slaveholding cruelty. He made the greatest pretensions to piety. His house was the house of prayer. He prayed morning, noon, and night. He very soon distinguished himself among his brethren, and was soon made a class-leader and exhorter. His activity in revivals was great, and he proved himself an instrument in the hands of the church in converting many souls. His house was the preachers' home. They used to take great pleasure in coming there to put up; for while he starved us, he stuffed them. We have had three or four preachers there at a time. The names of those who used to come most frequently while I lived there, were Mr. Storks, Mr. Ewery, Mr Humphry, and Mr. Hickey. I have also seen Mr. George Cookman at our house. We slaves loved Mr. Cookman. We believed him to be a good man. We thought him instrumental in getting Mr. Samuel Harrison, a very rich slaveholder, to emancipate his slaves; and by some means got the impression that he was laboring to effect the emancipation of all the slaves. When he was at our house, we were sure to be called in to prayers. When the others were there, we were sometimes called in and sometimes not. Mr. Cookman took more notice of us than either of the other ministers. He could not come among us without betraying his sympathy for us, and, stupid as we were, we had the sagacity to see it.

While I lived with my master in St. Michael's, there was a white young man, a Mr. Wilson, who proposed to keep a Sabbath school for the instruction of such slaves as might be disposed to learn to read the New Testament. We met but three times, when Mr. West and Mr. Fairbanks, both class-leaders, with many others, came upon with us with sticks and other missiles, drove us off, and forbade us to meet again. Thus ended our little Sabbath school in the pious town of St. Michael's.

I have said my master found religious sanction for his cruelty. As an example, I will state one of many facts going to prove the charge. I have seen him tie up a lame young woman, and whip her with a heavy cowskin upon her naked shoulders, causing the warm red blood to drip; and, in justification of the bloody deed, he would quote this passage of Scripture—"He that knoweth his master's will, and doeth it not, shall be beaten with many stripes."

Master would keep this lacerated young woman tied up in this horrid situation four or five hours at a time. I have known him to tie her up early in the morning, and whip her before breakfast; leave her, go to his store, return at dinner, and whip her again, cutting her in the places already made raw with his cruel lash. The secret of master's cruelty toward "Henny" is found in the fact of her being almost helpless. When quite a child, she fell into the fire, and burned herself horribly. Her hands were so burnt that she never got the use of them. She could do very little but bear heavy burdens. She was to master a bill of expense; and as he was a mean man, she was a constant offence to him. He seemed desirous of getting the poor girl out of existence. He gave her away once to his sister; but, being a poor gift, she was not disposed to keep her. Finally, my benevolent master, to use his own words, "set her adrift to take care of herself." Here was a recently-converted man, holding on upon the mother, and at the same time turning out her helpless child, to starve and die! Master Thomas was one of the many pious slaveholders who hold slaves for the very charitable purpose of taking care of them.

My master and myself had quite a number of differences. He found me unsuitable to his purpose. My city life, he said, had had a very pernicious effect upon me. It had almost ruined me for every good purpose, and fitted me for every thing which was bad. One of my greatest faults was that of letting his horse run away, and go down to his father-in-law's farm, which was about five miles from St. Michael's. I would then have to go after it. My reason for this kind of carelessness, or carefulness, was, that I could always get something to eat when I went there. Master William Hamilton, my master's father-in-law, always gave his slaves enough to eat. I never left there hungry, no matter how great the need of my speedy return. Master Thomas at length said he would stand it no longer. I had lived with him nine months, during which time he had given me a number of severe whippings, all to no good purpose. He resolved to put me out, as he said, to be broken; and, for this purpose, he let me for one year to a man named Edward Covey. Mr. Covey was a poor man, a farm-renter. He rented the place upon which he lived, as also the hands with which he tilled it. Mr. Covey had acquired a very high reputation for breaking young slaves, and this reputation was of immense value to him. It enabled him to get his farm tilled with much less expense to himself than he could have had it done without such a reputation. Some slaveholders thought it not much loss to allow Mr. Covey to have their slaves one year, for the sake of the training to which they were subjected, without any other compensation. He could hire young help with great ease, in consequence of this reputation. Added to the natural good qualities of Mr. Covey, he was a professor of religion—a pious soul—a member and a class-leader in the Methodist church. All of this added weight to his reputation as a "niggerbreaker." I was aware of all the facts, having been made acquainted with them by a young man who had lived there. I nevertheless made the change gladly; for I was sure of getting enough to eat, which is not the smallest consideration to a hungry man.

I left Master Thomas's house, and went to live with Mr. Covey, on the 1st of January 1833. I was now, for the first time in my life, a field hand. In my new employment, I found myself even more awkward than a country boy appeared to be in a large city. I had been at my new home but one week before Mr. Covey gave me a very severe whipping, cutting my back, causing the blood to run, and raising ridges on my flesh as large as my little finger. The details of this affair are as follows: Mr. Covey sent me, very early in the morning of one of our coldest days in the month of January, to the woods, to get a load of wood. He gave me a team of unbroken oxen. He told me which was the in-hand ox, and which the off-hand one. He then tied the end of a large rope around the horns of the in-hand ox, and gave me the other end of it, and told me, if the oxen started to run, that I must hold on upon the rope. I had never driven oxen before, and of course I was very awkward. I, however, succeeded in getting to the edge of the woods with little difficulty; but I had got a very few rods into the woods, when the oxen took fright, and started full tilt, carrying the cart against trees, and over stumps, in the most frightful manner. I expected every moment that my brains would be dashed out against the trees. After running thus for a considerable distance, they finally upset the cart, dashing it with great force against a tree, and threw themselves into a dense thicket. How I escaped death, I do not know.

There I was, entirely alone, in a thick wood, in a place new to me. My cart was upset and shattered, my oxen were entangled among the young trees, and there was none to help me. After a long spell of effort, I succeeded in getting my cart righted, my oxen disentangled, and again yoked to the cart. I now proceeded with my team to the place where I had, the day before, been chopping wood, and loaded my cart pretty heavily, thinking in this way to tame my oxen. I then proceeded on my way home. I had now consumed one half of the day. I got out of the woods safely, and now felt out of danger. I stopped my oxen to open the woods gate; and just as I did so, before I could get hold of my ox-rope, the oxen again started, rushed through the gate, catching it between the wheel and the body of the cart, tearing it to pieces, and coming within a few inches of crushing me against the gate-post. This twice, in one short day, I escaped death by the merest chance. On my return, I told Mr. Covey what had happened, and how it happened. He ordered me to return to the woods again immediately. I did so, and he followed on after me. Just as I got into the woods, he came up and told me to stop my cart, and that he would teach me how to trifle away my time, and break gates. He then went to a large gum-tree, and with his axe cut three large switches, and, after trimming them up neatly with his pocketknife, he ordered me to take off my clothes. I made him no answer, but stood with my clothes on. He repeated his order. I still made him no answer, nor did I move to strip myself. Upon this he rushed at me with the fierceness of a tiger, tore off my clothes, and lashed me till he had worn out his switches, cutting me so savagely as to leave the marks visible for a long time after. This whipping was the first of a number just like it, and for similar offences.

I lived with Mr. Covey one year. During the first six months, of that year, scarce a week passed without his whipping me. I was seldom free from a sore back. My awkwardness was almost always his excuse for whipping me. We were worked fully up to the point of endurance. Long before day we were up, our horses fed, and by the first approach of day we were off to the field with our hoes and ploughing teams. Mr. Covey gave us enough to eat, but scarce time to eat it. We were often less than five minutes taking our meals. We were often in the field from the first approach of day till its last lingering ray had left us; and at saving-fodder time, midnight often caught us in the field binding blades.

Covey would be out with us. The way he used to stand it, was this. He would spend the most of his afternoons in bed. He would then come out fresh in the evening, ready to urge us on with his words, example, and frequently with the whip. Mr. Covey was one of the few slaveholders who would and did work with his hands. He was a hard-working man. He knew by himself just what a man or a boy could do. There was no deceiving him. His work went on in his absence almost as well as in his presence; and he had the faculty of making us feel that he was ever present with us. This he did by surprising us. He seldom approached the spot where we were at work openly, if he could do it secretly. He always aimed at taking us by surprise such was his cunning that we used to call him, among ourselves, "the snake." When we were at work in the cornfield, he would sometimes crawl on his hands and knees to avoid detection and all at once he would rise nearly in our midst, and scream out, "Ha, ha! Come, come! Dash on, dash on!" This being his mode of attack, it was never safe to stop a single minute. His comings were like a thief in the night. He appeared to us as being ever at hand. He was under every tree, behind every stump, in every bush, and at every window, on the plantation. He would sometimes mount his horse, as if bound to St. Michael's, a distance of seven miles, and in half all hour afterwards you would see him coiled up in the corner of the wood-fence, watching every motion of the slaves. He would, for this purpose, leave his horse tied up in the woods. Again, he would sometimes walk up to us, and give us orders as though he was upon the point of starting on a long journey, turn his back upon us, and make as though he was going to the house to get ready; and, before he would get half way thither, he would turn short and crawl into a fence-corner, or behind some tree, and there watch us till the going down of the sun.

Mr. Covey's *forte* consisted in his power to deceive. His life was devoted to planning and perpetrating the grossest deceptions. Every thing he possessed in the shape of learning or religion, he made conform to his disposition to deceive. He seemed to think himself equal to deceiving the Almighty. He would make a short prayer in the morning, and a long prayer at night; and, strange as it may seem, few men would at times appear more devotional than he. The exercises of his family devotions were always commenced with singing; and, as he was a very poor singer himself, the duty of raising the hymn generally came upon me. He would read his hymn, and nod at me to commence. I would at times do so, at others, I would not. My non-compliance would almost always produce much confusion. To show himself independent of me, he would start and stagger through with his hymn in the most discordant manner. In this state of mind, he prayed with more than ordinary spirit. Poor man! such was his disposition, and success at deceiving, I do verily believe that he sometimes deceived himself to the solemn belief, that he was a sincere worshipper of the most high God; and this, too, at a time when he may be said to have been guilty of compelling his woman slave to commit the sin of adultery. The facts in the case are these: Mr. Covey was a poor man; he was just commencing in life; he was only able to buy one slave; and, shocking as is the fact, he bought her, as he said, for a breeder. This woman was named Caroline. Mr. Covey bought her from Mr. Thomas Lowe, about six miles from

St. Michael's. She was a large, able-bodied woman, about twenty years old. She had already given birth to one child, which proved her to be just what he wanted. After buying her, he hired a married man of Mr. Samuel Harrison, to live with him one year; and him he used to fasten up with her every night! The result was, that, at the end of the year, the miserable woman gave birth to twins. At this result Mr. Covey seemed to be highly pleased, both with the man and the wretched woman. Such was his joy, and that of his wife, that nothing they could do for Caroline during her confinement was too good, or too hard to be done. The children were regarded as being quite an addition to his wealth.

If at any one time of my life more than another, I was made to drink the bitterest dregs of slavery, that time was during the first six months of my stay with Mr. Covey. We were worked in all weathers. It was never too hot or too cold; it could never rain, blow, hail, or snow, too hard for us to work in the field. Work, work, work, was scarcely more the order of the day than of the night. The longest days were too short for him, and the shortest nights too long for him. I was somewhat unmanageable when I first went there, but a few months of this discipline tamed me. Mr. Covey succeeded in breaking me. I was broken in body, soul, and spirit. My natural elasticity was crushed, my intellect languished, the disposition to read departed, the cheerful spark that lingered about my eye died; the dark night of slavery closed in upon me, and behold a man transformed into a brute!

Sunday was my only leisure time. I spent this in a sort of beastlike stupor, between sleep and wake, under some large tree. At times I would rise up, a flash of energetic freedom would art through my soul, accompanied with a faint beam of hope that, flickered for a moment, and then vanished. I sank down again; mourning over my wretched condition. I was sometimes prompted to take my life, and that of Covey, but was prevented by a combination of hope and fear. My sufferings on this plantation seem now like a dream rather than a stern reality.

Our house stood within a few rods of the Chesapeake Bay, whose broad bosom was ever white with sails from every quarter of the habitable globe. Those beautiful vessels, robed in purest white, so delightful to the eye of freemen, were to me so many shrouded ghosts, to terrify and torment me with thoughts of my wretched condition. I have often, in the deep stillness of a summer's Sabbath, stood all alone upon the lofty banks of that noble bay, and traced, with saddened heart and tearful eye, the countless number of sails moving off to the mighty ocean. The sight of these always affected me powerfully. My thoughts would compel utterance; and there, with no audience but the Almighty, I would pour out my soul's complaint, in my rude way, with an apostrophe to the moving multitude of ships:

"You are loosed from your moorings, and are free; I am fast in my chains, and am a slave! You move merrily before the gentle gale, and I sadly before the bloody whip! You are freedom's swift-winged angels, that fly round the world; I am confined in bands of iron! O that I were free! Oh, that I were on one of your gallant decks, and under your protecting wing! Alas! betwixt me and you, the turbid waters roll. Go on, go on. O that I could also go! Could I but swim! If I could fly! O, why was I born a man, of whom to make a brute! The glad ship is gone; she hides in the dim distance. I am left in the hottest hell of unending slavery. O God, save me! God, deliver me! Let me be free! Is there any God? Why am I a slave? I will run away. I will not stand it. Get caught, or get clear, I'll try it. I had as well die with ague as the fever. I have only one life to lose. I had as well be killed running as die standing. Only think of it; one hundred miles straight north, and I am free! Try it? Yes! God helping me, I will. It cannot be that I shall live and die a slave. I will take to the water. This very bay shall yet bear me into freedom. The steamboats steered in a north-east course from North Point. I will do the same; and when I get to the head of the bay, I will turn my canoe adrift, and walk straight through Delaware into Pennsylvania. When I get there, I shall not be required to have a pass; I can travel without being disturbed. Let but the first opportunity offer, and, come what will, I am off. Meanwhile, I will try to bear up under the yoke. I am not the only slave in the world. Why should I fret? I can bear as much as any of them. Besides, I am but a boy, and all boys are bound to some one. It may be that my misery in slavery will only increase my happiness when I get free. There is a better day coming."

Thus I used to think, and thus I used to speak to myself; goaded almost to madness at one moment, and at the next reconciling myself to my wretched lot.

I have already intimated that my condition was much worse, during the first six months of my stay at Mr. Covey's, than in the last six. The circumstances leading to the change in Mr. Covey's course toward me form an epoch in my humble history. You have seen how a man was made a slave; you shall see how a slave was made a man. On one of the hottest days of the month of August, 1833, Bill Smith, William Hughes, a slave named Eli, and myself, were engaged in fanning wheat. Hughes was clearing the fanned wheat from before the fan. Eli was turning, Smith was feeding, and I was carrying wheat to the fan. The work was simple, requiring strength rather than intellect; yet, to one entirely unused to such work, it came very hard. About three o'clock of that day, I broke down; my strength failed me; I was seized with a violent aching of the head, attended with extreme dizziness; I trembled in every limb. Finding what was coming, I nerved myself up, feeling it would never do to stop work. I stood as long as I could stagger to the hopper with grain. When

I could stand no longer, I fell, and felt as if held down by an immense weight. The fan of course stopped; every one had his own work to do; and no one could do the work of the other, and have his own go on at the same time. Mr. Covey was at the house, about one hundred yards from the treading-yard where we were fanning. On hearing the fan stop, he left immediately, and came to the spot where we were. He hastily inquired what the matter was. Bill answered that I was sick, and there was no one to bring wheat to the fan. I had by this time crawled away under the side of the post and rail-fence by which the yard was enclosed, hoping to find relief by getting out of the sun. He then asked where I was. He was told by one of the hands. He came to the spot, and, after looking at me awhile, asked me what was the matter. I told him as well as I could, for I scarce had strength to speak. He then gave me a savage kick in the side, and told me to get up. I tried to do so, but fell back in the attempt. He gave me another kick, and again told me to rise. I again tried, and succeeded in gaining my feet; but, stooping to get the tub with which I was feeding the fan, I again staggered and fell. While down in this situation, Mr. Covey took up the hickory slat with which Hughes had been striking off the half-bushel measure, and with it gave me a heavy blow upon the head, making a large wound, and the blood ran freely; and with this again told me to get up. I made no effort to comply, having now made up my mind to let him do his worst. In a short time after receiving this blow, my head grew better. Mr. Covey had now left me to my fate. At this moment I resolved, for the first time, to go to my master, enter a complaint and ask his protection. In order to do this, I must that afternoon walk seven miles; and this, under the circumstances, was truly a severe undertaking. I was exceedingly feeble; made so as much by the kicks and blows which I received, as by the severe fit of sickness to which I had been subjected. I, however, watched my chance while Covey was looking in an opposite direction, and started for St. Michael's. I succeeded in getting a considerable distance on my way to the woods, when Covey discovered me, and called after me to come back, threatening what he would do if I did not come. I disregarded both his calls and his threats, and made my way to the woods as fast as my feeble state would allow; and thinking I might be overhauled by him if I kept the road, I walked through woods, keeping far enough from the road to avoid detection, and near enough to prevent losing my way. I had not gone far before my little strength again failed me. I could go no farther. I felt down, and lay for a considerable time. The blood was yet oozing from the wound on my head. For a time I thought I should bleed to death; and think now that I should have done so, but that the blood so matted my hair as to stop the wound. After lying there about three quarters of an hour, I nerved myself up again, and started on my way, through bogs and briers, barefooted and bareheaded, tearing my feet sometimes at nearly every step, and after a journey of about seven miles, occupying some five hours to perform it, I arrived at master's store. I then presented an appearance enough to affect any but a heart of iron. From the crown of my head to my feet, I was covered with blood. My hair was all clotted with dust and blood; my shirt was stiff with blood. My legs and feet were torn in sundry places with briers and thorns, and were also covered with blood. I suppose I looked like a man who had escaped a den of wild beasts, and barely escaped them. In this state I appeared before my master, humbly entreating him to interpose his authority for my protection. I told him all the circumstances as well as I could, and it seemed, as I spoke, at times to affect him. He would then walk the floor, and seek to justify Covey by saying he expected I deserved it. He asked me what I wanted. I told him, to set me get a new home; that as sure as I lived with Mr. Covey again, I should live with but to die with him; that Covey would surely kill me; he was in a fair way for it. Master Thomas ridiculed the idea that there was any danger of Mr. Covey's killing me, and said that he knew Mr. Covey; that he was a good man, and that he could not think of taking me from him; that, should he do so, he would lose the whole year's wages; that I belonged to Mr. Covey for one year, and that I must go back to him, come what might; and that I must not trouble him with any more stories, or that he would himself get hold of me. After threatening me thus, he gave me a very large dose of salts, telling me that I might remain in St. Michael's that night, (it being quite late), but that I must be off back to Mr. Covey's early in the morning; and that if I did not, he would get hold of me, which meant that he would whip me. I remained all night, and, according to his orders, I started off to Covey's in the morning, (Saturday morning), wearied in body and broken in spirit. I got no supper that night, or breakfast that morning. I reached Covey's about nine o'clock; and just as I was getting over the fence that divided Mrs. Kemp's fields from ours, out ran Covey with his cowskin, to give me another whipping. Before he could reach me, I succeeded in getting to the cornfield; and as the corn was very high, it afforded me the means of hiding. He seemed very angry, and searched for me a long time. My behavior was altogether unaccountable. He finally gave up the chase, thinking, I suppose, that I must come home for something to eat; he would give himself no further trouble in looking for me. I spent that day mostly in the woods, having the alternative before me,—to go home and be whipped to death, or stay in the woods and be starved to death. That night, I fell in with Sandy Jenkins, a slave with whom I was somewhat acquainted. Sandy had a free wife who lived about four miles from Mr. Covey's; and it being Saturday, he was on his way to see her. I told him my circumstances, and he very kindly invited me to go home with him. I went home with him, and talked this whole matter over, and got his advice as to what course it was best for me to pursue. I found Sandy an old adviser. He told me, with great solemnity, I must go back to Covey; but that before I went, I must go with him into another part of the woods, where there was a certain root, which, if I would take some of it with me, carrying it always on my right side, would render it impossible for Mr. Covey, or any other white man, to whip me. He said he had carried it for years; and since he had done so, he had never received a blow, and never expected to while he carried it. I at first rejected the idea, that the simple carrying of a root in my pocket would have any such effect as he had said, and was not disposed to take it; but Sandy impressed the necessity with much earnestness, telling me it could do no harm, if it did no good. To please him, I at length took the root, and, according to his direction, carried it upon my right side. This was Sunday morning. I immediately started for home; and upon entering the yard gate, out came Mr. Covey on his way to meeting. He spoke to me very kindly, bade me drive the pigs from a lot near by, and passed on towards the church. Now, this singular conduct of Mr. Covey really made me begin to think that there was something in the root which Sandy had given me; and had it been on any other day than Sunday, I could have attributed the conduct to no other cause then the influence of that root; and as it was, I was half inclined to think the root to be something more than I at first had taken it to be. All went well till Monday morning. On this morning, the virtue of the root was fully tested. Long before daylight, I was called to go and rub, curry, and feed, the horses. I obeyed, and was glad to obey. But whilst thus engaged, whilst in the act of throwing down some blades from the loft, Mr. Covey entered the stable with a long rope; and just as I was half out of the loft, he caught hold of my leg! and was about tying me. As soon as I found what he was up to, I gave a sudden spring, and as I did so, he holding to my legs, I was brought sprawling on the stable floor. Mr. Covey seemed now to think he had me, and could do what he pleased; but at this moment—from whence came the spirit I don't know—I resolved to fight and, suiting my action to the resolution, I seized Covey hard by the throat; and as I did so, I rose. He held on to me, and I to him. My resistance was so entirely unexpected, that Covey seemed taken all aback. He trembled like a leaf. This gave me assurance, and I held him uneasy, causing the blood to run where I touched him with the ends of my fingers. Mr. Covey soon called out to Hughes for help. Hughes came, and, while Covey held me, attempted to tie my right hand. While he was in the act of doing so, I watched my chance, and gave him a heavy kick close under the ribs. This kick fairly sickened Hughes, so that he left me in the hands of Mr. Covey. This kick had the effect of not only weakening Hughes, but Covey also. When he saw Hughes bending over with pain, his courage quailed. He asked me if I meant to persist in my resistance. I told him I did, come what might; that he had used me like a brute for six months, and that I was determined to be used so no longer. With that, he strove to drag me to a stick that was lying just out of the stable door. He meant to knock me down. But just as he was leaning over to get the stick, I seized him with both hands by his collar, and brought him by a sudden snatch to the ground. By this time, Bill came. Covey called upon him for assistance. Bill wanted to know what he could do. Covey said, "Take hold of him, take hold of him!" Bill said his master hired him out to work, and not to help to whip me; so he left Covey and myself to fight our own battle out. We were at it for nearly two hours. Covey at length let me go, puffing and blowing at a great rate, saying that if I had not resisted, he would not have whipped me half so much. The truth was, that he had not whipped me at all. I considered him as getting entirely the worst end of the bargain; for he had drawn no blood from me, but I had from him. The whole six months afterwards, that I spent with Mr. Covey, he never laid the weight of his finger upon me in anger. He would occasionally say, he didn't want to get hold of me again. "No," thought I, "you need not; for you will come off worse than you did before."

This battle with Mr. Covey was the turning-point in my career as a slave. It rekindled the few expiring embers of freedom, and revived within me a sense of my own manhood. It recalled the departed self-confidence, and inspired me again with a determination to be free. The gratification afforded by the triumph was a full compensation for whatever else might follow, even death itself. He only can understand the deep satisfaction which I experienced, who has himself repelled by force the bloody arm of slavery. I felt as I never felt before. It was a glorious resurrection, from the tomb of slavery, to the heaven of freedom. My long-crushed spirit rose, cowardice departed, bold defiance took its place; and I now resolved that, however long I might remain a slave in form, the day had passed forever when I could be a slave in fact. I did not hesitate to let it be known of me, that the white man who expected to succeed in whipping, must also succeed in killing me.

From this time I was never again what might be called fairly whipped, though I remained a slave four years afterwards. I had several fights, but was never whipped.

It was for a long time a matter of surprise to me why Mr. Covey did not immediately have me taken by the constable to the whipping-post, and there regularly whipped for the crime of raising my hand against a white man in defense of myself. And the only explanation I can now think of does not entirely satisfy me, but such as it is, I will give it. Mr. Covey enjoyed the most unbounded reputation for being a first-rate overseer and negro-breaker. It was of considerable importance to him. That reputation was at stake and had he sent me—a boy about sixteen years old—to the public whipping-post, his reputation would have been lost; so, to save his reputation, he suffered me to go unpunished.

My term of actual service to Mr. Edward Covey ended on Christmas day, 1833. The days between Christmas and New Year's day are allowed as holidays; and, accordingly, we were not required to perform any labor, more than to feed and take care of the stock. This time we regarded as our own, by the grace of our masters; and we therefore used or abused it nearly as we pleased. Those of us who had families at a distance, were generally allowed to spend the whole six days in their society. This time, however, was spent in various ways. The staid, sober, thinking and industrious ones of our number would employ themselves in making corn-brooms, mats, horse-collars, and baskets; and another class of us would spend the time hunting opossums, hares, and coons. But by far the larger part engaged in such sports and merriments as playing ball, wrestling, running foot-races, fiddling, dancing, and drinking whisky; and this latter mode of spending the time was by far the most agreeable to the feelings of our master. A slave who would work during the holidays was considered by our masters as scarcely deserving them. He was regarded as one who rejected the favor of his master. It was deemed a disgrace not to get drunk at Christmas; and he was regarded as lazy indeed, who had not provided himself with the necessary means, during the year, to get whisky enough to last him through Christmas.

From what I know of the effect of these holidays upon the slave, I believe them to be among the most effective means in the hands of the slaveholder in keeping down the spirit of insurrection. Were the slaveholders at once to abandon this practice, I have not the slightest doubt it would lead to an immediate insurrection among the slaves. These holidays serve as conductors, or safety-valves, to carry off the rebellious spirit of enslaved humanity. But for these, the slave would be forced up to the wildest desperation; and woe betide the slaveholder, the day he ventures to remove or hinder the operation of those conductors! I warn him that, in such an event, a spirit will go forth in their midst, more to be dreaded than the most appalling earthquake.

The holidays are part and parcel of the gross fraud, wrong, and inhumanity of slavery. They are professedly a custom established by the benevolence of the slaveholders; but I undertake to say, it is the result of selfishness, and one of the grossest frauds committed upon the down-trodden slave. They do not give the slaves this time because they would not like to have their work during its continuance, but because they know it would be unsafe to deprive them of it. This will be seen by the fact, that the slaveholders like to have their slaves spend those days just in such a manner as to make them as glad of their ending as of their beginning. Their object seems to be, to disgust their slaves with freedom, by plunging them into the lowest depths of dissipation. For instance, the slaveholders not only like to see the slave drink of his own accord, but will adopt various plans to make him drunk. One plan is, to make bets on their slaves, as to who can drink the most whisky without getting drunk; and in this way they succeed in getting whole multitudes to drink to excess. Thus, when the slave asks for virtuous freedom, the cunning slaveholder, knowing his ignorance, cheats him with a dose of vicious dissipation, artfully labeled with the name of liberty. The most of us used to drink it down, and the result was just what might be supposed: many of us were led to think that there was little to choose between liberty and slavery. We felt, and very properly too, that we had almost as well be slaves to man as to rum. So, when the holidays ended, we staggered up from the filth of our wallowing, took a long breath, and marched to the field,—feeling, upon the whole, rather glad to go, from what our master had deceived us into a belief was freedom, back to the arms of slavery.

I have said that this mode of treatment is a part of the whole system of fraud and inhumanity of slavery. It is so. The mode here adopted to disgust the slave with freedom, by allowing him to see only the abuse of it, is carried out in other things. For instance, a slave loves molasses; he steals some. His master, in many cases, goes off to town, and buys a large quantity; he returns, takes his whip, and commands the slave to eat the molasses, until the poor fellow is made sick at the very mention of it. The same mode is sometimes adopted to make the slaves refrain from asking for more food than their regular allowance. A slave runs through his allowance, and applies for more. His master is enraged at him; but, not willing to send him off without food, gives him more than is necessary, and compels him to eat it within a given time. Then, if he complains that he cannot eat it, he is said to be satisfied neither fill nor fasting, and is whipped for being hard to please! I have an abundance of such illustrations of the same principle, drawn from my own observation, but think the cases I have cited sufficient. The practice is a very common one. . . .

From *Incidents in the Life of a Slave Girl*

Harriet A. Jacobs

Perhaps the first thing that strikes us about the title of Harriet Jacobs's narrative is that it is not just about a "slave." It is about a slave "girl," about someone young and female, someone especially vulnerable—and vulnerable in a unique way. From the age of fifteen, Harriet Jacobs finds herself defined not only as property but also as sexual property. She is assaulted by the father of her young mistress and in spite of resistance and clear helplessness, accused by the wife of conniving in her own seduction.

Harriet Jacobs (1818–1896) wrote under the pseudonym of Linda Brent, assuming some of the tone of Victorian melodrama popular at the time; but the facts of her narrative are historically accurate and specifically autobiographical. Like Douglass, she escaped to the North, hid during the period of the Fugitive Slave Law, and worked for liberation with the support of New England abolitionists.

How does Jacobs's description of the slave experience compare with that of Frederick Douglass? What significance do you see in the role of religion and in the role of gender? What are the implications of sexual relations between whites and blacks in slave cultures and the effects on the families of both? What positive and negative legacy do you see in contemporary American society?

The Slaves' New Year's Day

Dr. Flint owned a fine residence in town, several farms, and about fifty slaves, besides hiring a number by the year.

Hiring-day at the south takes place on the first of January. On the second, the slaves are expected to go to their new masters. On a farm, they work until the corn and cotton are laid. They then have two holidays. Some masters give them a good dinner under the trees. This over, they work until Christmas eve. If no heavy charges are meantime brought against them, they are given four or five holidays, whichever the master or overseer may think proper. Then comes New Year's eve; and they gather together their little alls, or more properly speaking, their little nothings, and wait anxiously for the dawning of day.

Incidents in the Life of a Slave Girl, Written by Herself, chapters 3, 5, and 6.

At the appointed hour the grounds are thronged with men, women, and children, waiting, like criminals, to hear their doom pronounced. The slave is sure to know who is the most humane, or cruel master, within forty miles of him.

It is easy to find out, on that day, who clothes and feeds his slaves well; for he is surrounded by a crowd, begging, "Please, massa, hire me this year. I will work very hard, massa."

If a slave is unwilling to go with his new master, he is whipped, or locked up in jail, until he consents to go, and promises not to run away during the year. Should he chance to change his mind, thinking it justifiable to violate an extorted promise, woe unto him if he is caught! The whip is used till the blood flows at his feet; and his stiffened limbs are put in chains, to be dragged in the field for days and days!

If he lives until the next year, perhaps the same man will hire him again, without even giving him an opportunity of going to the hiring-ground. After those for hire are disposed of, those for sale are called up.

O, you happy free women, contrast your New Year's day with that of the poor bond-woman! With you it is a pleasant season, and the light of the day is blessed. Friendly wishes meet you every where, and gifts are showered upon you. Even hearts that have been estranged from you soften at this season, and lips that have been silent echo back, "I wish you a happy New Year." Children bring their little offerings, and raise their rosy lips for a caress. They are your own, and no hand but that of death can take them from you.

But to the slave mother New Year's day comes laden with peculiar sorrows. She sits on her cold cabin floor, watching the children who may all be torn from her the next morning; and often does she wish that she and they might die before the day dawns. She may be an ignorant creature, degraded by the system that has brutalized her from childhood; but she has a mother's instincts, and is capable of feeling a mother's agonies.

On one of these sale days, I saw a mother lead seven children to the auction-block. She knew that some of them would be taken from her; but they took all. The children were sold to a slave-trader, and their mother was bought by a man in her own town. Before night her children were all far away. She begged the trader to tell her where he intended to take them; this he refused to do. How could he, when he knew he would sell them, one by one, wherever he could command the highest price? I met that mother in the street, and her wild, haggard face lives today in my mind. She wrung her hands in anguish, and exclaimed, "Gone! All gone! Why don't God kill me?" I had no words wherewith to comfort her. Instances of this kind are of daily, yea, of hourly occurrence.

Slaveholders have a method, peculiar to their institution, of getting rid of *old* slaves, whose lives have been worn out in their service. I knew an old woman, who for seventy years faithfully served her master. She had become almost helpless, from hard labor and disease. Her owners moved to Alabama, and the old black woman was left to be sold to any body who would give twenty dollars for her.

The Trials of Girlhood

During the first years of my service in Dr. Flint's family, I was accustomed to share some indulgences with the children of my mistress. Though this seemed to me no more than right, I was grateful for it, and tried to merit the kindness by the faithful discharge of my duties. But I now entered on my fifteenth year—a sad epoch in the life of a slave girl. My master began to whisper foul words in my ear. Young as I was, I could not remain ignorant of their import. I tried to treat them with indifference or contempt. The master's age, my extreme youth, and the fear that his conduct would be reported to my grandmother, made him bear this treatment for many months. He was a crafty man, and resorted to many means to accomplish his purposes. Sometimes he had stormy, terrific ways, that made his victims tremble; sometimes he assumed a gentleness that he thought must surely subdue. Of the two, I preferred his stormy moods, although they left me trembling. He tried his utmost to corrupt the pure principles my grandmother had instilled. He peopled my young mind with unclean images, such as only a vile monster could think of. I turned from him with disgust and hatred. But he was my master. I was compelled to live under the same roof with him—where I saw a man forty years my senior daily violating the most sacred commandments of nature. He told me I was his property; that I must be subject to his will in all things. My soul revolted against the mean tyranny. But where could I turn for protection? No matter whether the slave girl be as black as ebony or as fair as her mistress. In either case, there is no shadow of law to protect her from insult, from violence, or even from death; all these are indicted by fiends who bear the shape of men. The mistress, who ought to protect the helpless victim, has no other feelings towards her but those of jealousy and rage. The degradation, the wrongs, the vices, that grow out of slavery, are more than I can describe. They are greater than you would willingly believe. Surely, if you credited one half the truths that are told you concerning the helpless millions suffering in this cruel bondage, you at the north would not help to tighten the yoke. You surely would refuse to do for the master, on your own soil, the mean and cruel work which trained bloodhounds and the lowest class of whites do for him at the south.

Every where the years bring to all enough of sin and sorrow; but in slavery the very dawn of life is darkened by these shadows. Even the little child, who is accustomed to wait on her mistress and her children, will learn, before she is twelve years old, why it is that her mistress hates such and such a one among the slaves. Perhaps the child's own mother is among those hated ones. She listens to violent outbreaks of jealous passion, and cannot help understanding what is the cause. She will become prematurely knowing in evil things. Soon she will learn to tremble when she hears her master's footfall. She will be compelled to realize that she is no longer a child. If God has bestowed beauty upon her, it will prove her greatest curse. That which commands admiration in the white woman only hastens the degradation of the female slave. I know that some are too much brutalized by slavery to feel the humiliation of their position; but many slaves feel it most acutely, and shrink from the memory of it. I cannot tell how much I suffered in the presence of these wrongs, nor how I am still pained by the retrospect. My master met me at every turn, reminding me that I belonged to him, and swearing by heaven and earth that he would compel me to submit to him. If I went out for a breath of fresh air, after a day of unwearied toil, his footsteps dogged me. If I knelt by my mother's grave, his dark shadow fell on me even there. The light heart which nature had given me became heavy with sad forebodings. The other slaves in my master's house noticed the change. Many of them pitied me; but none dared to ask the cause. They had no need to inquire. They knew too well the guilty practices under that roof; and they were aware that to speak of them was an offense that never went unpunished.

I longed for some one to confide in. I would have given the world to have laid my head on my grandmother's faithful bosom, and told her all my troubles. But Dr. Flint swore he would kill me, if I was not as silent as the grave. Then, although my grandmother was all in all to me, I feared her as well as loved her. I had been accustomed to look up to her with a respect bordering upon awe. I was very young, and felt shamefaced about telling her such impure things, especially as I knew her to be very strict on such subjects. Moreover, she was a woman of a high spirit. She was usually very quiet in her demeanor; but if her indignation was once roused, it was not very easily quelled. I had been told that she once chased a white gentleman with a loaded pistol, because he insulted one of her daughters. I dreaded the consequences of a violent outbreak; and both pride and fear kept me silent. But though I did not confide in my grandmother, and even evaded her vigilant watchfulness and inquiry, her presence in the neighborhood was some protection to me. Though she had been a slave, Dr. Flint was afraid of her. He dreaded her scorching rebukes. Moreover, she was known and patronized by many people; and he did not wish to have his villainy made public. It was lucky for me that I did not live on a distant plantation, but in a town not so large that the inhabitants were ignorant of each other's affairs. Bad as are the laws and customs in a slave-holding community, the doctor, as a professional man, deemed it prudent to keep up some outward show of decency.

O, what days and nights of fear and sorrow that man caused me! Reader, it is not to awaken sympathy for myself that I am telling you truthfully what I suffered in slavery. I do it to kindle a flame of compassion in your hearts for my sisters who are still in bondage, suffering as I once suffered.

I once saw two beautiful children playing together. One was a fair white child; the other was her slave, and also her sister. When I saw them embracing each other, and heard their joyous laughter, I turned sadly away from the lovely sight. I foresaw the inevitable blight that would fall on the little slave's heart. I knew how soon her laughter would be changed to sighs. The fair child grew up to be a still fairer woman. From childhood to womanhood her pathway was blooming with flowers, and overarched by a sunny sky. Scarcely one day of her life had been clouded when the sun rose on her happy bridal morning.

How had those years dealt with her slave sister, the little playmate of her childhood? She, also, was very beautiful; but the flowers and sunshine of love were not for her. She drank the cup of sin, and shame, and misery, whereof her persecuted race are compelled to drink.

In view of these things, why are ye silent, ye free men and women of the north? Why do your tongues falter in maintenance of the right? Would that I had more ability! But my heart is so full, and my pen is so weak! There are noble men and women who plead for us, striving to help those who cannot help themselves. God bless them! God give them strength and courage to go on! God bless those, every where, who are laboring to advance the cause of humanity!

The Jealous Mistress

I would ten thousand times rather that my children should be the half-starved paupers of Ireland than to be the most pampered among the slaves of America. I would rather drudge out my life on a cotton plantation, till the grave opened to give me rest, than to live with an unprincipled master and a jealous mistress. The felon's home in a penitentiary is preferable. He may repent, and turn from the error of his ways, and so find peace; but it is not so with a favorite slave. She is not allowed to have any pride of character. It is deemed a crime in her to wish to be virtuous.

Mrs. Flint possessed the key to her husband's character before I was born. She might have used this knowledge to counsel and to screen the young and the innocent among her slaves; but for them she had no sympathy. They were the objects of her constant suspicion and malevolence. She watched her husband with unceasing vigilance; but he was well practiced in means to evade it. What he could not find opportunity to say in words he manifested in signs. He invented more than were ever thought of in a deaf and dumb asylum. I let them pass, as if I did not understand what he meant; and many were the curses and threats bestowed on me for my stupidity. One day he caught me teaching myself to write. He frowned, as if he was not well pleased; but I suppose he came to the conclusion that such an accomplishment might help to advance his favorite scheme. Before long, notes were often slipped into my hand. I would return them, saying, "I can't read them, sir." "Can't you?" he replied; "then I must read them to you." He always finished the reading by asking, "Do you understand?" Sometimes he would complain of the heat of the tea room, and order his supper to be placed on a small table in the piazza. He would seat himself there with a well-satisfied smile, and tell me to stand by and brush away the flies. He would eat very slowly, pausing between the mouthfuls. These intervals were employed in describing the happiness I was so foolishly throwing away, and in threatening me with the penalty that finally awaited my stubborn disobedience. He boasted much of the forbearance he had exercised towards me, and reminded me that there was a limit to his patience. When I succeeded in avoiding opportunities for him to talk to me at home, I was ordered to come to his office, to do some errand. When there, I was obliged to stand and listen to such language as he saw fit to address to me. Sometimes I so openly expressed my contempt for him that he would become violently enraged, and I wondered why he did not strike me. Circumstanced as he was, he probably thought it was better policy to be forbearing. But the state of things grew worse and worse daily. In desperation I told him that I must and would apply to my grandmother for protection. He threatened me with death, and worse than death, if I made any complaint to her. Strange to say, I did not despair. I was naturally of a buoyant disposition, and always had a hope of somehow getting out of his clutches. Like many a poor, simple slave before me, I trusted that some threads of joy would yet be woven into my dark destiny.

I had entered my sixteenth year, and every day it became more apparent that my presence was intolerable to Mrs. Flint. Angry words frequently passed between her and her husband. He had never punished me himself, and he would not allow any body else to punish me. In that respect, she was never satisfied; but, in her angry moods, no terms were too vile for her to bestow upon me. Yet I, whom she detested so bitterly, had far more pity for her than he had, whose duty it was to make her life happy. I never wronged her, or wished to wrong her; and one word of kindness from her would have brought me to her feet.

After repeated quarrels between the doctor and his wife, he announced his intention to take his youngest daughter, then four years old, to sleep in his apartment. It was necessary that a servant should sleep in the same room, to be on hand if the child stirred. I was selected for that office, and informed for what purpose that arrangement had been made. By managing to keep within sight of people, as well as possible, during the day time, I had hitherto succeeded in eluding my master, though a razor was often held to my throat to force me to change this line of policy. At night I slept by the side of my great aunt, where I felt safe. He was too prudent to come into her room. She was an old woman, and had been in the family many years. Moreover, as a married man, and a professional man, he deemed it necessary to save appearances in some degree. But he resolved to remove the obstacle in the way of his scheme; and he thought he had planned it so that he should evade suspicion. He was well aware how much I prized my refuge by the side of my old aunt, and he determined to dispossess me of it. The first night the doctor had the little child in his room alone. The next morning, I was ordered to take my station as nurse the following night. A kind Providence interposed in my favor. During the day Mrs. Flint heard of this new arrangement, and a storm followed. I rejoiced to hear it rage.

After a while my mistress sent for me to come to her room. Her first question was, "Did you know you were to sleep in the doctor's room?"

"Yes, ma'am."

"Who told you?"

"My master."

"Will you answer truly all the questions I ask?"

"Yes, ma'am."

"Tell me, then, as you hope to be forgiven, are you innocent of what I have accused you?"

"I am."

She handed me a Bible, and said, "Lay your hand on your heart, kiss this holy book, and swear before God that you tell me the truth."

I took the oath she required, and I did it with a clear conscience.

"You have taken God's holy word to testify your innocence," said she. "If you have deceived me, beware! Now take this stool, sit down, look me directly in the face, and tell me all that has passed between your master and you."

I did as she ordered. As I went on with my account her color changed frequently, she wept, and sometimes groaned. She spoke in tones so sad, that I was touched by her grief. The tears came to my eyes; but I was soon convinced that her emotions arose from anger and wounded pride. She felt that her marriage vows were desecrated, her dignity insulted; but she had no compassion for the poor victim of her husband's perfidy. She pitied herself as a martyr; but she was incapable of feeling for the condition of shame and misery in which her unfortunate, helpless slave was placed.

Yet perhaps she had some touch of feeling for me; for when the conference was ended, she spoke kindly, and promised to protect me. I should have been much comforted by this assurance if I could have had confidence in it; but my experiences in slavery had filled me with distrust. She was not a very refined woman, and had not much control over her passions. I was an object of her jealousy, and, consequently, of her hatred; and I knew I could not expect kindness or confidence from her under the circumstances in which I was placed. I could not blame her. Slaveholders' wives feel as other women would under similar circumstances. The fire of her temper kindled from small sparks, and now the flame became so intense that the doctor was obliged to give up his intended arrangement.

I knew I had ignited the torch, and I expected to suffer for it afterwards; but I felt too thankful to my mistress for the timely aid she rendered me to care such about that. She now took me to sleep in a room adjoining her own. There I was an object of her especial care, though not of her especial comfort, for she spent many a sleepless night to watch over me. Sometimes I woke up, and found her bending over me. At other times she whispered in my ear, as though it was her husband who was speaking to me, and listened to hear what I would answer. If she startled me, on such occasions, she would glide stealthily away; and the next morning she would tell me I had been talking in my sleep, and ask who I was talking to. At last, I began to be fearful for my life. It had been often threatened; and you can imagine, better than I can describe, what an unpleasant sensation it must produce to wake up in the dead of night and find a jealous woman bending over you. Terrible as this experience was, I had fears that it would give place to one more terrible.

My mistress grew weary of her vigils; they did not prove satisfactory. She changed her tactics. She now tried the trick of accusing my master of crime, in my presence, and gave my name as the author of the accusation. To my utter astonishment, he replied, "I don't believe it; but if she did acknowledge it, you tortured her into exposing me." Tortured into exposing him! Truly, Satan had no difficulty in distinguishing the color of his soul! I understood his object in making this false representation. It was to show me that I gained nothing by seeking the protection of my mistress; that the power was still all in his own hands. I pitied Mrs. Flint. She was a second wife, many years the junior of her husband; and the hoary-headed miscreant was enough to try the patience of a wiser and better woman. She was completely foiled, and knew not how to proceed. She would gladly have had me flogged for my supposed false oath; but, as I have already stated, the doctor never allowed any one to whip me. The old sinner was politic. The application of the lash might have led to remarks that would have exposed him in the eyes of his children and grandchildren. How often did I rejoice that I lived in a town where all the inhabitants knew each other! If I had been on a remote plantation, or lost among the multitude of a crowded city, I should not be a living woman at this day.

The secrets of slavery are concealed like those of the Inquisition. My master was, to my knowledge, the father of eleven slaves. But did the mothers dare to tell who was the father of their children? Did the other slaves dare to allude to it, except in whispers among themselves? No, indeed! They knew too well the terrible consequences.

My grandmother could not avoid seeing things which excited her suspicions. She was uneasy about me, and tried various ways to buy me; but the never changing answer was always repeated: "Linda does not belong to me. She is my daughter's property, and I have no legal right to sell her." The conscientious man! He was too scrupulous to sell me; but he had no scruples whatever about committing a much greater wrong against the helpless young girl placed under his guardianship, as his daughter's property. Sometimes my persecutor would ask me whether I would like to be sold. I told him I would rather be sold to any body than to lead such a life as I did. On such occasions he would assume the air of a very injured individual, and reproach me for my ingratitude. "Did I not take you into the house, and make you the companion of my own children?" he would say. "Have I ever treated you like a negro? I have never allowed you to be punished, not even to please your mistress. And this is the recompense I get, you ungrateful girl!" I answered that he had reasons of his own for screening me from punishment, and that the course he pursued made my mistress hate me and persecute me. If I wept, he would say, "Poor child! Don't cry! don't cry! I will make peace for you with your mistress. Only let me arrange matters in my own way. Poor, foolish girl! you don't know what is for your own good. I would cherish you. I would make a lady of you. Now go, and think of all I have promised you."

I did think of it.

Reader, I draw no imaginary pictures of southern homes. I am telling you the plain truth. Yet when victims make their escape from this wild beast of Slavery, northerners consent to act the part of bloodhounds, and hunt the poor fugitive back into his den, "full of dead men's bones, and all uncleanness." Nay, more, they are not only willing, but proud, to give their daughters in marriage to slaveholders. The poor girls have romantic notions of a sunny clime, and of the flowering vines that all the year round shade a happy home. To what disappointments are they destined! The young wife soon learns that the husband in whose hands she has placed her happiness pays no regard to his marriage vows. Children of every shade of complexion play with her own fair babies, and too well she knows that they are born unto him of his own household. Jealousy and hatred enter the flowery home, and it is ravaged of its loveliness.

Southern women often marry a man knowing that he is the father of many little slaves. They do not trouble themselves about it. They regard such children as property, as marketable as the pigs on the plantation; and it is seldom that they do not make them aware of this by passing them into the slavetrader's hands as soon as possible, and thus getting them out of their sight. I am glad to say there are some honorable exceptions.

I have myself known two southern wives who exhorted their husbands to free those slaves towards whom they stood in a "parental relation"; and their request was granted. These husbands blushed before the superior nobleness of their wives' natures. Though they had only counseled them to do that which it was their duty to do, it commanded their respect, and rendered their conduct more exemplary. Concealment was at an end, and confidence took the place of distrust.

Though this bad institution deadens the moral sense, even in white women, to a fearful extent, it is not altogether extinct. I have heard southern ladies say of Mr. Such a one, "He not only thinks it no disgrace to be the father of those little niggers, but he is not ashamed to call himself their master. I declare, such things ought not to be tolerated in any decent society!"

Part 7

European Settlers in Asia and Ideologies of Racism

This World War II–era American illustration of a Japanese soldier drew on deep-seated racial and sexual fears.

In the centuries after 1500 Europeans settled throughout the world, in Asia as well as the Americas. Larger European populations settled in the Americas than in Asia for a couple of reasons. Most important, Native Americans lacked immunities to disease that were shared by Europeans and Asians and thus were decimated, leaving behind large areas of fertile land without strong populations to protect it. This was not the case in Asia. In India, the Portuguese encountered an expanding Mughal empire as well as Indian princes, who together were in control of the subcontinent. Even if the Portuguese had come (as to Brazil) to establish plantations, they would have been limited in the amount of land available to them. In fact, they came in smaller numbers—to trade, rather than to plant. They expected (and received) enormous returns by buying East Indian spices and selling them in Europe. The Portuguese and then the Dutch, English, and French initially established commercial facilities in Indian ports, gaining access to interior markets and lands only in the eighteenth century.

Unlike the Portuguese, the Dutch initiated some settlements in Java and the Banda islands (in what is today Indonesia) and turned a supply station on the southern tip of Africa into a pastoral economy. Most Europeans were effectively excluded from Japan after 1600, but the Spanish made effective use of Manila as a port for shipping Mexican silver from Acapulco for Chinese silks and ceramics. None of these European ports, however, attracted large numbers of European settlers. Nor did they import a large amount of African slaves, since there was a sufficient number of local laborers and a ready source of Chinese migrants to the Philippines and maritime southeast Asia.

Nevertheless, ideas of race were easily transferable from one part of the world to another. Asian colonies were in contact with American ones, and the exchange of personnel only increased with improvements in transportation. Even before the age of the clipper ship, at the end of the eighteenth century, Lord Cornwallis, defeated by the American colonial forces at Yorktown, moved on to serve as British viceroy in Ireland and Governor General in India.

So, we might ask, what ideas of race developed in, or were transferred to, these Asian outposts of settlement and trade? Did Europeans view Asian Indians differently from American Indians? Did they view Asians differently from Africans? Are there signs of "racism" in the initial stages of European settlement in Asia? Or, did racism (as Michael Adas argues here) develop later?

We also look in these readings at the development of ideologies of racism in Europe and America, especially in the nineteenth century. If European settlers in Asia were only arrogant or ethnocentric in the sixteenth and seventeenth centuries, by the last half of the nineteenth century, the signs of racism are clear. To what extent was this related to new ideas in Europe and America about race, new scientific fads of measuring differences among people, and a new pride in European and American power and technology?

From *Machines as the Measure of Men: Science, Technology, and Ideologies of Western Dominance*

Michael Adas

Michael Adas is a modern historian of colonialism. In the book excerpted here he argues that machines, or technological ability, were the measure that Europeans used to devalue colonial peoples. Cultural differences were less important. He points out that all non-Europeans (except Ethiopians) were non-Christians, so in terms of culture they were all equal—pagans. But in technology (which became increasingly important to Europeans themselves) there were differences. Consequently, Europeans generally viewed Chinese (with the most advanced technology) as superior to Indians (of India) and Indians as superior to Africans.

Adas argues that this technological measure became more important for Europeans in the Industrial age (the nineteenth century) than it was earlier. In the sixteenth and seventeenth centuries (before the industrial revolution), European technology was not appreciably more advanced than non-European technologies; so it was not until the nineteenth century that Europeans viewed Africans as seriously and permanently inferior (i.e., in a racist way).

In the first selection included here, "The Limits of Diffusion," Adas argues that racism developed only in the second half of the nineteenth century. Before the 1860s, Europeans believed their civilization was superior, but they did not believe that they were racially (biologically) superior. Racism came late in the nineteenth century as the disparity between European and non-European technology widened and as the "scientific racism" of European scientists and social scientists was disseminated among the public, educators, and colonial administrators who, as a consequence of this new pseudo knowledge, limited the opportunities of colonized people.

In "The First Generation of Improvers," Adas refers to the great debate among English colonizers in India as to whether the Indians ought to learn English and study European literature and science. Many English coloniz- ers, and some Indians, stressing the value of Indian culture and languages, argued against English education. Other English colonizers, and again some Indians, argued that Indians ought to be exposed to European civi- lization, languages, and schools. The latter won the debate and this has sometimes been interpreted as a sign of British racism. But here too Adas argues that this was a case of cultural arrogance and ethnocentrism but cetainly not racism. It can hardly be called racism for the British to teach Indians what the British considered the great learning of British civiliza- tion.

Implicit in this effort was the assumption that Indians could learn as much as the British; they could become British. A racist could not have accepted that assumption. Adas makes a similar case in discussing Euro- pean attitudes toward the Chinese and French policy in Africa. Do you agree or disagree with his argument that these policies were not racist?

In the last selection, "The Age of Industrialization: The Search for Sci- entific and Technological Proofs of Racial Inequality," Adas discusses the scientific racism of the second half of the nineteenth century in Europe and America. Why, according to Adas, did it suddenly become necessary for these Western scientists to find physical and biological bases for supposed Asian and African inferiority? How could phrenology and craniometry (es- sentially measuring head size and facial bumps) become scientifically re- spectable? How do you think otherwise intelligent people could be so seriously misinformed? Why was this biological explanation of behavioral difference more damaging than mere prejudice or preference for Western ways?

The Limits of Diffusion

Contrary to the impression given in much of the recent literature on nineteenth-century European colonization, in which there is a tendency to reduce European interaction with Africans and Asians to stereotypes of racist exclusivism and condescension, European responses to racial thinking varied widely in this era. To begin with, the meaning of the term "race" itself was often vague; its application changed significantly from one writer to another and even within the same work of a single author. The term "race" was used rather routinely to indicate divisions within humanity as a whole, but there was little agreement on which divisions were appropriate or even how many different races could be distinguished. In addition, as contemporary critics of racist thinking such as R.P. Lesson and Theodor Waitz pointed out, opinions varied widely among nineteenth-century writers as to which characteristics should be decisive in deciding racial boundaries. Not surprisingly, there was little consistency in the Victorians' usage when it came to the term "race." References can be found in nineteenth-century works to the human race; the Hindu or Islamic race; primitives as a race; the British and French or Anglo-Saxon and Celtic races; the African or European race; the Bantu or Tamil race; the Aryan and Semitic races; and of course the Negro and Caucasian, or Negroid and Caucausoid, races. As these examples suggest, the problems of agreeing upon the number of races and how to distinguish them were compounded by the fact that the same group could be classified in several different ways.

Different classifications could result in conflicting, even blatantly contradictory assessments of the racial attributes and potential of a given group. For example, linguistic and archeological evidence uncovered over the course of the century convinced many thinkers that Hindu civilization in northern India had been developed by a branch of the Aryan "race" (not language family, as present-day scholars would argue). This view clashed with the tendency of some writers to classify all Indians as part of the "brown" or "black" race, and especially with the decidedly racist attitudes that dominated British social interaction with the Indians from the last decades of the nineteenth century. The notion that the northern Indians or Hindus represented a branch of the Aryan race that had been degraded by centuries of life in an enervating climate and constant intermarriage with lesser racial types provided a way to reconcile the two views. But it did little to resolve questions regarding the Indians' historic achievements and future potential.

A survey of nineteenth-century works dealing with racial categories suggests that only a minority of writers used the term "race" to differentiate between and rank human groups on the basis of hereditary biological differences. Though most Europeans clearly considered themselves superior to African or Asian peoples, until the last decades of the century their conviction of superiority at the level of ideas, as distinct from that of social interaction, was based primarily on cultural attainments rather than physical differences. There is, of course, in European writings of this period a narcissistic preference for white skin and straight hair, but the notion that biological factors were responsible for Europe's achievements and global dominance was not widely argued or accepted until the latter part of the century. . . .

The fact that virtually all nineteenth-century European thinkers accepted without question the assumption that Europeans were technologically and scientifically superior to all other peoples but did not necessarily draw from this the conclusion that Europeans were racially superior suggests that we may need to reevaluate the place of racism in its more restricted sense in the intellectual discourse of this era. Though many authors who made racist arguments paid little attention to or altogether ignored European scientific and technological advances, racism was more often ideologically subordinate to a more fundamental set of European convictions that arose out of their material accomplishments. In addition, at the level of intellectual exchange as opposed to popular sentiment, scientific and technological gauges antedated racial distinctions as important proofs of European superiority. They have also (despite setbacks) shown more staying power in the twentieth century, when national liberation and civil rights struggles and Nazi atrocities have done much to discredit racist arguments.

Questions relating to the capacity of Africans and Asians to adopt Western science and technology tended to be debated at two levels: among the physicians, anthropologists, and social theorists who developed, or disputed, the racist theories that peaked in sophistication in this era; and among administrators and missionary spokesmen who shaped educational policies in the colonies. For most of the first half of the century, there was little interaction between the two groups. The impact of racist theory on colonial decision-making was negligible, and colonial officials and missionaries were only marginally involved in developing instruments to measure racial differences with scientific precision and supplying information about overseas societies to confirm theories based on the assumption of innate racial differences. In the last decades of the century, when both theories of racial supremacy and scientific and technological gauges of human worth were widely accepted by European politicians and intellectuals, the interplay of ideas became more intense. In lectures, memoirs, and newspaper articles, explorers and former colonial administrators recounted personal experiences and missionaries and anthropologists provided field evidence that supported racist theories. These racist ideas in turn played a major role in late nineteenth-century debates over colonial policy. The following discussion gives special attention to the impact, or lack of it, of racist thinking on British and French educational policies in their colonial possessions. As we shall see, a tautological relationship developed: scientific and technological achievements were frequently cited as gauges of racial capacity, and estimates of racial capacity determined the degree of technical and scientific education made available to different non-Western peoples.

The First Generations of Improvers

Race was not an issue in the controversy over higher education in India that pitted Orientalists against Evangelicals and Utilitarians in the 1820s and 1830s. The victory of the pro-Anglicizing Evangelicals and Utilitarians was sealed by the 1835 resolution of Governor-General Lord William Bentinck, committing the British to "the promotion of European literature and science among the natives of India." Bentinck's decision, one of the most momentous in the history of European colonization, was based on the assumption (which none of the British officials engaged in the debate had challenged) that Indians were intellectually able to master the English language and Western learning, including advanced mathematics and science. In fact, the British desire to supplant what they viewed as hopelessly antiquated and superstition-ridden Indian views of the natural world had been one of the main objectives of the Evangelical and Utilitarian factions from the outset of the campaign to win increased government support for English education for Indians, particularly at the university level. Their assaults on Sanskrit and Persian learning were culturally arrogant, but they were free of the racial prejudice that is often assumed to have been synonymous with British rule in nineteenth-century India.

The original impetus for the drive to win government support for the use of English in higher education can be traced to Charles Grant's 1792 critique of Indian civilization and his official efforts to enact a far-reaching program of reform in the British-controlled portions of the subcontinent. As President of the Board of Trade in Calcutta and later Chairman of the Court of Directors of the East India Company, Grant was in a superb position to push his proposals for administrative and legal reform. He was also one of the more prominent members of the Evangelical clique that was active in the late eighteenth and early nineteenth centuries in a wide range of reformist causes, including the campaign to abolish the slave trade. He viewed moral uplift as the sine qua non of his program to rescue the Indians from the degraded state to which they had fallen. Therefore, Christian education was central to his proposals for reform in India, though he also envisaged a major role for science and technology. Grant was confident that instruction in the revealed truths of Christianity and in the advanced sciences and technology that the British had developed through their "great use of reason in all subjects" would be sufficient to weaken the Indians' attachment to what he viewed as repulsive customs and "superstitious chimeras," and to arouse them from centuries of lethargy and passivity. The mere sight of the wonderful machines devised by the British, Grant asserted, would convince the Hindus of the superiority of European "natural philosophy" and attract them to English-language schools. Through English education and Christian instruction, Indian youths could be awakened to a spirit of invention, a desire for improvement, and a taste for British manufactured goods. Having mastered the "principles of mechanics" devised by European thinkers and engineers over the centuries, educated Indians would be able to work for improvements in agricultural production and the "useful arts" which would benefit the whole population of the subcontinent.

Though Grant did refer to the racial origins of British moral superiority over the Indians, his estimate of the potential for Indian improvement was decidedly nonracist. Reflecting the views of most eighteenth century thinkers, he held that an enervating climate and centuries of despotic rule were the main causes of Indian character flaws and India's backwardness. He shared the confidence of most Enlightenment thinkers that "all branches of the human race" could be "improved through reason and science." Hindu inferiority, he argued, arose from "moral causes" not "physical origin[s]." The Bengalis were as capable as the ancient Britons of raising themselves up from the lowly state to which they had fallen, and Grant had no doubt about their desire to do so. Presumably on the basis of personal conversations, he insisted that Indians who had been in close contact with Westerners conceded the "immense superiority" of European thought and technology. He inferred that they would welcome the widespread introduction of both European ideas and machines into the subcontinent. He was convinced that these would serve as key agents of the process of social and intellectual regeneration which he had come to see as a central purpose of British rule.

Interestingly, Grant was anxious to assuage the concern not of those who doubted the Indian capacity to master Western learning but of those who feared that the Indian acquisition of it would result in a rebellion against British authority—similar to that which had recently deprived the British of their valuable colonies in North America. Grant reasoned that the lethargic and servile Indians were unlikely to respond in the same way as the energetic and aggressive Americans, who had been nurtured by a temperate climate and English freedoms.

In the early 1800s, Grant found numerous allies in his campaign for government-supported education in India. After 1813, when Christian proselytization was allowed for the first time in areas controlled by the East India Company, missionaries such as William Carey and John Samuel founded private colleges in which instruction in English and Western sciences was promoted. Carey envisioned a somewhat elementary course of instruction in the sciences for Indian youths. Samuel's approach stressed the practical and applied over the theoretical. The college that he proposed in 1813 resembled a technical school in its approach to the sciences, and he made much of the need for rigorous physical education to inculcate the virtues of industry, activity, and bodily fitness among the Bengalis, whom the British regarded as languid, soft, and passive.

The privately financed efforts of Western missionaries and prominent Englishmen to establish English-language colleges in the early 1800s were bolstered by a growing demand for English education on the part of Indian leaders themselves. Hindu notables and British improvers joined forces in 1817 to found the Calcutta School Book Society and the Hindu College, which were aimed in part at the dissemination of Western scientific thought in English as well as in Indian languages. The special interest in English education evinced by the Kayasthas and similar caste groups whose members had traditionally served as scribes and government officials, and the rapidly growing Indian commercial classes in port cities such as Calcutta arose from more than an opportunistic desire to secure positions in the colonial bureaucracy. As the 1823 petition by Raja Rammohan Roy to Governor-General Lord Amherst made clear, English education was viewed as a means of unlocking the secrets of the Western sciences that had contributed so much to the advancement of European societies. Roy, who was among the boldest of the early Indian leaders favoring sweeping reforms of Indian society and extensive Anglicization, charged that the perpetuation of the government's policy of confining its support to Sanskrit (and Arabic-Persian) education would serve only to "keep [India] in darkness." If, however, the object of government was the "improvement of the native population," Roy declared, it should "promote a more liberal and enlightened system of instruction, embracing Mathematics, Natural Philosophy, Chemistry, Anatomy and other useful sciences . . . which the nations of Europe have carried to a degree of perfection that has raised them above the inhabitants of other parts of the world."

Of the forces joined in the early campaign for English education in India, the Utilitarians ultimately played the most critical role in both England and India. Through his relentless critiques of virtually all aspects of Indian society, James Mill helped to prepare the way for English-language instruction, even though he opposed the ultra-Anglicizing policies advocated by other Utilitarians. His lengthy commentary on the dismal condition of the "arts" and sciences in the subcontinent made it clear that the introduction of Western learning and technology were essential features of his wide-ranging plans for reform in India. His official dispatches too left no doubt that he thought the Indians intellectually able to acquire Western scientific learning and adopt Western technology. The hopes of Mill and other Utilitarians that their programs to "improve" India's laws, political economy, customs, and learning would be translated into government legislation were finally realized when Lord William Bentinck was appointed Governor-General in 1829. . . .

The growing awareness of the scientific and technological backwardness of China in the era of industrialization did little to diminish the confidence of most European observers that the Chinese were capable of adopting, if they chose to do so, the technology and scientific ideas of the West. The majority view that China had once been a great civilization persisted throughout the nineteenth century. Evidence of the technological accomplishments of that civilization—its bridges and canals, sailing vessels and water mills—served as reminders of the great feats of invention and engineering that the Chinese had once performed and could again achieve. As we have seen, most Western observers linked China's stagnation to the policies of a succession of despotic regimes and the Chinese people's excessive reverence for past precedents and established custom.

Though a number of writers in the mid-nineteenth century suggested that the servility and passivity of the Chinese might be racial traits and thus difficult to overcome, most missionaries and diplomats in this period emphasized Chinese xenophobia, not innate intellectual deficiencies, as the major barrier to Chinese borrowing. The three missionaries who produced the brief 1838 essay "Intellectual Character of the Chinese," for example, declared that without exception the "natural [mental] endowment" of the Chinese was equal to that of "any other people on earth." An anonymous essay published a half-decade earlier had deplored the cultural arrogance of the Chinese because it had blocked the introduction of Western learning. But the author insisted that the potential for spreading the science and technology of the West was greater in China than in any other Asiatic society. He noted that the Chinese already had a substantial scientific tradition to build upon, a large number of literate individuals, and a highly adaptable language. He proposed exposing the Chinese to European inventions and establishing a society to introduce them to the superior scientific knowledge of the West as the most effective way of rousing the Chinese from their lethargy and making them aware of their backwardness.

In the reports of the Medical Missionary Society in the late 1830s and the 1840s, there were repeated references to the need to instruct young Chinese in Western medicine, chemistry, and inductive reasoning and to bring to their attention the practical applications of Western mathematics and mechanics. Members of the society, who earnestly professed their faith in the unity of mankind, foresaw little difficulty in disseminating European learning and technology once Chinese political restrictions had been removed. As early as the 1830s the missionary Peter Parker had worked to turn his brightest students into competent medical doctors, and his efforts were periodically though haphazardly taken up by other missionaries throughout the middle decades of the century. Though opportunities for educating the Chinese were greatly restricted until after the British and French military incursions of the late 1850s, missionary opinion in general was reflected in the views of Evariste Huc, one of the most respected and widely quoted visitors to China in the mid-nineteenth century. Noting the abundance of China's resources and the intelligence and industriousness of its people, Huc concluded that the Chinese "nation" would industrialize rapidly once its leaders committed it to the acquisition and use of Western ideas and machines.

Except for enclaves such as Sierre Leone, where freed slaves were settled under European sponsorship, British or French control over the education of Africans in the first decades of the nineteenth century was almost as limited as their access to the Chinese. The available evidence, however, suggests that both missionary and official opinion regarding the intellectual capacity of the Africans was only marginally, if at all, affected by the thinking of those who sought to demonstrate racial or biological reasons for the perceived inferiority of the Africans. The predominant view among administrators and missionaries at work in the coastal enclaves where Europeans exercised some control was rooted in the Enlightenment assumption that all branches of the human family possessed equivalent mental and physical faculties and were thus inherently improvable. Of course, the "imperial humanitarians" were certain that the Africans were decidedly inferior to the Europeans, but they stressed cultural rather than biological deficiencies in attempting to explain African backwardness. Therefore, though missionaries such as John Philip believed that "the speculations of science" and the "pursuits of literature" were "above the comprehension" of the "untutored savage" and accordingly stressed religious education, they generally concurred with Philip's view that it was not the quality of the African's mind that created the obstructions but rather the "objects it is used to contemplating."

Perhaps the fullest insights in this period into European estimates of the African potential for adopting Western technology and for education in European sciences can be found in the views expressed by French colonial officials and educators with regard to the proper instruction for Africans living in the French commercial enclaves of Goree and St. Louis in Senegal. In contrast to the deliberations over educational policy in India, the role of the colonial administration and the language of instruction were not central to the policy disputes in Senegal. In the first half of the nineteenth century, virtually all administrators and missionaries in areas colonized by France adhered to the policy of assimilation. This approach rested on two convictions that were somewhat contradictory: the belief that all human groups have similar intellectual capacities, which we have seen was dominant in the Enlightenment and Revolutionary eras; and a strong sense of French cultural superiority over Africans or Asians. In the towns of St. Louis and Goree, where the doctrines of assimilation in their various guises were most fully applied, it was assumed that young Africans who attended French schools could be transformed into full citizens of France through their mastery of the French language, French literature, and other aspects of French culture. . . .

The Age of Industrialization: The Search for Scientific and Technological Proofs of Racial Inequality

In the eighteenth century the effort to demonstrate the scientific validity of the belief that there were innate differences in mental and moral capacity between racial groups had been confined to small circles of physicians and essayists. From the early 1800s, it grew into one of the central preoccupations of European and North American intellectuals. A substantial literature has developed on the decisive shift in this period from skin color to skull configuration as the key determinant of racial identity and the main gauge of racial potential. But both science and technology played other roles in nineteenth-century attempts to delineate racial boundaries and to provide empirical support for the belief that European peoples were intrinsically superior to all others. Scientific and technological achievements were increasingly cited as evidence of racial abilities or racial ineptitude. These were used as key criteria by which to rank different racial groups in the hierarchies of civilized, barbarian, and savage peoples which nineteenth-century thinkers were so fond of constructing. The ability of African or Asian peoples to use Western tools or firearms was also frequently cited as evidence of their potential as races for improvement. Though the ways in which gauges based on scientific or technological accomplishment were used remained fairly constant, the frame of reference for arguments about racial capacity changed significantly between the first half and the last decades of the century. In the earlier period, a static view of racial divisions and attributes prevailed; from the 1860s onward a more fluid, evolutionary view of racial development gained increasing acceptance both in intellectual circles in Europe and among colonial policymakers and educators.

As the focus of racial thinking shifted from eighteenth-century speculation about the origins of racial differentiation to an extended debate in the early nineteenth century over the consequences of racial differences, the efforts of such physicians as White and Soemmering to quantify physical distinctions between human groups came to dominate scientific thinking on the issue of race. Though measurements of arm length or genital size continued to be made, the skull became the focus of investigation. Technology, in the guise of instruments from simple calipers to Gratton's craniometer, was enlisted in the search for an accurate technique of skull measurement and comparison. Some investigators stressed the need to measure cranial capacity (Samuel Morton used white peppers and then lead gunshot; Friedrich Tiedemann used millet seed); others such as Anders Retzius and George Combe insisted that what mattered was the shape of the head or the proportions of different parts of the skull or brain. The usefulness of Camper's facial angle was debated, and it was gradually replaced by a bewildering variety of new phrenological gauges, including the cephalic index, the nose index, the vertical index, and the cephalo-orbital index. Thousands and then tens of thousands of skulls were measured in innumerable ways. The obsession with craniometry culminated at century's end with A. von Torok's thousands of measurements of a single skull. As Stephen Gould has observed, few endeavors illustrate as well as

phrenology and craniology the "allure of numbers" for nineteenth-century prac-
titioners of the human sciences and their "faith that rigorous measurement
could guarantee irrefutable precision, and might mark the transition between
subjective speculation and a true science as worthy as Newtonian physics."

Despite vigorous challenges throughout the century, the enduring influence
of phrenology and craniometry rested on the assumption, first fully elaborated
in George Combe's System of Phrenology, that a correspondence between
intelligence and skull shape or brain size could be scientifically demonstrated
for entire racial groups. Some writers also sought to link cranial capacity to
the temperament or moral development of various races. The American physician Samuel Morton, for example, one of the most prominent craniologists
of the century, characterized the Hindus on the basis of skull measurements
as "mild, sober and industrious" but "prone to fantastic religions," and the
Turks as violent, passionate, cruel, and vindictive. Victor de l'Isle opined that
the different races could be divided into conquerors and slaves on the basis of
head shape and size, while Georges Cuvier suggested that there was a connection between the "beautiful form" of the Caucasians' heads and the do-
minion that they had historically exerted over most of the rest of humankind.
The fact that a priori conclusions had been reached about the most desirable
sort of skull is made evident by descriptions of the Caucasian type, which are
invariably exercises in European or American self-adulation. It is even more
disturbingly apparent in the very unscientific efforts of craniologists such as
Morton and Paul Broca to ignore or explain away anomalies in their data and
outright contradictions between their data and conclusions.

From *The Mismeasure of Man*

Stephen Jay Gould

*Stephen Jay Gould taught biology, geology, and the history of science at
Harvard University. He was also the Frederick P. Rose Honorary Curator
in Invertebrates at the American Museum of Natural History.*

In this section from his book, the author studies the early development of scientific racism in nineteenth-century Europe and America. He shows how even the most enlightened and liberal scientists of the age failed to challenge popular racist stereotypes. Indeed, these racist stereotypes were held by some of the most democratic political leaders as well. Why do you think such ideas could be held so pervasively by so many thoughtful and otherwise well-intentioned people? What does this selection tell you about the strength of racist ideas?

In what ways does Gould's discussion of eighteenth- and nineteenth-century thought differ from that of Adas in the previous reading? How do you resolve their differences? Was there a great difference between the English attitude toward the people of India and white American attitudes toward blacks?

In assessing the impact of science upon eighteenth- and nineteenth-century views of race, we must first recognize the cultural milieu of a society whose leaders and intellectuals did not doubt the propriety of racial ranking—with Indians below whites, and blacks below everybody else. Under this universal umbrella, arguments did not contrast equality with inequality. One group—we might call them "hard-liners"—held that blacks were inferior and that their biological status justified enslavement and colonization. Another group—the "soft-liners," if you will—agreed that blacks were inferior, but held that a people's right to freedom did not depend upon their level of intelligence. "Whatever be their degree of talents," wrote Thomas Jefferson, "it is no measure of their rights."

Soft-liners held various attitudes about the nature of black disadvantage. Some argued that proper education and standard of life could "raise" blacks to a white level; others advocated permanent black ineptitude. They also disagreed about the biological or cultural roots of black inferiority. Yet, throughout the egalitarian tradition of the European Enlightenment and the American revolution, I cannot identify any popular position remotely like the "cultural relativism" that prevails (at least by lip-service) in liberal circles today. The nearest approach is a common argument that black inferiority is purely cultural and that it can be completely eradicated by education to a Caucasian standard.

All American culture heroes embraced racial attitudes that would embarrass public-school mythmakers. Benjamin Franklin, while viewing the inferiority of blacks as purely cultural and completely remediable, nonetheless expressed his hope that America would become a domain of whites, undiluted by less pleasing colors.

I could wish their numbers were increased. And while we are, as I may call it, scouring our planet, by clearing America of woods, and so making

this side of our globe reflect a brighter light to the eyes of inhabitants
in Mars or Venus, why should we . . . darken its people? Why increase
the Sons of Africa, by planting them in America, where we have so fair
an opportunity, by excluding all blacks and tawneys, of increasing the
lovely white and red? (*Observations Concerning the Increase of Mankind*, 175).

Others among our heroes argued for biological inferiority. Thomas Jefferson
wrote, albeit tentatively: "I advance it, therefore, as a suspicion only, that the
blacks, whether originally a distinct race, or made distinct by time and circumstances are inferior to the whites in the endowment both of body and of mind"
(in Gossett, 1965, p. 243). Lincoln's pleasure at the performance of black
soldiers in the Union army greatly increased his respect for freedmen and
former slaves. But freedom does not imply biological equality, and Lincoln
never abandoned a basic attitude, so strongly expressed in the Douglas debates
(1858).

There is a physical difference between the white and black races which
I believe will forever forbid the two races living together on terms of
social and political equality. And inasmuch as they cannot so live, while
they remain together there must be the position of superior and inferior,
and I as much as any other man am in favor of having the superior
position assigned to the white race.

Lest we choose to regard this statement as mere campaign rhetoric, I cite this
private jotting, scribbled on a fragment of paper in 1859:

Negro equality! Fudge! How long, in the Government of a God great
enough to make and rule the universe, shall there continue knaves to
vend, and fools to quip, so low a piece of demagogism as this (in Sinkler,
1972, p. 47).

I do not cite these statements in order to release skeletons from ancient
closets. Rather, I quote the men who have justly earned our highest respect in
order to show that white leaders of Western nations did not question the propriety of racial ranking during the eighteenth and nineteenth centuries. In this
context, the pervasive assent given by scientists to conventional rankings arose
from shared social belief, not from objective data gathered to test an open
question. Yet, in a curious case of reversed causality, these pronouncements
were read as independent support for the political context.

All leading scientists followed social conventions. In the first formal definition of human races in modern taxonomic terms, Linnaeus mixed character with anatomy (*Systema Naturae*, 1758). *Homo sapiens afer* (the African black), he proclaimed, is "ruled by caprice"; *Homo sapiens europaeus* (European man) is "ruled by customs." Of African women, he wrote: . . ."Women without shame, breasts lactate profusely." The men, he added, are indolent and anoint themselves with grease.

The three greatest naturalists of the nineteenth century did not hold blacks in high esteem. Georges Cuvier, widely hailed in France as the Aristotle of his age, and a founder of geology, paleontology and modern comparative anatomy, referred to native Africans as the most degraded of human races, whose form approaches that of the beast and whose intelligence is nowhere great enough to arrive at regular government (Cuvier, 1812, p. 105). Charles Lyell, the conventional founder of modern geology, wrote:

> the brain of the Bushman . . . leads towards the brain of the Simiadae [monkeys]. This implies a connexion between want of intelligence and structural assimilation. Each race of Man has its place, like the inferior animals (in Wilson, 1970, p. 347).

Charles Darwin, the kindly liberal and passionate abolitionist, wrote about a future time when the gap between human and ape will increase by the anticipated extraction of such intermediates as chimpanzees and Hottentots.

> The break will then be rendered wider, for it will intervene between man in a more civilized state, as we may hope, than the Caucasian, and some ape as low as a baboon, instead of as at present between the negro or Australian and the gorilla (*Descent of Man*, 1871, p. 201).

Even more instructive are the beliefs of those few scientists often cited in retrospect as cultural relativists and defenders of equality. J.F. Blumenbach attributed racial differences to the influences of climate. He protested rankings based on beauty or presumed mental ability and assembled a collection of books written by blacks. Nonetheless, he did not doubt that white people set a standard from which all other races must be viewed as departures:

> The Caucasian must, on every physiological principle, be considered as the primary or intermediate of these five principal Races. The two extremes into which it has deviated, are on the one hand the Mongolian, and on the other the Ethiopian (African blacks) (1825, p. 37).

Alexander von Humboldt, world traveler, statesman, and greatest popularizer of nineteenth-century science, would be the hero of all modern egalitarians who seek antecedents in history. He, more than any other scientist of his time, argued forcefully and at length against ranking on mental or aesthetic grounds. He also drew political implications from his convictions, and campaigned against all forms of slavery and subjugation as impediments to the natural striving of all people to attain mental excellence. He wrote in the most famous passage of his five-volume *Cosmos*:

> Whilst we maintain the unity of the human species, we at the same time repel the depressing assumptions of superior and inferior races of men. There are nations more susceptible of cultivation than others—but none in themselves nobler than others. All are in like degree designed for freedom (1849, p. 368).

Yet even Humboldt invoked innate mental differences to resolve some dilemmas of human history. Why, he asks in the second volume of *Cosmos*, did the Arabs explode in culture and science soon after the rise of Islam, while Scythian tribes of southeastern Europe stuck to their ancient ways; for both peoples were nomadic and shared a common climate and environment? Humboldt did find some cultural differences—greater contact of Arabs with surrounding urbanized cultures—for example. But, in the end, he labeled Arabs as a "more highly gifted race" with greater "natural adaptability for mental cultivation" (1849, p. 578).

Alfred Russel Wallace, codiscoverer of natural selection with Darwin, is justly hailed as an antiracist. Indeed, he did affirm near equality in the innate mental capacity of all peoples. Yet, curiously, this very belief led him to abandon natural selection and return to divine creation as an explanation for the human mind—much to Darwin's disgust.

From *Essay on the Inequality of Human Races*

Arthur de Gobineau

Gobineau's four-volume Essai sur l'inegalité des races humaines, *published between 1835 and 1855, became a bible for racists, influencing generations especially in Germany, into the twentieth century. It is a simpleminded book that asserts truths already under assault by science and common sense, but the unambiguous quality of his declarations had a wide appeal. There are three races, Gobineau asserted, at a time when even European head-measurers grappled with a confusing variety of human types. Each of the three—white, black, and yellow—is a pure race, each with its own characteristics. Civilizations decline and fall when the races are mixed. Race mixture dilutes pure bloodlines and leads to false doctrines of equality.*

Gobineau, born into a middle-class household, held a conviction that he was descended from nobility. (He styled himself Joseph Arthur Comte de Gobineau.) His vision of race shared the elements of his personal search for aristocracy. Like many aristocrats, real and imagined, in Europe in the middle of the nineteenth century, he feared the modern world of the middle-class and of immigrant labor. Who are the laborers, middle class, and aristocrats of Gobineau's world view of the races?

I have shown the unique place in the organic world occupied by the human species, the profound physical, as well as moral, differences separating it from all other kinds of living creatures. Considering it by itself, I have been able to distinguish, on physiological grounds alone, three great and clearly marked types, the black, the yellow, and the white. However uncertain the aims of physiology may be, however meager its resources, however defective its methods, it can proceed thus far with absolute certainty.

The negroid variety is the lowest, and stands at the foot of the ladder. The animal character, that appears in the shape of the pelvis, is stamped on the negro from birth, and foreshadows his destiny. His intellect will always move within a very narrow circle. He is not however a mere brute, for behind his low receding brow, in the middle of his skull, we can see signs of a powerful energy, however crude its objects. If his mental faculties are dull or even non-

---

Essai sur l'inegalité des races humaines, translated by Adrian Collins (New York: G.P. Putnam's Sons, 1915), pp. 205–210 [spelling Americanized].

existent, he often has an intensity of desire, and so of will, which may be called terrible. Many of his senses, especially taste and smell, are developed to an extent unknown to the other two races.

The very strength of his sensations is the most striking proof if his inferiority. All food is good in his eyes, nothing disgusts or repels him. What he desires is to eat, to eat furiously, and to excess; no carrion is too revolting to be swallowed by him. It is the same with odors; his inordinate desires are satisfied with all, however coarse or even horrible. To these qualities may be added an instability and capriciousness of feeling, that cannot be tied down to any single object, and which, so far as he is concerned, do away with all distinctions of good and evil. We might even say that the violence with which he pursues the object that has aroused his senses and inflamed his desires is a guarantee of the desires being soon satisfied and the object forgotten. Finally, he is equally careless of his own life and that of others: he kills willingly, for the sake of killing; and this human machine, in whom it is so easy to arouse emotion, shows, in face of suffering, either a monstrous indifference or a cowardice that seeks a voluntary refuge in death.

The yellow race is the exact opposite of this type. The skull points forward, not backward. The forehead is wide and bony, often high and projecting. The shape of the face is triangular, the nose and chin showing none of the coarse protuberances that mark the negro. There is further a general proneness to obesity, which, though not confined to the yellow type, is found there more frequently than in the others. The yellow man has little physical energy, and is inclined to apathy; he commits none of the strange excesses so common among negroes. His desires are feeble, his will-power rather obstinate than violent; his longing for material pleasures, though constant, is kept within bounds. A rare glutton by nature, he shows far more discrimination in his choice of food. He tends to mediocrity in everything; he understands easily enough anything not too deep or sublime. He has a love of utility and a respect for order, and knows the value of a certain amount of freedom. He is practical, in the narrowest sense of the word. He does not dream or theorize; he invents little, but can appreciate and take over what is useful to him. His whole desire is to live in the easiest and most comfortable way possible. The yellow races are thus clearly superior to the black. Every founder of a civilization would wish the backbone of his society, his middle class, to consist of such men. But no civilized society could be created by them; they could not supply its nerve-force, or set in motion the springs of beauty and action.

We come now to the white peoples. These are gifted with reflective energy, or rather with an energetic intelligence. They have a feeling for utility, but in a sense far wider and higher, more courageous and ideal, than the yellow races; a perseverance that takes account of obstacles and ultimately finds a means of overcoming them; a greater physical power, an extraordinary instinct for order, not merely as a guarantee of peace and tranquility, but as an indispensable means of self-preservation. At the same time, they have a remarkable, and even extreme, love of liberty, and are openly hostile to the formalism under which the Chinese are glad to vegetate, as well as to the strict despotism which is the only way of governing the negro.

The white races are, further, distinguished by an extraordinary attachment to life. They know better how to use it, and so, as it would seem, set a greater price on it; both in their own persons and those of others, they are more sparing of life. When they are cruel, they are conscious of their cruelty; it is very doubtful whether such a consciousness exists in the negro. At the same time, they have discovered reasons why they should surrender this busy life of theirs, that is so precious to them. The principal motive is honor, which under various names has played an enormous part in the ideas of the race from the beginning. I need hardly add that the word honor, together with all the civilizing influences connoted by it, is unknown to both the yellow and the black man. . . .

Such is the lesson of history. It shows us that all civilizations derive from the white race, that none can exist without its help, and that society is great and brilliant only so far as it preserves the blood of the noble group that created it, provided that this group itself belong to the most illustrious branch of our species.

The Internal Brand of the Scarlet "W"

Stephen Jay Gould

In this essay, Gould discusses one of the scientific strategies used in the United States in the 1920s to limit immigration (especially the immigration of Jews). Notice how a new scientific theory (in this case Mendel's "particulate" theory, replacing the idea of genes "blending") is enlisted in this anti-immigration campaign. How were scientists like Davenport involved in

With permission from *Natural History,* March 1998. Copyright the American Museum of Natural History 1998, pp. 23–25, 70–72.

this campaign? What role do you see in the backing and funding of impor-
tant families and institutions in the United States of the period? Was the
idea of a "nomadic race" racist?
     While Gould does not use the term "racism" in this article, he examines
the core of racist assumptions by revealing the effort and the absurdity of
linking physical features (in this case, genes or chromosomes) with complex
behavioral traits (like wanderlust). Do we still do this today? If so, why?

As a setting for an initial welcome to a new home, the international arrivals
hall at Kennedy Airport pales before the spaciousness, the open air, and the
symbol of fellowship in New York's harbor. But the plaque that greets airborne
immigrants of our time shares one feature with the great lady who graced the
arrival of so many seaborne ancestors, including all my grandparents in their
childhood. The plaque on Kennedy's wall and the pedestal of the Statue of
Liberty bear the same inscription: Emma Lazarus's poem "The New Colos-
sus"—but with one crucial difference. The airport version reads:

> Give me your tired, your poor,
> Your huddled masses yearning to breathe free . . .
> Send these, the homeless, tempest-tost to me:
> I lift my lamp beside the golden door.

One might be excused for supposing that the elision represents a large and
necessary omission to fit the essence of a longer poem onto a smallish plaque.
But only one line, easily accommodated, has been cut—and for a reason that
can only reflect thoughtless (as opposed to merely ugly) censorship, therefore
inviting a double indictment on independent charges of stupidity and cowardice. (As a member of the last public school generation trained by forced mem-
orization of a holy historical canon, including the Gettysburg Address, the
Preamble to the Constitution, Mr. Emerson on the rude bridge that arched the
flood, and Ms. Lazarus on the big lady with the lamp, I caught the deletion
right away and got sufficiently annoyed to write a *New York Times* Op-Ed
piece a couple of years ago. Obviously, I am still seething, but at least I now
have the perverse pleasure of using the story for my own benefit to introduce
this essay.) I therefore restore the missing line (along with Emma Lazarus's
rhyming scheme and syntax):

The wretched refuse of your teeming shore

Evidently, the transient wind of political correctness precludes such a phrase
as "wretched refuse," lest any visitor read the line too literally or personally.
Did the authorities at our Port Authority ever hear about metaphor and its

prominence in poetry? Did they ever consider that Lazarus might be describing the disdain of a foreign elite toward immigrants whom we would welcome, nurture, and value?

This story embodies a double irony that prompted my retelling. We hide Emma Lazarus's line today because we misread its true intention, and because contemporary culture has so confused (and often even equated) inappropriate words with ugly deeds. But the authorities of an earlier generation invoked the false and literal meaning—the identification of most immigrants as wretched refuse to accomplish a deletion of persons rather than words. That is, the supposed genetic inferiority of most refugees (an innate wretchedness that American opportunity could never overcome) became an effective rallying cry for a movement that did succeed in imposing strong restrictions on immigration beginning in the 1920s. These laws, strictly enforced despite pleas for timely exceptions, immured thousands of Europeans who sought asylum because Hitler's racial laws had marked them for death, while our quotas on immigration precluded any addition of their kind. These two stories of past exclusion and truncated present welcome surely illustrate the familiar historical dictum that significant events tend to repeat themselves—the first time as tragedy, the second as farce.

In 1925, Charles B. Davenport, one of America's foremost geneticists, wrote to his friend Madison Grant, the author of a best-selling book, *The Passing of the Great Race*, on the dilution of America's old (read northern European, not Native American) blood by recent immigration: "Our ancestors drove Baptists from Massachusetts Bay into Rhode Island, but we have no place to drive the Jews to." Davenport faced a dilemma. He sought a genetic argument for innate Jewish undesirability, but conventional stereotypes precluded the usual claim for inherent stupidity. So Davenport opted for weakness in moral character rather than intellect. In his 1911 book, *Heredity in Relation to Eugenics*—not, by the way, a political tract but his generation's leading textbook in the developing science of genetics—he wrote:

> In earning capacity both male and female Hebrew immigrants rank high and the literacy is above the mean of all immigrants. . . . On the other hand, they show the greatest proportion of offenses against chastity and in connection with prostitution, the lowest of crimes. . . . The hordes of Jews that are now coming to us from Russia and the extreme southeast of Europe, with their intense individualism and ideals of gain at the cost of any interest, represent the opposite extreme from the early English and the more recent Scandinavian immigration, with their ideals of community life in the open country, advancement by the sweat of the brow, and the uprearing of families in the fear of God and love of country.

The rediscovery and publication of Mendel's laws in 1900 had initiated the modern study of genetics. Earlier theories of heredity had envisaged a "blending" or smooth mixture and dilution of traits by interbreeding, whereas Mendelism featured a "particulate" theory of inheritance, with traits coded by discrete and unchanging genes that need not be expressed in all offspring independent and undiluted, but that remain in the hereditary constitution, awaiting expression in some future generation.

In an understandable initial enthusiasm for this great discovery, early geneticists committed their most common error in trying to identify single genes as causes for nearly every feature of the human organism, from discrete bits of anatomy to complex facets of personality. The search for single genetic determinants seemed reasonable for simple, discrete, and discontinuous characters and contrasts (like blue versus brown eyes). But the notion that complex behaviors might also emerge from a similar root in simple heredity of single genes never made much sense, for two major reasons: (1) a continuity in expression that precludes any easy definition of traits supposedly under analysis (I may know blue eyes when I see them, but where does a sanguine personality end and melancholia take over?); and (2) a virtual certainty that environments can substantially mold such characters, whatever their underlying genetic influence (my eyes may become blue whatever I eat, but my inherently good brain may end up residing in a stupid adult if poor nutrition starved my early growth and poverty denied me any education).

Nonetheless, most early human geneticists searched for "unit characters"—supposed traits that could be interpreted as the product of a single Mendelian factor—with abandon, even in complex, continuous, and environmentally labile features of personality or accomplishment in life. (These early analyses proceeded primarily by the tracing of pedigrees. I can envisage accurate data, and reliable results, for a family chart of eye color, but how could anyone trace the alleged gene for "optimism," "feeble inhibition," or "wanderlust"—not to mention such largely situational phenomena as "pauperism" or "communality." Was great-uncle George a jovial back-slapper or a reclusive cuss?)

Whatever the dubious validity of such overextended attempts to reduce complex human behaviors to effects of single genes, this strategy certainly served the aims and purposes of the early twentieth century's most influential social crusade with an allegedly scientific foundation: the eugenics movement, with its stated aim of "improving" America's hereditary stock by preventing procreation among the supposedly unfit (called "negative eugenics") and encouraging more breeding among those deemed superior in bloodline ("positive eugenics"). The abuses of this movement have been extensively documented in many excellent books covering such subjects as the hereditarian theory of mental testing and the passage of legislation for involuntary sterilization and restriction of immigration from nations deemed inferior in hereditary stock.

Many early geneticists played an active role in the eugenics movement, but none more zealously than the aforementioned Charles Benedict Davenport (1866–1944), who received a Ph.D. in zoology at Harvard in 1892, taught at the University of Chicago, and then became head of the Carnegie Institution's Station for Experimental Evolution at Cold Spring Harbor, New York, where he also established and directed the Eugenics Record Office, beginning in 1910. This office, with its mixed aims of supposedly scientific documentation and overt political advocacy, existed primarily to establish and compile detailed pedigrees in attempts to identify the hereditary basis of human traits. The hyper-enthusiastic Davenport secured funding from several of America's leading (and, in their own judgment, therefore eugenically blessed) families, particularly from Mrs. E. H. Harriman, the guardian angel and chief money-bags for the entire movement.

In his 1911 textbook, dedicated to Harriman "in recognition of the generous assistance she has given to research in eugenics," Davenport stressed the dependence of effective eugenics upon the new Mendelian "knowledge" that complex behavioral traits may be caused by single genes. Writing of the 5,000 immigrants who passed through Ellis Island every day, Davenport states:

> Every one of these peasants, each item of that "riff-raf" of Europe, as it is sometimes carelessly called, will, if fecund, play a role for better or worse in the future history of this nation. Formerly, when we believed that factors blend, a characteristic in the germ plasm of a single individual among thousands seemed not worth considering: it would soon be lost in the melting pot. But now we know that unit characters do not blend; that after a score of generations the given characteristic may still appear, unaffected by repeated unions. . . . So the individual, as the bearer of a potentially immortal germ plasm with innumerable traits, becomes of the greatest interest.

That is, of our "greatest interest" to exclude by restricting immigration, lest American heredity be overwhelmed with a deluge of permanent bad genes from the wretched refuse of foreign lands.

To illustrate Davenport's characteristic style of argument, and to exemplify his easy slippage between supposed scientific documentation and overt political advocacy, we may turn to his influential 1915 monograph entitled *The Feebly Inherited* (publication number 236 of his benefactor, the Carnegie Institution of Washington), especially to part 1 on "Nomadism, or The Wandering Impulse, With Special Reference to Heredity." The preface makes no bones about either sponsorship or intent. With three of America's wealthiest and most conservative families on board, one could hardly expect disinterested neutrality toward the full range of possible results. The Carnegies had endowed the general show, while Davenport paid homage to specific patrons: "The cost of training the field-workers was met by Mrs. E. H. Harriman, founder and principal patron of the Eugenics Record Office, and Mr. John D. Rockefeller, who paid also the salaries of many of the field-workers."

Davenport's preface also boldly admits his political position and purposes. He wishes to establish "feeble inhibition" as a category of temperament leading to inferior morality. Such a formulation will provide a one-two punch for identification of the eugenically unfit—bad intellect and bad morals. The genetic basis of stupidity had already been documented in numerous studies of the feebleminded. But eugenics now needed to codify the second reason for excluding immigrants and discouraging reproductive rights of the native unfit-bad moral character (as in Davenport's fallback position, documented earlier in this essay, for restricting Jewish immigration when he could not invoke the usual charge of intellectual inferiority). Davenport writes:

> A word may be said as to the term "feebly inhibited" used in these studies. It was selected as a fit term to stand as co-ordinate with "feeble-minded" and as the result of a conviction that the phenomena with which it deals should properly be considered apart from those of feeble-mindedness.

To allay any doubt about his motivations, Davenport then makes his political point: Feeble inhibition, leading to immorality, may be even more detrimental than feeblemindedness, leading to stupidity.

> I think it helps to consider separately the hereditary basis of the intellect and the emotions. It is in this conviction that these studies are submitted for thoughtful consideration. For, after all, the chief problem in administering society is that of disordered conduct, conduct is controlled by emotions, and the quality of the emotions is strongly tinged by the hereditary constitution.

Davenport then selects nomadism as his primary example of a putatively simple Mendelian trait—the product of a single gene—based on feeble inhibition and leading almost inevitably to immoral behavior. He encounters a problem of definition at the very outset of his work, as expressed in an opening sentence that must be ranked as one of the least profound statements in the entire history of science. "A tendency to wander in some degree is a normal characteristic of man, as indeed of most animals, in sharp contrast to most plants."

How, then, shall the "bad" form of wanderlust, defined as a compulsion to flee from responsibility, be distinguished from the meritorious sense of bravery and adventure—leading to "good" wanderlust—that motivated our early (largely northern European) immigrants to colonize and subdue the frontier. In his 1911 book, Davenport had warmly praised as "the enterprising restlessness of the early settlers . . . the ambitious search for better conditions. The abandoned farms of New England point to the trait in our blood that entices us to move on to reap a possible advantage elsewhere."

In a feeble attempt to put false labels on segments of complex continua, Davenport identified the "bad" form as "nomadism," defined as an inability to inhibit the urge we all occasionally feel to flee from our duties, but that decent folks suppress. Nomads are society's tramps, bums, hoboes, and gypsies— "those who, while capable of steady and effective work, at more or less regular periods run away from the place where their duties lie and travel considerable distances."

Having defined his quarry (albeit in a fatally subjective way), Davenport then required two further arguments to make his favored link of a "bad" trait to a single gene that eugenics might labor to breed down and out: he needed to prove the hereditary basis and then to find the "gene" for nomadism.

His arguments for a genetic basis must be judged as astonishingly weak, even by the standards of his generation. He simply argued, based on four dubious analogies, that features akin to nomadism emerge whenever situations veer toward "raw" nature (where genetics must rule) and away from environmental refinements of modern human society. Nomadism must be genetic because analogous features appear as "the wandering instinct in great apes," among "primitive peoples," in children (then regarded as akin to primitives under the false view that ontogeny recapitulates phylogeny), and in adolescents (in whom raw instinct temporarily overwhelms social inhibition in the Sturm und Drang of growing up). The argument about "primitive" people seems particularly weak since a propensity for wandering might be regarded as well suited to a lifestyle based on hunting mobile game, rather than identified as a mark of inadequate genetic constitution (or any kind of genetic constitution at all). But Davenport, reversing the probable route of cause and effect, would not be daunted:

If we regard the Fuegians, Australians, Bushmen and Hottentots as the most primitive men, then we may say that primitive man is nomadic. . . .

It is frequently assumed that they are nomadic because they hunt, but it
is more probable that their nomadic instincts force them to hunting rather
than agriculture for a livelihood.

Davenport then pursues his second claim—nomadism as the product of a
single gene—by tracing pedigrees stored in his Eugenics Record Office. On
the subjective criterion of impressions recorded by fieldworkers, or written
descriptions of amateur informants, Davenport marked all nomads in his table
with a scarlet *W* for *Wanderlust*, the common German term for an urge to
roam. He then examined the distribution of *W*s through families and generations to reach one of the most peculiar and improbable conclusions ever advanced in a famous study: nomadism, he argued, is caused by a single gene,
a sex-linked recessive located on what would later be identified as the female
chromosome.

Davenport reached this conclusion because he thought that nomadism ran
through family pedigrees in the same manner as hemophilia, color blindness,
and the other truly sex-linked recessive traits. This status can be legitimately
inferred from several definite patterns of heredity. For example, fathers with
the trait do not pass it to their sons (since the relevant gene resides on the X-
chromosome and males pass only a Y-chromosome on to their sons). Mothers
with the trait pass it to all their sons, but none of their daughters, when the
father lacks the trait. (Since the feature is recessive, an afflicted mother must
carry the gene on both X-chromosomes. She passes a single X to her son, who
must then express the trait, for he has no other X-chromosome. But a daughter
will receive one afflicted X-chromosome from her mother and one normal X-
chromosome from her father; she will therefore not express that trait because
the father's normal copy of the gene is dominant.) Davenport knew these rules,
so his study didn't fail on this account. Rather, his criteria for identifying
nomadism as a discrete and scorable "thing" were so subjective, and so biased
by his genetic assumptions, that his pedigree data turned out to be worthless.

Davenport's summary reached (and preached) a eugenic crescendo: "The
wandering instinct," he stated, "is a fundamental human instinct, which is,
however, typically inhibited in intelligent adults of civilized peoples." Unfortunately, people who possess the bad gene W (the scarlet letter of wanderlust)
cannot achieve this healthy inhibition, and they become feckless nomads who
run from responsibility by literal flight. The trait is genetic, racial, and unde-
sirable. Immigrants marked by W should be excluded (and many immigrants
must be shiftless wanderers rather than brave adventurers), while nomadic
natives should be strongly encouraged, if not compelled, to desist from breeding. Davenport concludes:

The new light brought by our studies is this: The nomadic impulse is, in all the cases, one and the same unit character. Nomads, of all kinds, have a special racial trait—are, in a proper sense, members of the nomadic race. This trait is the absence of the germinal determiner that makes for sedentariness, stability, domesticity.

Of course, no one would now defend Davenport's extreme view of single genes determining nearly every complex human behavior. Most colleagues eventually rejected Davenport's theory; he lived into the 1940s, long past the early flush of Mendelian enthusiasm and well into the modern era of understanding that complex traits usually record the operation of many genes, each with a small and cumulative effect (not to mention a strong, and often predominant, influence from nongenetic environmental contexts of growth and expression). A single gene for anger, conviviality, contemplation, or wanderlust now seems as absurd as a claim that one assassin's bullet, and nothing else, caused World War I, or that Darwin discovered evolution all by himself, and we would still be creationists if he had never been born.

Nonetheless, in our modern age of renewed propensity for genetic explanations (a valid and genuine enthusiasm when properly pursued), Davenport's general style of error resurfaces on an almost daily basis, albeit in much more subtle form, but with all the vigor of his putative old gene—yes, he did propose one—for stubbornly persistent behavior.

We are not questioning whether genes influence behavior; of course they do. We are not arguing that genetic explanations should be resisted because they have negative political, social, or ethical connotations—a charge that must be rejected for two primary reasons. First, nature's facts stand neutral before our ethical usages. We have, to be sure, often made dubious, even tragic, decisions based on false genetic claims. But, in other contexts, valid arguments about the innate and hereditary basis of human attributes can be profoundly liberating.

Consider only the burden lifted from loving parents who raise beautiful and promising children for twenty years and then "lose" them to the growing ravages of schizophrenia—almost surely a genetically based disease of the mind, just as many congenital diseases of bodily organs also appear in the third decade of life, or even later. Generations of psychologists had subtly blamed parents for unintentionally inducing such a condition, then viewed as entirely environmental in origin. What could be more cruel than a false weight of blame added to such an ultimate tragedy? Second, we will never get very far, either in our moral deliberations or our scientific inquiries, if we disregard genuine facts because we dislike their implications. In the most obvious case, I cannot think of a more unpleasant fact than the inevitable physical death of each human body, but a society built on the premise that King Prospero will reign in his personal flesh forever will not flourish for long.

However, if we often follow erroneous but deeply rooted habits of thinking to generate false conclusions about the role of heredity in human behavior, then these habits should be exposed and corrected—all the more vigorously if such arguments usually lead to recommendations for action that most people would also regard as ethically wrong (involuntary sterilization of the mentally retarded, for example). I believe that we face such a situation today and that the genetic fallacies underlying our misusages bear a striking similarity in style and logic to Davenport's errors, however much we have gained in subtlety of argument and factual accuracy.

Throughout the history of genetics, the most common political misuses have rested on claims for "biological determinism"—the argument that a given behavior or social situation can't be helped because people are "made that way" by their genes. Once we attribute something we don't like to genes, we tend either to make excuses or to make less effort for change. For example, many people still argue that we should deny educational benefits and social services to groups falsely judged as genetically inferior. Their poverty and misfortune lie in their own heredity, the argument goes, and therefore their condition cannot be significantly ameliorated by social intervention. Thus, history shows a consistent linkage between genetic claims in this mold and conservative political arguments for maintenance of an unjust status quo of great benefit to people currently in power.

Group Definition and the Idea of "Race" in Modern China (1793–1949)

Frank Dikotter

Western scientific racism and pseudo-scientific studies of race developed in the context of Western imperialism at the end of the nineteenth century. Before the nineteenth century, European travelers, administrators, and scholars expressed a good deal of respect for aspects of non-Western cultures, especially Indian and Chinese. But the widening technological gap between industrialized Europe and the colonial world at the end of the nineteenth century led Europeans to argue that their superiority was inborn, not merely learned, that Western dominance was racial rather than cultural. The assumption that the colonized people were incapable of learning European ways fit nicely with the refusal of the Europeans to encourage the educational or political aspirations of colonized people. Whatever the causes of "scientific racism," it became identified, even in the colonies, with the other products of European science and technology: the steam engine, railroads, machine guns, and the telegraph.

Thus, as Chinese scholars faced the agents of Western expansion in the wake of the opium war in the mid-nineteenth century, they borrowed Western "scientific" ideas of race along with the rest of Western science. Like earlier Europeans, earlier Chinese believed that important human differences were cultural rather than biological. But in the context of European expansion and increased colonial settlement and conflict, the fashionably modern racial ideas replaced traditional Confucian cultural categories. To what extent are the origins of Chinese racism distinctly Chinese, and to what extent are they a result of the Chinese encounter with the West? Is racism universal or was scientific racism a global export?

Precious little attention has been paid in Western historiography to racial ideas in non-Western countries. In the Chinese case, the idea of "race" (zhong, "seed," "species," "race") started to dominate the intellectual scene at the end of the nineteenth century and continued to be considered a vital problem by many intellectuals until the end of the 1940s. The emergence of a social cos-

From "Group Definition and the Idea of 'Race' in Modern China (1793–1949)," *Ethnic and Racial Studies*, 13, no. 3 (1990), pp. 420–31.

mology guided by a racial interpretation of foreign people represented a radical departure from the cultural universalism which characterized traditional China. This article examines the transition from cultural exclusiveness to racial exclusiveness in modern China. The transition started in the middle of the last century and was completed in the 1920s. Even a cursory survey of this historical development is of more than academic interest, as it contributes to a better understanding of how a quarter of mankind came to formulate its vision of the world.

Thought in ancient China was oriented towards the world, or *tianxia*, "all under heaven." The world was perceived as one homogeneous unity named "great community" (*datong*) The Middle Kingdom [China], dominated by the assumption of its cultural superiority, measured outgroups according to a yardstick by which those who did not follow the "Chinese ways" were considered "barbarians." A theory of "using the Chinese ways to transform the barbarian" was strongly advocated. It was believed that the barbarian could be culturally assimilated. In the Age of Great Peace, the barbarians would flow in and be transformed: the world would be one.

Western incursions from the end of the eighteenth century onward blatantly contradicted this traditional conceptual framework: Westerners were unwilling to pay homage to the Chinese court (the Macartney mission of 1793): they rejected the tribute system which had traditionally regulated contracts with barbarians; they refused to be culturally assimilated; and mysteriously, they failed to turn into Chinese.

The most dramatic consequence of this new historical development was that the sheer physical presence of Westerners in the beginning of the nineteenth century demonstrated the relativity of China's own world-view. Chinese literati increasingly discovered that the well-established symbolic universe in which they operated was neither total nor absolute. . . .

Absence of familiarity with physically dissimilar people contributed to the gradual appearance of a racial consciousness in China after the middle of the last century. Racial consciousness often first appears among those who had extended contact with a phenotypically different outgroup. The Canton area in particular and the coastal regions generally first developed a sense of racial identity that was to spread gradually to most of the country. Familiarity with outgroups led both to an increased relativization of the ingroup's cosmological position and to an increased specification of the ingroup's identity.

Intellectuals directly exposed to foreigners were vital in the activation of a racial consciousness. After the 1840s, scholar-officials involved in foreign affairs became increasingly aware of the need for a less Sino-centric perspective. Officials . . . compiled world geographies concerned with more practical valuations of the outside world. By a process of positive differentiation between themselves and other non-Western people, they enhanced their own identity. . . . Africans functioned as a negative identity for those who attempted to depart from the culturalistic assumptions of the traditional Chinese universe. Stereotypes and misperceptions largely facilitated the emergence of a racial identity, which was vital in the process of relativization and adaptation. . . .

The New Culture Movement (1915–1949) was characterized by a totalistic and iconoclastic attack on the traditional cultural heritage. Many new scholars, often educated in either Japan or the West, were determined to integrate foreign science and culture into the intellectual revolution of their country. The invited the youth to part with the stagnant elements of traditional culture and to accept foreign democracy, science and culture as the founding elements of a new order.

Spurred by this intellectual revolution, the idea of race made rapid progress, infiltrating most domains of intellectual activity. The successive attacks unleashed against the traditional heritage since the middle of the nineteenth century had dramatically undermined the bases of a well-established collective identity and had led to the artificial separation of race and culture. Racial exclusiveness was the warrant for successful cultural iconoclasm. With the New Culture Movement, Western social sciences became an instrument to debunk the traditional culture and to boost racial identity. Science and age-old stereotypes constantly intermingled to accommodate ethnocentric feelings of biological exclusiveness.

The concept of the evolution of species led to the idea of original purity. Vision of a pure and vibrant race were projected into an idealized past to compensate for the nation's degraded position in the new world order created by the West. Science and myth wove a fabric on which the frustrated mind could visualize its fantasies. . . .

The transition from cultural universalism to racial nationalism took place in an age dominated by Western racial theories. . . .

Doubts about the biological foundations of the race led to the flourishing of eugenics, the pseudo-science of race improvement. The pressure of the superiority-inferiority complex felt by many educated Chinese was relieved by dichotomization: intellectuals were designated as the superior elements of the race, whereas the lower classes were branded inferior. . . .

It was only after 1949 that the concepts of race and class would merge, giving the country a new sense of identity. Racial discrimination was expressly forbidden by the Chinese Communist Party after 1949. Widespread propaganda under the supervision of reformed anthropologists attempted to rectify racial thinking; it also fostered the idea that only Westerners could indulge in "racism," as the Chinese were now the leader of the victimized coloured people in the historical struggle against white "imperialism." . . . During the Sino-

Soviet rift, race made an official reappearance when the Communist party increasingly harped on the theme of biological differences between Soviets and Chinese. With the gradual rapprochement of the two superpowers nowadays, the idea of racial identity could prove to be dangerously tempting in an isolated China.

Part 8

Imperialism and Settler Racism

Racial stereotypes of various groups in America abound in this late nineteenth century political cartoon on who has the power and right to control and own the land. (*McGee's Illustrated Weekly, March 6, 1880*)

The period between 1880 and 1940 was the high water mark of European imperialism. Political leaders who had convinced themselves and their nations that overseas colonies were too expensive and unnecessary as recently as the early 1870s, changed their minds with the economic contraction that began in 1873 and leaped over each other to create an empire in Africa after 1880. The "scramble for Africa" that carved up the entire continent between 1880 and 1914 was echoed less dramatically in Asia, where the French took Indo-China, the United States seized the Philippines and Hawaii, and both joined England, Germany, and Japan in winning territories and trading concessions in China.

This period was also the high point of Western racism. Leading the way was a movement that since has been called "scientific racism," a movement that began before 1850 with the skull measurers and abstract classifiers, but became more serious and insidious after Darwin. Post-Darwinian biologists accepted the extinction of peoples (like the Tasmanians) as a fact of evolutionary development. Anthropologists lumped the people of the colonies into "savages" and "barbarians," saving the more advanced state of "civilization" for themselves. A spate of scholarly studies distinguished between "how natives think" or "the mind of primitive man" (illogical, emotional, like children) and the superior, rational, intelligence of scientific, civilized mankind. Colonial administrators took their cue to reduce the scientific and literary education of colonials, switching to more practical skills. Inferior education in the colonies confirmed studies designed to prove that Asians and Africans were not as intelligent as Europeans.

In the Americas, the period between 1880 and 1920 was the great age of immigration. In the United States, immigrants from southern and eastern Europe (especially Italians and Jews) replaced earlier waves of immigrants from northwestern Europe. Racist alarms were raised against both Italians and Jews. In New Orleans, in 1891, eleven Italians were lynched by a mob as the major local newspapers and business leaders looked on in approval. Jews were threatened and stoned as anti-Semitic demonstrations came to the United States in the late 1880s, reaching a peak in 1893. Italian immigrants received a much more welcome reception in Brazil and Argentina, where more Italians had already emigrated in the previous decades and achieved considerable success economically and politically. In Brazil, after the abolition of slavery in 1887, the coffee planters of São Paulo actively recruited workers in Italy, partly so they would not have to employ the blacks of the Brazilian northeast.

In the great age of immigration, old immigrants like the Irish "became white" (Ignatiev 1995) while the new immigrants took their place. "You don't call an Italian a white man?" a construction boss was asked. "No sir," he replied, "an Italian is a Dago" (Higham 1978, 66). Asian immigration slowed with the passage of the Chinese exclusion act in 1882, but the Chinese and

Indians and other "orientals" (as you will see in the excerpt from *Burmese Days*) were typically thought of as "black," regardless of their appearance, and were lumped together with Africans at the bottom of a racist hierarchy.

For African Americans, emancipation from slavery did not mean equal citizenship or opportunity with whites. Physical segregation by race was actually a product of post-slavery society, developing in the South after 1877 and throughout the United States after 1890 (Woodward 1974) as was the rise of the Ku Klux Klan, and lynching.

References

Higham, John. 1978. *Strangers in the Land: Patterns of American Nativism 1860–1925*. New York: Atheneum.
Ignatiev, Noel. 1995. *How the Irish Became White*. New York: Routledge.
Woodward, C. Vann. 1974. *The Strange Career of Jim Crow*. New York: Oxford University Press.

Racism in the United States and South Africa

Kevin Reilly

The United States and South Africa were products of the first wave of European expansion and settlement that lasted from 1500 to 1800. This essay compares the evolution of the United States and South Africa from those early days of colonial status through the period of the "new imperialism." Compare the American frontiersmen with the Afrikaners. In what ways were these frontier people like the bandeirantes of Brazil? Were European governments in the eighteenth century restraints on colonial racism? Was colonial independence a setback for racial justice? Did nationalist movements in colonial countries unite only white people, or even unite whites against blacks? Can a society overcome both racial and class tensions, or is one achieved at the cost of the other? What do you think of the distinction between dominative and aversive racism? Has racism declined since 1940, or has it merely changed?

It is particularly ironic that racial barriers were constructed in the United States and South Africa at the very time that class differences were increasing—during the period of rapid industrialization between 1870 and 1914. Normally the process of capitalist industrialization creates social classes: workers and employers; skilled and unskilled; manufacturers and miners; industrial and service personnel; rich and poor. Normally capitalist industrialization erases all inequalities except class: it makes money, wages, income, and property more important than race, gender, nationality, religion, or background. While such changes occurred among most white workers in the United States and South Africa, the presence of black Africans (or African-Americans) altered that process for whites as well as blacks. Racial identity was often more important than class identity. People often thought of themselves (and others) as members of a race, rather than as representatives of a particular social class, income group, religion, or even gender. The white boss (a redundancy in itself) saw the African first as a black, then as an individual who happened to be Christian, poor, or male.

The purpose of this [essay] is to try to understand why this happened in the United States and South Africa. A comparison of these two bastions of white supremacy helps us to understand both the causes and the direction of change in the two countries.

South Africa and North America: Colonies and Conquest

There are striking parallels in the early history of race relations in North America and South Africa. Both areas were settled by Europeans in the seventeenth century. In each case there was an initial confrontation with indigenous inhabitants—the Native Americans of North America and the Khoikhoi (or Khoisan) of South Africa. In North America the land was taken for European settlement, and the Native Americans were virtually annihilated. In South Africa the Khoikhoi surrendered both their land and their labor to the Europeans.

The process of European conquest was slower in South Africa than in North America. The South African settlement at the Cape of Good Hope was originally intended by the East India Company of Holland to be a supply station for the Dutch ships en route to the East Indies. The company initially discouraged settlement beyond Cape Town, feeling that a larger colony would be too difficult to govern. The Khoikhoi were pastoralists who provided the Europeans with cattle, but as the European colony grew, its demand for meat outstripped Khoikhoi ambitions or intentions. The area of white occupation increased tenfold between 1703 and 1780 as former company employees seized Khoikhoi land for their own farms and pastures. Those Khoikhoi who were not killed by war or smallpox epidemics (as the Native Americans were) be-came the herders and wagon drivers for the new Dutch masters (called Boers).

Thus, in one important respect the racial situation in South Africa was dif-ferent from that of North America around 1770. While most coastal American Indians had been annihilated, sent to the West Indies as slaves, or pushed beyond the Appalachians, the survivors among the original Khoikhoi inhabi-tants of the Cape region of South Africa became a class of subordinate servants.

Initially neither North American nor South African colonists justified their dominance in racial terms. Rather, they justified European settlement econom-ically. The North American colonists drew on Lockeian theories of labor and private property to assert that agricultural work was more desirable than hunt-ing because agriculture involved the addition of one's own labor to nature. Thus, according to this rationale, Europeans were improving the land, while Native Americans were only draining it. This rationale ignored the fact that Native Americans were also agriculturalists and concentrated on their more marginal hunting and gathering activities. In the case of South Africa both the Boers and the Khoikhoi were pastoralists, so the Boers could not argue that their use of the land was more worthy. Instead, the Boers argued that by taking Khoikhoi land they were spreading Christian civilization, a claim that became louder (if not more accurate) with the passage of time. These economic and religious justifications suggest the absence of racist feelings in the early stages of colonization. Indeed, the Native Americans were called noble savages and portrayed as bronzed Europeans. Intermarriage between Boers and Khoikhoi was not uncommon, and Khoikhoi did not experience racial discrimination.

British, Boer, and Bantu: Redcoats, Rebels, and Redskins

Settler movement beyond the initial frontiers occurred in both North America and South Africa around 1770. In both cases the government had hoped to keep the Europeans and indigenous peoples apart. In North America, when the British defeated the French in the French and Indian War in 1763, the British issued the Proclamation of 1763, which prohibited European settlement beyond the Appalachian Mountains. In South Africa the Dutch East India Company had originally attempted to keep the Europeans in Cape Town. When that effort failed, they attempted to restrict Europeans' movement to the area bounded by the Great Fish River. By then Boer and Khoikhoi mixed as masters and ser-vants. There were, however, different, less Westernized Africans beyond the Great Fish River that the Dutch (and after 1795 their successors, the British

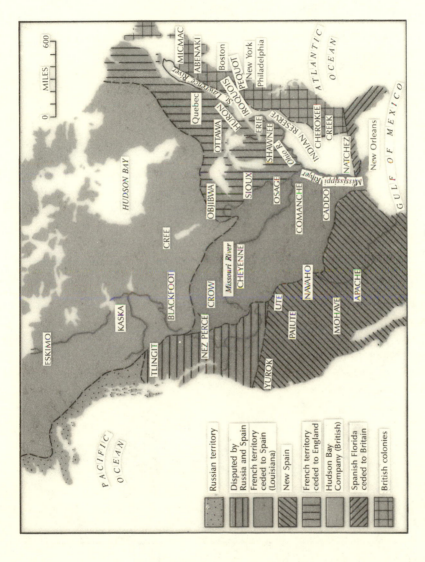

North America in 1763 after the Seven Years War. (*Kevin Reilly*)

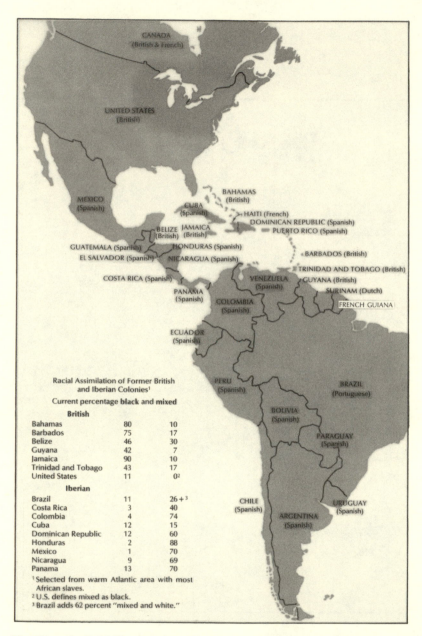

Racial Assimilation of Former British and Iberian Colonies[1]

Current percentage **black and mixed**

British		
Bahamas	80	10
Barbados	75	17
Belize	46	30
Guyana	42	7
Jamaica	90	10
Trinidad and Tobago	43	17
United States	11	0[2]

Iberian		
Brazil	11	26 + [3]
Costa Rica	3	40
Colombia	4	74
Cuba	12	15
Dominican Republic	12	60
Honduras	2	88
Mexico	1	70
Nicaragua	9	69
Panama	13	70

[1] Selected from warm Atlantic area with most African slaves.
[2] U.S. defines mixed as black.
[3] Brazil adds 62 percent "mixed and white."

The "Bronzing" Of The Americas. The Mexican idea of the "bronzing" of the Americas is much closer to reality in those countries that were colonized by the Iberians (Spanish and Portuguese) than in former British colonies. *(Kevin Reilly)* government) wanted to keep separate. These were the Bantu peoples (generally taller, darker-skinned Africans who had migrated south from the Sudan for over a thousand years). The Bantu peoples constituted many nations. In 1800 the Zulu, Swazi, and Basuto emerged as the strongest in southeastern Africa beyond the Great Fish River.

The Bantu peoples were a more formidable barrier to European migration than either the Khoikhoi or the Native Americans. The Bantu were far more numerous. Further, since the great Bantu migration had originated on the southern edge of European settlement and trade in Sudanic Africa, these peoples had already developed immunities to European diseases (which devastated the Native Americans).

The American white settler economy was also more expansive than the Boer South African. While the American economy provided important shipping supplies for the enormously productive West Indian sugar plantations of the British empire, the Cape Colony of South Africa remained essentially a subsistence pastoral economy and a food supplier for passing ships until the discovery of gold and diamonds at the end of the nineteenth century. The American settlers were therefore more powerful politically than their Boer counterparts. While there were sporadic Boer rebellions against Dutch (and later British) control of the frontier, there was nothing approaching an American Revolution in South Africa. In the end, the American settlers were successful in displacing the Native Americans because of the American Revolution. Thomas Jefferson and other early presidents insisted on protecting the Native Americans by incorporating them into American civilization. But by the 1828 election of Andrew Jackson, a veteran Native American fighter, the policy of the federal government was to remove the Native Americans in order to make way for white settlement. Even Native American nations that had attempted to adopt the ways of the white society were unceremoniously forced to move; the Cherokee, for example, were sent on a forced march to Oklahoma that was so brutal that four thousand out of fifteen thousand died along the way.

The Boers, unable to convince the Dutch before 1795 of their expansionist needs, became greatly suspicious of the British administration that took over after 1795. In the frontier conflicts with the neighboring Xhosa and Bantu peoples, the Boers believed that the British government was on the side of the Africans. In the period of the 1820s to 1850s many Boers took matters into their own hands in a different way than did the North American revolutionaries. They left British protection entirely by driving their wagons, families, cattle, and Khoikhoi herders beyond the Great Fish River and north to the high plains (or Meld) outside the colony. This migration became the national epic of the Boers, the equivalent of the American War of Independence. But the story of the Great Trek also resembles the later North American stories of war with the Native Americans: wagon trains in a circle to fend off attacks; crossing deserts and mountains with only Bibles, muskets, and determination; establishing "free" and independent states that depended on the expulsion of the original inhabitants.

Race and Slavery

We have said nothing so far of slavery. There was, of course, slavery in both North America and South Africa, but neither the Native Americans nor the South African Khoikhoi became slaves in great numbers. Even most of the South African Bantu remained outside the system of slavery. The Khoikhoi were indentured servants, as were many Europeans who came to America in the colonial period. The Bantu (like the Native Americans) could not be easily captured, enslaved, and assimilated. The slaves of South Africa were the mixed group of Asian and African peoples that South Africans bought from slave markets or imported from other Dutch colonies (especially Indonesia). Since these slaves were not drawn from a particular racial or ethnic group, slavery was not identified with race. Thus, slavery in South Africa actually had little to do with South African racial ideas.

If South African slavery was less racially specific than North American, it was also more widespread. There were more slaves, and more white slave owners. Slave ownership was more "democratic" (if such a word can be used): in 1750 half the whites in South Africa owned slaves, a higher percentage even than in Southern colonies of British America. Further, most South African slave owners owned only a few slaves. This was because South African slavery was not plantation slavery. There were no large estates equivalent to the sugar, coffee, and cotton plantations of the Americas. South African slaves worked in smaller units on farms, on the range, and in the city, usually under a single, extended family. They worked alongside Khoikhoi servants and employees— that is, among dependent workers of varying races and obligations.

Thus, ironically, though slavery was more widespread in South Africa than it was in the United States, white South African society was less dependent on it. Slavery was just one of the many systems of dependent labor in South Africa. For that reason the British abolition of slavery between 1834 and 1838 met with less diehard resistance than the abolitionist movement in the Southern United States. South African whites had become accustomed to having their menial work done by nonwhites, but slavery was not the only way of accomplishing that. While the plantation owners of the American South went to war to preserve slavery, some Boers turned to other methods of labor control. Others took their slaves, families, and herds on the Great Trek out of the country.

The American Civil War

There are historians who will tell you that slavery was not the main cause of the Civil War in America. They will tell you that the South seceded from the Union in order to preserve states' rights, not slavery. They will say that Lincoln went to war to preserve the Union, not to end slavery. And they will say that most Northerners did not want to fight a war to force the South to abolish slavery.

It is possible that a majority of white Southerners thought they were fighting a war of independence and principle. It is also possible that a majority of Northerners were against freeing the slaves when the war broke out in 1860. But majorities, like individuals, often delude themselves or get lost in the rush of events.

What does seem indisputable is that there were two social systems inhabiting the body politic of the United States in 1860, and those two systems had become increasingly incompatible. Whether we call those systems "free" and "slave," as Lincoln did, or "competitive" and "paternal," as Southern slave-holders did, the difference in labor systems was the point of conflict for the powerful in the North and the South. The expanding industry of the North depended on a wage labor system, and the Southern plantation depended on slavery. As both groups eyed the new territories in Texas and the West, these contrary systems, each of which seemed exclude the other, offered more than economic competition. As the conflict intensified, each system came to stand for a way of life. Slavery meant agriculture, Southern gentility, honor, the traditions and values of past generations of planters. Wage labor meant free labor, free land, free men, opportunity, progress, and industry. And as these worldviews diverged and hardened, the future states of the American West represented the political battleground in which the national government would be won or lost. Lincoln's election victory in 1860 signaled the ultimate loss of that battleground, the government of the Union, for Southern planters. It seemed to them the defeat of their class and their way of life—if they remained to accept it.

It might have been possible for a slave system and a capitalist wage labor system to exist side by side indefinitely. The growth of capitalism in the North (and in England) owed much to the slave labor of the cotton plantations in the South. The initial stages of capitalist industrialization depended on cotton and slavery. In many ways the plantation owners of the South even operated like capitalists. "A great plantation was as difficult to operate as a complicated modern factory, which in important respects it resembled. Hit-or-miss methods could not be tolerated, endless planning and anxious care were demanded."[1]

Different economies, even class systems, might have remained compatible. The cultures, values, ideals, and ideas that those social systems engendered proved less open to compromise. The war of nerves that preceded the war of armies was waged with words. As tensions increased, Northern publicists and politicians became more indignant about slavery, and Southern planters revived older visions of agricultural harmony, natural order, and civilized grace, which they contrasted with the money-grubbing ways of the North. Some Southerners saw Northern moralistic rhetoric as a program to abolish Southern property. To understand Southern fears today, one might imagine the reaction of modern Americans to a Soviet-controlled Canada's sending spies and agitators, growing stronger economically than the United States, and threatening to nationalize all corporations in order to "free" the workers.

The Civil War was a radical revolution. Charles Beard, the great American historian, called it "the Second American Revolution." In some ways the Civil War was even more radical than the "first" American Revolution. The Revolution of 1776 has often been called a "conservative revolution" because it transferred power from an English ruling class to a colonial ruling class. The Civil War enshrined the conviction of the Revolution that "all men are created equal." It took seriously the radically democratic message of the middle-class capitalist revolution. It drew on the resources of the most egalitarian elements of capitalism. Not coincidentally was a Midwestern lawyer the candidate of the new Republican party in 1860. Lincoln spoke for frontiersmen who had become successful farmers. By the 1850s they had created a third America, as agricultural as the South but without slavery. Instead of siding with the South, the new West found its allies in the more radical spokesmen of the Northeast.

The union of frontier farmer and Northern capitalist did not, however, last much beyond the war. Only a few of its statesmen were willing to unseat the ruling elite of the South once they had been defeated. Fewer still were willing to break up the old plantations and distribute the land to the former slaves so that they might become independent farmers themselves. A small band of radical Republicans (that did not include Lincoln) saw slavery as a remnant of a dying world of feudalism and sought to "reconstruct" the South according to the Northern principles of "free speech, free toil, schoolhouses, and ballot boxes." Thaddeus Stevens, their most eloquent spokesman, proposed that the large plantations be confiscated to provide forty acres for each former slave family, a measure that had been carried out on a smaller scale by the Union army in the last year of the war. Horace Greeley, editor of the *New York Tribune* and a former abolitionist, spoke for many when he answered Stevens's bill: he objected to what he saw as warfare on Southern property; he praised the wealthier class of Southerners as enlightened and humane; and he warned against social upheaval. A radical revolution, even a democratic capitalist one, was not to endure.

Still, the accomplishments of the era of Reconstruction (1865–1877) were considerable. The Thirteenth Amendment to the Constitution freed the slaves in 1865. The Fourteenth Amendment gave the freedmen citizenship and civil rights by 1868. The Fifteenth Amendment provided black men the vote by 1870. Civil rights legislation and the radical wing of the Republican party guaranteed blacks full political participation. There was, however, no social revolution for the former slaves. The plantations were not divided to give freed slaves "forty acres and a mule." Without land or capital, former slaves became tenant farmers and sharecroppers who had to mortgage their futures for seed.

The reason that Stevens's bill failed in Congress and no other attempt was made at land redistribution for the former slaves was that there was simply no consensus, even in the North, for fully integrating the former slaves into American society as equals. There were other drawbacks, to be sure. The confiscation of Southern land struck fear into the hearts of others besides Horace Greeley. There was also a long-standing belief in Anglo-American political thought, going back to John Locke, that legal equality and the ballot box were all anyone needed to compete on life's playing field and that government should provide nothing more. However, since Northern businessmen were persuading the government to give them tariffs, a strong central banking system, railroads, and a huge chunk of federal land, we cannot take such principles too seriously. The more important reason Congress rejected the bill seems to be a general unwillingness to integrate independent blacks into American society.

Dominative Versus Aversive Racism

In a book called *White Racism: A Psychohistory*, Joel Kovel suggests a distinction between two kinds of racism, which he calls dominative and aversive. Dominative racism, he says, is the racism of slave society. Domination is legal and accepted. Slaves know their place, even if they resent it. In some cases the domination is so complete that it goes unquestioned, thus allowing whites to view the slaves as good-humored children grateful for their protection. In these cases bonds of loyalty and affection can develop between masters and slaves, who pretend to ignore the reality of domination because it is so complete, legal, and unquestioned. Then, when breaches occur, they are punished with the most severe brutality, almost as if a sacred trust has been violated, and the very inequality of the relationship is revealed.

The vice president of the Confederacy, Alexander Stephens, sounded the tune of dominative racism in 1861:

> Many governments have been founded on the principles of subordination and serfdom of certain classes of the same race; Such were, and are, in

violation of the laws of nature. Our system commits no such violation of nature's laws. With us, all the white race, however high or low, rich or poor, are equal in the eyes of the law. Not so with the Negro. Subordination is his place. He, by nature, or by the curse against Canaan, is fitted for that condition which he occupies in our system. . . . Its foundations are laid, its "cornerstone" rests upon the great truth that the Negro is not equal to the white man, that slavery—subordination to the superior race—is his natural or normal condition.[2]

Aversive racism is different from dominative racism, according to Kovel. Aversive racism is the racism that existed in the North before the Civil War and became the American attitude, North and South, after the war. The aversive racist accepts the notion of legal equality, at least reluctantly. Unable to achieve "legal distance," he or she seeks "physical distance" from blacks. The aversive racist has an aversion to blacks and attempts to turn away and avoid them. This is the racism of segregation, legal and "voluntary." It is the racism of those who wish the blacks would "just go away." As a psychological state of avoidance it is more difficult to confront than dominative racism. The aversive racist can also turn away from the recognition that his or her own behavior is racist. It is part of the avoidance to insist that "I'm not racist, but . . ."

Not everyone in the North was an aversive racist, but many of those who were antislavery were also antiblack and hoped to get rid of blacks as well as slavery. Many Republicans, including Lincoln, answered charges by their opponents in the election of 1860 that they were in favor of racial equality and amalgamation by declaring their support of plans to deport the black population. Indeed, the colonization of Liberia in Africa was supported by Northern abolitionists as well as Southerners.

It was racial segregation, however, that was the core practice of aversive racism, just as slavery was the core of dominative racism. And it is racial segregation that unites South African and United States history, because both societies made an important investment in racial segregation in the twentieth century. We might date the reign of racial segregation in the United States from the Supreme Court decision of *Plessy v. Ferguson* in 1896 to that of *Brown v. Board of Education* in 1954, although it began earlier and has continued in residential and other "voluntary" forms since. In South Africa we may date segregation from shortly after the founding of the Union of South Africa in 1910 to the present.

South Africa, 1834–1910

We have already seen that there was no South African equivalent of the Civil War. When slavery was abolished by the British government in 1834, the

Boers had already developed alternative forms of forced labor. The end of slavery did not mean the end of cheap black labor, and so it could be tolerated. What was more galling to the Boers was the British insistence that blacks and whites be treated equally before the law. British humanitarianism they could not stomach. And so, while they did not go to war, some ten thousand Boers between 1836 and 1846 walked away from British authority in their Great Trek. The Boer governments of the Orange Free State (after 1848) and the Transvaal, or (officially) South African Republic (after 1880), were sufficiently independent of British authority that we must speak of a number of South Africas before the Union of 1910.

The Boer republics received British recognition on the condition that they not revive slavery. They complied in word only, replenishing their stock of "apprentices" with "orphans" captured in Bantu wars. Their constitutions were unabashedly white supremacist. One declared there would be "no equality between colored people and the white inhabitants of the country." Another barred political participation to anyone of mixed race "down to the tenth degree."

The British colonies, on the other hand, professed racial equality while allowing discrimination. The British government of Natal declared "there shall not be in the eye of law any distinction of color, origin, race, or creed; but the protection of the law, in letter and substance, shall be extended impartially to all alike."[3] It proceeded to exclude the majority Zulus and other Africans from any citizenship by beginning the process of ruling them in separate "homelands." Only in the Cape Colony were Africans theoretically allowed to vote, and there a property qualification limited the suffrage to a token few. While whites and blacks were presumed to be equal before the law, the Cape Colony passed a series of "Masters and Servant" laws, which dictated strict control and punishment of unruly "servants," all of whom, of course, were black.

A union of such divergent societies and racial policies seemed unlikely at mid-century. There could be no South African civil war because there was no South African Union. The establishment of Boer republics and African homelands was a process of fragmentation rather than unification. Two events changed all that. One was the discovery of diamonds in 1867. The other was the discovery of gold in 1884. Both discoveries in Boer republics required African labor and British capital. They provided an industrial base that required a far more extensive transportation and communication network than the rural and landlocked Boer republics could build on their own. Gold and diamonds created a unified South Africa by 1910.

The "Union" of South Africa that was created was a union of whites: British and Boers. The Africans paid the bill for the new white harmony. The Boer model of racial policy, not that of the British colonies, became the national model for the Union, despite the fact that British arms had imposed unity in the Boer War (1899–1902). One might say that the British won the war but gave away the peace. But that is not quite accurate. By 1902 the British were not as concerned about racial equality as they had been in the 1830s. By accepting Boer racism they were not giving up very much.

That judgment might be more true of the defeat of radical reconstruction in the Northern United States. The North, which won the Civil War in 1865, gave away the peace in 1877. In the United States, as in South Africa, a peace was made between white ruling classes that excluded blacks. In the United States in 1877 and in South Africa in 1910, national unions were forged for whites only. There lie the origins of racial segregation and subordination in each.

From Reconstruction to Segregation: Uniting the States, 1877–1914

The disputed presidential election of 1876, in which Rutherford B. Hayes ran against Samuel Tilden, provided an opportunity for the conservative white South to regroup to aid the conservative Republicans of the North. They elected Republican Hayes, and he pledged his presidency to undo the work of the radical wing his own party and to return the South to the whites. Federal troops were withdrawn from the South, and the federal government looked the other way as one Southern state after another began to restrict the civil rights of blacks.

Segregation, the hallmark of aversive racism, began in the North before the Civil War, but it was made into a system of race relations in the 1870s. This occurred in the South in new cities, such as Birmingham, not in the older plantation-area cities, such as New Orleans. Until the 1890s, "social contact between the races resisted, particularly at New Orleans, in a variety of sports, on the beaches of Lake Pontchartrain, and in some churches and bars," writes C. Vann Woodward.

> One source of leadership and strength that Louisiana Negroes enjoyed and that blacks of no other state shared was a well-established upper class of mixed racial origin in New Orleans with a strong infusion of French and other Latin intermixtures. Among the people were descendants of the "Free People of Color," some of them men of culture, education, and wealth, often with a heritage of several generations of freedom. Unlike the great majority of Negroes, they were city people with an established professional class and a high degree of literacy. Their views found expression in at least four Negro newspapers that existed simultaneously in New Orleans in the 1880s. By ancestry as well as by residence, they were associated with Latin cultures that were in some

ways at variance with Anglo-American ideas of race relations. Their forebears had lived under the Code Noir decreed for Louisiana by Louis XIV, and their city faced out upon Latin America. This group had taken the lead in fighting for Negro rights during Reconstruction and were in a natural position to resist the tide of legal segregation. When it touched their shores they were the first to speak out.[4]

But touch their shores it did. On 10 July 1890, a bill requiring separate railroad for blacks passed the Louisiana state legislature, despite the work of militant leaders and eighteen black members of the state legislature (as well as the railroad, which regarded segregation as an added expense). The opposition organized to challenge the constitutionality of the law under the Fourteenth Amendment. Homer Adolph Plessy, a black, bought a ticket in New Orleans and sat in the car reserved for whites. He was arrested and convicted before Judge John H. Ferguson of the Criminal District Court of the Parish of New Orleans. The case *Plessy v. Ferguson* came to the U.S. Supreme Court. "Justice is pictured blind; her daughter, the Law, ought at least to be color-blind," Plessy's attorney, Albion Tourgee, argued. "Why not require all colored people to walk on one side street and the white on the other?" he asked scornfully.[5]

With the Supreme Court's decision on *Plessy v. Ferguson*, in May 1896, Tourgee's taunt became a reality. White segregationists cheered the decision of Justice Henry Billings Brown for the majority that "separate but equal" facilities were constitutional. By 1900 all Southern states had separate railway cars, and segregation was spreading to stations, streetcars, public parks, hospitals, and prisons. Some towns prohibited blacks altogether. Many cities imposed compulsory residential segregation. North Carolina and Florida required white and black students to use different textbooks in the public schools. New Orleans even created separate districts for white and black prostitutes.

Segregation measures were sometimes executed with platitudes of enlightened liberalism. President Woodrow Wilson stated in 1912 that he wished to see "justice done to the colored people in every matter; and not mere grudging justice, but justice executed with liberality and cordial good feeling."[6] Then he proceeded to segregate the eating and toilet facilities of federal civil service workers.

Blacks were systematically disenfranchised as well in the decades after *Plessy*. Poll taxes, "general understanding" tests, "good character" tests were among the obstacles used to prevent blacks from voting. In 1896 there were over 130,000 registered black voters in Louisiana. By 1904 there were fewer than 1,350.[7]

Frenzied racist propaganda led to "white supremacy elections," in which white mobs attacked and destroyed black neighborhoods and engaged in wide-spread lynching and looting. Between 1890 and 1920 four thousand blacks were put to death without trial. The brutal violence of dominative racism did not disappear in the age of aversive racism. Intimidation and separation, domination and aversion, were often employed together by whites concerned with "keeping blacks in their place."

Blacks too learned the survival skills of a white supremacist society. "Just the other day my Laura started getting sassy about white children," one black mother told an interviewer much later:

> My husband told her to hold her tongue and do it fast. It's like with cars and knives, you have to teach your children to know what's dangerous and how to stay away from it, or else they sure won't live long. White people are a real danger to us until we learn how to live with them. So if you want your kids to live long, they have to grow up scared of whites; and the way they get scared is through us; and that's why I don't let my kids get fresh about the white man even in their own house. If I do there's liable to be trouble to pay. They'll forget, and they'll say something outside, and that'll be it for them, and us too. So I make them store it in the bones, way inside, and then no one sees it. Maybe in a joke we'll have once in a while, or something like that, you can see what we feel inside, but mostly it's buried. But to answer your question, I don't think it's only from you it gets buried. The colored man, I think he has to hide what he really feels even from himself. Otherwise there would be too much pain—too much.[8]

Booker T. Washington expressed that attitude for many American blacks in the generation after the Civil War. Born a slave on a Virginia plantation in 1859, he worked his way to become head of a new college for blacks, the Tuskegee Institute of Alabama in 1881. Convinced that Southern whites would not accept education for blacks if it challenged white supremacy, Washington dismissed academic education as dangerous. Instead he urged vocational training and imbued his students with conservative values. He wrote in his 1901 autobiography, *Up from Slavery*:

> We wanted to teach the students how to bathe, how to care for their teeth and clothing. We wanted to teach them what to eat, and how to eat it properly, and how to care for their rooms. Aside from this, we wanted to give them such a practical knowledge of some one industry, together with the spirit of industry, thrift, and economy, that they could

be sure of knowing how to make a living after they had left us. We wanted to teach them to study actual things instead of mere books alone.[9]

In an age when blacks were being excluded from trades as well as professions Washington's gradualism had its supporters.

By the 1890s, it also had its critics. William Edward Burghardt Du Bois was born into a middle-class black family in Boston three years after the Civil War. In his *Souls of Black Folks* (1903) Du Bois accused Washington of making a compromise that relegated blacks to a new slavery. He urged confrontation instead of compromise. In 1909 he called for the organization of a committee for racial equality, the right to vote, and full education. The following year that committee became the National Association for the Advancement of Colored People. In the pages of *Crisis*, its monthly journal, Du Bois lashed out at everything from American imperialism overseas to the timidity of black preachers at home. An internationalist, he organized Pan-African congresses that brought African and American blacks together, and he taught his readers both critical citizenship as Americans and a wider African cultural heritage. His own struggle between a defensive black nationalist separatism and a cosmopolitan, international democratic socialism continued to be a principal concern of black intellectuals after the war.

Segregation in South Africa: Boer War to World War I

While the Anglo-Boer War in South Africa pitted one group of whites, the British, against another, the Dutch-descended Boers, it was not like the American Civil War, because British and Boers had never been part of the same society. And although British racial policy was more liberal than Boer, the war was not fought on behalf of the Africans. There was in fact a kind of white gentlemen's agreement not to arm the Africans on either side. Britain was victorious because, like the North in the American Civil War, it enjoyed a superior economy and technology and was ruthless (including devising the concentration camp for its Boer prisoners). The defeat of the Boers in 1902, like the defeat of the South in 1865, did provide the opportunity for a commitment to racial justice. As we have seen, that commitment was made, if incompletely, by Northern republicans between 1860 and 1877. It was barely made by the British in South Africa at all.

Perhaps postwar radical reconstruction was never possible in the Transvaal or Orange Free State in 1902. The "white man's peace," the Treaty of Vereeniging in 1902, required the Boers, or Afrikaners, to become British citizens but limited citizenship to whites and allowed some Afrikaner soldiers to retain their rifles for defense against Africans. The enormous numerical superiority of Africans (70 percent) and "coloreds" (10 percent) over whites was enough to ensure compromise.

Alfred Milner, the postwar British governor of the two Afrikaner colonies, had the power to dictate some racial reform. Instead, he chose to convert the defeated Afrikaners to the fact of British administration by aiding their economic development. That meant an alliance with wealthy farmers and mining magnates and involved assistance in their quest for cheap labor.

Conquered Africans had provided cheap labor as squatters on Afrikaner farms since the Great Trek. Heavy work had generally been seasonal, however, and it was never organized on a massive scale. The mines were different. The discovery of diamonds in 1867 and gold in 1884 transformed the interior economy (especially the Transvaal) infinitely more than partial industrialization had changed the American South in the 1890s. The Witwatersrand, the gold-mining area of the Transvaal, demanded 42,500 African workers in 1894 and nearly 100,000 in 1899.[10]

Further, the poor quality of gold made its extraction expensive. The problem for the mine owners was how to ensure that an increasing number of Africans would work in the mines for the extremely low wages that would make it profitable. In fact, Africans in the years after the war "were staying at home in large numbers, somehow contriving to support their families on their small plots, unwilling to come out to work for the reduced level of wages that mining magnates, industrialists, large farmers, and government officials all agreed 'the country' in such straitened circumstances could afford to pay."[11]

There were many answers to the labor problem after the war. Milner himself was interested in importing Chinese laborers (and did in fact bring in fifty thousand between 1904 and 1910).[12] Others, like the defeated Afrikaner general and future prime minister Louis Botha, insisted that African labor would be ample if only sufficient force were applied. Taxes might be increased, especially on the unemployed. But Botha, a farmer who had always relied on African squatters close at hand and attentive to his needs, said nothing about segregation when he addressed Milner's Transvaal Labour Commission in 1903. The word was first used about 1910 by future Nationalist party leader J. B. M. Hertzog. Segregation was still a new idea in 1903.[13]

"I would like you to give me your opinion on this scheme." Mr. Thompson, member of the Native Affairs Commission, was questioning the Reverend B. Kumalo and other African members of the Native Vigilance Association of the Orange River Colony on September 23, 1904. "If the Government of the Orange River Colony were today to move you all . . . to a spot a couple or three miles out of Bloemfontein, there right out of town, away from the white people, would that meet your idea?" Mr. Kumalo's "idea" had been that Africans ought to hold property and vote. "Not fully," he replied, "because that would not give the black man the right to buy land in town. He ought to have the right to buy land in the town even, and to speculate if he wishes to."

"But answer this first," Mr. Thompson interjected. "Would you not like to see, in the first place, all the Natives moved from these slums and all about, and put a couple of miles out of the town, with a proper railway system to bring them out in the morning, and take them back at night, ring the curfew bell at night, at nine o'clock, and keep them in their town. Do you not think that would be in the interests of the Natives as a whole round Bloemfontein?"[14]

A proper railway to bring them to work in the morning and return them at night: who could ask for anything more? Segregation was the recommendation of the Native Affairs Commission in 1905 because the commissioners had found a way of combining physical separation with labor control. On the farms, Africans had to be close by to be useful. Whole separate towns could be built for Africans near the labor-hungry mines. "Plots of half-acres" might not be affordable after all. The ghetto was to be a more appropriate model.

Actually the territorial segregation the Native Affairs Commission envisioned led to two types of ghettos. One was the separate black "townships" suggested by the commission to get blacks out of the cities. The second was the barrack compounds near the mines for black workers, men forced to live for weeks or months without women or families. The mine compounds were barely disguised prisons.

> Eight, twelve, or sixteen men slept in concrete bunks stacked four deep along the walls. Their washing hung from string tied to the top bunks, so that you had to duck and plough your way to the door. The single light bulb was always burning. . . . Men came and went at all hours . . . the food was prepared and dished out to tin plates by shovel in the cookhouse.[15]

The townships, designed not for the sleeping hours of contract workers, but as the homes of families lured or forced from the cities, were less obviously prisons. Typically the government built thousands of identical small cement houses arranged in rows for miles in each direction with only a single road for entry or exit; transit into or out of the townships required the presentation of a pass at the guard house.

The restriction of blacks to mining camps and special townships that deprived of rights and basic amenities was part of a larger plan to accomplish two contrary goals. South African whites wanted blacks to be readily available to provide cheap labor in the mines, cities, and farms throughout the country, but they wanted them to disappear after work. Outnumbered by blacks almost ten to one, South African whites sought a way to live off black labor in a white country. The Native Land Act of 1913 declared that certain designated black reserves were the only places blacks could live, unless whites gave them temporary permission to live elsewhere. "The town is a European area," the Native Affairs Commission of 1921 declared. "The native men, women, and children should only be permitted within municipal areas in so far and for so long as their presence is demanded by the wants of the white population," another commission added the following year. The Natives (Urban Areas) Act of 1923 and succeeding amendments established a system of "influx controls" and "passes." Based on the disingenuous assumption that all blacks reside in the 13 percent of South African territory designated as reserves or tribal home-lands, these laws required permission and passes for blacks to be in the towns, cities, and mining areas—the only areas where white South Africans allowed them to work. An African without a proper pass could be imprisoned, sent to a remote "resettlement camp," or forced into convict labor.

Since it is "inconceivable" (as Jan Hofmeyr, a deputy prime minister in the 1940s, put it) for whites to do without black labor and "just as inconceivable" for blacks to find sufficient work in the homelands, the existence of these homelands as anything but a labor reserve is a convenient fiction. Thus, when the South African government began in the 1960s to give "independence" to these "Bantu homelands" and assign South African blacks to "citizenship" in these tribal reserves, it strengthened its claim that the blacks were alien "guest workers" in South Africa. Blacks who were born in the cities of South Africa and declined to move to remote homelands or accept "tribal citizenship" were often deprived of internal passes, passports, and any remaining rights. One South African recounted:

> I'm a Zulu, but I was born and raised in Johannesburg. My grandparents and mother are buried in Johannesburg. The [officials] wanted my father, brothers and sisters, and I to go to what they called a Zulu homeland. First they refused to give me a passport. Then they just destroyed our home. I came back one day and it had been bulldozed to the ground: our furniture was on the street.[16]

Apartheid and Segregation

Apartheid was enshrined as official South African policy by the Nationalist party government after its victory in 1948. As official government policy, apartheid led to increasing discrimination against blacks and an escalating level of protest, culminating in the violence in Sharpeville in 1960, Soweto in 1976, and throughout South Africa until it was abandoned in 1989, the year in which

Nelson Mandela was released from prison and the ban on his African National Congress party was lifted. Finally, in 1994, Mandela was elected President of South Africa, and the country has struggled to create a multi-racial democracy.

The comparison of South African apartheid and North American segregation illuminates some issues and confuses some others. The comparison points out the similar turn to racial discrimination in two parts of the world at about the same time. That is instructive. Both developments were products of white settler societies after a period of slavery when they were beginning to industrialize and required large numbers of workers. But the comparison falls short when we push it further. In South Africa, apartheid, or "separate development," was part of a system of beliefs that became official government policy. It gained its "philosophical" defenders. Commissions, studies, and books were presented to argue that "separate development" was better for blacks as well as for whites. South Africa, they argued, was a country of minorities, different tribes, "white and black," each of which should be allowed to go its own way. The white tribes were urban, the black tribes rural. Each of the black tribes had unique native traditions that, they argued, should be preserved rather than mixed in a melting pot.

The "melting pot" became an American ideal, at least for whites. Segregation in America was rarely defended as anything but a pragmatic solution (usually temporary) to a difficult problem. It's not that Americans were unable to be philosophical racists. Southern slaveholders had produced their share of books and speeches proving the superiority of slavery over wage labor. But America took segregation less seriously. American segregation was equivalent to what South Africans called "petty apartheid," the smaller, less important signs of separation: the "whites only" facilities from washrooms to cemeteries that dotted the landscape of both countries in the middle of the twentieth century. For South Africans the issue of separate washrooms was always a minor matter compared with the issues of exclusion from the cities; restriction to homelands, camps, and townships; lack of citizenship or the vote; and the need for all blacks (but no whites) to carry passes. Thus, as blacks were removed from the white cities and neighborhoods, segregated facilities became less necessary. . . .

One of the main differences between South African and United States history is that in North America the Europeans annihilated the native inhabitants (intentionally or not) and took the land. The "American Bantu" were quickly decimated, and their descendants were put on reservations. They never approached a majority of the population. The second main difference follows from this. The American Indians could never provide the abundant and inexpensive labor necessary for economic growth and industrialization. African slaves played that role in the very important agricultural stage of American economic growth, but the American Civil War created a society with a different set of needs and values. It is true that some of the freedmen of the South were employed in the new Southern mill towns after the Civil War, especially in new cities, such as Birmingham. By and large, however, by the 1880s most former slaves were relegated to a new kind of serfdom as tenant farmers and sharecroppers. They became indebted, often to their old masters, on the land they had formerly worked as slaves. In this respect, their participation in the second stage of American industrialization was curtailed.

The workers who built America between the Civil War and the First World War were, for the most part, immigrants rather than former slaves. Successive waves of new arrivals came (especially from Europe) with the hope of making a better life for themselves in the New World. Only after 1920, with the large-scale internal migration of blacks to Northern cities, did blacks again play a crucial role in the industrial work force, and that created new racial tensions. In effect, the captains of American industry chose to import masses of cheap immigrant workers at about the same time that South African mine owners decided to employ native blacks. Both societies created color lines. In South Africa blacks were the unskilled laborers and whites were skilled. In the United States blacks were left with marginal subsistence on the farms, while each new wave of immigrants was brought in to struggle with its predecessor.

The tensions between the waves of immigrants were often racial, their sentiments racist. This was the case even when one ethnic group opposed another ethnic group of the same "race," and perhaps especially true in the conflicts over Chinese labor. But since such "racism" could be directed against Irish or Italians as easily as against Indians or Chinese, it was less a matter of race than of class.

Notes

1. Allan Nevins, *Ordeal of the Union. Volume I: Douglas, Buchanan and Party Chaos, 1857–1859* (New York: Charles Scribner's Sons, 1950), p. 438.

2. George M. Fredrickson, *White Supremacy: A Comparative Study in American and South African History* (New York: Oxford University Press, 1981), pp. 161–162.

3. Ibid., p. 176.

4. C. Vann Woodward, *American Counterpoint: Slavery and Racism in the North-South Dialogue* (Boston: Little Brown, 1971), pp. 213–214.

5. Ibid.

6. Cited in Joel Kovel, *White Racism: A Psychohistory* (New York: Random House, 1970), p. 31.

7. Ronald Segal, *The Race War* (New York: Viking, 1967), p. 208.

8. Robert Coles, *Children of Crisis* (New York: Dell, 1968), p. 66.

9. Booker T. Washington, *Up from Slavery* (New York: Lancer Books, 1968), p. 129.

10. Martin Legassick, "The Analysis of 'Racism' in South Africa: The Case of the Mining Economy" (presented at IDEP/UN International Seminar, Dar es Salaam, 1975).

11. John W. Cell, *The Highest Stage of White Supremacy: The Origins of Segregation in South Africa and the American South* (Cambridge: Cambridge University Press, 1982), p. 46.

12. Terence O'Brien, *Milner* (London: Constable, 1979), p. 216.

13. Cell, *The Highest Stage*, pp. 47 and 49.

14. Minutes of Evidence, South African Native Affairs Commission, 1903–1904. Extracts in Sheridan Johns III, *Protest and Hope, 1882–1934*, p. 39. This is the first volume of Thomas Karis and Gwendolen M. Carter, *From Protest to Challenge: A Documentary History of African Politics in South Africa, 1882–1964* (Stanford: Hoover Institute Press, 1972).

15. John Ya-Otto, *Battle-Front Namibia* (Westport, Conn.: Lawrence Hill, 1981), p. 14.

16. Interview with anonymous informant, July 1984.

From *Max Havelaar*

Multatuli

Max Havelaar *is the great Dutch novel of the nineteenth century, often called the* Uncle Tom's Cabin *of Dutch literature. It awakened popular awareness to the inequities of colonialism in the Dutch East Indies much the way Harriet Beecher Stowe's novel focused sentiment in the United States in the 1850s on slavery.*

Multatuli (Latin for "I suffered much") was the pen name of Eduard Douwes Dekker (1820–1887) who went to Java in 1838 to serve in the East Indian Civil Service. In 1856 he became a colonial official in Java, but within three months he resigned in protest against the treatment of the Javanese. His experiences and grievances were presented in the character of Max Havelaar when the book was published in 1859.

While the book sent a shiver down the spine of Dutch middle-class society and was responsible for many reforms of the colonial system, it did little for its author, who died in obscurity in Germany (much as his Dutch contemporary, Vincent van Gogh, died in exile in France).

This section of the novel is an interlude in which Dekker explores Dutch colonial attitudes toward Europeans of "mixed blood," usually Dutch fathers and "native" women. This distinction between the two parts of "European society" could have been made in British India, French Algeria, or Indochina or anywhere else in the European colonial world of the nineteenth century.

Notice that this is a special kind of racism, directed not at the indigenous Other (in this case the Javanese) but at the partial Other, who because of half European parentage must be counted among "European society," but because of half Javanese parentage is doomed to inferior status.

Notice also what sort of Dutch colonials, according to the author, carry the greatest prejudice against these "half-caste" people. What is Dekker saying about the social origins of racism in the Dutch colonies? Why would the least educated and least prosperous Dutch be the most racist, and why would their racism be most virulently expressed against the "liplaps?" Do you see any similarities with racism in the United States or South Africa?

European society in the Dutch East Indies is rather sharply divided into two parts: the real Europeans, and those who—although legally enjoying exactly the same rights—were not born in Europe, and have more or less "native" blood in their veins. In fairness to the conceptions of humanity in the East Indies I hasten to add here that, however sharp the line which is drawn in social life between the two classes of individuals who, for the genuine natives, both equally bear the name of *Hollander*, this distinction has nothing of the barbarous character which prevails in the American status differentiation. I cannot deny that, even so, there is still much in this mutual relationship which is unjust and repellent, and that the name *liplap* (half-caste) has often grated on my ear as proof of the distance which separates many a non-half-caste, a "white" person, from real civilization. It is true that only in exceptional cases is the half-caste admitted into European society, and that generally, if I may use a very slangy expression, he is not regarded as "one hundred per cent." But few people would present or defend such exclusion or disparagement as a *just principle*. Everyone is, of course, at liberty to choose his own environment and company, and one cannot blame the full European for preferring to mix with his own kind rather than with persons who—irrespective of their greater or lesser moral or intellectual value—do not share his impressions and ideas, or—and this, in a presumed difference in civilization, is perhaps very often the main thing—*whose prejudices have taken a different direction from his.*

A *liplap*—if I wanted to use the official, more polite term, I should have to say a *"so-called native child,"* but I beg leave to keep to an idiom which seems born of alliteration; I intend nothing impolite by it, and what does the word mean anyway?—a liplap may have many good qualities. The European may also have many good qualities. Both have many that are bad, and in this too they resemble each other. But the good and the bad qualities inherent in both are too divergent for commerce between them to be, as a rule, mutually satisfactory. Besides—and for this the Government is largely responsible—the liplap is often ill educated. We are not concerned here with what the European would be like if his mental development had been thus impeded from his youth; but it is certain that *in general* the liplap's poor schooling hinders his being placed on an equality with the European, even when some *individual* liplap may perhaps deserve to be ranked above some *individual* European, as regards culture or scientific or artistic attainments.

In this too there is nothing new. It was, for instance, the policy of William the Conqueror to raise the most insignificant Norman above the most accomplished Saxon, and every Norman would appeal to the superiority of the Normans *in general*, in order to assert himself in particular, where he would have been the inferior *without* the influence of his countrymen as the dominant party.

Such a state of affairs naturally gives rise to a certain awkwardness in social intercourse, which nothing could remove except philosophical, broad-minded views and measures on the part of the Government.

It is obvious that the European, who is the gainer by such a relationship, feels perfectly comfortable in his artificial ascendancy. But it is often ludicrous to hear someone who acquired most of his culture and grammar in Zandstraat in Rotterdam jeer at the liplap because, in speaking Dutch, he makes *glass* or *government* masculine, *sun* or *moon* neuter.

A liplap may be well-bred, well-educated, even learned—there are such! But no sooner has the European who shammed sick in order to stay away from the ship on which he washed dishes, and who bases his claims to good manners on "ow are yer?" and "Beg pardon" become head of the commercial undertaking which made such "stupendous" profits out of indigo in 1800-and-something . . . nay, long before he becomes owner of the *toko*, the general store in which he sells hams and fowling-pieces—no sooner has this European noticed that the most well-bred liplap has difficulty in distinguishing between *h* and *g*, than he laughs at the stupidity of the man who does not know the difference between *hot* and *got*.

But, to take the grin off his face, our European would have to know that in Arabic and Malay those two consonants are expressed by one letter, that *Hieronymus* passes via *Geronimo* into *Jerome,* that from *buano* we make *guano,* that our *hand* fits into a French *gant,* that *kous* in Dutch is *hose* in English, and that for *Guild Heaume* we say in Dutch *Huillem* or *Willem.* So much erudition is too much to ask from someone who made his fortune "in" indigo and got his education from success in throwing dice . . . or worse!

And such genuine Europeans surely cannot be expected to hobnob with liplaps!

I understand how *Willem* comes from *Guillaume*, and I must admit that, especially in the Moluccas, I have often met liplaps who amazed me by the extent of their knowledge and who gave me the idea that we Europeans, in spite of all the resources at our disposal, are often—and *absolutely*, not merely *relatively*—far behind these poor pariahs, who have to contend from the very cradle with artificial, studied, unjust subordination and with silly prejudice against their colour.

From *Burmese Days*

George Orwell

This is a chapter from one of the great novels on colonialism. George Orwell captures the life of the British colonial class in a remote "up-country" town in Burma in the 1920s. The chapter takes place in the European Club. The principal character is Flory, the only Englishman at all sympathetic to the Burmese, who has befriended the Indian physician, Dr. Veraswami, but is too weak to propose him as the first "native" member of the club. The other main characters are Westfield, district superintendent of police; Ellis, local company manager and the most racist of the group; Lackersteen, local manager of a timber company who is usually drunk; Maxwell, a forest officer; and Macgregor, deputy commissioner and secretary of the club.

Why does the club loom so large in the lives of these Englishmen? Since they complain a lot, why are they in Burma? Does Burma offer them advantages they would not have at home? How was colonial life changing in the 1920s? How do you account for the virulent racism of men like these? Why does Ellis correct the butler's English?

Flory's house was at the top of the maidan [parade ground], close to the edge of the jungle. From the gate the maidan sloped sharply down, scorched and khaki-coloured, with half a dozen dazzling white bungalows scattered round it. All quaked, shivered in the hot air. There was an English cemetery within a white wall half-way down the hill, and nearby a tiny tin-roofed church. Beyond that was the European Club, and when one looked at the Club—a dumpy one-storey wooden building—one looked at the real centre of the town. In any town in India the European Club is the spiritual citadel, the real seat of the British power, the Nirvana for which native officials and millionaires pine in vain. It was doubly so in this case, for it was the proud boast of Kyauktada Club that, almost alone of Clubs in Burma, it had never admitted an Oriental to membership. Beyond the Club, the Irrawaddy flowed huge and ochreous, glittering like diamonds in the patches that caught the sun; and beyond the river stretched great wastes of paddy fields, ending at the horizon in a range of blackish hills.

The native town, and the courts and the jail, were over to the right, mostly hidden in green groves of peepul trees. The spire of the pagoda rose from the trees like a slender spear tipped with gold. Kyauktada was a fairly typical Upper Burma town, that had not changed greatly between the days of Marco Polo and 1910, and might have slept in the Middle Ages for a century more if it had not proved a convenient spot for a railway terminus. In 1910 the Government made it the headquarters of a district and a seat of Progress— interpretable as a block of law courts, with their army of fat but ravenous pleaders, a hospital, a school, and one of those huge, durable jails which the English have built everywhere between Gibraltar and Hong Kong. The population was about four thousand, including a couple of hundred Indians, a few score Chinese and seven Europeans. There were also two Eurasians named Mr. Francis and Mr. Samuel, the sons of an American Baptist missionary and a Roman Catholic missionary respectively. The town contained no curiosities of any kind, except an Indian fakir who had lived for twenty years in a tree near the bazaar, drawing his food up in a basket every morning.

Flory yawned as he came out of the gate. He had been half drunk the night before, and the glare made him feel liverish. "Bloody, bloody hole!" he thought, looking down the hill. And, no one except the dog being near, he began to sing aloud, "Bloody, bloody, bloody, oh, how thou art bloody" to the tune of "Holy, holy, holy, oh how Thou art holy," as he walked down the hot red road, switching at the dried-up grasses with his stick. It was nearly nine o'clock and the sun was fiercer every minute. The heat throbbed down on one's head with a steady, rhythmic thumping, like blows from an enormous bolster. Flory stopped at the Club gate, wondering whether to go in or to go farther down the road and see Dr. Veraswami. Then he remembered that it was "English mail day" and the newspapers would have arrived. He went in, past the big tennis screen, which was overgrown by a creeper with starlike mauve flowers.

In the borders beside the path swathes of English flowers, phlox and lark-spur, hollyhock and petunia, not yet slain by the sun, rioted in vast size and richness. The petunias were huge, like trees almost. There was no lawn, but instead a shrubbery of native trees and bushes—gold mohur trees like vast umbrellas of blood-red bloom, frangipanis with creamy, stalkless flowers, pur-ple bougainvillea, scarlet hibiscus, and the pink, Chinese rose, bilious-green crotons, feathery fronds of tamarind. The clash of colours hurt one's eyes in the glare. A nearly naked *mali* [gardener], watering-can in hand, was moving in the jungle of flowers like some large nectar-sucking bird.

On the Club steps a sandy-haired Englishman, with a prickly moustache, pale grey eyes too far apart, and abnormally thin calves to his legs, was stand-ing with his hands in the pockets of his shorts. This was Mr. Westfield, the District Superintendent of Police. With a very bored air he was rocking himself backwards and forwards on his heels and outing his upper lip so that his moustache tickled his nose. He greeted Flory with a slight sideways movement of his head. His way of speaking was clipped and soldierly, missing out every word that well could be missed out. Nearly everything he said was intended for a joke, but the tone of his voice was hollow and melancholy.

"Hello, Flory me lad. Bloody awful morning, what?

"We must expect it at this time of year, I suppose," Flory said. He had turned himself a little sideways, so that his birth marked cheek was away from Westfield.

"Yes, dammit. Couple of months of this coming. Last year we didn't have a spot of rain till June. Look at that bloody sky, not a cloud in it. Like one of those damned great blue enamel saucepans. God! What'd you give to be in Piccadilly now, eh?"

"Have the English papers come?"

"Yes, Dear old *Punch*, *Pink'un*, and *Vie Parisienne*. Makes you homesick to read 'em, what? Let's come in and have a drink before the ice all goes. Old Lackersteen's been fairly bathing in it. Half pickled already."

They went in, Westfield remarking in his gloomy voice, "Lead on, Mac-duff." Inside, the Club was a teak-walled place smelling of earth-oil, and con-sisting of only four rooms, one of which contained a forlorn "library" of five hundred mildewed novels, and another an old and mangy billiard-table—this, however, seldom used, for during most of the year hordes of flying beetles came buzzing round the lamps and littered themselves over the cloth. There were also a card-room and a "lounge" which looked towards the river, over a wide veranda; but at this time of day all the verandas were curtained with green bamboo chicks. The lounge was an unhomelike room, with coco-nut matting on the floor, and wicker chairs and tables which were littered with shiny illustrated papers. For ornament there were a number of "Bonzo" pictures, and the dusty skulls of sambhur. A punkah, lazily flapping, shook dust into the tepid air.

There were three men in the room. Under the punkah a florid, fine-looking, slightly bloated man of forty was sprawling across the table with his head in his hands, groaning in pain. This was Mr. Lackersteen, the local manager of a timber firm. He had been badly drunk the night before, and he was suffering for it. Ellis, local manager of yet another company, was standing before the notice board studying some notice with a look of bitter concentration. He was a tiny wiry-haired fellow with a pale, sharp-featured face and restless movements. Maxwell, the acting Divisional Forest Officer, was lying in one of the long chairs reading the *Field*, and invisible except for two large-boned legs and thick downy forearms.

"Look at this naughty old man," said Westfield, taking Mr. Lackersteen half affectionately by the shoulders and shaking him. "Example to the young, what? There, but for the grace of God and all that. Gives you an idea what you'll be like at forty."

Mr. Lackersteen gave a groan which sounded like brandy.

"Poor old chap," said Westfield; "regular martyr to booze, eh? Look at it oozing out of his pores. Reminds me of the old colonel who used to sleep without a mosquito net. They asked his servant why and the servant said: 'At night, master too drunk to notice mosquitoes; in the morning, mosquitoes too drunk to notice master.' Look at him boozed last night and then asking for more. Got a little niece coming to stay with him, too. Due tonight, isn't she, Lackersteen?"

"Oh, leave that drunken sot alone," said Ellis without turning round. He had a spiteful cockney voice. Mr. Lackersteen groaned again, "-the niece! Get me some brandy, for Christ's sake."

"Good education for the niece, eh? Seeing uncle under the table seven times a week.-Hey, butler! Bringing brandy for Lackersteen master!"

The butler, a dark, stout Dravidian with liquid, yellow-irised eyes like those of a dog, brought the brandy on a brass tray. Flory and Westfield ordered gin. Mr. Lackersteen swallowed a few spoonfuls of brandy and sat back in his chair, groaning in a more resigned way. He had a beefy, ingenuous face, with a toothbrush moustache. He was really a very simple-minded man, with no ambitions beyond having what he called "a good time." His wife governed him by the only possible method, namely, by never letting him out of her sight for more than an hour or two. Only once, a year after they were married, she had left him for a fortnight, and had returned unexpectedly a day before her time, to find Mr. Lackersteen, drunk, supported on either side by a naked Burmese girl, while a third up-ended a whisky bottle into his mouth. Since then she had watched him, as he used to complain, "like a cat over a bloody mousehole." However, he managed to enjoy quite a number of "good times," though they were usually rather hurried ones.

"My Christ, what a head I've got on me this morning," he said. "Call that butler again, Westfield. I've got to have another brandy before my missus gets here. She says she's going to cut my booze down to four pegs a day when our niece gets here. God rot them both!" he added gloomily.

"Stop playing the fool, all of you, and listen to this," said Ellis sourly. He had a queer wounding way of speaking, hardly ever opening his mouth without insulting somebody. He deliberately exaggerated his cockney accent, because of the sardonic tone it gave to his words. "Have you seen this notice of old Macgregor's? A little nosegay for everyone. Maxwell, wake up and listen!"

Maxwell lowered the *Field.* He was a fresh-coloured blond youth of not more than twenty-five or six—very young for the post he held. With his heavy limbs and thick white eyelashes he reminded one of a carthorse colt. Ellis nipped the notice from the board with a neat, spiteful little movement and began reading it aloud. It had been posted by Mr. Macgregor, who, besides being Deputy Commissioner, was secretary of the Club.

"Just listen to this. 'It has been suggested that as there are as yet no Oriental members of this club, and as it is now usual to admit officials of gazetted rank, whether native or European, to membership of most European Clubs, we should consider the question of following this practice in Kyauktada. The matter will be open for discussion at the next general meeting. On the one hand it may be pointed out'—oh, well, no need to wade through the rest of it. He can't even write out a notice without an attack of literary diarrhoea. Anyway, the point's this. He's asking us to break all our rules and take a dear little nigger-boy into this Club. *Dear* Dr. Veraswami, for instance. Dr. Very-slimy, I call him. That *would* be a treat, wouldn't it? Little pot-bellied niggers breathing garlic in your face over the bridge-table. Christ, to think of it! We've got to hang together and put our foot down on this at once. What do you say, Westfield? Flory?"

Westfield shrugged his thin shoulders philosophically. He had sat down at the table and lighted a black, stinking Burma cheroot.

"Got to put up with it, I suppose," he said. "B——s of natives are getting into all the Clubs nowadays. Even the Pegu Club, I'm told. Way this country's going, you know. We're about the last Club in Burma to hold out against 'em."

"We are; and what's more, we're damn well going to go on holding out.

I'll die in the ditch before I'll see a nigger in here." Ellis had produced a stump of pencil. With the curious air of spite that some men can put into their tiniest action, he re-pinned the notice on the board and pencilled a tiny, neat "B. F." against Mr. Macgregor's signature "There, that's what I think of his idea. I'll tell him so when he comes down. What do *you* say, Flory?"

Flory had not spoken all this time. Though by nature anything but a silent man, he seldom found much to say in Club conversations. He had sat down at the table and was reading G.K. Chesterton's article in the *London News*, at the same time caressing Flo's head with his left hand. Ellis, however, was one of those people who constantly nag others to echo their own opinions. He repeated his question, and Flory looked up, and their eyes met. The skin round Ellis's nose suddenly turned so pale that it was almost grey. In him it was a sign of anger. Without any prelude he burst into a stream of abuse that would have been startling, if the others had not been used to hearing something like it every morning.

"My God, I should have thought in a case like this, when it's a question of keeping those black, stinking swine out of the only place where we can en'oy ourselves, you'd have the decency to back me up. Even if that pot-bellied, greasy little sod of a nigger doctor *is* your best pal. I don't care if you choose to pal up with the scum of the bazaar. If it pleases you to go to Veraswami's house and drink whisky with all his nigger pals, that's your look-out. Do what you like outside the Club. But, by God, it's a different matter when you talk of bringing niggers in here. I suppose you'd like little Veraswami for a Club member, eh? Chipping into our conversation and pawing everyone with his sweaty hands and breathing his filthy garlic breath in our faces. By God, he'd go out with my boot behind him if ever I saw his black snout inside that door. Greasy, pot-bellied little ——!" etc."

This went on for several minutes. It was curiously impressive, because it was so completely sincere. Ellis really did hate Orientals hated them with a bitter, restless loathing as of something evil or unclean. Living and working, as the assistant of a timber firm must, in perpetual contact with the Burmese, he had never grown used to the sight of a black face. Any hint of friendly feeling towards an Oriental seemed to him a horrible perversity. He was an intelligent man and an able servant of his firm, but he was one of those Englishmen—common, unfortunately—who should never be allowed to set foot in the East.

Flory sat nursing Flo's head in his lap, unable to meet Ellis's eyes. At the best of times his birthmark made it difficult for him to look people straight in the face. And when he made ready to speak, he could feel his voice trembling—for it had a way of trembling when it should have been firm; his features, too, sometimes twitched uncontrollably.

Steady on," he said at last, sullenly and rather feebly. "Steady on. There's no need to get so excited. I never suggested having any native members in here."

"Oh, didn't you? We all know bloody well you'd like to, though. Why else do you go to that oily little babu's house every morning, then? Sitting down at table with him as though he was a white man, and drinking out of glasses his filthy black lips have slobbered over. It makes me spew to think of it."

"Sit down, old chap, sit down," Westfield said. "Forget it. Have a drink on it. Not worth while quarrelling. Too hot."

"My God," said Ellis a little more calmly, taking a pace or two up and down, "my god, I don't understand you chaps. I simply don't. Here's that old fool Macgregor wanting to bring a nigger into this Club for no reason whatever, and you all sit down under it without a word. Good God, what are we supposed to be doing in this country? If we aren't going to rule, why the devil don't we clear out? Here we are, supposed to be governing a set of damn black swine who've been slaves since the beginning of history, and instead of ruling them in the only way they understand, we go and treat them as equals. And all you silly b——s take it for granted. There's Flory, makes his best pal of a black babu who calls himself a doctor because he's done two years at an Indian so-called university. And you, Westfield, proud as Punch of your knock-kneed, bribe-taking cowards of policemen. And there's Maxwell, spends his time running after Eurasian tarts. Yes, you do, Maxwell; I heard about your goings-on in Mandalay with some smelly little bitch called Molly Pereira. I supposed you'd have gone and married her if they hadn't. You all seem to *like* the dirty black brutes. Christ, I don't know what's come over us all. I really don't."

"Come on, have another drink," said Westfield. "Hey, butler! Spot of beer before the ice goes, eh? Beer, butler!"

The butler brought some bottles of Munich beer. Ellis presently sat down at the table with the others, and he nursed one of the cool bottles between his small hands. His forehead was sweating. He was sulky, but not in a rage any longer. At all times he was spiteful and perverse, but his violent fits of rage were soon over, and were never apologised for. Quarrels were a regular part of the routine of Club life. Mr. Lackersteen was feeling better and was studying the illustrations in *La Vie Parisienne.* It was after nine now, and the room, scented with the acrid smoke of Westfield's cheroot, was stifling hot. Everyone's shirt stuck to his back with the first sweat of the day. The invisible chokra who pulled the punkah rope outside was falling asleep in the glare.

"Butler!" yelled Ellis, and as the butler appeared, "go and wake that bloody chokra up!"

"Yes Master."

"And butler!"

"Yes, master?"

"How much ice have we got left?"

"Bout twenty pounds, master. Will only last to-day, I think. I find it very difficult to keep ice cool now."

"Don't talk like that, damn you—'I find it very difficult!' Have you swallowed a dictionary? 'Please, master, can't keeping ice cool'—that's how you ought to talk. We shall have to sack this fellow if he gets to talk English too well. I can't stick servants who talk English. D'you hear, butler?"

"Yes, master," said the butler, and retired.

"God! No ice till Monday," Westfield said. "You going back to the jungle, Flory?"

"Yes. I ought to be there now. I only came in because of the English mail."

"Go on tour myself, I think. Knock up a spot of Travelling Allowance. I can't stick my bloody office at this time of year. Sitting there under the damned punkah, signing one chit after another. Paper-chewing. God, how I wish the war was on again!"

"I'm going out the day after to-morrow," Ellis said. "Isn't that damned padre coming to hold his service this Sunday? I'll take care not to be in for that, anyway. Bloody knee-drill."

"Next Sunday." said Westfield. "Promised to be in for it myself. So's Macgregor. Bit hard on the poor devil of a padre, I must say. Only gets here once in six weeks. Might as well get up a congregation when he does come."

"Oh, hell! I'd snivel psalms to oblige the padre, but I can't stick the way these damned native Christians come shoving into our church. A pack of Madrassi servants and Karen school-teachers. And then those two yellow-bellies, Francis and Samuel—they call themselves Christians too. Last time the padre was here they had the nerve to come up and sit on the front pews with the white men. Someone ought to speak to the padre about that. What bloody fools we were ever to let those missionaries loose in this country! Teaching bazaar sweepers they're as good as we are. 'Please, sit, me Christian same like master.' Damned cheek."

On the Exclusion of Chinese Workers

Senator John F. Miller

Settler racism was expressed not only by settlers in foreign lands, but also against foreign settlers at home. In settler societies, foreign immigration was always a potential trigger of racist sentiment. This is ironic since settler societies were made up of immigrants. But each new wave of immigration threatened some degree of change in the nature of the settled society. In highly mobile industrial capitalist societies, new immigrants also represented cheap sources of labor. As such they were frequently welcomed by employers, but feared by existing laborers, their unions, and their political representatives.

As each new wave of immigrants established themselves in the factories, unions, and political parties of their new society, they sought to close the door to new immigrants seen as potential competitors for their jobs and fortunes. The Irish, vilified in their own immigrant days by the English, turned on the Italians and Jews who came in great numbers to the United States after 1860. After the completion of the transcontinental railroad in 1869, which relied on Irish labor in the East and new Chinese immigrants in the West, and the series of economic downturns that began in 1873, the Irish joined other Europeans in opposing further Chinese immigration.

The move to exclude Chinese workers from the United States took on a special force in California, the "golden gate" of immigration from Asia. In the United States Congress of the 1870s, the anti-Chinese forces were led by Aaron Sargent, a Republican of California (who incidently was also the leading champion of woman's suffrage). By the time the Chinese Exclusion Act came to the consideration of the U.S. Congress in 1882, its leading spokesmen was another Californian, Senator John F. Miller.

The Chinese Exclusion Act called for the curtailment of immigration by Chinese "skilled and unskilled laborers and Chinese employed in mining." In this selection, taken from the Congressional Record, *Senator Miller spoke on behalf of Chinese exclusion.*

Notice Miller's use of Darwinian imagery of the "survival of the fittest." How does Miller make the Chinese seem something less than human? Judging from this passage, what seems to be the most important reason for the passage of the Chinese Exclusion Act in 1882? Recognizing that many of

Congressional Record, 47–1. February 28, 1882, pp. 1482–1485.

Miller's constituents face real problems, what would be a non-racist response to these problems?

If mankind existed now in one grand co-operate society, in one universal union, under one system of laws, in a vast homogeneous brotherhood, serenely beatified, innocent of all selfish aims and unholy desires, with one visible temporal ruler, whose judgements should be justice and whose sway should be eternal, then there would be no propriety in this measure.

But the millennium has not yet begun, and man exists now, as he has existed always—in the economy of Providence—in societies called nations, separated by the peculiarities if not the antipathies of race. In truth the history of mankind is for the most part descriptive of racial conflicts and the struggles between nations for existence. . . .

During the late depression in business affairs, which existed for three or four years in California, while thousands of white men and women were walking the streets, begging and pleading for an opportunity to give their honest labor for any wages, the great steamers made their regular arrivals from China and discharged at the wharves of San Francisco their accustomed cargoes of Chinese, who were conveyed through the city to the distributing dens of the Six Companies, and within three or four days after arrival every Chinaman was in his place at work, and the white people unemployed still went about the streets. This continued until the white laboring men rose in their desperation and threatened the existence of the Chinese colony, when the influx was temporarily checked; but now, since business has revived and the pressure is removed, the Chinese come in vastly increased numbers, the excess of arrivals over departures averaging about 1,000 per month at San Francisco alone. The importers of Chinese find no difficulty in securing openings for their cargoes now, and when transportation from California to Eastern States is cheapened, as it soon will be, they will extend their operation into the Middle and Eastern States, unless prevented by law, for wherever there is a white man or woman at work for wages, whether at the shoe bench, in the factory, or on the farm, there is an opening for a China Man. . . .

To those who have not studied the history of race conflicts, nor witnessed the social and industrial phenomena now open to view in the Pacific States, it may seem strange and improbable that the apparently insignificant, dwarfed, leathery little man of the Orient should, in the peaceful contest for survival, drive the Anglo-Saxon from the field. . . .

During the thousands of years of training which this race of men has undergone, in which they have been accustomed to incessant toil and insufficient food, the individuals who were too weak to endure the strain have fallen out, and none but the "fittest" have survived to become the progenitors of their race. The laborers of China are therefore men, who by long training and a heredity which is stamped upon them and ground into them through centuries of time, have become machine-like in every physical characteristic. They are of obtuse nerve, but little affected by heat or cold, wiry, sinewy, with muscles of iron; they are automatic engines of flesh and blood; they are patient, stolid, unemotional, and persistent, with such a marvelous frame and digestive apparatus that they can dispense with the comforts of shelter and subsist on the refuse of other men, and grow fat on less than half the food necessary to sustain life in the Anglo-Saxon. We have found that these men bring with them these wonderful qualities, and never lose them through all the changes of climate and food which they meet in this country; and they never change or abandon their habits or methods no matter what their surroundings may be. They herd together like beasts in places where white men could not live; they clothe themselves in the cheapest raiment as they have always done in China, and subsist on cheap food imported for their use and the refuse of our markets.

No matter how low the wages of the white man are fixed, the Chinese underbid him. Competition with such a machine by the free white man is impossible. To compete with the Chinese the white man must become such a man as the China Man is. He must work as the China Man works, subsist on as cheap food, inure himself to the same disgusting and parsimonious diet. He must adopt the packing habit, in which the shelter and space now required for one with be sufficient for ten; the unmarried must not marry, and those who have wives or children must give up home and resort to the hovel. . . .

Forty centuries of Chinese life has made the Chinaman what he is. An eternity of years cannot make him such a man as the Anglo-Saxon. It is as impossible to bring the Chinaman up to the American standard as it is cruel and wicked to risk, by any experiment, the degradation of the American laborer to the Chinese standard. The experiment now being tried in California is to subject American free labor to competition with Chinese servile labor, and so as it has gone, it has put into progress the displacement of American laborers, and the substitution of Chinese for white men. This process will continue if permitted until the white laborer is driven out into other fields, or until those who remain in the contest come down to the Chinese level.

As illustrative of this process I will submit the following undeniable facts. In San Francisco the Chinese began some fifteen years ago to enter the manufacturing establishments as operatives, then operated entirely by white people. They were dexterous and apt, and the work of displacement of the whites went steadily on. Wages were cut down, and still the Chinese underbid the white man, and in some of the factories the whole number of white employees were supplanted. The more intelligent Chinese, who had learned the art and business in which they had been employed, began a co-operative system of Chinese manufacture, and numerous factories sprung up, carried on wholly by Chinese in competition with their old employers. Chinese proprietors imported laborers from China, who came under contracts for a term of years, as they all come, and work out their passage money at the wages paid in China, three or four dollars a month. For example, I will cite the manufacture of boots and shoes. The number of boot and shoe factories in San Francisco is 60. The number carried on by white proprietors is 12. The number carried on by Chinese is 48. The number of slipper factories is 50: all carried on by Chinese. The number of Chinese employed in making boots, shoes, etc. is 5,700. Number of white people so employed is 1,100. . . .

The San Francisco Assembly of Trades certified that there are 8,265 Chinese employed in laundries. It is a well-known fact that white women who formerly did this work have been quite driven out of that employment. The same authority certifies that the number of Chinese now employed in the manufacture of clothing in San Francisco is 7,510, and the number of whites so employed is 1,000. In many industries the Chinese have entirely supplanted the white laborers and thousands of our white people have quit California and sought immunity from this grinding competition in other and better favored regions. . . .

But it has been said that all the argument we make against the admission of the Chinese cooly into direct competition with our free America laborer apply with equal force to the immigrants who come from Europe, and that most of the objections we make against the Chinese apply to immigrants from beyond the Atlantic particularly the Irish. Now, if this were true it would furnish no argument in favor of the introduction of Chinese. It might be an argument against the European immigrants, but it is not true.

European immigrants are men of the like mental and physical characteristics of the American laborer. They are of the same or a kindred race, trained under a like civilization, with similar aspirations, hopes, and tendencies. Their wants and necessities are the same, and they conform their habits, methods, and manners to those of the people by whom they are surrounded. The requirements of their social condition expand with their improving fortunes. They assimilate with American society and become a part of the America people. The competition in the field of labor between such men and the American is a contest between equals. While the European immigrant augments production he become a liberal consumer. The Chinaman clothes himself in cheap imported fabrics and his principal article of food is imported rice. The European immigrants built homes, rear families, and surround themselves with the luxuries and refinements of modern life. The Chinese take shelter in the hovel, or mass themselves in houses like swine in the sty, and send their wages to China. The accumulations of the European immigrants remain in the country and swell the aggregate wealth of the nation. Moreover, they are free, independent men, who control their own labor and their own destiny. They soon become the earnest defenders of free institutions and republican government.

Part 9

Racism Against the "Internal Other": Anti-Semitism

The Nazis exploited a popular superstition that Jews killed Christian children for their blood. This etching appeared on the front page of the Nazi publication *Der Stuermer*. The caption reads, "In 1476 the Jews of Regensburg murdered six boys. They extracted their blood and put them to death as martyrs. The judges found the bodies of the deceased in a subterranean space, which belonged to the Jew Josfal. On an alter there stood a stone plate flecked with blood." *(Virginius Dabney, courtesy of United States Holocaust Memorial Museum Photo Archives)*

Our distinction between settler societies with indigenous or imported foreign Others and societies with "internal Others" is a relative one. Over time, any foreign population can become internal. To the extent to which the foreigners assimilate, their Otherness disappears quickly. To the extent to which they do not or cannot, they remain an internal Other.

Throughout history Jews, like other people, moved, settled, assimilated, and held on to ancestral identity. Jewish emigration from Palestine was particularly heavy in the Babylonian empire of the sixteenth century B.C.E., the Greek empire of Alexander the Great and his successors, and after the Roman destruction of the temple in Jerusalem in 70 C.E. The last of these led to the great modern diaspora of Jews throughout Europe.

One of the props of anti-Semitism in Christian Europe was the image of Jews as non-Christians, "anti-Christs," and even "Christ killers." In the readings from medieval Europe, we see the poisonous power of this imagery. Religious intolerance was no doubt an important engine of anti-Semitism in Christian Europe; but it was not the only one.

It is sometimes argued that anti-Semitism existed in the ancient world long before the rise of Christianity. As early as 525 B.C.E., Persian conquerors of the Middle East enlisted Jews as allies in ruling Egypt. Later conquerors, including the Greeks and Romans, used Jews as agents of empire. In return for the patronage of foreign rulers, these Jews won the enmity of subject populations in Egypt and elsewhere. In 270 B.C.E., an Egyptian priest, Manetho, published in Greek a *History of Egypt* sometimes called the first anti-Semitic piece of literature. It was at least anti-foreign.

Thus, the second prop of anti-Semitism was the use by emperors and kings of Jews as a special caste, a minority given special favors and responsibilities, agents who could be trusted because they were different. No doubt the anti-Semitic literary images made Jews less assimilable and more useful as middlemen of monarchs. The particular duties that Jews performed may have varied somewhat. Their generally high rates of literacy may have made some Jews useful in governmental administration in the ancient world. In addition the need of European monarchs to fund their armies and opulence, combined with Christian proscriptions against usury, increased the usefulness of Jews as money lenders and financiers. In consequence, Jews were formed into and perceived as a separate caste whose power or wealth elicited the envy and contempt of the poor.

By the time of the Spanish Inquisition of the fourteenth and fifteenth centuries, in which 30,000 people were burned at the stake, Jews were beginning to be thought of as a race as well as a religion. The Marranos who were executed in the Inquisition were themselves converts to Christianity or descendants of Christian converts, recognized as Christians by the King and the

Pope. However, popular resentment had grown to a point that, once unleashed, it cared little for conversion or confession of faith.

As you read these selections, ask yourself what role religion played in the history of anti-Semitism. What role did Jewish functional identity play? When did the hatred of Jews become racism? How?

Chronicle

Solomon bar Simson

This selection is part of a chronicle of the first crusade (1096) written in Hebrew by a Jewish observer around 1140.

Notice the Christians see the Jews as an internal Other. Who in Christian society seems willing or able to protect the Jews? Why? Why did Christians attack Jews before going off to the Holy Land? How did Solomon bar Simson understand this event? How do you understand it?

Are these Christians racist? Do they view the Jews as a separate race or merely as believers in a different religion?

I will now recount the event of this persecution in other martyred communities as well—the extent to which they clung to the Lord, God of their fathers, bearing witness to His Oneness to their last breath.

In the year four thousand eight hundred and fifty-six, the year one thousand twenty-eight of our exile, in the eleventh year of the cycle Ranu, the year in which we anticipated salvation and solace, in accordance with the prophecy of Jeremiah: "Sing with gladness for Jacob, and shout at the head of the nations," etc.—this year turned instead to sorrow and groaning, weeping and outcry. Inflicted upon the Jewish People were the many evils related in all the admonitions; those enumerated in Scripture as well as those unwritten were visited upon us.

At this time arrogant people, a people of strange speech, a nation bitter and impetuous, Frenchmen and Germans, set out for the Holy City, which had

---

Reprinted from *The Jews and the Crusaders: The Hebrew Chronicles of the First and Second Crusades*, trans. and ed. Shlomo Eidelberg (Madison: University of Wisconsin Press, 1977), pp. 21–22, 121–23. Reprinted by permission of Shlomo Eidelberg.

been desecrated by barbaric nations, there to seek their house of idolatry and banish the Ishmaelites [Muslims] and other denizens of the land and conquer the land for themselves. They decorated themselves prominently with their signs, placing a profane symbol—a horizontal line over a vertical one—on the vestments of every man and woman whose heart yearned to go on the stray path to the grave of their Messiah. Their ranks swelled until the number of men, women, and children exceeded a locust horde covering the earth; of them it was said: "The locusts have no king yet go they forth all of them by bands." Now it came to pass that as they passed through the towns where Jews dwelled, they said to one another: "Look now, we going a long way to seek out the profane shrine and to avenge ourselves on the Ishmaelites, when here, in our very midst, are the Jews—they whose forefathers murdered and crucified him for no reason. Let us first avenge ourselves on them and exterminate them from among the nations so that the name of Israel will no longer be remembered, or let them adopt our faith and acknowledge the offspring of promiscuity."

When the Jewish communities became aware of their intentions, they resorted to the custom of our ancestors, repentance, prayer, and charity. The hands of the Holy Nation turned faint at this time, their hearts melted, and their strength flagged. They hid in their innermost rooms to escape the swirling sword. They subjected themselves to great endurance, abstaining from food and drink for three consecutive days and nights, and then fasting many days from sunrise to sunset, until their skin was shriveled and dry as wood upon their bones. And they cried out loudly and bitterly to God.

But their Father did not answer them; He obstructed their prayers, concealing Himself in a cloud through which their prayers could not pass, and He abhorred their tent, and He removed them out of His sight—all of this having been decreed by Him to take place "in the day when I visit"; and this was the generation that had been chosen by Him to be His portion, for they had the strength and the fortitude to stand in His Sanctuary, and fulfill His word, and sanctify His Great Name in His world. It is of such as these that King David said: "Bless the Lord, ye angels of His, ye almighty in strength, that fulfill His word," etc. . . .

The leaders of the Jews gathered together and discussed various ways of saving themselves. They said: "Let us elect elders so that we may know how to act, for we are consumed by this great evil." The elders decided to ransom the community by generously giving of their money and bribing the various princes and deputies and bishops and governors. Then, the community leaders who were respected by the local bishop approached him and his officers and servants to negotiate this matter. They asked: "What shall we do about the news we have received regarding the slaughter of our brethren in Speyer and Worms?" They [the Gentiles] replied: "Heed our advice and bring all your money into our treasury. You, your wives, and your children, and all your belongings shall come into the courtyard of the bishop until the hordes have passed by. Thus will you be saved from the errant ones."

Actually, they gave this advice so as to herd us together and hold us like fish that are caught in an evil net, and then to turn us over to the enemy, while taking our money. This is what actually happened in the end, and "the outcome is proof of the intentions." The bishop assembled his ministers and courtiers— mighty ministers, the noblest in the land—for the purpose of helping us; for at first it had been his desire to save us with all his might, since we had given him and his ministers and servants a large bribe in return for their promise to help us. Ultimately, however, all the bribes and entreaties were of no avail to protect us on the day of wrath and misfortune.

It was at this time that Duke Godfrey [of Bouillon], may his bones be ground to dust, arose in the hardness of his spirit, driven by a spirit of wantonness to go with those journeying to the profane shrine, vowing to go on this journey only after avenging the blood of the crucified one by shedding Jewish blood and completely eradicating any trace of those bearing the name "Jew," thus assuaging his own burning wrath. To be sure, there arose someone to repair the breach—a God-fearing man who had been bound to the most holy of altars—called Rabbi Kalonymos, the Parnass of the community of Mainz. He dispatched a messenger to King Henry in the kingdom of Pula, where the king had been dwelling during the past nine years, and related all that had happened.

The king was enraged and dispatched letters to all the ministers, bishops, and governors of all the provinces of his realm, as well as to Duke Godfrey, containing words of greeting and commanding them to do no bodily harm to the Jews and to provide them with help and refuge. The evil duke then swore that he had never intended to do them harm. The Jews of Cologne nevertheless bribed him with five hundred zekukim of silver, as did the Jews of Mainz. The duke assured them of his support and promised them peace.

However, God, the maker of peace, turned aside and averted His eyes from His people, and consigned them to the sword. No prophet, seer, or man of wise heart was able to comprehend how the sin of the people infinite in number was deemed so great as to cause the destruction of so many lives in the various Jewish communities. The martyrs endured the extreme penalty normally indicted only upon one guilty of murder. Yet, it must be stated with certainty that God is a righteous judge, and we are to blame.

Then the evil waters prevailed. The enemy unjustly accused them of evil acts they did not do, declaring: "You are the children of those who killed our object of veneration, hanging him on a tree; and he himself had said: 'There will yet come a day when my children will come and avenge my blood.' We are his children and it is therefore obligatory for us to avenge him since you are the ones who rebel and disbelieve in him. Your God has never been at peace with you. Although He intended to deal kindly with you, you have conducted yourselves improperly before Him. God has forgotten you and is no longer desirous of you since you are a stubborn nation. Instead, He has departed from you and has taken us for His portion, casting His radiance upon us."

When we heard these words, our hearts trembled and moved out of their places. We were dumb with silence, abiding in darkness, like those long dead, waiting for the Lord to look forth and behold from heaven.

And Satan—the Pope of evil Rome—also came and proclaimed to all the nations believing in that stock of adultery—these are the stock of Seir—that they should assemble and ascend to Jerusalem so as to conquer the city, and journey to the tomb of the superstition whom they call their god. Satan came and mingled with the nations, and they gathered as one man to fulfill the command, coming in great numbers like the grains of sand upon the seashore, the noise of them clamorous as a whirlwind and a storm. When the drops of the bucket had assembled, they took evil counsel against the people of the Lord and said: "Why should we concern ourselves with going to war against the Ishmaelites dwelling about Jerusalem, when in our midst is a people who disrespect our god—indeed, their ancestors are those who crucified him. Why should we let them live and tolerate their dwelling among us? Let us commence by using our swords against them and then proceed upon our stray path."

The heart of the people of our God grew faint and their spirit flagged, for many sore injuries had been inflicted upon them and they had been smitten repeatedly. They now came supplicating to God and fasting, and their hearts melted within them. But the Lord did as He declared, for we had sinned before Him, and He forsook the sanctuary of Shiloh—The Temple-in-Miniature—which He had placed among His people who dwelt in the midst of alien nations. His wrath was kindled and He drew the sword against them, until they remained but as the flagstaff upon the mountaintop and as the ensign on the hill, and He gave over His nation into captivity and trampled them underfoot. See, O Lord, and consider to whom Thou hast done thus: to Israel, a nation despised and pillaged, Your chosen portion! Why have You uplifted the shield of its enemies, and why have they gained in strength? Let all hear, for I cry out in anguish; the ears of all that hear me shall be seared: How has the staff of might been broken, the rod of glory—the sainted community comparable to fine gold, the community of Mainz! It was caused by the Lord to test those that fear Him, to have them endure the yoke of His pure fear.

Regulation of the Jewish Community, Florence, 1463

During the Renaissance, Florence had a reputation for considerable tolerance. There were no witch hunts or pogroms.

What is the reason given for this regulation of 1463? The regulation involves certain prior agreements. What are they? Are these agreements made with each individual Jew or with a larger entity?

[The priors] have considered that a large number of Jews have come to settle in Florence, and scarcely any of them wear a sign, so that there is considerable confusion, and it is difficult to distinguish between Jews and Christians. There have been numerous errors and mistakes in the past, and it is obvious that there will be others in the future. They are determined to remedy this unsatisfactory situation, which will require some modification of the contract made by the Commune of Florence, or by those authorized by it to make this agreement, granting permission to these Jews named in the contract to engage in money lending in Florence for ten years, beginning on June 18, 1459. . . . Having examined this matter with those Jews to whom this permission was granted in the agreement, who also have demonstrated their desire to correct this unfortunate situation, the following provisions have been established.

Every Jew, male or female above the age of twelve, whether or not named in the Florentine agreement, and whether or not a resident of the city of Florence, shall be required to wear a sign of O in the city of Florence. This yellow O shall be worn on the left breast, over the clothing in a visible place; it shall be at least one foot in circumference and as wide as the thickness of a finger. A penalty of 25 lire shall be levied on every occasion that this sign is not worn, with two witnesses required. . . . Outside of the city, those Jews who are not engaged in moneylending operations in the *contado* or district of Florence, and all foreign Jews who are passing through en route to some place, shall not be required to carry this sign in the *contado* or district. And if any Jew arrives in Florence, he shall be permitted to enter the city without any sign, and to go to his house or hotel where he is lodging and there he may deposit

Cassuto, *Gli ebrei a Firenze nell'età del Rinascimento* (Florence, 1918). Provisions of January 24, 1406 and June 12, 1430. Translated in Gene Brucker, ed., *The Society of Renaissance Florence* (New York: Harper, 1971), pp. 362–65.

his baggage. But thereafter, he may not go in the city without carrying the sign. . . . This provision is not to be construed to mean that the Jews named in the agreement are required to wear the sign in their house, or within ten yards of their house.

To prevent any large concentration of Jews in Florence, or a greater number than is necessary, in future the Jews engaged in moneylending in Florence may not number more than seventy persons in their houses and in their shops, working as factors and apprentices. Included in this number of seventy are Jews of both sexes, masculine and feminine, large and small. And if this number be exceeded, and those additional Jews remain in Florence for more than five days, the community will be fined 50 florins for each person and for each violation. And all other Jews not included in this community of seventy may not stay in the city of Florence or its suburbs for more than five days in any single visit . . . and having left the city, they cannot return again . . . before one month. . . .

The present addition to the agreement . . . has been drawn up with the consent of the above named Jews and in particular, in accordance with the wishes of the heads of the community, who have desired [to make] their future life and business activity more honest, less dangerous, and less subject to opprobrium. . . . This clause is added, namely, that all Hebrew books which pertain to the faith, law, or church of these Jews, and also all scholarly books of whatever discipline, may be possessed, read, studied, and copied by the Jews of this community. . . . This is not to include the possession, reading, and study of any book like those which have brought infamy and opprobrium to the Jews living in Cortona, or any similar book against the Christian faith which may appear in future. The community, and each above-named Jew, is to be permitted—without penalty or prejudice—to perform and recite the ceremonies and offices in the synagogues and houses in which they live . . . according to the mode and customs which is practiced by the Italian Jews. . . .

On the Jews, 1543

Martin Luther

Martin Luther, the father of the Protestant Reformation, initially believed that Jews were closer to Christ than Christians, who had been corrupted by the Roman papacy. Before his break with the Roman church, he wrote: "The Jews are blood-relations of our Lord; if it were proper to boast of flesh and blood, the Jews belong more to Christ than we. I beg, therefore, my dear Papist, if you become tired of abusing me as a heretic, that you begin to revile me as a Jew."

When, however, Luther established his own purified Christianity, and the Jews did not throng to convert, Luther turned on them with the venom and imagery that often bubbled to the surface of Christian discussions of Jews. Without excusing the poisonous language of these passages, it would be ahistorical to read the later Nazi agenda into Luther. For Luther, Jewish religious identity was offensive to God and so Jewish means of continuing that identity had to be ended. This is still short of the nineteenth-century idea of Jewish religion as a biologically fixed or racial identity, beyond the possibility of conversion and redemption.

What traditional Christian or European images of Jews does Luther draw on? In what sense did Luther views Jews as an "internal other"?

What shall we Christians do with this rejected and condemned people, the Jews? Since they live among us, we dare not tolerate their conduct, now that we are aware of their lying and reviling and blaspheming. If we do, we become sharers in their lies, cursing and blasphemy. Thus we cannot extinguish the unquenchable fire of divine wrath, of which the prophets speak, nor can we convert the Jews. With prayer and the fear of God we must practice a sharp mercy to see whether we might save at least a few from the glowing flames. We dare not avenge ourselves. Vengeance a thousand times worse than we could wish them already has them by the throat. I shall give you my sincere advice:

First, to set fire to their synagogues or schools and to bury and cover with dirt whatever will not burn, so that no man will ever again see a stone or cinder of them. This is to be done in honor of our Lord and of Christendom,

---

From *Luther's Works*, Volume 47: *The Christian in Society* IV, trans. Martin H. Bertram (Philadelphia: Fortress Press, 1971), pp. 290–93.

so that God might see that we are Christians, and do not condone or knowingly tolerate such public lying, cursing, and blaspheming of his Son and of his Christians. For whatever we tolerated in the past unknowingly—and I myself was unaware of it—will be pardoned by God. But if we, now that we are informed, were to protect and shield such a house for the Jews, existing right before our very nose, in which they lie about, blaspheme, curse, vilify, and defame Christ and us . . . it would be the same as if we were doing all this and even worse ourselves, as we very well know.

In Deuteronomy 13 [:12 ff.] Moses writes that any city that is given to idolatry shall be totally destroyed by fire, and nothing of it shall be preserved. If he were alive today, he would be the first to set fire to the synagogues and houses of the Jews. For in Deuteronomy 4 [:2] and 12 [:32] he commanded very explicitly that nothing is to be added to or subtracted from his law. And Samuel says in I Samuel 15 [:23] that disobedience to God is idolatry. Now the Jews' doctrine at present is nothing but the additions of the rabbis and the idolatry of disobedience, so that Moses has become entirely unknown among them (as we said before), just as the Bible became unknown under the papacy in our day. So also, for Moses' sake, their schools cannot be tolerated; they defame him just as much as they do us. It is not necessary that they have their own free churches for such idolatory.

Second, I advise that their houses also be razed and destroyed. For they pursue in them the same aims as in their synagogues. Instead they might be lodged under a roof or in a barn, like the gypsies. This will bring home to them that they are not masters in our country, as they boast, but that they are living in exile and in captivity, as they incessantly wail and lament about us before God.

Third, I advise that all their prayer books and Talmudic writings, in which such idolatry, lies, cursing and blasphemy are taught, be taken from them.

Fourth, I advise that their rabbis be forbidden to teach henceforth on pain of loss of life and limb. For they have justly forfeited the right to such an office by holding the poor Jews captive with the saying of Moses (Deuteronomy 17 [:10 ff.]) in which he commands them to obey their teachers on penalty of death, although Moses clearly adds: "what they teach you in accord with the law of the Lord." Those villains ignore that. They wantonly employ the poor people's obedience contrary to the law of the Lord and infuse them with this poison, cursing, and blasphemy. In the same way the pope also held us captive with the declaration in Matthew 16 [:18], "You are Peter," etc., inducing us to believe all the lies and deceptions that issued from his devilish mind. He did not teach in accord with the word of God, and therefore he forfeited the right to teach.

Fifth, I advise that safe-conduct on the highways be abolished completely for the Jews. For they have no business in the countryside, since they are not lords, officials, tradesmen, or the like. Let them stay at home. . . .

Sixth, I advise that usury be prohibited to them, and that all cash and treasure of silver and gold be taken from them and put aside for safekeeping. The reason for such a measure is that, as said above, they have no other means of earning a livelihood than usury, and by it they have stolen and robbed from us all they possess. Such money should now be used in no other way than the following: Whenever a Jew is sincerely converted, he should be handed one hundred, two hundred, or three hundred florins, as personal circumstances may suggest. With this he could set himself up in some occupation for the support of his poor wife and children, and the maintenance of the old or feeble. For such evil gains are cursed if they are not put to use with God's blessing in a good and worthy cause. . . .

Seventh, I commend putting a flail, an ax, a hoe, a spade, a distaff, or a spindle into the hands of young, strong Jews and Jewesses and letting them earn their bread in the sweat of their brow, as was imposed on the children of Adam (Gen 3 [:19]). For it is not fitting that they should let us accursed Goyim toil in the sweat of our faces while they, the holy people, idle away their time behind the stove, feasting and farting, and on top of all, boasting blasphemously of their lordship over the Christians by means of our sweat. No, one should toss out these lazy rogues by the seat of their pants.

The Discovery of Anti-Semitism in Vienna

Adolf Hitler

This selection from Hitler's Mein Kampf *shows how Hitler wanted to present his evolution toward anti-Semitism. Among other things, it reminds us of the range and respectability of anti-Semitism in Austrian Vienna after*

World War I. What forces in Viennese society seem to benefit from anti-Semitism?

Notice how Hitler perceived Jews as both foreign and insiders. This is an example of the racism based on fear of pollution or corruption by an internal Other. Notice how so much seems to Hitler to depend on whether he can distinguish Jews from non-Jews. Notice the metaphor of seduction. To what extent is Hitler motivated by fear of Marxists or communists in the Social Democratic party? To what extent does he feel threatened by pro-French intellectuals and internationalists? How do all of these fears come together in Hitler's image of Jews?

Today it is difficult, if not impossible, to say when the word, "Jew," first gave me ground for special thoughts. At home I do not remember having heard the word during my father's lifetime. I believe that the old gentleman would have regarded any special emphasis on this term as cultural backwardness. In the course of his life he had arrived at more or less cosmopolitan views which, despite his pronounced national sentiments, not only remained intact, but also affected me to some extent.

Likewise at school I found no occasion which could have led me to change this inherited picture. At the *Realschule,* to be sure, I did meet one Jewish boy who was treated by all of us with caution, but only because various experiences had led us to doubt his discretion and we did not particularly trust him; but neither I nor the others had any thoughts on the matter.

Not until my fourteenth or fifteenth year did I begin to come across the word "Jew," with any frequency, partly in connection with political discussions. This filled me with a mild distaste, and I could not rid myself of an unpleasant feeling that always came over me whenever religious quarrels occurred in my presence.

At that time I did not think anything else of the question.

There were few Jews in Linz. In the course of the centuries their outward appearance had become Europeanized and had taken on a human look; in fact, I even took them for Germans. The absurdity of this idea did not dawn on me because I saw no distinguishing feature but the strange religion. The fact that they had, as I believed, been persecuted on this account sometimes almost turned my distaste at unfavorable remarks about them into horror.

Thus far I did not so much as suspect the existence of an organized opposition to the Jews.

Then I came to Vienna.

Preoccupied by the abundance of my impressions in the architectural field, oppressed by the hardship of my own lot, I gained at first no insight into the inner stratification of the people in this gigantic city. Notwithstanding that Vienna in those days counted nearly two hundred thousand Jews among its two million inhabitants, I did not see them. In the first few weeks my eyes and my senses were not equal to the flood of values and ideas. Not until calm gradually returned and the agitated picture began to clear did I look around me more carefully in my new world, and then among other things I encountered the Jewish question.

I cannot maintain that the way in which I became acquainted with them struck me as particularly pleasant. For the Jew was still characterized for me by nothing but his religion, and therefore, on grounds of human tolerance, I maintained my rejection of religious attacks in this case as in others. Consequently, the tone, particularly that of the Viennese anti-Semitic press, seemed to me unworthy of the cultural tradition of a great nation. I was oppressed by the memory of certain occurrences in the Middle Ages, which I should not have liked to see repeated. Since the newspapers in question did not enjoy an outstanding reputation (the reason for this, at that time, I myself did not precisely know), I regarded them more as the products of anger and envy than the results of a principled, though perhaps mistaken, point of view.

I was reinforced in this opinion by what seemed to me the far more dignified form in which the really big papers answered all these attacks, or, what seemed to me even more praiseworthy, failed to mention them; in other words, simply killed with silence.

I zealously read the so-called world-press (*Neue Freie Presse, Wiener Tageblatt*, etc.) and was amazed by the scope of what they offered its readers and the objectivity of individual articles. I respected the exalted tone, though the flamboyance of the style sometimes caused me inner dissatisfaction, or even struck me unpleasantly. Yet this may have been due to the rhythm of life in the whole metropolis.

Since in those days I saw Vienna in that light, I thought myself justified in accepting this explanation of mine as a valid excuse. . . .

It was this which caused me little by little to view the big papers with greater caution.

And on one such occasion I was forced to recognize that one of the anti-Semitic papers, the *Deutsches Volksblatt*, behaved more decently.

Another thing that got on my nerves was the loathsome cult for France which the big press, even then, carried on. A man couldn't help feeling ashamed to be a German when he saw these saccharine hymns of praise to the "great cultural nation." This wretched licking of France's boots more than once made me throw down one of these "world newspapers." And on such occasions I sometimes picked up the *Volksblatt* which, to be sure, seemed to me much smaller, but in these matters somewhat more appetizing. I was not in agreement with the sharp anti-Semitic tone, but from time to time I read arguments which gave me some food for thought.

At all events, these occasions slowly made me acquainted with the man and the movement, which in those days guided Vienna's destinies: Dr. Karl Lueger and the Christian Social Party.

When I arrived in Vienna, I was hostile to both of them.

The man and the movement seemed "reactionary" in my eyes.

My common sense of justice, however, forced me to change this judgment in proportion as I had occasion to become acquainted with the man and his work; and slowly my fair judgment turned to unconcealed admiration. Today, more than ever, I regard this man as the greatest German mayor of all times.

How much of my basic principles were upset by this change in my attitude toward the Christian Social Party!

My views with regard to anti-Semitism thus succumbed to the passage of time, and this was my greatest transformation of all.

It cost me the greatest inner soul struggles, and only after months of battle between my reason and my sentiments did my reason begin to emerge victorious. Two years later, my sentiment had followed my reason, and from then on became its most loyal guardian and sentinel.

At the time of this bitter struggle between spiritual education and cold reason, the visual instruction of the Vienna streets had performed invaluable services. There came a time when I no longer, as in the first days, wandered blindly through the mighty city; now with open eyes I saw not only the buildings but also the people.

Once, as I was once strolling through the Inner City, I suddenly encountered an apparition in a black caftan with black hair locks. Is this a Jew? was my first thought.

For, to be sure, they had not looked like that in Linz. I observed the man furtively and cautiously, but the longer I stared at this foreign face, scrutinizing feature for feature, the more my first question assumed a new form:

Is this a German?

As always in such cases I now began to try to relieve my doubts by books. For a few hellers I bought the first anti-Semitic pamphlets of my life. Unfortunately, they all proceeded from the supposition that in principle the reader knew or even understood the Jewish question to a certain degree. Besides, the tone for the most part was such that doubts again arose in me, due in part to the dull and amazingly unscientific arguments favoring the thesis.

I had a relapse for weeks at a time, once even for months.

The whole thing seemed to me so monstrous, the accusations so boundless, that, tormented by the fear of doing injustice, I again became anxious and uncertain.

Yet, I could no longer very well doubt that the objects of my study were not Germans of a special religion, but a people in themselves; for since I had begun to concern myself with this question and to take cognizance of the Jews, Vienna appeared to me in a different light than before. Wherever I went, I began to see Jews, and the more I saw, the more sharply they became distinguished in my eyes from the rest of humanity. Particularly the Inner City and the districts north of the Danube Canal swarmed with a people which even outwardly had lost all resemblance to Germans.

And whatever doubts I may still have nourished were finally dispelled by the attitude of a portion of the Jews themselves.

Among them there was a great movement, quite extensive in Vienna, which came out sharply in confirmation of the national character of the Jews: this was the *Zionists.*

It looked, to be sure, as though only a part of the Jews approved this viewpoint, while the great majority condemned and inwardly rejected such a formulation. But when examined more closely, this appearance dissolved itself into an unsavory vapor of pretexts advanced for mere reasons of expedience, not to say lies. For the so-called liberal Jews did not reject the Zionists as non-Jews, but only as Jews with an impractical, perhaps even dangerous, way of publicly avowing their Jewishness.

Intrinsically they remained unalterably of one piece.

In a short time this apparent struggle between Zionistic and liberal Jews disgusted me; for it was false through and through, founded on lies and scarcely in keeping with the moral elevation and purity always claimed by this people.

The cleanliness of this people, moral and otherwise, I must say, is a point in itself. By their very exterior you could tell that these were no lovers of water, and, to your distress, you often knew it with your eyes closed. Later I often grew sick to my stomach from the smell of these caftan-wearers. Added to this, there was their unclean dress and their generally unheroic appearance.

All this could scarcely be called very attractive; but it became positively repulsive when, in addition to their physical uncleanliness, you discovered the moral stains on this "chosen people."

In a short time I was made more thoughtful than ever by my slowly rising insight into the type of activity carried on by the Jews in certain fields.

Was there any form of filth or profligacy, particularly in cultural life, without at least one Jew involved in it?

If you cut even cautiously into such an abscess, you found, like a maggot in a rotting body, often dazzled by the sudden light—a kike!

What had to be reckoned heavily against the Jews in my eyes was when I became acquainted with their activity in the press, art, literature, and the theater. All the unctuous reassurances helped little or nothing. It sufficed to look at a billboard, to study the names of the men behind the horrible trash they

This racist German depiction of sexual depravity shows a Nazi image of the Jewish boss. *(Courtesy of United States Holocaust Memorial Museum Photo Archives)*

Another racist German depiction of sexual depravity shows a French-African soldier guarding the Rhine River with a belt of naked German women. *(Courtesy of United States Holocaust Memorial Museum Photo Archives)*

advertised, to make you hard for a long time to come. This was pestilence, spiritual pestilence, worse than the Black Death of olden times, and the people was being infected with it! It goes without saying that the lower the intellectual level of one of these art manufacturers, the more unlimited his fertility will be, and the scoundrel ends up like a garbage separator, splashing his filth in the face of humanity. And bear in mind that there is no limit to their number; bear in mind that for one Goethe Nature easily can foist on the world ten thousand of these scribblers who poison men's souls like germ-carriers of the worse sort, on their fellow men.

It was terrible, but not to be overlooked, that precisely the Jew, in tremendous numbers, seemed chosen by Nature for this shameful calling.

Is this why the Jews are called the chosen people? . . .

And I now began to examine my beloved "world press" from this point of view.

And the deeper I probed, the more the object of my former admiration shriveled. The style became more and more unbearable; I could not help rejecting the content as inwardly shallow and banal; the objectivity of exposition now seemed to me more akin to lies than honest truth; and the writers were—Jews.

A thousand things which I had hardly seen before now struck my notice and others, which had previously given me food for thought, I now learned to grasp and understand.

I now saw the liberal attitude of this press in a different light; the lofty tone in which it answered attacks and its method killing them with silence now revealed itself to me as a trick as clever as it was treacherous; the transfigured raptures of their theatrical critics were always directed at Jewish writers, and their disapproval never struck anyone but Germans. The gentle pinpricks against William II revealed its methods by their persistency, and so did its commendation of French culture and civilization. The trashy content of the short story now appeared to me as outright indecency, and in the language I detected the accents of a foreign people; the sense of the whole thing was so obviously hostile to Germanism that this could only have been intentional.

But who had an interest in this?

Was all this a mere accident?

Gradually, I became uncertain.

The development was accelerated by insights which I gained into a number of other matters. I am referring to the general view of ethics and morals which was quite openly exhibited by a large part of the Jews, and the practical application of which could be seen.

Here again the streets provided an object lesson of a sort which was sometimes positively evil.

The relation of the Jews to prostitution and, even more, to the white-slave traffic, could be studied in Vienna as perhaps in no other city of Western Europe, with the possible exception of the southern French ports. If you walked at night through the streets and alleys of Leopoldstadt,* at every step you witnessed proceedings which remained concealed from the majority of the German people until the War gave the soldiers on the eastern front occasion to see similar thing, or, better expressed, forced them to see them.

When thus for the first time I recognized the Jew as the cold-hearted, shameless, and calculating director of this revolting vice traffic in the scum of the big city, a cold shudder ran down my back.

But then a flame flared up within me. I no longer avoided discussion of the Jewish question; no, now I sought it. And when I learned to look for the Jew in all branches of cultural and artistic life and its various manifestations, I suddenly encountered him in a place where I would least have expected to find him.

When I recognized the Jew as the leader of the Social Democracy, the scales dropped from my eyes. A long soul struggle had reached its conclusion.

Even in the daily relations with my fellow workers I observed the amazing adaptability with which they adopted different positions on the same question, sometimes within an interval of a few days, sometimes in only a few hours. It was hard for me to understand how people who, when spoken to alone, possessed some sensible opinions, suddenly lost them as soon as they came under the influence of the masses. it was often enough to make one despair. When, after hours of argument, I was convinced that now at last I had broken the ice or cleared up some absurdity, and was beginning to rejoice at my success, on the next day to my disgust I had to begin all over again; it had all been in vain. Like an eternal pendulum their opinions seemed to swing back again and again to the old madness.

All this I could understand: that they were dissatisfied with their lot and cursed the Fate which often struck them so harshly; that they hated the employers who seemed to them the heartless bailiffs of Fate; that they cursed the authorities who in their eyes were without feeling for their situation; that they demonstrated against food prices and carried their demands into the streets: this much could be understood without recourse to reason. But what inevitably remained incomprehensible was the boundless hatred they heaped upon their own nationality, despising its greatness, besmirching its history, and dragging its great men into the gutter.

---

*Second District of Vienna, separated from the main part of the city by the Danube Canal. Formerly the ghetto, it still has a predominantly Jewish population.

This struggle against their own species, their own clan, their own homeland, was as senseless as it was incomprehensible. It was unnatural.

It was possible to cure them temporarily of this vice, but only for days or at most weeks. If later you met the man you thought you had converted, he was just the same as before.

His old unnatural state had regained full possession of him

* * *

I gradually became aware that the Social Democratic press was directed predominantly by Jews; yet I did not attribute any special significance to this circumstance, since conditions were exactly the same in the other papers. Yet one fact seemed conspicuous: there was not one paper with Jews working on it which could have been regarded as truly national, according to my education and way of thinking.

I swallowed my disgust and tried to read this type of Marxist press production, but my revulsion became so unlimited in so doing that I endeavored to become more closely acquainted with the men who manufactured these compendiums of knavery.

From the publisher down, they were all Jews.

I took all the Social Democratic pamphlets I could lay hands on and sought the names of their authors: Jews. I noted the names of the leaders; by far the greatest part were likewise members of the "chosen people," whether they were representatives in the Reichsrat or trade-union secretaries, the heads of organizations or street agitators. It was always the same gruesome picture. the names of the Austerlitzes, Davids, Adlers, Ellenbogens, etc. will remain forever graven in my memory. One thing had grown clear to me: the party with whose petty representatives I had been carrying on the most violent struggle for months was, as to leadership, almost exclusively in the hands of a foreign people; for, to my deep and joyful satisfaction, I had at last come to the conclusion that the Jew was no German.

Only now did I become thoroughly acquainted with the seducer of our people.

A single year of my sojourn in Vienna had sufficed to imbue me with the conviction that no worker could be so stubborn that he would not in the end succumb to better knowledge and better explanations. Slowly I had become an expert in their own doctrine and used it as a weapon in the struggle for my own profound conviction.

Success almost always favored my side.

The great masses could be saved, if only with the gravest sacrifice in time and patience.

But a Jew could never be parted from his opinions.

At that time I was still childish enough to try to make the madness of their doctrine clear to them; in my little circle I talked my tongue sore and my throat hoarse, thinking I would inevitably succeed in convincing them how ruinous their Marxist madness was; but what I accomplished was often the opposite. It seemed as though their increased understanding of the destructive effects of Social Democratic theories and their results only reinforced their determination.

The more I argued with them, the better I came to know their dialectic. First they counted on the stupidity of their adversary, and then, when there was no other way out, they themselves simply played stupid. . . . Whenever you tried to attack one of these apostles, your hand closed on a jelly-like slime which divided up and poured through your fingers, but in the next moment collected again. But if you really struck one of these fellows so telling a blow that, observed by the audience, he couldn't help but agree, and if you believed that this had taken you at least one step forward, our amazement was great the next day. The Jew had not the slightest recollection of the day before, he rattled off his same old nonsense as though nothing as all had happened, and, if indignantly challenged, affected amazement; he couldn't remember a thing, except that he had proved the correctness of his assertions the previous day.

Sometimes I stood there thunderstruck.

I didn't know what to be more amazed at: the agility or their tongues or their virtuosity at lying.

Gradually, I began to hate them.

All this had but one good side: that in proportion as the real leaders or at least the disseminators of Social Democracy came within my vision, my love for my people inevitably grew. For who, in view of the diabolical craftiness of these seducers, could damn the luckless victims? How hard it was, even for me, to get the better of this race of dialectical liars! And how futile was such success in dealing with people who twist the truth in your mouth, who without so much as a blush disavow the word they have just spoken, and in the very next minute take credit for it all.

No. the better acquainted I became with the Jew, the more forgiving I inevitably became toward the worker. . . .

. . . [I]t was the duty of every thinking man to force himself to the forefront of the ill-starred movement, thus perhaps averting catastrophe . . . however, the original founders of this plague of the nations must have been veritable devils; for only in the brain of a monster—not that of a man—could the plan of an organization assume form and meaning, whose activity must ultimately result in the collapse of human civilization and the consequent devastation of the world.

In this case the only remaining hope was struggle, struggle with all the weapons which the human spirit, reason, and will can devise, regardless on which side of the scale Fate should lay its blessing.

Thus I began to make myself familiar with the founders of this doctrine, in order to study the foundations of the movement. If I reached my goal more quickly than at first I had perhaps ventured to believe, it was thanks to my newly acquired, though at that time not very profound, knowledge of the Jewish question. This alone enabled me to draw a practical comparison between the reality and the theoretical flim-flam of the founding fathers of Social Democracy, since it taught me to understand the language of the Jewish people, who speak in order to conceal or at least to veil their thoughts; their real aim is not therefore to be found in the lines themselves, but slumbers well concealed between them.

For me this was the time of the greatest spiritual upheaval I have ever had to go through.

I had ceased to be a weak-kneed cosmopolitan and become an anti-Semite.

Just once more—and this was the last time—fearful, oppressive thoughts came to me in profound anguish.

When over long periods of human history I scrutinized the activity of the Jewish people, suddenly there rose up in me the fearful question whether inscrutable Destiny, perhaps for reasons unknown to us poor mortals, did not with eternal and immutable revolve, desire the final victory of this little nation.

Was it possible that the earth had been promised as a reward to this people which lives only for this earth?

Have we an objective right to struggle for our self-preservation, or is this justified only subjectively within ourselves.

As I delved more deeply into the teachings of Marxism and thus in tranquil clarity submitted the deeds of the Jewish people to contemplation, Fate itself gave me its answer.

The Jewish doctrine of Marxism rejects the aristocratic principle of Nature and replaces the eternal privilege of power and strength by the mass of numbers and their dead weight. Thus it denies the value of personality in man, contests the significance of nationality and race, and thereby withdraws from humanity the premise of its existence and its culture. As a foundation of the universe, this doctrine would bring about the end of any order intellectually conceivable to man. And as, in this greatest of all recognizable organisms, the result of an application of such a law could only be chaos, on earth it could only be destruction for the inhabitants of this planet.

If, with the help of his Marxist creed, the Jew is victorious over the other peoples of the world. his crown will be the funeral wreath of humanity and this planet will, as it did thousands of years ago, move through the ether devoid of men.

Eternal Nature inexorably avenges the infringement of her commands.

Hence today I believe that I am acting in accordance with the will of the Almighty Creator: *by defending myself against the Jew, I am fighting for the work of the Lord.*

Blacks in Germany During the Third Reich: Star of David Not Required

Stephen Kaufman

Anti-Semitism was not the only kind of racism practiced by the Nazis. Like other European countries, Germany also had a history of white racism directed against Africans. In this selection, the author explores the meeting of anti-Semitism and white racism in Hitler's racial mythology. Why was the occupation of the Rhineland so important in the development of this mythology of Aryan racial purity? How did Hitler implicate the Jews in the "negrification" of Germany? Notice the images that introduce this and the next part. How did the Nazis draw on political, racial, and sexual fears in producing their racist propaganda?

Blacks in Germany during the Third Reich were all too visible to require special insignia, but despite their visibility, the actions and policies of the Nazi regime varied considerably by circumstance, locale and time. Traditional perceptions of Blacks and Nazis are framed against the triumphs of Joe Louis in the boxing ring and Jesse Owens during the 1936 Olympics. Recent books and articles have expanded our understanding of the complex relationships between Nazis and Blacks.

Blacks falling under Nazi control included those who had German citizenship, those who were citizens of other European countries later occupied by Germany, *ex-patriot* Americans and citizens of other non-European countries and prisoners of war. This essay focuses on Blacks who were German citizens as were most German Jews.

Germany, like other European states, participated in the colonization and partition of Africa in the 1880s, fifty years before the Nazis came to power. German occupation of Kamerun, German South West Africa, and German East Africa. manifested the prejudice and racist behavior of other European colonies in Africa.

Not surprisingly, despite this imperialist attitude, Blacks came to live in Germany. The exact number is unknown but is considered small. Some ap-

---

Original publication for this book.

"Degenerate Music." Illustration used for the "Degenerate Art" exhibit in Düsseldorf, Germany, during the Reich Music Festival of 1938. *(Permission of the Bildarchiv Preussischer Kulturbesitz)*

"The Rhineland Bastards." Nazi propaganda exploited the image of interracial children born to German women and the occupying French-Moroccan troops who had been stationed in the Rhineland until the late 1920s. *(Library of Congress, courtesy of United States Holocaust Memorial Museum Photo Archives)*

parently came for economic reasons while others came to serve the African states from which they originated. It is estimated that as many as 25,000 Blacks were living in Germany by 1933. German classification of Blacks often included people from North Africa and neighboring Islamic states.

In some cases, Blacks residing in Germany fathered children with German women. Hans Massaquoi, a German citizen and the son of a Black African father and a German woman, recently wrote an illuminating autobiography in which he recounts his experiences growing up in Germany during the entire Nazi. His father left Germany, and he was raised by his mother. While he experienced taunting, job discrimination and the occasional fight, he was not systematically rounded up, interrogated, thrown into a concentration or internment camp or subjected to medical operations.

Massaquoi's relatively benign experience contrasts sharply with that of a group of African-Germans who came to be known as the Rhineland Bastards. These German citizens were the biracial children of the Allied occupation of the Rhineland after World War I. France used soldiers from its African colonies to occupy the industrial and populated Rhineland. Though hard numbers are difficult to come by, estimates place as many as 30–40,000 colonial troops in Germany. These troops came from both sub-Saharan Africa and North Africa. German reactions were swift and forceful. Diplomatic initiatives were undertaken to have the Black colonial soldiers removed, and large scale public relations campaigns across Europe and the United States were initiated to force the removal of the troops. Posters, editorial cartoons and an extra-ordinary commemorative coin expressed German attitudes towards the use of Black soldiers.

Many of the drawings clearly expressed the sexual character of German concerns. At the core of many of the protests was the charge that Black soldiers were raping German women. It is important to note that military tribunals investigating these assaults found no basis for the allegations. The children were apparently the result of voluntary sexual relationships including lovers as well as prostitutes

As the troops were moved out, numerous letters and cards were sent by German women to their colonial lovers attesting to the voluntary character of the relationships. Nonetheless sufficient political pressures were applied to have the Black colonial soldiers removed. The children from these sexual liaisons remained behind as is often the case with departing occupying armies. Born in occupied Germany, they were German citizens, but to many Germans they were known as the Schwarze Schande, the Black Shame.

Hitler himself would make use of the German resentment at the Allied use of Black colonial troops after World War I. In *Mein Kampf*, he rails against the "negrification" of Europe and manages to see Jews as the culprits. Hitler further goes on to discuss the reasons by which one gains citizenship in Germany. He writes about birthplace as the key reason and decries the citizenship granted to the Rhineland Bastards who, he said, were destroying the character of the Aryan gene pool.

Soon after the Nazi regime came to power it set out to deal with the issue of race and the case of the Rhineland Bastards was a flash point. The Nuremburg Laws and other guidelines established a framework for controlling the character of the Aryan gene pool. The Rhineland Bastards were identified. Histories and photographs were taken and then forwarded to the Wilhelm Kaiser Anthropological Institute. There the portfolios were evaluated. After secret hearings, those children judged to be Rhineland Bastards were forcibly taken to nearby hospitals and sterilized to ensure that they would not continue their pollution of the Aryan gene pool.

Some historians have suggested that German treatment of Blacks was not more brutal because Blacks were neither numerous nor perceived as powerful within the boundaries of the Third Reich and that German political strategy as it related to expanded interests in sub-Saharan Africa required a less confrontational approach.

Other Blacks came under Nazi Control as Germany expanded its territorial base. The treatment of these people varied considerably. There is some evidence to suggest that Black soldiers were often singled out for punishment in direct contravention of the Geneva Accords, but so frequently were White Allied soldiers.

Anecdotal stories of Blacks in the Netherlands, France and Poland suggest that some enjoyed privileges not shared by other victims of the Nazi regime. In France, an OSS Black spy was allowed to roam freely until he was identified as a spy. Only then was he sent to a concentration camp. A Black artist in the Netherlands was sent to an internment camp. There both his wife and the camp commandant supplied him with painting supplies. He and his paintings survived the war. An ex-patriot American Black jazz band leader played extensively in Warsaw before Nazi soldiers and had free run of the city. These anecdotal stories plus those of other Blacks under the fist of the Nazi regime suggest that they were treated differently from other groups designated as enemies of the state. Surely they were persecuted because of their racial designation, but most escaped the cruelest attention directed towards many other victims of the Holocaust.

Part 10

The Holocaust and
Twentieth-Century Genocide

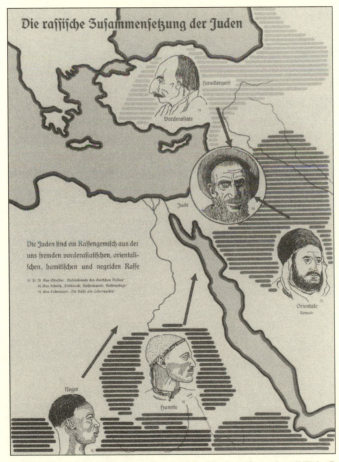

The classification of the races was a keystone of "scientific racism." This German version places the Jew in the chain of African and "Oriental" races. *(Hans Pauli, courtesy of United States Holocaust Memorial Museum Photo Archives)*

The Holocaust—the Nazi murder of millions of Jews, as well as gypsies, homosexuals, socialists, communists, and the Polish—was a central event of European history in the twentieth century. The sheer scale and incomprehensible inhumanity of the Nazi concentration camps forever altered Western conceptions of human nature. That such horrors could be perpetrated at the heart of a civilization that prided itself on its beliefs in human perfectability, the brotherhood of man, and the rights of the individual—the culture of Goethe and Beethoven and Heine—made it all the more incomprehensible. Of course, as the readings in Part 9 make depressingly clear, traditions of intolerance had grown alongside those of enlightenment and universalism. Christian Europe had long indulged itself in anti-Semitic prejudice against Jews, and the extreme ethnic nationalism of the age could be a volatile brew in periods of economic stress or political turmoil—especially in the hands of unscrupulous demagogues. Racism grew not only in the dark; it prospered also in daylight, from the chicanery of pseudodemocratic politics in a manipulable mass society. Before they were killed by the state, Jews were deprived of their property and their rights by law (like the infamous Nuremberg Laws of 1935).

The Holocaust was unique; but in a sense every historical event is unique, and we do not learn from uniqueness. We learn only by comparing one event with another. Only by comparison can we discern uniqueness. In the twentieth century, there were other attempts by one people to annihilate another. Hitler himself remarked in reference to the Turkish massacre of Armenian civilians in 1915: "No one remembers the Armenians." The Japanese allies of Germany during World War II had already by 1940 offered a model for systematic extermination of civilian populations in wartime. They had also taught ordinary soldiers and scientists how to regard a subject foreign population as being beneath contempt.

Since Hitler, the world has witnessed bouts of genocidal brutality in places like Cambodia, Yugoslavia, and Rwanda and Burundi. Not all of these were racist. The annihilation of Cambodian urban dwellers by the Maoist Khmer Rouge in the 1970s could hardly be considered racist since the urban population was not considered a separate race. The cases of Yugoslavia and Rwanda/Burundi are more complex. Where does ethnocentrism, or even religious intolerance, fade into racism? Does the distinction matter?

How does racism turn into genocide? All of the cases discussed here were cases of racism directed against an internal Other. While the distinction can never be absolute, these were fewer cases of settler societies. It is true that Poland was not part of Nazi Germany before 1939, or China part of Japan before 1931, but genocide occurred (or was at least attempted) in places where an occupying power was supreme. Some historians have written of the holocaust or genocide of the Native American population in the course of European colonization and expansion. Settlement can result in the annihilation of an indigenous population. In general, however, colonialists are more likely to push the indigenes beyond the frontier—at least those who survive.

The Armenian Genocide

Robert F. Melson

The author outlines a set of similarities between Armenian genocide and Hitler's Holocaust. What do you think of these comparisons? What, according to the author, were the differences between the Armenian genocide and the Holocaust? In what ways were Nigeria and Yugoslavia responsible for similar acts of genocide? Do you agree that the Armenian genocide was a precursor and model of both the Holocaust and contemporary cases of genocide? Why does the author believe that the Armenian genocide was a closer model for late-twentieth-century genocides than the Holocaust was? Do you agree, or disagree?

Twentieth-Century Genocide

During this century, the world has experienced four tidal waves of national and ethnic conflict and genocide in the wake of collapsing states and empires. These were punctuated by the First and Second World Wars and by the post-colonial and post-Communist eras. During the First World War and its aftermath the Ottoman empire collapsed, and it committed the first total genocide of the twentieth century against its Armenian minority. In the same period, the disintegration of the German and Austro-Hungarian empires set off *Volkisch*, nationalist and fascist movements that repressed minorities and precipitated the Second World War. In the context of that war, the Nazis attempted to exterminate the Jews and Gypsies and committed partial genocide against other peoples. Following the Second World War, as former European colonial em-

From *Is the Holocaust Unique? Perspectives on Comparative Genocide*, edited by Alan S. Rosenbaum. Copyright © 1996 by Westview Press, Member of Perseus Books Group. Reprinted by permission of Westview Press, a member of Perseus Books, L.L.C. pp. 87–98.

pires—notably Britain and France—withdrew from their possessions, they led behind fragile regimes that lacked legitimacy. Such "Third World" governments frequently ruled over culturally plural societies and tried to impose the hegemony of one ethnic group over the rest. In reaction, minorities rebelled and sought self-determination. This led to ethnic wars and genocide in places like Indonesia, Burundi, Sri Lanka, Nigeria, Pakistan, Ethiopia, Sudan, and Iraq. In the wake of the recent collapse of Communist regimes in the Soviet Union and former Yugoslavia, we are experiencing the fourth wave of nationalist upsurge, ethnic conflicts, and genocide. Meanwhile, as in contemporary Rwanda, it should be noted that the third wave of postcolonial genocide has not yet spent its force.

This chapter puts forth the position that the Armenian genocide was not only the first total genocide of the twentieth century but that it also served as the prototype for genocides that came after. In particular, the Armenian genocide approximates the Holocaust; but at the same time its territorial and national aspects, which distinguish it from the Holocaust, make it an archetype for ethnic and national genocides in the Third World, as well as in the post-Communist states.

This chapter offers a brief historical overview of the Armenian genocide, then compares that event first to the Holocaust and also to the Nigerian and Yugoslav genocides. The second set of cases represents contemporary instances of genocide in the Third World and the post-Communist states, respectively. The chapter concludes by raising a number of questions about the Armenian genocide and about genocide in general.

The Armenian Genocide

In traditional Ottoman society, Armenians—like other Christians and Jews— were defined as a *dhimmi millet*, a non-Muslim religious community of the empire. Their actual treatment by the state varied to some extent with the military fortunes of the empire, with the religious passions of its elites, and with the encroachment upon their land of Muslim refugees from the Balkans and the Caucasus and of Kurdish pastoralists.

Although by and large *dhimmis* (religious minorities) were free to practice their religion, they were considered to be distinctively inferior in status to Muslims.[1] However, in the nineteenth century, the Armenians challenged the traditional hierarchy of Ottoman society as they became better educated, wealthier, and more urban. In response, despite attempts at reforms, the empire became more repressive, and Armenians, more than any other Christian minority, bore the brunt of persecution.[2]

Throughout the nineteenth century, the Ottoman sultans were caught in the vise between great power pressures on the one hand and the demand for self-determination among their minorities on the other. By the time Abdul Hamid II came to power in 1876, he had set a course of political and social repression and technological modernization. Nevertheless, he could not halt the military and political disintegration of his regime, and he was replaced in 1908 by a political revolution of Young Turks with new and radical ideas of how to address the Ottoman crisis.

In the first instance, the Committee of Union and Progress (CUP), the political organization formed by the Young Turks, attempted radically to transform the regime following liberal and democratic principles that had been embodied in the earlier constitution of 1876. They hoped for the support of the Great Powers for their reforms, but neither the European powers nor the minorities reduced their pressures. On the contrary, they took the opportunity of internal Ottoman disarray and revolutionary transformation to press their demands, and between 1908 and 1912 they succeeded in reducing the size of Ottoman territory by 40 percent and its population by 20 percent.[3]

Concluding that their liberal experiment had been a failure, CUP leaders turned to Pan-Turkism, a xenophobic and chauvinistic brand of nationalism that sought to create a new empire based on Islam and Turkish ethnicity. This new empire, stretching from Anatolia to western China, would exclude minorities or grant them nominal rights unless they became Turks by nationality and Muslim by religion.

This dramatic shift in ideology and identity, from Ottoman pluralism to an integral form of Turkish nationalism, had profound implications for the emergence of modern Turkey.[4] At the same time, Pan-Turkism had tragic consequences for Ottoman minorities, most of all for the Armenians. From being once viewed as a constituent *millet* of the Ottoman regime, they suddenly were stereotyped as an alien nationality. Their situation became especially dangerous because of their territorial concentration in eastern Anatolia on the border with Russia, Turkey's traditional enemy. Thus, the Armenians, at one and the same time, were accused of being in league with Russia against Turkey and of claiming Anatolia, the heartland of the projected Pan-Turkic state.

This was the situation even before the First World War. When war broke out, however, the Young Turks, led by Talaat Pasha, the minister of interior, and Enver Pasha, the minister of war, joined the German side in an anti-Russian alliance that would allow Turkey to expand at Russia's expense. It was in this context of revolutionary and ideological transformation and war that the fateful decision to destroy the Armenians was taken.

By February 1915, Armenians serving in the Ottoman army were turned into labor battalions and were either worked to death or killed. By April, the remaining civilians were deported from eastern Anatolia and Cilicia toward the deserts near Aleppo in an early form of ethnic cleansing. The lines of Armenian deportees were set upon again and again by Turkish and *Kurdish villagers who were often incited and led by specially designated killing squads, Teshkilat-i Makhsusiye*. These units had been organized for their murderous purposes at the highest levels of the CUP.[5] Those Armenians who escaped massacre were very likely to perish of famine on the way. In this manner, between 1915 and the armistice in 1918, some 1 million people—out of a population of 2 million—were killed. Later, a half-million more Armenians perished as Turkey sought to free itself of foreign occupation and to expel minorities. Thus, between 1915 and 1923 approximately one-half to three-quarters of the Armenian population was destroyed in the Ottoman empire.

The Armenian Genocide and the Holocaust

The Armenian genocide and the Holocaust are the principal instances of total domestic genocide in the twentieth century. In both cases, a deliberate attempt was made by the government of the day to destroy in whole an ethno-religious community of ancient provenance. When one compares the situation and history of the Armenians in the Ottoman empire to the Jews in Europe, a pattern leading to genocide becomes apparent. It is a pattern that also reveals some significant differences, and it is those differences that link the Armenian genocide not only to the Holocaust but to contemporary instances of that crime. Let us first consider the similarities between the Armenian genocide and the Holocaust:

1. Under the prerevolutionary regimes in the Ottoman empire and Germany, Armenians and Jews were ethno-religious minorities of inferior status that had experienced rapid social progress and mobilization in the nineteenth century. These circumstances helped to create what came to be known as the "Armenian question" and the "Jewish problem." Armenians raised a question and Jews created a "problem" because neither the Muslim Ottoman empire nor Christian Europe were prepared to deal with low-status religious minorities that had become increasingly assertive and successful in the modern world.

2. Under the prerevolutionary regimes, Armenians may have suffered massacres, and Jews may have experienced discrimination in Germany as well as pogroms in Russia; but in none of these cases was a policy of total destruction formulated or implemented to resolve "questions" or to solve "problems." Genocide followed in the wake of revolutions in the Ottoman empire and Germany.

3. Following the reversals of 1908–1912, the CUP rejected Pan-Islam and Ottomanism as legitimating ideologies linking state to society and turned to Turkish nationalism and Pan-Turkism. The CUP identified the Turkish ethnic

group as the authentic political community on which the Turkish state could and should rely, and by implication it excluded the Armenians from the Turkish nation.

The Armenians were in danger of being conceived as enemies of Turkey and of the Turkish revolution once Ottoman Turks came to view themselves not in religious terms but in ethnic terms. What made the Armenian situation significantly more dangerous than that of other minorities was the Armenian *millet's* concentration in eastern Anatolia, an area that Turkish nationalists claimed to be the heartland of the Turkish nation. Moreover, the eastern *vilayets* (provinces) of Anatolia were on the Russian border, Turkey's traditional enemy, casting the Armenian presence in a sinister light.

In a similar fashion, a revolutionary situation in Germany allowed the Nazis to recast German identity and ideology. The German revolution destroyed the Weimar Republic, undermined democratic and socialist conceptions of legitimacy, and enabled the Nazis to come to power. Once the Nazis controlled the apparatus of the state, they set about recasting German political identity in terms of their racial and antisemitic ideology. They did this by excluding and expelling those whom they defined as "non-Aryans" and "Jews" from the newly valued and invented "Aryan" community.

4. When the First World War broke out, the CUP enthusiastically joined the Ottoman empire to the Germans against the Russians. This permitted Talaat and Enver to claim that the internal Armenian enemy was in league with the external Russian foe. Wartime circumstances then were used to justify the deportation and destruction of the Armenian community.

Similarly, the Nazis launched the Second World War in order to carve out an empire for Germany, and it was under wartime circumstances that they implemented their policies of partial genocide against Poles, Russians, and others and their extermination against the Jews. In particular, they viewed the Soviet Union as their principal foreign foe, and they assumed that it was ruled by a "world Jewish conspiracy." Thus, in 1941, at the same time that they invaded the Soviet Union, they launched the "Final Solution."

Thus did ideological vanguards use the opportunities created by revolution and war to destroy ancient communities that had been judged to he "problematic" under the prerevolutionary regimes and "enemies" under revolutionary and wartime circumstances. These elements—the prerevolutionary statuses of the victims and revolutionary and wartime circumstances—may be said to account for some of the essential similarities between the two genocides. There were, however, significant differences as well.

The perpetrators of the Armenian genocide were motivated by a variant of nationalist ideology, the victims were a territorial ethnic group that had sought autonomy, and the methods of destruction included massacre, forced deportation, and starvation. In contrast, the perpetrators of the Holocaust were motivated by racism and antisemitism and ideologies of global scope; the victims were not a territorial group, and so, for the most part, they had sought integration and assimilation instead of autonomy, and the death camp was the characteristic method of destruction. A word needs to be said about these factors that differentiate the Armenian genocide from the Holocaust. It will be shown, however, that it is precisely these differences that link the Armenian genocide to contemporary events.

Differences Between the Armenian Genocide and the Holocaust

Like these similarities, the differences between the Armenian genocide and the Holocaust may be plotted along the same dimensions: Jews and Armenians differed in status in the two empires; Nazi racist antisemitism differed significantly from the Pan-Turkist nationalism of the Young Turks; and the killers of the Armenians relied mostly on massacre and starvation rather than the death camps.

Like the Armenians in the Ottoman empire, the Jews were an ethno-religious community of low status in Christian Europe. Unlike the Armenians, however, who were the subject of contempt for being non-Muslims, the Jews of feudal Europe became a pariah caste stigmatized as "killers of the Son of God." Thus, Jews were not only despised in most parts of Europe, they were also hated and feared in a way the Armenians in the Ottoman empire were not.

In the nineteenth century, to the extent that the state became bureaucratic, the society meritocratic, and the economy capitalistic, Armenians and Jews began to advance in status and wealth. Indeed, it has been suggested that Armenian and Jewish progress was viewed as illegitimate and subversive, which precipitated antagonistic reactions both in the Ottoman empire and in imperial Germany.[6]

Here at least two variations may be noted. Whereas Armenians were a territorial group that increasingly made known its demands for greater autonomy and self-administration within the Ottoman system, Jews were geographically dispersed and thus, with the exception of the Zionists who sought a Jewish state in Palestine, most made no territorial demands on the larger societies in which they lived.[7] Instead, to the extent that they accepted the modern world, most Jews sought assimilation to the culture and integration into the wider society.

The reaction against Jewish progress, assimilation, and attempts at integration became a wide movement of European antisemitisim, a form of racism

that set up unbridgeable obstacles to Jewish inclusion. According to antisemites, Eugen Duhring, for example, not even conversion would allow Jews to
become the equals of Germans or other Europeans. Already in 1881, he wrote:

> A Jewish question would still exist, even if every Jew were to turn his
> back on his religion and join one of our major churches. Yes, I maintain
> that in that case, the struggle between us and the Jews would make itself
> felt as ever more urgent . . . It is precisely the baptized Jews who infiltrate
> furthest, unhindered in all sectors of society and political life.[8]

According to Wilhelm Marr (another nineteenth-century antisemite), for example, Jews were not only an alien race, they constituted an international
conspiracy whose aim was the domination of Germany, Europe, indeed, the
whole world. Thus, antisemites founded not only a movement that opposed
Jewish progress and assimilation, they formulated a far-reaching ideology that
helped them to explain the vacillations and crises of the modern world. It was
an ideology that came to rival liberalism and socialism in its mass appeal.

By way of contrast, no such ideology of anti-Armenianism developed in the
Ottoman empire. Armenians may have been popularly despised for being
dhimmis, or Gavur (infidels), and later, under the Young Turks, they may have
been feared as an alien nation supposedly making claims to Anatolia, the heartland of the newly valued "Turkey." However, even Pan-Turkism left the door
open to conversion and assimilation of minorities, something that racism and
antisemitism explicitly rejected.

Moreover, though the Young Turks may have claimed that the Armenians
were in league with their international enemies, especially the Russians, there
was no equivalent in the Pan-Turkish view of the Armenians to the Nazis'
hysterical struggle against the "Jewish spirit" that was said to linger in Germany and Europe even after most of the Jews had been murdered. Saul Friedlander has noted:

> It was the absolutely uncompromising aspect of the exterminatory drive
> against the Jews, as well as the frantic extirpation of any elements ac-
> tually or supposedly linked to the Jews or to the "Jewish Spirit" . . .
> which fundamentally distinguished the anti-Jewish actions of the Nazis
> from their attitude toward another group.[9]

Thus, the Holocaust became centered not only in Germany but evolved into
an international policy of mass murder and cultural destruction that included
Europe and even the whole world. Finally, the death camp, a conception of
the Nazi state, was an extraordinary organization, not seen before or since. It

was a factory managed by the SS but staffed at all levels by the inmates themselves. Its primary aim was to dehumanize and kill its prisoners after confiscating their property and making use of their labor. Although Jews, like Armenians, perished in massacres and by starvation, the use of the death camp as a method of extermination differentiates the Holocaust from the Armenian genocide.

At the same time that these differences—the nationalist ideology of the perpetrators, the territoriality of the victims, and the methodology of destruction, especially expulsion and starvation—differentiate the Armenian genocide from the Holocaust, they link that earlier genocide to contemporary destructions in the Third World and in the post-Communist states. In that sense, as has already been noted, the Armenian genocide predates and partly encompasses both kinds of genocide and is, thereby, a prototype for genocide in our time. We now turn to an examination of the Nigerian and Yugoslav genocides and to their comparison to the Armenian prototype.

Nigeria

Genocide has been committed throughout the Third World. Following are a few examples: Indonesia, Burundi, Rwanda, Sudan, East Pakistan, and Iraq. In all of these instances, a shaky and hardly legitimate postcolonial state ruling over a culturally plural society attempted to establish the hegemony of a leading ethnic group over other ethnic segments of society. This attempt at domination provoked movements of resistance and self-determination, which the postcolonial state then tried to halt by force, including massacre and partial genocide.

Nigeria gained its independence from Great Britain in 1960. It was organized as a federation of three states, each centering on a major ethnic group. The northern state was dominated by the Hausa-Fulani, the western by the Yoruba, and the eastern by the Ibos. The major ethnic groups jockeyed for power at the federal level, but each had its "minorities" that felt discriminated against at the state level of the federation. The postindependence government, dominated by Hausa-Fulani Muslims, was resisted by southern, largely non-Muslim groups, especially the Ibos. In 1966, after a failed military coup, thousands of Ibos were massacred in northern Nigeria. In 1967, a year after the massacres, the Ibos tried to secede. They called eastern Nigeria "Biafra" and fought a war of self-determination until 1970, when their secession attempt collapsed.

During the war, over 1 million Biafrans starved to death as a result of the deliberate Nigerian policy of blockade and disruption of agricultural life. Thus, between 1966 and 1970, a "genocide-in-part" occurred in Nigeria, following the United Nations (UN) definition. It is important, however, to recall that what happened in Biafra differed from the Holocaust and the Armenian genocide in that the policies of the Nigerian Federal Military Government (FGM) did not include extermination of the Ibos.

Yugoslavia

A definitive history of the recent conflict in former Yugoslavia does not yet exist, but it is possible to render a provisional sketch. The Yugoslav disaster stems from the failure of the Communist regime to establish legitimate political institutions, a viable economy, and a compelling political culture. After Marshal Tito's death in 1980, ethnically based nationalist movements started to mobilize and to demand greater autonomy if not yet self-determination. The process of dissolution and disintegration was drastically accelerated with the rise of Slobodan Milosevic, who articulated an integral form of Serbian nationalism and irredentism that called for the creation of a Yugoslavia dominated by Serbia such as had existed after the First World War. This frightened the other nationalities and encouraged intransigent elements.

Milosevic's integral Serbian nationalism, in a context of Yugoslav and Communist institutional decay and insecurity, helped to sharpen ethnic enmities, strengthen centrifugal forces throughout the federation, and accelerate the processes of disintegration. Thus, on September 27, 1989, the parliament of Slovenia allocated amendments to its constitution giving the republic the right to secede from Yugoslavia. Thousands of Serbs demonstrated in Novi Sad, fearing for their status in an independent Slovenia. On July 3, 1990, the Slovenian parliament declared that the laws of the republic took precedence over those of Yugoslavia; on December 22, 1990, Slovenia reported that 95 percent of the voters supported a plebiscite on independence; and on June 25, 1991, Slovenia declared its independence from Yugoslavia.

A similar march of events occurred in Croatia, which declared its independence on the same day. The big difference between Slovenia and Croatia, however, was the presence of a large Serbian minority in the latter. Moreover, no sooner was independence declared in Croatia than the Franjo Tudjman regime launched an anti-Serb campaign that would have alarmed the Serbs, even if nationalist elements among them had not been earlier mobilized by Milosevic. Now that their kin were being threatened in Croatia, Milosevic and other Serbian nationalists could call forth the terrible history of the Ustasha genocide of the Second World War to mobilize the Serbs against Croatian independence and in support of Serbian irredenta [Serbs in Croatia and other non-Serbian areas].

After June 25, 1991, when Slovenia and Croatia, in declaring their independence, thereby created Serbian minorities—especially in Croatia—the Serb radicals, using the cover of the Yugoslav army, launched an attack intended to incorporate Serbian-populated Croatian territory. To this end, Serbian forces not only initiated hostilities but set out on a path of terrorism and massacre in order to drive Croats out of areas that they desired to incorporate into Greater Serbia

This policy of terrorism and ethnic cleansing accelerated with even greater ferocity against Bosnia when it declared independence on March 3, 1992. Indeed, in time, both Serb and Croat forces descended on Bosnia with the clear intention of carving up and destroying a state that initially had tried to stand aside from ethnic nationalism and had opted for a pluralist society. However, both Serb and Croat nationalists were intent on either carving up and destroying Bosnia or making it a rump state that would in time collapse. To this end, the Bosnian Serbs led by their leader, Radovan Karadzic, a psychiatrist of Montenegran origin, especially practiced massacre, ethnic cleansing, and cultural destruction against those they called the "Turks." Taken together, such policies of destruction on a wide scale are called genocide.

Keeping Nigeria and Yugoslavia in mind, it is also important to note the great fear and insecurity that possess everyone when a government is challenged and a state begins to disintegrate. This great fear, especially in culturally plural societies leads people to seek the shelter of families and kin and persuades various groups to band together for protection and to view one another as potential enemies.

Indeed, before a culturally plural state like Nigeria or Yugoslavia disintegrates, its politics may revolve about various ethnic issues of group status and the distribution of scarce goods; but once a state crashes, for whatever reasons, ethnic groups begin to fear for their lives, as well they should. Once a political order disintegrates, who can guarantee an ethnic group that its mortal enemies won't come to power and try to dominate it or even destroy it? It is this great fear that has seized all the groups in Yugoslavia, including those Serbs who are the main perpetrators of partial genocide.

The Armenian and Nigerian Genocides

In both the Nigerian and Bosnian cases, we can see some parallels to the Armenian genocide. A dominant ethnic group in a culturally plural society attempted to establish its hegemony. It was resisted by minorities that attempted to gain some form of autonomy or self-determination. In reaction, the dominant group perpetrated repression and genocide. Yet there are significant differences that may be even more instructive.

The crucial difference between a total domestic genocide, as occurred in the Armenian case, and a partial one, as occurred in Nigeria, can also be seen by comparing the two. Unlike the Armenians, once Biafra was defeated and the danger of secession passed, the Ibos were not massacred or further expelled from Nigeria. On the contrary, there was a genuine attempt to reintegrate the Ibo population into Nigeria when the war ended.

This difference may be due to two reasons. First, although the FGM was dominated by Hausa-Fulani elements, it included minorities in its leadership; indeed, General Yakubu Gowon, its commander, was a Christian from the north. Thus, the FGM never developed an ideology of "northernization" or "Muslimization" the way the Young Turks relied on Turkification and sought to create an ethnically homogeneous Turkey.

Second, the territorial issue, a crucial element in the Armenian case, was present in the Biafran case, but it worked in favor of the Ibos. The Ibos of the north were "strangers" and not "sons of the soil"; thus, they could not make a legitimate claim to northern territory. Moreover, it is significant that the Ibos had their own area, which, except for its oil, the north did not covet. Once the Ibos were driven from the north back into their space and the Biafran secession was defeated, the northern elements in the army and elsewhere had succeeded in their major aims. Further massacre and starvation of the Ibos was unnecessary for ideological, territorial, or any other reasons, and the partial genocide ceased.

The Biafran state was never claimed as the "homeland" of the Hausa-Fulani in the manner that Anatolia had been staked out by the Turks. Thus, a federal solution to ethnic conflict could be implemented in Nigeria the way it could not in the Ottoman empire. The Armenians could not be driven back to "their" lands, since their lands were claimed to be the heartland of Turkey. Indeed, it may be suggested that this Turkish claim to Armenian lands was a major reason why the Armenian genocide, unlike the mass death of Biafra, became total in the manner of the Holocaust.

The Armenian and Bosnian Genocides

Two major similarities between the Armenian genocide and the partial genocide occurring in Bosnia should be apparent. Like the Young Turks, the Serbian—and to some extent the Croat—nationalists are also dreaming of a large state that would include their peoples and exclude other ethnic and national groups. Like the Armenians, the Bosnian Muslims, an ethno-religious community making claims to land, were being massacred and driven out by Serb and Croat nationalist movements that sought to incorporate their lands, "cleanse" the area of their presence, anal destroy their culture.

However, the status of Bosnia as an independent state recognized by the international community marks a significant difference between the situations of Ibos in Nigeria and of Armenians in the Ottoman empire. Neither Armenians nor Biafrans were widely recognized as members of independent states while their destructions were in processes.

Armenians were largely abandoned to their fate, in part because the genocide occurred in the midst of a world war. During the cold war, both the Eastern and Western blocs discouraged movements of self-determination, fearing superpower involvements and the African states did the same, fearing their own disintegration along ethnic lines. This may explain, in part, why Ibos, like Armenians, were also abandoned, except for some humanitarian relief.

That "partial" and not "total" genocide occurred in Bosnia, unlike Armenia, should be very cold comfort for the world community. Eighty years after the Armenian genocide and fifty years after the Holocaust, a European state practiced genocide while Europe, the United States, and the United Nations seemed unable or unwilling to halt the slaughter. If genocide cannot be halted in Europe, it cannot be stopped or prevented anywhere else, certainly not in places like Rwanda or Burundi. This, then, is the "New World Order" we face as we stand at the threshold of the third millennium.

Conclusion

The Armenian genocide was a precursor and prototype for the Holocaust in that a minority of traditionally low status that had successfully begun to enter the modern world was set upon and nearly destroyed in the context of revolution and war. However, the Holocaust was not an identical replay of the Armenian genocide. The Armenian case differed from the Holocaust in three dimensions: First, the Young Turks were largely motivated by an ideology of nationalism, whereas the Nazis were moved by an ideology heavily influenced by social Darwinism and racism. Second, the Armenians were a territorial group concentrated in the eastern vilayets of the empire, and they had historical claims to the land. In contrast, the Jews were not a territorial group. To destroy the Jews, the Nazis had to formulate a policy of genocide that transcended Germany and even Europe. Lastly, the method of destruction of the Armenians centered on their deportation, shooting, and starvation, whereas in the Holocaust the majority of Nazi victims perished in death camps. This is not to deny that a large percentage of Nazi victims also perished by shootings and starvation in the manner of their Armenian predecessors.

It should be noted, however, that it is precisely these differences that enable the Armenian genocide to be a precursor and prototype for contemporary genocide. Indeed, one conclusion we can draw from this analysis is that the Armenian genocide is a more accurate archetype than is the Holocaust for current mass murders in the postcolonial Third World and in the contemporary post-

Communist world. In Nigeria and Yugoslavia, for example, as in the Armenian case and unlike the Holocaust, the perpetrators were driven by a variant of nationalism, the victims were territorial ethnic groups aiming at some form of autonomy or self-determination, and the methods of destruction involved massacre and starvation.

I have tried to show that the Armenian genocide was a precursor and prototype both for the Holocaust and for contemporary nationalist genocides. In no case was it an exact template for later genocides, nor were these duplicates of the Armenian case; nevertheless, the Armenian pattern of destruction set a terrible precedent for our century and for the future.

Notes

1. See Roderic H. Davison, "Turkish Attitudes Concerning Christian-Muslim Equality in the Nineteenth Century," *American Historical Review* 4 (1954): 844–864.

2. See Robert F. Melson, *Revolution and Genocide: On the Origins of the Armenian Genocide and the Holocaust* (Chicago: University of Chicago Press, 1992), pp. 43–69.

3. See Feroz Ahmad, *The Young Turks* (Oxford: Clarendon Press, 1969), p. 153.

4. See Bernard Lewis, *The Emergence of Modern Turkey* (New York: Oxford University Press, 1961).

5. See Vahakn N. Dadrian, "Genocide as a Problem of National and International Law: The World War I Armenian Case and Its Contemporary Legal Ramifications" *Yale Journal of International Law* 2 (Summer 1989): 221–334.

6. See Melson, *Revolution and Genocide*, p. 137.

7. For discussions of the ideological crosscurrents that affected Jews in this period, see Jonathan Frankel, *Prophesy and Politics: Socialists, Nationalism, and the Russian Jews, 1862–1917* (Cambridge: Cambridge University Press, 1981), and Ezra Mendelsohn, *The Jews of East Central Europe Between the World Wars* (Bloomington: Indiana University Press, 1983).

8. Cited in Paul R. Mendes-Flohr and Jehuda Reinharz, *The Jews in the Modern World: A Documentary History* (New York: Oxford University Press, 1980), p. 273.

9. See Saul Friedlander, "On the Possibility of the Holocaust: An Approach to a Historical Synthesis," in *The Holocaust as Historical Experience*, ed. Yehuda Bauer and Nathan Rotenstreich (New York: Homes and Meier, 1981), p. 2.

The Nanking Holocaust: Tragedy, Trauma and Reconciliation

Peter Li

Peter Li is professor of East Asian studies at Rutgers University and editor of East Asia: An International Quarterly. *In this essay, he reviews six recent books dealing with the Japanese atrocities in China during World War II. In what ways were Japanese atrocities motivated by racism? What similarities and differences do you see between the Japanese massacre of Chinese and the other examples of twentieth-century genocide mentioned in the previous selection?*

As Auschwitz has become a symbol of the Jewish Holocaust and Nazi atrocities in World War II, Nanking has become the symbol of the Japanese military's monstrous and savage cruelty in the Asian Pacific War from 1931–1945. But in comparison to the Jewish Holocaust, relatively little has been written about the atrocities perpetrated by the Japanese military in China, Korea, the Philippines, Singapore, and Indonesia, where close to 50 million people died at the hands of Japanese aggression. In China alone, an estimated 30 million people lost their lives.

While there are thousands of volumes, numerous museum exhibits, documentaries and feature films about the Holocaust, literature about the Japanese atrocities has been scant in the more than fifty years since the end of the war. In fact Eugene B. Sledge has written that "the best kept secret about World War II is the truth about the Japanese atrocities."

Japanese designs on China began as early as the 1890s, after Japan's successful program of modernization during the Meiji period (1868–1912) and culminated in its first assault on the continent and China's defeat in the Sino-Japanese War of 1894–95. From that time on, China lost all respect and dignity in the eyes of the Japanese, who looked upon China as territory to be exploited as a colony or semi-colony. In a manner similar to the European and American claims on Asia and Africa, the Japanese viewed the conquest of China as Japan's "manifest destiny."

Reprinted by permission of Transaction Publishers, "The Nanking Holocaust: Tragedy, Trauma and Reconciliation" by Peter Li. *Society* (January/February 2000). Copyright © 2000 by Transaction Publishers; all rights reserved.

In the 1930s, at the height of the worldwide depression, Japan's expansionists and militarists once again looked at China as their rightful claim. Lt. Colonel Ishiwara wrote in 1930: "Japan's survival depends upon a favorable resolution of the problem of Manchuria and Mongolia. . . ." "Japan must expand overseas to achieve political stability at home. . . . " "The future of Manchuria and Mongolia will only be satisfactorily decided when Japan obtains those areas. . . ." and "Japan must be willing to fight America to achieve our national objectives" (Ienaga 1968, 11). Thus, the blueprint for the Asian-Pacific War was laid. On September 18, 1931, the Japanese staged an incident in Mukden (present-day Shenyang), later called the Manchurian Incident, which led to the seizure and occupation of the whole of Manchuria. For the militarists, Manchuria was still not enough—they eyed the whole of China. In 1937, the Japanese instigated the "Marco Polo Bridge Incident" outside Beijing, which led to allout war and the occupation of much of China. There is no question that the war that ensued from 1937–1945 was one of the bloodiest in human history. Wherever the Japanese soldiers went, there were atrocities committed on both civilians and combatants; the Japanese considered POWs a burden.

While these events have not occupied headline news recently, within the past ten years, there has been a gradual awakening of interest in the history of the Asian-Pacific region, and a flurry of books have appeared about the Asia Pacific War including the seven books listed above. However, it is Iris Chang's recent volume, *The Rape of Nanking: The Forgotten Holocaust of World War II*, that ignited a ground swell of interest in the Asia Pacific War which even shocked the Japanese ambassador to the United States, Kunihiko Saito, who at a press conference on April 21, 1998, criticized the book and the attention that it was getting.

The Chinese Perspective

For over half a century the Chinese and others have remained relatively reticent about the Japanese atrocities. This should not be taken to mean, however, that there has been any lack of pain, suffering, and anguish among the surviving victims, or friends and relatives of the victims. In fact, Iris Chang's family is a good example of how memories of the war were passed on from one generation to the next. Iris Chang received her inspiration to write about Nanking from her maternal grandparents, who escaped the Nanking massacre by just one month, and from her own parents. Since the war experience was an integral part of the family memory, it was frequently the subject of conversation at the Chang family gatherings.

It was not until 1992, however, that the ideas about the subject began to coalesce, and two more years of gestation before the ideas evolved into a book project. The immediate cause was a conference sponsored by the Global Alliance for Preserving the History of World War II in Asia (AOHWA) held in Cupertino, California, which presented poster-sized photographs of the Rape of Nanking. Chang described them as "some of the most gruesome photographs I had ever seen in my life" (Chang 1997, 9). After more than two years of intensive research, the final product is *The Rape of Nanking: The Forgotten Holocaust of World War II*, which has been reprinted seventeen times to date with 130,000 copies currently in print.

During the course of her research, Chang would have nightmares. She woke up in the middle of the night shaking with anger; she lost weight, lost hair, and had trouble sleeping and eating.

There was also an urgency about Chang's book, in that the survivors and witnesses to the massacre at Nanking were fast disappearing.

The seven books listed above are not pleasant to read. Many sections are unbearably gruesome to read for more than four or five pages at a time. In fact, it might have been better if these seven volumes, totaling approximately 2,500 pages, had never been written at all. It would have been even better, though, if the realities depicted on those pages had never happened. Yet since these are realities, we cannot and should not be spared the painful burden of an account of these events. For a wide range of reasons, some justifiable and others not, over fifty years have passed, the atrocities committed by the Japanese military during the Second World War have not yet reached the eyes and ears of the world at large, and the government of Japan has yet to face up to its past. However, with the publication of *The Rape of Nanking: The Forgotten Holocaust of World War II* in November 1997, on the sixtieth anniversary of the fall of the Nanking to the Japanese in 1937, things have begun to change. The book rose to number eleven on *The New York Times* best-seller list in February 1998.

The publication of Chang's book has initiated a slow awakening of the world at large, that aside from the horrors of the Jewish Holocaust under Nazi Germany, there had been another awful tragedy perpetrated by the Japanese during the Asian Pacific War in which victims of slaughter, rape, and savage brutality numbered in the millions, some estimate 30 million in China itself. The numbers killed in the city of Nanking alone, in a period of seven weeks from December 13, 1937 to February 1938, according to the International Military Tribunal of the Far East (IMTFE), was an estimated 260,000. The Memorial Hall of the Victims of the Nanking Massacre in Nanjing, established in 1984, claims that at least 300,000 Chinese were killed in the seven-week period of the Nanking Massacre (Chang 1997, 99–104). Japanese sources significantly underestimate the numbers; they "range from as few as 3,000 to 6,000 made by individuals whose accounts have been discredited, to as high as 200,000.

One of Japan's leading historians of the war, Hata Ikuhito, wrote in 1986 that 'illegal murders' at Nanking ranged from 38,000 to 42,000" (Cook 1992, 39).

Iris Chang has produced, as much as possible, a balanced and multi-sided view of the tragedy at Nanking from three perspectives: (1) the culture, strategy, and behavior of the invading Japanese forces, (2) the suffering of the victims of the massacre, and (3) the courageous but futile efforts of the foreign nationals staying in the International Safety Zone who tried to protect at least some people.

The city of Nanking took on special significance for the Japanese because at the time Nanking was the capital of the Republic of China, and victory there would have meant the symbolic defeat of China. Japan had taken Shanghai, the much coveted center of international trade and gateway to central China after more than three months of fierce fighting. The Nationalists lost 300,000 troops and ten generals. It was a great prize for the Japanese, but the greater prize would be the capture of the capital. The Japanese then realized that taking China would not come as easily as expected; some had predicted that China could be taken in three months.

In the march from Shanghai to Nanking during the month of November, the Japanese troops already began their bloodthirsty spree of indiscriminate killing. Their 200,000-man force advanced on Nanking with a vengeance, killing, looting, raping, and burning as they proceeded. Wherever they went, they left "in their wake scorched earth and scattered bodies." It is estimated that another 300,000 civilians were killed on the three routes taken by the Japanese troops (Yin 1996, 21).

Upon entering Nanking, the Japanese were shocked at the number of soldiers who surrendered without firing a shot. The surrendering Chinese soldiers often outnumbered the invading forces. Japanese soldiers, who had been trained in a military culture "in which suicide was infinitely preferable to capture" found it incomprehensible that the Chinese soldiers would surrender rather than fight. Thus, the Japanese regarded the Chinese prisoners with great contempt.

The perspective of the Japanese soldier probably can be garnered from the diary of a Japanese soldier, Azuma Shiro, who was in Nanking and felt secretly ashamed that he had been afraid of the Chinese. Azuma wrote in his diary: "They [the surrendered Chinese soldiers] all walked in droves. like ants crawling on the ground. They looked like a bunch of homeless people, with ignorant expressions on their faces. . . . They hardly looked like the enemy who only yesterday was shooting at and troubling us. It was impossible to believe that they were the enemy soldiers. I felt quite foolish to think we had been fighting to the death against these ignorant slaves. And some of them were even twelve- or thirteen-year-old boys" (Chang 1997, 44).

The massacre, arson, looting, and brutal assault on women that ensued are graphically depicted in James Yin and Shi Young's powerful book, *Rape of Nanking: An Undeniable History, in Photographs*, which contains some 450 photographs that leave an unforgettable record of Japanese atrocities. The order from above was: "Kill All Captives." The methods of killing ranged from beheading, bayoneting, live burial, burning, and freezing; killing was a form of entertainment. "There seemed to be no limit to the Japanese capacity for human degradation and sexual perversion in Nanking. Just as some soldiers invented killing contests to break the monotony of murder, so did some invent games of recreational rape and torture when wearied of the glut of sex. Perhaps one of the most brutal forms of Japanese entertainment was the impalement of vaginas. In the streets of Nanking corpses of women lay with their legs splayed open, their orifices pierced with wooden rods, twigs and weeds" (Chang 1997, 94).

Among the different methods of execution, beheading with the sword seemed to bring the most satisfaction to many Japanese soldiers because of the association with military culture of the samurai bushido (the way of the warrior). It was also used as a method of building up courage and stamina in the novice soldier inexperienced in killing. Corporal Kazuo Sone reporting on his first decapitation wrote:

"Of course I was reluctant to show my weakness in front of others. My last bit of courage was brought out when I screamed "Kill!" and brought down the sword against the prisoner's neck. . . . The severed head dropped to the ground and rolled like a ball down the embankment to the water. The whole process lasted only a few seconds. But it seemed like hours to me. Thus, I had now obtained the unusual experience of a beheading" (Yin 1996, 132).

If the image of the samurai sword had once evoked heroic acts of bravery and courage, the numerous souvenir pictures taken by Japanese soldiers of themselves wielding swords about to behead the bound, helpless, kneeling victim should put an end to those romantic conceptions. The swords had now become symbols of something much more sinister. There were contests devised to see who could behead the greatest number of persons in the shortest time. Photographs of severed heads lined up neatly in a row or placed on fence posts were taken for souvenirs.

Other methods included bayoneting of local civilians and POWs. Tens of thousands of Chinese prisoners were used for live bayonet practice. They were tied to posts with ropes or wires and new recruits were forced to practice stabbing their victims to death with their 15-inch bayonets to build up their morale and courage. Kazuo Sone wrote in his *A Japanese Soldier's Confession*, "This kind of killing experience was every soldier's test and ordeal. After this they would be fearless in real battle, and would glory in the act of killing. War made people cruel, bestial and insane. It was an abyss of inhuman crimes"

(Yin 1996, 156). We often read about the terror of a soldier's first experience in hand-to-hand combat or his first experience in killing another human being written about in war literature. In the Japanese case, on the other hand, the soldiers were already conditioned before combat in live bayonet practice.

Live burial was another method of getting rid of captives. This method of killing was slow and excruciating: "Chinese captives were also bound hand and foot and planted neck deep in the earth, leaving their protruding heads to terrorize people . . . some were jabbed with bayonets, some trampled by horses, some doused with boiling water, some crushed under tank tracks" (Yin 1996, 168). The terrified screaming and miserable howls of the victims could be heard up to several miles away. Some of the captives were buried up to their waist in the ground, then set upon by German shepherds.

There were also burnings, committed by first dousing the prisoners with gasoline and then shooting them, thus igniting the fumes, and ending with a spectacular conflagration. The Japanese also derived great joy from devising new ways of killing; they laughed and applauded as the victims struggled in agony. In this respect, the Japanese surpassed their German counter-parts in the cruelty and ingenuity of their methods. A Japanese soldier wrote in his diary: "Recently, when we were very bored, we had some fun killing Chinese. We caught some innocent Chinese and either buried them alive, or pushed them into a fire, or beat them with clubs, or killed them by other cruel means" (Yin 1996, 178).

The worst of the atrocities were the brutal assaults on the unfortunate Chinese women who crossed the paths of the Japanese. It is estimated that upwards of 80,000 women were raped by the invading Japanese soldiers, and this is the reason the Nanjing massacre is often referred to as the "Rape of Nanking." The women were not only assaulted and brutalized, but also humiliated and insulted. Case after case was enumerated at the International Military Tribunal of the Far East (IMTFE) totaling some 435 documented instances of rape and subsequent mutilation. The undocumented cases remain buried with the victims themselves. Occasionally, instances of fierce resistance paid off, as in case of Ms. Liu Xiuyung, who survived to tell her ordeal. Liu was 18 years old at the time, and she fought back with such ferocity that the Japanese soldiers were shocked. But finally, outnumbered, the soldiers aimed their bayonets at her head, slashing her face with their blades and knocking out her teeth. Her mouth filled with blood, which she spit into their eyes, "Blood was on the walls, on the bed, on the floor, everywhere," Liu remembered. "I had no fear in my mind. I was furious. My only thought was to fight and kill them." Finally a soldier plunged his bayonet into her belly and everything went black for her (Chang 1997, 98).

Now 79, Ms. Liu has brought her case to a Tokyo court demanding compensation from the Japanese government, together with nine other survivors of the massacre. Her indomitable spirit was still very much in evidence as she told reporters, "I want to tell the world that [the Nanking Massacre] really happened. . . . The Japanese people must tell their children the truth and let them know that war must never happen again between our two nations."

Another survivor told how he refused to lead Japanese soldiers to the women they desperately wanted. Xue Jialin recounted that day in December 1937 when Japanese soldiers appeared in his village: "They came to our village and forced me to lead them to where the 'flower girls' hid. I would rather die than do this kind of inhuman thing. I refused and angered them, An officer cut my lips open with his sword and chopped off my teeth" (Yin 1996, 214).

A valuable lesson was to be learned from all this. After the experience of Nanking, the savage brutality of the Japanese Army became known and their promises of good treatment were never to be believed. When the Japanese first took Nanjing, they dropped leaflets saying "Those Chinese soldiers who are not willing to fight and who are holding up white flags or both of their hands to surrender to the Japanese Army with this certificate [Preferential Certificate], will be treated leniently by the Imperial Army. No harm will come them; no one will be killed. Jobs will be offered to them. Intelligent soldiers, come!" (Yin 1996, 30). This turned out to be a total lie; those who surrendered were indiscriminately shot and killed. From this battle onward, very few Chinese Nationalist soldiers ever surrendered to the Japanese. They would fight to the end rather than surrender.

On the other hand, if the Chinese army had been better organized and led, there would not have been such a large scale massacre. The Chinese command was marked by chaos and disorder, In the midst of the fighting, General Tang Shengzhi, who had been earlier ordered by Chiang Kai-shek to defend Nanking at all cost, was suddenly ordered to retreat. Chiang seemed to be playing dice with the lives of his own troops. "Not surprisingly, the order to retreat threw the Chinese military into an uproar. Some officers ran about the city haphazardly informing anyone they came into contact with to pull out. . . . Other officers told no one, not even their own troops. . . . In their haste and confusion to leave the city, at least one Chinese tank rolled over countless Chinese soldiers in its path, stopping only when blown up by a hand grenade" (Chang 1997, 76). It must be admitted there was also a callous disregard for human life on the part of the Chinese Nationalist Army, but there was not the deliberate cruelty. Often times the surrendering troops outnumbered their captors; if there had been any organized resistance, the Japanese soldiers would have been overcome and killed. But there was no resistance. Most of the prisoners watched passively as their comrades were killed by the Japanese knowing all the time that they would be next.

The third perspective that Chang presented is from that of the foreign nationals that stayed behind to protect and care for the some 250,000 Chinese who sought refuge in the International Safety Zone that was set up in the heart of Nanking by some two dozen foreigners "mostly American, but also German, Danish, Russian, and Chinese." Chief among them were John Rabe, a German Nazi who also came to be known as the "Living Buddha of Nanking" because of his heroic stance to establish the International Safety Zone; Robert Wilson, an American surgeon who elected to stay behind in Nanking while other doctors left, and Wilhelmina (Minnie) Vautrin, known as the "the living Goddess of Mercy of Nanking," who was dean at Ginling Women's Arts and Science College and the only woman who remained to face the brutal Japanese invaders.

While researching the life of John Rabe, who went to China in 1908 and worked for Siemens China Company selling telephones and electrical equipment to the Chinese government, Iris Chang discovered he had kept an extensive diary of the daily events that took place during the Rape of Nanking. She went to Germany to seek out Rabe's granddaughter and secured the diaries that are now available to the public. This has become the most recent and most important of the incontrovertible collaborative evidence regarding what had happened in Nanking. But Rabe did more than just set up the Safety Zone and supervise the activities; he roamed the city streets as well to prevent atrocities through his personal intervention. He was appalled by the rapes in the city and personally intervened to stop them. "There were girls under the age of 8 and women over the age of 70 who were raped and then, in the most brutal way possible, knocked down and beat up. We found corpses of women on beer glasses and others who had been lanced with bamboo shoots" (Rabe's diary quoted in Chang 1997, 119). But not all his attempts to save the Chinese were successful. Rabe persuaded thousands of Chinese to lay down their arms, believing the propaganda of the Japanese posters: "Trust Our Japanese Army They Will Protect and Feed You." But much to the soldiers' and Rabe's dismay, the Japanese never kept their word. The soldiers were rounded up and shot.

Another heroine of the Rape of Nanking was Wilhelmina (Minnie) Vautrin, who became virtually the head of the Ginling College when most of the other faculty fled the city. She was an avid diarist and left an invaluable record of her days in China. At the height of the terror, one thousand refugees a day were passing through the city. In three days, the compounds of Ginling College were filled with three thousand women. Because Ginling was a women's college, Minnie Vautrin specifically looked after women, girls, and children. She herself also became vulnerable to the rapacious Japanese soldiers, who were on the look-out for women for military prostitution and rape. Vautrin was, like Rabe, at times duped by the deception of the Japanese. She was tricked into sending innocent women into the hands of the Japanese soldiers. Vautrin, not unlike the men, was sometimes threatened with physical abuse. She was slapped by Japanese soldiers more than once. When the rape of Nanking began on December 13, there were also reporters from Japanese, British, and American newspapers on hand who reported on the events. Yoshio Moriyama of the *Asahi Shimbun*, Tillman Durdin of the *New York Times*, and H.J. Timperley of the *Manchester Guardian* in their respective newspapers reported on the ugly incidents occurring in Nanking. The Japanese, American, and British reporters were all in agreement regarding the mass exterminations that were taking place. Moriyama reported on December 14: "At one time, after Nanking was captured, more than 30,000 Chinese were driven to the foot of the city wall. Machine guns then swept the crowd and grenades were thrown from atop the wall. The 30,000 people were all killed, most of them women, children, and the elderly" (Yin 1996, 50). Durdin telegraphed an urgent dispatch to the *New York Times* on December 17 stating: "During the first three days of the occupation, the situation developed in an unpredictable fashion; large scale looting, sexual assault on women and tyrannized killing of innocent people, civilians driven out of their houses . . . all of these turned Nanking into a city of terror" (Yin 1996, 52). George Fitch, an American and longtime resident of Nanking, wrote: The city is "laid waste, ravaged, completely looted, much of it burned. Complete anarchy has reigned for ten days—it has been hell on earth" (Yin 1996, 56). The atrocities had been so horrendous that even Prince Mikasa, the youngest brother of Emperor Hirohito, wrote a report, "Reflections as a Japanese on the Sino-Japanese War," in which he revealed to his brother the atrocities he had witnessed in China and wished desperately to bring the war to a close (Yin 1996, 58).

The horrors of the Rape of Nanking and the moral questions they raised remain unresolved and not completely understood to this day. The reasons for the savage brutality of the Japanese soldiers are many: ranging from the Japanese military culture stemming from the traditional training of Japanese samurai, and the brutal military training in the army to the long years of indoctrination on the superiority of the Japanese race, and the Japanese contempt for the Chinese after the First Sino-Japanese War of 1894–95. Generalizing on human nature, the Japanese movie director and comedian Takeshi Kitano said: "I believe that even the most normal-seeming people have the potential for violence. The most extreme example might be found among the Japanese soldiers during World War II who committed atrocities in China. Most of them were probably the sons of farmers" (*New York Times*, March 15, 1998).

Others believe that human cruelty will never cease to exist even with the progress of civilization: "It is an error to imagine that civilization and savage cruelty are antithesis. . . . In our times the cruelties, like most other aspects of our world, have become far more effectively administered than before. They have not and will not cease to exist" (Bauman 1989, 9). Probably this ingenious explanation came from General Matsui Iwane himself, the general nominally in charge of the Nanking campaign: "The struggle between Japan and China was always a fight between brothers within the 'Asian Family.' . . . It had been my belief during all these days that we must regard this struggle as a method of making the Chinese undergo self-reflection. We do not do this because we hate them, but on the contrary we love them too much" (Chang 1997, 219). If this is the way the Japanese show brotherly love, then the Chinese could certainly have done with less of it.

Before we leave Iris Chang and James Yin and Shi Young's two volumes on the Rape of Nanking, we must briefly touch on Sledge's statement mentioned at the beginning, "The best kept secret of World War II is the truth about the Japanese atrocities." Why has this part of World War II been kept from the world, and why has the Japanese government not faced up to its militarist past and eluded justice? For one thing, the Japanese government has utilized, for all that it was worth, its position as the primary victim of the war because of the atomic bombing of Hiroshima and Nagasaki. Because the United States felt guilty and responsible for the bombings, we helped Japan rebuild and nurtured Japan's victim status. Next came the Cold War which made it necessary for the United States to cultivate Japan as an ally to counter the Soviet and Chinese threat. Therefore, its past transgressions were overlooked. China has also played a significant part in not publicizing the wartime atrocities because it was engaged in a vicious civil war of its own after World War II. And after the civil war concluded, both China and Taiwan "needed Japan to play off against each other" and subsequently needed Japan as a trading partner ("The Forgotten Victims of World War II"). Therefore, China has never demanded an apology or reparations.

Probably the most important reason for Japan's reticence and lack of remorse and continued denials is what has been called the Showa-era continuum, or the transwar continuities in Japan. The most important symbol of this continuity is the reign of Emperor Hirohito after the war. He was exonerated from any responsibility for the war crimes through a secret arrangement with General MacArthur, who engineered the surrender of Japan and the U.S. occupation. Emperor Hirohito, therefore, remained in power until his death in 1989. This is the equivalent of exonerating Hitler from war crimes committed by Germany during World War II.

Along with the emperor, a great number of politicians, bureaucrats, and technocrats continued their positions in the public sector after a brief respite. They received a slap on the wrist and then went back to work. It is because of this continuity that Japan would never admit to the rape of Nanking, preferring to regard it as a lie, a fabrication, and just a part of war. It is equally regrettable that Emperor Hirohito's Imperial Rescript, delivered on the occasion of Japan's surrender, he never mentioned remorse, guilt, or responsibility for the war in the Pacific. He denied any aggression on the part of Japan, stating that war was declared on America and Britain "to assure Japan's self-preservation and the stabilization of East Asia" nor did Japan intend "to infringe upon the sovereignty of other nations or embark upon territorial aggrandizement" (Imperial Rescript, August 15, 1945). Therefore, he admitted no wrongdoing nor the committing of any war crimes. Japan came away with a clean bill of health. As the century draws to a close, however, there are renewed calls to bring Japan to justice. Japan must come to terms with its past. As the Nobel Laureate for literature, Oe Kenzaburo aptly noted: "[Japan's] unwillingness to come to terms with its past is not just morally offensive, it prevents Japan from playing its proper role in Asia" ("Denying History Disables Japan," *New York Times*, July 2, 1995).

Yin and Young's book is an oversized volume with text in both English and Chinese. It also has a foreword by the Most Revered Desmond Tutu of South Africa, who writes: "To sweep under the carpet the atrocities which occurred in Nanking in 1937–38 and turn a blind eye to the truth is at best a gross disservice to future generations and at worst to be criminally negligent and irresponsible. A record such as this book is an essential part of our history. However horrible, we must not be sheltered from the evils of our past" (Yin 1996, ix–x). Professor Ying-shih Yu of Princeton University has also written a short insightful preface to the volume commenting on the disruption of China's modernization program by the Japanese incursions.

Japanese Biological Warfare

Whereas the rampant destruction and massacre in Nanking were generally known to the public, the experiments in biological warfare were conducted in great secrecy. The center of Japan's effort to develop effective weapons of biological warfare was located in Pin-fang, near Harbin in China's northeast province of Heilungjiang, with satellite sites in other places in China and beyond. As germ or chemical warfare was outlawed by the Geneva convention, these experiments had to be conducted in secret. Known as Unit 731 and headed by Lt. General Ishii Shiro, this center of research, consisting of more than 70 buildings occupying about six square kilometers, became the ground for some of the most gruesome experiments involving human subjects. It has gradually come to light that "an estimated three thousand Manchurians, Chinese, Russians, Koreans, Europeans, and Americans were killed" by the

Imperial Japanese Army's Unit 731. These human victims were subjected to various forms of experimentation in four main areas: cholera, epidemic hemorrhagic fever (EHF), bubonic plague, and frostbite.

Located in the newly conquered territory of Manchuria, the Japanese utilized the virtually unlimited supply of human subjects selected from among the illiterate peasants in the surrounding villages on whom they could perform their experiments. These innocent subjects were artificially infected with disease. And as the disease advanced, these human subjects were dissected either with or without anesthetics to observe the state of deterioration of the internal organs: "As soon as the symptoms were observed, the prisoner was taken from his cell and into the dissection room. He was stripped and placed on the table, screaming, trying to fight back. He was strapped down, still screaming frightfully. One of the doctors stuffed a towel into his mouth, then with one quick slice of the scalpel he was opened up" (Gold 1996, 44). His intestines and internal organs were removed and examined. Sometime during the vivisection, the subject died, but it was of no concern to the doctors. The bodies were disposed of afterwards in the crematorium.

Sheldon H. Harris, author of *Factories of Death*, began his study of Japan's biological warfare experimentation program in 1985 at the instigation of his Chinese colleagues at Northeast Normal University in Changchun, China, where he initially learned about the activities of Unit 100 based in that city. As his research expanded, he enlisted the help of Mr. Han Xiao of the Unit 731 Museum in Pingfang near Harbin. In the United States, Harris scoured the National Archives in Washington, D.C. and in Suitland, Maryland on Japanese biological warfare and the subsequent American cover-up. Part II of Harris' book is a detailed account of the United States government's part in covering up and silencing all information concerning Unit 731's activities in developing biological warfare weapons. This occurred because the United States wanted to obtain the results of Lt. General Ishii Shiro's experiments. Therefore, Ishii was pardoned from prosecution by the United States government in exchange for his secret reports on his germ warfare experiments. Ishii became a free man, as did at least nineteen others who worked at Pingfang. This was certainly one of the dark pages of American history.

The documents declassified under the Freedom of Information Act were also instrumental in the writing of Hal Gold's book, *Unit 731: Testimony*, a companion volume to Harris' *Factories of Death*. Part I of Gold's book gives an historical overview of Japanese experiments in biological warfare; part two consists of testimonies of twenty-four individuals from all walks of life, male and female, civilian and military who worked at Unit 731 and came forward voluntarily to tell their stories. Credit must be given to these courageous individuals who told of their work experience with the various units. In fact, it was the exhibition that inspired Hal Gold to write *Unit 731: Testimony* because he was able to obtain the testimony of the doctors, nurses, and other workers who were employed in the various units.

Some of their accounts detailed unimaginable cruelty. In an experiment on the treatment of frostbite, for example, four or five human subjects were led out into freezing weather dressed in warm clothing—only their arms were exposed to be frozen. Their arms were then made to freeze more quickly with the help of large fans. "This was done until their frozen arms, when struck with a short stick, emitted a sound resembling that which a board gives out when it is struck" (Harris 1994, 70). Then the experts experimented with different kinds of treatments. The unfortunate victims, however, sometimes lost their limbs, their lives, or both.

Aside from the main center located in Pingfang, there were more than a dozen facilities located at other cities in China. There was the Beijing-based Unit 1855, which was a combined prison and experiment center for research into plague, cholera, and typhus. Unit 8604, based in Guangzhou, performed starvation experiments and used rats in spreading plague to the population. Unit 100 was located in present-day Changchun; it was a bacteria factory producing large quantities of glanders (an equine disease), anthrax, and other pathogens. There was also the Nanjing-based Unit 1644, which mixed plague germs with wheat, corn, clothing scraps, and cotton, which were then dropped from the air. Another center, Unit 9420, located in Singapore, used infected fleas to transmit plague pathogens. These fleas, bred in large quantities, were shipped to be used in Thailand.

As early as 1932, an Epidemic Prevention Research Laboratory was set up in the Army hospital in Tokyo with Ishii in charge. The term "prevention" was an euphemism for the development of bacteriological and chemical attack weapons. It was Ishii's goal to develop bacteria and chemicals into weapons for the Imperial Army. In China, these units were set up under the cloak of "AntiEpidemic Water Supply and Purification Bureaus" which attracted no undue attention until near the war's end when attempts were made to destroy all evidence. In all, eighteen or more of these units were ultimately established in Manchuria and in other parts of China proper (Harris 1994, 31–33). Some have called this murder by "medical research" as opposed the wanton killings described elsewhere (William F. Harvey, e-mail communication, April 26, 1998).

From July 1993 to December 1994, after Japanese citizens discovered the existence of these biological warfare stations, an exhibition featuring the activities of Unit 731 was organized to inform the Japanese people of the atrocities committed by the Japanese military in Asia. It was an exhibition organized by the citizens of Japan who had to raise their own money, rent exhibition space, etc., because they wanted to educate the public. The exhibition was shown at sixty-one locations across Japan. Speakers who had worked in those "factories of death" volunteered to speak about their experiences. This is evidence that the Japanese people were willing to come to terms with the atrocities committed by their military units, whereas the government was not.

An example of how the American government has participated in the cover-up of the biological warfare episode was the experience of the American soldier, Frank James, a POW captured by the Japanese in November 1942. He became a subject of biological experimentation at Unit 731 when he was sent to Mukden and given injections upon his arrival and subjected to many extractions of blood samples. But he was forced to remain silent about his experience. "When he returned to the United States in 1945, the U.S. Army made him sign a document swearing never to discuss his 731 experience. For forty years, he kept silent." He finally testified before Congress in 1986 and told his story. It was indeed a grave mistake and a shameful act on the part of the United States government to have kept this secret from the American people.

The Japanese Perspective

The next two works, Frank Gibney's *Senso* and Haruko and Theodore Cook's *Japan at War* offer us another perspective on the war. Up to this point we have heard mostly from the victims of the atrocities; in *Senso* and *Japan at War* we get a more complicated side of the story from the Japanese themselves; we hear the voices of the victimizers. From July 10, 1986 to August 29, 1987, the *Asahi Shimbun* received about 4,000 letters to the editor from its readers reminiscing about World War II. Of these 4,000 letters, 1,100 were printed, The writers were soldiers and civilians, women as well as men, wives, mothers, and children, They described their lives as prisoners of war, in military camps, during the evacuation of school children. under military control, and so on. Out of these 1,100 letters, 300 were selected and translated by Frank Gibney and included in his book, *Senso: The Japanese Remember the Pacific War.*

In August 1988, on the eve of the death of Emperor Hirohito, the husband and wife team of Haruko and Theodore Cook began criss-crossing Japan searching for prospective interviewees for their book, *Japan at War: An Oral History.* Hundreds of people were contacted for the book, yet many were hesitant to tell their stories. Locating interviewees was a daunting task; people did not wish to talk about their experiences. This reveals much about how the Japanese deal with the war experience. The experience of war is not forgotten but suppressed. The war is strangely disembodied; it is anchored neither in time nor in the public memory.

The interviews and letters that were obtained, however, do reveal the reasons for the brutality of the Japanese military. They enable us to better understand the cause of such monstrous behavior. They describe the transformation of ordinary normal men into murdering demons. Taminaga Shozo, a university graduate and a second lieutenant in the 232nd Regiment of the 39th Division who was sent to central China, vividly described one such transformation. In a period of a few months "Good sons, good daddies, good elder brothers at home were brought to the front to kill each other. Human beings turned into murdering demons. Everyone became a demon within three months. Men were able to fight courageously only when their human characteristics were suppressed. So we believed. It was a natural extension of our training back in Japan. This was the Emperor's Army" (Cook 1992, 43).

What was the army training like? The experiences of Inanaga Hitoshi, a grade school teacher and antiwar pacifist, and Sakata Tsuyoshi may serve as examples. The new recruits in the Japanese Imperial Army were degraded, abused, and dehumanized. Inanaga wrote: "The abuse by veterans toward new recruits was termed 'lessons.' 'Take off your glasses!' 'Stand firm!' Then the clenched fists would strike full force on his face. The following morning's salty miso soup stung his lips. The beating caused his back teeth to crumble" (Gibney 1995, 30). Several of his fellow soldiers committed suicide, and some deserted. Sakata wrote in his letter to the *Asahi Shimbun* of this army training:

"Until the end, my military life was filled with training and beatings. Training began as soon as the reveille sounded. . . . Before inflicting punishments, they [the senior soldiers] always said they were indoctrinating us with the military man's spirit. We were made to form a single line and stand at attention and then ordered to clench our teeth. Then they hit us with their fists. This was better than the occasion when they struck us with the leather straps of their swords or with their leather indoor shoes. . . . The number of blows I received, which I vowed I would never forget was 264" (Gibney 1995, 54).

The Japanese training of their new recruits give us some insight into why the Japanese soldiers were capable of such brutality. It was a case of "the transfer of oppression." The arbitrary and cruel treatment that the military inflicted on its own officers and soldiers was transferred to their treatment of the enemy. The hierarchical and authoritarian nature of Japanese society was another factor which contributed to the harsh treatment of POWs and enemy combatants.

Another part of the toughening process for new recruits, in addition to their military training, was practice in beheadings and the bayoneting of live prisoners in the field. Tominaga described his initiation in beheading a Chinese prisoner after watching his superior officer's demonstration.

"I was tense, thinking I couldn't afford to fail. I steadied myself, holding the sword at a point above my right shoulder, and swung down with one breath.

The head flew away and the body tumbled down, spouting blood. The air reeked from all the blood. I washed the blood off the blade then wiped it with the paper provided. Fat stuck to it and wouldn't come off. I noticed, when I sheathed it, that my sword was slightly bent" (Cook 1992, 42).

The practice in beheading seemed to change something inside the soldier: "[After having beheaded a prisoner] I don't know how to put it, but I gained strength somewhere in my gut." And he soon developed what was called "evil eyes" without realizing what had happened. It was not until some of the women in the National Defense Women's Association mentioned that they had never seen men with such evil eyes that he realized a transformation had taken place. "Everybody becomes bloodthirsty on the battlefield. The men received their baptism of blood when they went into combat. They were victimizers. I joined them by killing a prisoner" (Cook 1992, 42).

In reflecting on the atrocities committed by the Japanese soldiers, Kimizuka Kiyoshi awakened to the outrageousness of their behavior in China:

"When I look back at the brutal treatment given to military prisoners of war and the whole population of China after the invasion of China, I cannot but feel that the time-honored courteousness of the Japanese people and our sense of chivalry had sunk so low that Japanese soldiers had been reduced to madmen." It is true that the state of mind of those involved in a kill-or-be-killed war is abnormal. The Japanese, however, were particularly prone to flaunt a sense of superiority over the Chinese. . . . For some reason, while flattering themselves that they were the world's best peoples. the Germans and the Japanese were capable of outrageous behavior (Gibney 1995, 69).

Cook and Gibney's works raise larger issues regarding Japanese reaction to the war. The veterans talked about their experiences during the war in moving, personal terms and in the most excruciating details, yet when it came to coming to terms with larger issues of the war, they refused to draw any conclusions. Some of the common characteristics were:

1. There is no well-established overall narrative for telling the defeat of Japan;
2. The war responsibility is not clearly established in the minds of many Japanese today, no matter how certain the rest of the world may be about it;
3. The people introduced the notion of "a good defeat";
4. The interviewees rarely invoked an enemy, or hatred for the enemy somehow the war became an "enemy-less" conflict;
5. Few of the interviewees looked back and tried to reach some sort of conclusion about the overall experience of the war.

There is no sense of closure to the war, no consciousness of moral responsibility nor remorse for their actions. The war occurred "like some natural cataclysm" and not the result of anything they had done, and there was no sense of responsibility for their past crimes. The reason for this lack of drawing any general conclusions may be due to the fact that the people have never been fully informed about the war by the government. From the emperor's Imperial Rescript of August 15, 1945, it was announced that "We must endure the unendurable and bear the unbearable." The emperor has admitted to no wrong doing to the present-day, and the Japanese people have yet to be told the whole truth about the war, or Japan's role in it, by their own political leaders.

Japan at War contains sixty-eight interviews with Japanese survivors who experienced the war and gives us a rare glimpse into the minds of the Japanese people. Among those interviewed included Ienaga Saburo. One of Japan's leading historians, he was not afraid to speak out frankly about the Asian Pacific War and fought in the courts for over twenty years for his right to speak out uncensored by the Ministry of Education. Ienaga is a man of conscience who regretted that he had failed earlier in his career to fight against the militarism that had overtaken Japan in the 1930s, and he is determined to speak out now.

The case of Captain Tominaga Shozo is another interesting example of one who had come to terms with the past. He was a soldier who joined the Japanese Imperial Army in 1941, fought in China, committed many atrocities, and was captured by the Russians and held as a POW after the war. Finally he was transferred to a People's Liberation Army camp where he was treated with kindness and consideration. There, transformation began to take place slowly: "We began to realize that human beings should be treated this way and began to reflect on our treatment of Chinese during the war." One day he and the other prisoners were given ten sheets of paper and told to write their personal histories. As the imprisonment continued, the prisoners came to a new consciousness and a sense of responsibility for their own actions; Tominaga and his friends wrote another self-examination from this new perspective. Before their release, a war crimes trial was held in accordance with the Potsdam Declaration. Captain Tominaga and forty-five other prisoners were indicted for having committed atrocities, but were nevertheless released to return to Japan because, as he wrote, "we showed clear signs of repentance and had admitted our guilt" (Cook 1992, 467). Tominaga was finally released in 1956 after spending fifteen years in China.

On the whole, the two volumes amply confirmed the worst allegations of American propaganda during the conflict. With fanatical disregard for human life, Japanese soldiers committed countless atrocities against both enemy combatant and innocent civilians (Karnow, "Collective Amnesia").

Forgiveness and Reconciliation

The Railway Man by Eric Lomax is a moving odyssey of a British soldier who became a POW under the Japanese and survived two years of brutal torture by his Japanese interrogator, a member of the Kempeitai (Japanese equivalent of the Gestapo), Nagase Takashi. Lomax was captured while serving in Singapore and subsequently sent to work on the Burma-Siam Railway in a camp called Kanburi (short for Kanchanaburi) in present-day Thailand. Arrested and interrogated for having in his possession a secretly-built radio, Lomax had to suffer two years of dreadful torture, starvation, and physical beatings at the hands of his English-speaking interrogator, Nagase Takashi, and his subordinates. After the war, for fifty years Lomax suffered from the aftereffects of his two years of torture, humiliation, and dehumanization. And he often thought of confronting his hated interrogator with murderous intent.

By coincidence, while visiting a friend he was given a photocopy from the *Japan Times* for August 15, 1989 with a picture of and an article about Nagase Takashi, who was described as devoting much of his life to "make up for the Japanese Army's treatment of prisoners-of-war." When he first heard about the good deeds that Nagase was performing, Lomax was filled with disbelief. His hatred of the Japanese was so strong that he did not care to see another Japanese for the rest of his life. And he doubted Nagase's sincerity:

"[My friend Henry Cecil Babb] gave me some information about his correspondent Nagase Takashi, who claimed to have become active in charitable causes near Kanburi in the postwar years, and who had just built a Buddhist temple close to the railway there. I read about his activities with cold scepticism and found the very thought of him distasteful. I could not believe the idea of a Japanese repentance. He had organized a meeting of 'reconciliation' at the River Kwae Bridge . . . I had not seen a Japanese since 1945 and had no wish ever to meet one again. His reconciliation assembly sounded to me like a fraudulent publicity stunt" (Lomax 1995, 232).

Lomax had a total distrust of the Japanese and had no desire to meet Nagase. Through more coincidences, however, they corresponded and finally arranged to meet in Kanburi in Thailand. Lomax had learned that Nagase's repentance was genuine and sincere. It was not merely words. Nagase had gone back to Thailand more than sixty times since 1963. And his reparations were not an occasional thing but had become a way of life. He built a Temple of Peace on the River of Kwae Bridge and had become a devout Buddhist. He often spoke out against militarism and is known to have said critically of Japan:

"Japan is a very strange country, truth cannot prevail. So I am a citizen of the world and not a Japanese." He accuses the Japanese royal family of being a family of war criminals and claims that 80 percent of the Japanese today do not know that Japan had ever invaded another country.

Because of Nagase's sincere remorse and demonstration of his repentance with good deeds and actions, Eric Lomax was finally moved to give Mr. Nagase the forgiveness he desired. They met alone in a hotel room in Tokyo, and Lomax handed Nagase a handwritten letter. He writes in the letter: "The war had been over for almost fifty years; that I had suffered much; and that I knew that although he too had suffered throughout this time, he had been most courageous and brave in arguing against militarism and working for reconciliation. I told him that while I could not forget what happened at Kanburi in 1943, 1 assured him of my total forgiveness" (Lomax 1995, 275).

Lasting Distrust of Japan

"Unlike many in the West who have come to see Japan as a reformed militarist nation, a 'civil power,' many East Asians, in varying degrees, still view Japan with suspicion in terms of its militarist past. In other words, unlike those in the West who see the Japanese militaristic culture of the 'sword' has given way to an anti-militaristic culture of the 'chrysanthemum,' many East Asians see the revival of militarism as by no means a foregone scenario of a future Japan" (Deng, "Asianization"). Distrust of Japan dating back to the days of Pearl Harbor was echoed in Ruth Benedict's classic anthropological study of the contradictory nature of Japanese personality and character, *The Chrysanthemum and the Sword* (1946). For East Asians, particularly those who had directly suffered the brutality of Japanese militarism, the memory is still painfully clear; it is especially important for Japan to make a sincere, unambiguous apology and pay reparations to its victims even though the compensation will not erase the pain and suffering.

At the moment a decision is pending in a suit representing 33,000 U.S. POWs, 14,000 civilian internees, and thousands more Dutch, Australian, and New Zealand survivors filed in the Tokyo District Court on January 30, 1995. The suit asks for an official apology and compensation of $20,000 per individual from the Japanese government. Ms. Liu Xiuyung, the Nanking massacre survivor, and nine others have also filed suit in the Tokyo District Court asking for an apology and compensation. Her quest is supported by a courageous group of 200 Japanese lawyers, scholars, and others who wanted the Japanese people to become better informed about Japan's past actions. Individuals such as Azuma Shiro, a retired veteran of World War II, historian Ienaga Saburo, Eric Lomax's Kempeitai interrogator, Nagase Takashi, and Nobel Laureate novelist Oe Kenzaburo have all spoken out courageously about the fact that the Japanese government has not faced up to its past.

Recently a bill was introduced into the House, HCR 126, that condemns the Japanese for their wartime atrocities and calls for: (1) the Japanese government to issue formally a clear and unambiguous apology and: (2) immediately pay compensation to all victims of Japanese World War II war crimes. With her new book, Iris Chang has now added her voice in challenging the sixty years of denials and deceits by the Japanese government that have kept her own people and the world from knowing the truth about the atrocities committed by the Japanese military in China and elsewhere in Asia.

Many complex factors came into play to bring about the conflict in the Pacific: the world-wide economic depression in the 1930s, Japan's late-stage adoption of imperialism and colonialism, racism and prejudice, cultural conflict, modernization, militarism, expansionism, and Japan's perceived need for self-preservation. However, in order to close this bloody chapter of modern history, Japan must come to terms with her past. In order to achieve a meaningful reconciliation, a fuller discussion of the complex and multifaceted issues of the Asia Pacific War, perhaps will help provide a common ground upon which to build a satisfactory settlement among the Pacific rim countries. Furthermore, the dialogue must continue not only among the many voices of the Pacific region, but need to include also the voices of Americans, Canadians, English, Dutch, Australians, and all those who have suffered the pains of hunger, torture, and disease under the Japanese military. The issue is not merely an East Asian one, but a transnational one that involves America and Europe.

References

Bauman, Zygmunt. 1989. *Modernity and the Holocaust.* Ithaca, NY: Cornell University Press.

Chang, Iris. 1997. *The Rape of Nanking: The Forgotten Holocaust of World War II.* New York: Basic Books.

Cook, Haruko Taya, and Theodore F. Cook. 1992. *Japan at War: An Oral History.* New York: New Press.

Gibney, Frank, ed. 1995. *Senso: The Japanese Remember the Pacific War. Letters to the Editor of Asahi Shimbun.* Armonk, NY: M.E. Sharpe.

Gold, Hal. 1996. *Unit 731: Testimony.* Tokyo: Yenbooks.

Harris, Sheldon. 1994. *Factories of Death: Japanese Biological Warfare, 1932–45, and the American Cover-up.* London and New York: Routledge.

Ienaga, Saburo. 1968. *The Pacific War 1931–1945.* New York: Pantheon Books.

Lomax, Eric. 1995. *The Railway Man: A POW's Searing Account of War Brutality and Forgiveness.* New York: W.W. Norton.

Yin, James Yin, and Shi Young. 1996. *Rape of Nanking: An Undeniable History, in Photographs*. Chicago: Triumph Books.

The Nuremberg Laws, 1935

In 1930, Jews constituted about 1 percent of the German population. Most were well assimilated and thought of themselves as Germans. Many had intermarried with German Catholics and Protestants, had friends and business partners who were Christians, and were indistinguishable from other Germans. Their shock at the rise of anti-Semitism under Hitler is reflected in the large numbers who never left Germany.

Two months after Hitler was chosen by Chancellor Hindenburg to form a minority government, in April 1933, he began his attack on the Jews. He directed his SA "brown shirt" Nazi vigilantes to boycott Jewish stores. The campaign was called off because of pressure from other governments, but the experiment showed Hitler that the German people were unwilling to protest or challenge such blatant anti-Jewish actions by the government.

In 1933, Jews were excluded from holding public office and from employment in the civil service, journalism, radio, theater, film, teaching, and farming. In 1934, Jews were banned from the stock exchanges and severely restricted in law, medicine, and business, all of which became official prohibitions by 1938.

These acts and the Nuremberg Laws of September 15, 1935, were carried out in full public view (though all were edicts of Hitler under the "emergency" powers he assumed after the fire in the parliamentary building, the Reichstag, in February 1933).

What further restrictions did the Nuremberg laws place on German Jews? In what ways were these even more serious than deprivation of livelihood in certain professions?

The Reich Citizenship Law of September 15, 1935

THE REICHSTAG HAS ADOPTED by unanimous vote the following law which is herewith promulgated.

Article 1

(1) A subject of the state is one who belongs to the protective union of the German Reich, and who, therefore, has specific obligations to the Reich.

(2) The status of subject is to be acquired in accordance with the provisions of the Reich and the state Citizenship Law.

Article 2

(1) A citizen of the Reich may be only one who is of German or kindred blood, and who, through his behavior, shows that he is both desirous and personally fit to serve loyally the German people and the Reich.

(2) The right to citizenship is obtained by the grant of Reich citizenship papers.

(3) Only the citizen of the Reich may enjoy full political rights in consonance with the provisions of the laws.

Article 3

The Reich Minister of the Interior, in conjunction with the Deputy to the *Fuehrer*, will issue the required legal and administrative decrees for the implementation and amplification of this law.

Promulgated: September 16, 1935. *In force*: September 30, 1935.

First Supplementary Decree of November 14, 1935

On the basis of Article III of the Reich Citizenship Law of September 15, 1935, the following is hereby decreed:

Article 1

(1) Until further provisions concerning citizenship papers, all subjects of German or kindred blood who possessed the right to vote in the *Reichstag* elections when the Citizenship Law came into effect, shall, for the present, possess the rights of Reich citizens. The same shall be true of those upon whom the Reich Minister of the Interior, in conjunction with the Deputy to the *Fuehrer* shall confer citizenship.

(2) The Reich Minister of the Interior, in conjunction with the Deputy to the *Fuehrer*, may revoke citizenship.

Article 2

(1) The provisions of Article I shall apply also to subjects who are of mixed Jewish blood.

(2) An individual of mixed Jewish blood is one who is descended from one

or two grandparents who, racially, were full Jews, insofar that he is not a Jew according to Section 2 of Article 5. Full-blooded Jewish grandparents are those who belonged to the Jewish religious community.

Article 3

Only citizens of the Reich, as bearers of full political rights, can exercise the right of voting in political matters, and have the right to hold public office. The Reich Minister of the Interior, or any agency he empowers, can make exceptions during the transition period on the matter of holding public office. The measures do not apply to matters concerning religious organizations.

Article 4

(1) A Jew cannot be a citizen of the Reich. He cannot exercise the right to vote; he cannot hold public office.

(2) Jewish officials will be retired as of December 31, 1935. In the event that such officials served at the front in the World War either for Germany or her allies, they shall receive as pension, until they reach the age limit, the full salary last received, on the basis of which their pension would have been computed. They shall not, however, be promoted according to their seniority in rank. When they reach the age limit, their pension will be computed again, according to the salary last received on which their pension was to be calculated.

(3) These provisions do not concern the affairs of religious organizations.

(4) The conditions regarding service of teachers in public Jewish schools remains unchanged until the promulgation of new laws on the Jewish school system.

Article 5

(1) A Jew is an individual who is descended from at least three grandparents who were, racially, full Jews . . .

(2) A Jew is also an individual who is descended from two full-Jewish grandparents if:

(a) he was a member of the Jewish religious community when this law was issued, or joined the community later;
(b) when the law was issued, he was married to a person who was a Jew, or was subsequently married to a Jew;

    (c) he is the issue from a marriage with a Jew, in the sense of Section I, which was contracted after the coming into effect of the Law for the Protection of German Blood and Honor of September 15, 1935;

    (d) he is the issue of an extramarital relationship with a Jew, in the sense of Section I, and was born out of wedlock after July 31, 1936.

Article 6

(1) Insofar as there are, in the laws of the Reich or in the decrees of the National Socialist German Workers' Party and its affiliates, certain requirements for the purity of German blood which extend beyond Article 5, the same remain untouched. . . .

Article 7

The *Fuehrer* and Chancellor of the Reich is empowered to release anyone from the provisions of these administrative decrees.

* * *

Law for the Protection of German Blood and German Honor
September 15, 1935

Thoroughly convinced by the knowledge that the purity of German blood is essential for the further existence of the German people and animated by the inflexible will to safe-guard the German nation for the entire future, the Reichstag has resolved upon the following law unanimously, which is promulgated herewith:

Section 1

1. Marriages between Jews and nationals of German or kindred blood are forbidden. Marriages concluded in defiance of this law are void, even if, for the purpose of evading this law, they are concluded abroad.

2. Proceedings for annulment may be initiated only by the Public Prosecutor.

Section 2

Relation outside marriage between Jews and nationals for German or kindred blood are forbidden.

Section 3

Jews will not be permitted to employ female nationals of German or kindred blood in their households.

Section 4

1. Jews are forbidden to hoist the Reich and national flag and to present the colors of the Reich.
2. On the other hand they are permitted to present the Jewish colors. The exercise of this authority is protected by the state.

Section 5

1. A person who acts contrary to the prohibition of section 1 will be punished with hard labor.
2. A person who acts contrary to the prohibition of section 2 will be punished with imprisonment or with hard labor.
3. A person who acts contrary to the provisions of section 3 or 4 will be punished with imprisonment up to a year and with a fine or with one of these penalties.

Section 6

The Reich Minister of the Interior in agreement with the Deputy of the *Fuehrer* will issue the legal and administrative regulations which are required fro the implementation and supplementation of this law.

Section 7

The law will become effective on the day after the promulgation, section 3 however only on 1 January, 1936.

Nuremberg, the 15th day of September 1935 at the Reich party Rally of Freedom.

The Fuehrer and Reich Chancellor Adolf Hitler
The Reich Minister of the Interior Frick
The Reich Minister of Justice Dr. Goertner
The Deputy of the Fuehrer R. Hess

Kristallnacht

Stephen Kaufman

*On November 9 and 10, 1938, German citizens, urged by the Nazi govern-
ment, unleashed an evening of terror upon the Jewish community that later
became known as "Kristallnacht," the Night of Broken Glass. The name
refers to the thousands of windows broken in Jewish homes, businesses and
synagogues. Many argue that this event was the beginning of the Holocaust.
What were the causes of Kristallnacht? According to the author, what lessons should we draw from this event today?*

On November 9, 1938, a storm was unleashed that would soon engulf the Jews
of Europe. The winds that preceded the storm had been occasionally calm,
occasionally mild and occasionally violent. Storm warnings were found in the
pogroms and other virulent anti-Semitic acts found throughout Europe. My
maternal grandparents, mother and father were among the millions who fled
Europe, partly in response to the pogroms. I still recall the stories related to
me by my mother about the Cossacks who came through their small shtetl of
Stari Strelyska in what is now the Ukraine and vandalized the town and tortured its Jewish inhabitants—my great-grandfather among them.

To the extent that Germany was a refuge from the pogroms of Russia and
Eastern Europe, the ascension of the Nazi regime changed all this. With the
willing compliance of the German electorate, Hitler became chancellor in 1933
and began his unrelenting attack on the Jews.

In the years preceding Kristallnacht one might easily excuse the world for
inaction because German Jews and others thought that this storm warning
would pass like all others. Life would return to normal and Jews would only
be buffeted by the governments that turned a blind eye to the violence against
them. But Kristallnacht was different because of the events that preceded it.

The first real turning point was the passing of the Nuremberg Laws and
German Laws of Citizenship which effectively denied the Jews of Germany
their rightful place in German society. By force of law, Jews who were one
day citizens in a highly educated country were no longer entitled to the same
rights and privileges and protection under the law. The state had legitimized

---

From remarks before temple Bet Tikva in Flemington, NJ, to commemorate the sixtieth
anniversary of Kristallnacht, November 9, 1998.

Germans pass by the shattered shop window of a Jewish-owned business that was destroyed during Kristallnacht, 1938. *(National Archives, courtesy of United States Holocaust Memorial Museum Photo Archives)*

"SCIENTIFIC INVESTIGATIONS."

Australian cartoon mocking the value of scientific investigations of aborigines on the grounds that the aborigines are all the same and uneducable. (Sydney *Punch*, 1878.) *(Ross Woodrow and The University of Newcastle)*

the inferior status of Jews and the laws of the state supported not only denial of rights but persecution as well.

This condition persisted for three and a half years with increasing incidents of psychological terror, economic deprivation and social isolation. With increasing rhetoric directed against the Jewish community from the state leadership and Nazi party leadership, the results were inevitable. The rhetoric was also accompanied by a widening circle of government decrees which further isolated German Jews from the society and imposed economic hardships.

Against this, the specific historical acts which precipitated Kristallnacht occurred. The details are relevant to the extent that we understand the incendiary nature of the situation and the pre-meditated actions which followed. Polish Jews in increasing numbers following World War I had moved to Germany to seek economic relief and escape from Polish anti-Semitism. In the period immediately before Kristallnacht, it was estimated that there were more than 50,000 Polish Jews living in Germany.

As part of the growing restrictions against Jews, Germany in 1938 had declared that these Polish Jews would need to return to Poland—no need for alien Jews in Germany, let alone Jews of German citizenship. In the meantime, Poland had decreed that Polish Jews living outside the country for a period of more than five years would have to ask for re-entry permits. It is believed that Poland issued this decree in the hopes of forcing many of the expatriate Polish Jews into remaining outside of Poland. The orders were given not to issue the necessary Polish permits. Thus the Jews were caught in a no man's land between a Germany which wished to exile them and a Poland which did not wish them to return. Thousands of Jews were stuck in deplorable conditions in Poland just across the border from Germany. That neither country cared for Jews made the situation difficult for the Jews caught stuck between the two countries.

The roundups in Germany began on October 27, 1938. One family caught in the early sweeps was that of Hershl Grynzspan. His family had moved to Germany in 1914 and lived in Hanover. His parents and the rest of his family were caught in the detention camps. Hershl left for Paris in 1936 to seek a better future. He received a postcard which described the difficult living conditions of those caught in the roundup.

After receiving the card, he went to the German Embassy in Paris on November 7, 1938. Distraught about the fate of his parents, he sought out a German consular officer. Upon gaining entry to an office, he shot and mortally wounded Ernest vom Rath, a minor administrative secretary in the German Embassy. This specific act was the one that precipitated the event known as Kristallnacht.

The news of the assassination followed the next day and the postcard from his family shortly after their internment and the news of the exiled Jews hit the newspapers.

The Nazi machine began the preparations for the incendiary activities. An editorial appeared in the Nazi organ *Volkisher Beobachter*, calling for meetings in each city and town. Nazi leaders fomented the mobs to seek revenge for the wounding of the German embassy official. In the morning of November 9 vom Rath died, and the news, coupled with the preparations, unleashed Kristallnacht.

Coincidentally, the German leadership including Hitler was meeting in Munich to celebrate the anniversary of the 1923 Munich Putsch. Hitler left the meeting early upon learning of vom Rath's death and was heard to say: "Let the Storm Troopers have a fling."

Orders were issued to make it appear as if the "demonstrations" were spontaneous. Reinhard Heydrich, a senior Nazi, officer developed the guidelines under which the terrorism was to occur. A copy of the orders was preserved. A partial transcript follows.[1]

> Kristellnacht
>
> Message from SS-Grupenfuehrer Heydrich to all State Police Main Offices and Field Offices, November 10:
>
> Regards: Measures against Jews tonight. . . . Only such measures may be taken which do not jeopardize German life or property (for instance, burning of synagogues; only if there is no danger of fires for the neighborhoods).
>
> Business establishments and homes of Jews may be destroyed but not looted. The police have been instructed to supervise the execution of these directives and to arrest looters.
>
> In business streets special care is to be taken that non-Jewish establishments will be safeguarded at all cost against damage. . . .
>
> As soon as the events of this night permit, the use of the designated officers, as many Jews, particularly wealthy ones, as the local jails will hold, are to be arrested in all districts. Initially only healthy male Jews, not too old, are to be arrested. After the arrests have been carried out the appropriate concentration camp is to be contacted immediately with a view to a quick transfer of the Jews to the camps. . . .

The results are well known—the destruction of Jewish synagogues, businesses, schools and homes. Personal effects were often tossed into the street and burned. Nearly a hundred Jews were killed, thousands subjected to violent acts, and nearly 30,000 arrested and sent to Buchenwald, Dachau, and Sachsenhausen. A giant step forward had been taken towards the Shoah.

Events immediately following Kristallnacht also provide for a provocative insight into the position of Jews within Germany. Claims could be made by Jews for the damage from the insurance companies to cover their losses. But these payments were then confiscated by the German government on the grounds that German Jewry was itself responsible for the riot. In addition, German Jews were fined one billion reich marks.

The laws, decrees, and support of the state and the creation of a culture which reviled Jews made Kristallnacht and the Shoah possible. That officers of the state were elected on platforms of discrimination against Jews sent clear messages of the intent of the German state. It is important to remember that the world stood by as these laws and decrees were enacted.

What can we learn from Kristallnacht?

Surely, we should remember the victims from that night. Surely, we should remember Kristallnacht's historical position in relation to the Shoah. Surely, we should remember that too little action was taken by the world community to protest Kristallnacht. And surely, we must remember that we must depend upon one another. We must ask ourselves as we recall Kristallnacht what we have done in response to the current seminal flares of the last years of this century. As we anguish about the failure of others to act in the 1930s, we must also anguish about our inaction over events in Bosnia, Herzegovina, Rwanda, Timor, Tibet, Burma, Guatemala, and many other places where mass murder or genocide has taken place. And what have you done? What have I done?—not enough.

I recall the mourner's Kaddish recited by Jews on the day of Yom HaShoah. Interspersed between the lines are the major death and concentration camps where Jews died by the millions. We could just as easily substitute the names of distant lands and people who just in the last twenty to thirty years suffered a similar fate—that of state-sponsored death.

We must remember the victims of the Holocaust and Kristallnacht, not only because they are Jews but because they are victims. A small minority group cannot hope by themselves to feel immune to the injustices of a society bent on persecution of its minority groups. Comfort and security can only come from within when all individuals and groups are valued—when all are recognized with the same rights and privileges as human beings. We must collectively work towards these goals.

And so the most fitting tribute and commemoration for Kristallnacht is for the community to become more vigilant against the denial of human rights everywhere. Insist that education at all levels include the study of the Holocaust and genocide. Insist that the education include not only examples of man's inhumanity to man, but also examples of people working collectively on behalf of human rights.

The actions of Danes and Bulgarians to protect their Jews are models for us all. We need look no further than the United States where the civil rights movement, while perhaps not moving quickly and far enough, is testimony to positive changes—to South Africa where a system not unlike that of pre-World War II Germany was changed.

We must learn that actions can make a difference. I look forward to a time when an Avenue of Righteous becomes unnecessary. A time when people's ordinary reactions to injustice is to stop it. Where it is not necessary to raise these people to the stature of heroes, but instead to a time when those that do not speak up or act to prevent racism are questioned by their neighbors. Nations can and must create cultural norms which value the rights of all citizens. Nations can also create norms which ask governments to intercede quickly and strongly in the face of inhumanity. This is a lasting commemoration to Kristallnacht.

Note

1. Before "Kristallnacht," the "night of broken glass," *Nazi Conspiracy and Aggression,* vol III (Washington, DC: Government Printing Office, 1946), pp. 545–547.

Testimony at Nuremberg

Rudolf Hoess

Rudolf Hoess (no relation to Hitler's aide, Rudolf Hess) was born in 1900, joined the SS in 1933, and after serving five years as a convicted murderer was chosen to head the extermination camp of Auschwitz. This is his signed testimony (in part) at the Post-War Trials of Major War Criminals held at

From Rudolf Franz Ferdinand Hoess, "Affidavit, 5 April 1946," in *Trial of the Major War Criminals Before the International Tribunal, Nuremberg, 14 November 1945– October 1946* (Nuremberg: Secretariat of the International Military Tribunal, 1949), Doc. 3868–PS, vol. 33, 275–79.

Nuremberg. What do you make of his attitude toward the death camps and of his own role in the Holocaust?

I, RUDOLF FRANZ FERDINAND HOESS, being first duly sworn, depose and say as follows:

1. I am forty-six years old, and have been a member of the NSDAPI since 1922; a member of the SS since 1934; a member of the Waffen-SS since 1939. I was a member from 1 December 1934 of the SS Guard Unit, the so-called Deathshead Formation (Totenkopf Verband).

2. I have been constantly associated with the administration of concentration camps since 1934, serving at Dachau until 1938; then as Adjutant in Sachsenhausen from 1938 to 1 May, 1940, when I was appointed Commandant of Auschwitz. I commanded Auschwitz until 1 December, 1943, and estimate that at least 2,500,000 victims were executed and exterminated there by gassing and burning, and at least another half million succumbed to starvation and disease, making a total dead of about 3,000,000. This figure represents about 70% or 80% of all persons sent to Auschwitz as prisoners, the remainder having been selected and used for slave labor in the concentration camp industries. Included among the executed and burnt were approximately 20,000 Russian prisoners of war (previously screened out of Prisoner of War cages by the Gestapo) who were delivered at Auschwitz in Wehrmacht transports operated by regular Wehrmacht officers and men. The remainder of the total number of victims included about 100,000 German Jews, and great numbers of citizens (*mostly* Jewish) from Holland, France, Belgium, Poland, Hungary, Czechoslovakia, Greece, or other countries. We executed about 400,000 Hungarian Jews alone at Auschwitz in the summer of 1944.

4. Mass executions by gassing commenced during the summer 1941 and continued until fall 1944. I personally supervised executions at Auschwitz until the first of December 1943 and know by reason of my continued duties in the Inspectorate of Concentration Camps WVHA2 that these mass executions continued as stated above. All mass executions by gassing took place under the direct order, supervision and responsibility of RSHA. I received all orders for carrying out these mass executions directly from RSHA.

6. The "final solution" of the Jewish question meant the complete extermination of all Jews in Europe. I was ordered to establish extermination facilities at Auschwitz in June 1941. At that time there were already in the general government three other extermination camps: BELZEK, TREBLINKA and WOLZEK. These camps were under the Einsatzkommando of the Security Police and SD. I visited Treblinka to find out how they carried out their exterminations. The Camp Commandant at Treblinka told me that he had liquidated 80,000 in the course of one-half year. He was principally concerned

with liquidating all the Jews from the Warsaw Ghetto. He used monoxide gas and I did not think that his methods were very efficient. So when I set up the extermination building at Auschwitz, I used Cyclon B, which was a crystallized Prussic Acid which we dropped into the death chamber from a small opening. It took from 3 to 15 minutes to kill the people in the death chamber depending upon climatic conditions. We knew when the people were dead because their screaming stopped. We usually waited about one-half hour before we opened the doors and removed the bodies. After the bodies were removed our special commandos took off the rings and extracted the gold from the teeth of the corpses.

7. Another improvement we made over Treblinka was that we built our gas chambers to accommodate 2,000 people at one time, whereas at Treblinka their 10 gas chambers only accommodated 200 people each. The way we selected our victims was as follows: we had two SS doctors on duty at Auschwitz to examine the incoming transports of prisoners. The prisoners would be marched by one of the doctors who would make spot decisions as they walked by. Those who were fit for work were sent into the Camp. Others were sent immediately to the extermination plants. Children of tender years were invariably exterminated since by reason of their youth they were unable to work. Still another improvement we made over Treblinka was that at Treblinka the victims almost always knew that they were to be exterminated and at Auschwitz we endeavored to fool the victims into thinking that they were to go through a delousing process. Of course, frequently they realized our true intentions and we sometimes had riots and difficulties due to that fact. Very frequently women would hide their children under the clothes but of course when we found them we would send the children in to be exterminated. We were required to carry out these exterminations in secrecy but of course the foul and nauseating stench from the continuous burning of bodies permeated the entire area and all of the people living in the surrounding communities knew that exterminations were going on at Auschwitz.

8. We received from time to time special prisoners from the local Gestapo office. The SS doctors killed such prisoners by injections of benzine. Doctors had orders to write ordinary death certificates and could put down any reason at all for the cause of death.

9. From time to time we conducted medical experiments on women inmates, including sterilization and experiments relating to cancer. Most of the people who died under these experiments had been already condemned to death by the Gestapo.

10. Rudolf Mildner was the chief of the Gestapo at Kattowicz and as such was head of the political department at Auschwitz which conducted third degree methods of interrogation from approximately March 1941 until September

1943. As such, he frequently sent prisoners to Auschwitz for incarceration or execution. He visited Auschwitz on several occasions. The Gestapo Court, the SS Standgericht, which tried persons accused of various crimes, such as escaping Prisoners of War, etc., frequently met within Auschwitz, and Mildner often attended the trial of such persons, who usually were executed in Auschwitz following their sentence. I showed Mildner throughout the extermination plant at Auschwitz and he was directly interested in it since he had to send the Jews from his territory for execution at Auschwitz.

I understand English as it is written above. The above statements are true; this declaration is made by me voluntarily and without compulsion; after reading over the statement, I have signed and executed the same at Nurnberg, Germany on the fifth day of April 1946.

Once Chosen, Tribal Elites Now Suffer Consequences

William E. Schmidt

The continuation of racial or ethnic genocide after the Nazi massacre of Jews is one of the most disturbing phenomena of the modern world. One of the most recent outbreaks occurred in the central African Great Lake states of Rwanda and Burundi in the early 1990s. In this article, the author examines some of the roots of the Hutu massacre of Tutsis shortly after it happened. How were European ideas of race related to these events in Africa? In what ways were these events similar to, and different from, the other examples in this chapter?

They are tall and narrow featured, and during the colonial era in central Africa, the Tutsi were among Africa's most remarkable elites. While they numbered only a small minority among the majority Hutu, the Tutsi not only administered Rwanda and neighboring Burundi, but the Germans and later, the Belgians celebrated them with a kind of Wagnerian romanticism, assuring them the best

From *The New York Times*, April 17, 1994, p. 43. Copyright © 1994 by The New York Times Co. Reprinted by permission.

jobs and favored treatment. Even entrance to school was fixed in the Tutsi's favor; admission to college was limited to those who could pass a minimum height test.

But over the last 40 years, after the Belgians left Africa and Rwanda began to grapple with the uncertainties and turbulence of majority rule, the Tutsi sinecure unraveled. Tribal uprisings among the Hutu singled out the Tutsi for reprisal; hundreds of thousands fled, tens of thousands were massacred. Last week, in the latest and most horrific spasm of ethnic and political violence yet, uncounted thousands of Tutsi were slaughtered by Hutu gangs and soldiers, who went on a bloody rampage after the Hutu presidents of both Rwanda and Burundi died in a suspicious plane crash.

Beyond central Africa, far away from the streets of Kigali, where machete-wielding youth dragged victims from their houses and hacked them to death on the spot, the scale of the violence seems beyond rational accounting. Yet even before the end of the cold war and the collapse of Soviet rule unleashed hidden ethnic fury and hatred within places like the former Yugoslavia, Africa and much of the developing world have been struggling for nearly half a century to come to terms with grinding ethnic and tribal rivalries that remain, in a way, one of the most enduring legacies of their colonial past.

To varying degrees, the Maronites in Lebanon and the Copts in Egypt, the Sikhs in India and the Vietnamese in Cambodia have also paid, like the Tutsi, the price of having been singled out. These were groups that had been disproportionately chosen to fill the bureaucracies or staff the schools or run the armies of European empire, much to the resentment of others in the population whom they helped to rule, and whose own grievances sometimes took violent form in the year following independence.

For the French or the British or the Germans, the tendency to settle on one group among many underscored, at heart, a practical and economic necessity: To administer their far-flung holdings, the European powers needed locals to rule in their place. But too often, said Amitav Ghosh, an Indian novelist who was trained as a sociologist, the Europeans deliberately settled on selected minority groups to serve as their collaborators. "The idea was to create a kind of client community, and dependency," said Mr. Ghosh. "It was a way of insuring loyalty."

In superimposing what in some cases was a new hierarchy atop an existing social system, colonialism gave a new shape and tension to relationships between different ethnic groups, even if it did not reorder them entirely. In Rwanda, the Tutsi historically had been the feudal overlords, although their pre-colonial relations with the Hutu were marked by a great degree of flexibility.

Under the Belgians, however, said Alison DesForge, an African historian, the system was made more rigid. "The colonial system reinforced the status of the Tutsi, by emphasizing the differences between the groups." Among other things, the Belgians even introduced identity cards that required that everyone be identified by their tribal origin.

All of this created a rich broth of grievances and resentments that, in the post-colonial period, easily lent itself to the manipulations of local politicians looking to excite popular support. In Rwanda, the awful bloodshed and reprisal killings by Hutu against Tutsi last week were not entirely spontaneous; for years, the regime of President Juvenal Habyarimana, the Hutu strongman who was killed in the plane crash 10 days ago, had stoked the fires of ethnic hatred, providing weapons and direction for tribal gangs.

"In a way, it is a self-perpetuating process," said Gareth Austin, a professor of history at the London School of Economics. "Just as the Europeans were able to divide and rule, by choosing one group or another as their surrogates, so are the post-colonial political leaders, who now wield tribalism and ethnicity as a kind of flag to whip up political support. The long-term lesson is, tribalism and ethnicity works."

In some ways, the very tribalism or contemporary ethnic rivalries that have contributed to the polarization of ethnic politics in northern India or parts of Africa were, at root, Eurpean inventions, reflecting a mix of political expediency and, at times, spurious racial science. It was the British, for example, who filled their colonial armies with Sikhs or Ghurkas or Masai, because the British concluded that they were "martial races," courageous and disciplined by nature.

Even more bald was the attachment Europeans developed toward the Tutsi, an attraction that was, at root, racial. In the late 19th century, the Tutsi were even celebrated among Europeans as the descendants of the biblical patriarch Ham, a lighter-skinned people whose narrower features reminded Europeans of themselves. In western Africa, too, said Peter Ekeh, the head of African-American Studies at Buffalo University, the British and the Germans turned to the Fulani, a minority people who were the existing elite, because of the regal bearing. But in Guinea, the French passed them over for the very same reason.

"The French had just come out of their own revolution, and they found the Fulani too aristocratic," said Mr. Ekeh.

It is wrong to suggest that the colonial era is the direct cause of the bloodshed and ethnic tension that has afflicted Rwanda or other parts of the developing world. In recent years, growing poverty, disease and corruption have also stretched the frayed social fabric of these societies, and given rise to a post-colonial class structure where education and jobs are increasingly hard to come by.

"The structure of post-colonial society has perpetuated these conditions, and, if anything, created an even greater emphasis on ethnicity," said David Newbury, of the University of North Carolina.

"One should not undervalue the underlying indigenous forces," said Ms. DesForge, a central African specialist. "But power relationships within these societies have been shifted in ways that no one could perceive or predict. If nothing else, this legacy has increasingly provided ruthless or ambitious people with opportunities to manipulate these tensions to their own advantage."

Part 11

Overcoming Racism in Twentieth-Century Settler Societies

Linked arm-in-arm, civil rights leaders march in Montgomery, Alabama, March 17, 1965. From left are Ralph Abernathy, James Foreman, Martin Luther King, Jr., S. L. Douglas, and John Lewis. *(Associated Press Photo)*

"Settler society" is a term which we have used so far to designate early colonized societies—especially in the wake of the Columbian encounter in the "colonial era." But many of these same societies of the Americas remained "settler societies" into the twentieth century. The great age of trans-Atlantic migration from Europe to the Americas extended from the 1880s to the 1920s. The "closing of the frontier" in the United States, presaged by Frederick Jackson Turner in 1893, was not completed until well into the twentieth century. (One is tempted to date the end with President John F. Kennedy's call for "new frontiers" in 1961.)

The first victims of the European settlement in the Americas were called Indians. As European settlers moved further west to new frontiers, Americans developed a literature and in the twentieth century a cinematic genre called "the Western" that mirrored that encounter with "Indians" in the movement westward. But like any mirror, the mythology of the Western reversed positions of invaders and invaded. The Western also provided a template for "white" experiences with people of other colors, from America's first experiments in extra-frontier imperialism in Hawaii and the Philippines in 1898 to the American war in Vietnam.

Chronologically, the second victims of European settlement in the Americas were the African slaves who were settled to work plantations on land seized from Indians. Legally subservient as slaves until the Civil War era, and legally second-class citizens until 1954, the descendants of those forced settlers suffered the prejudice of European color-coding and the discrimination of a caste apart, relegated to the lower rungs of the economy and society. The American dream of equal opportunity was a dream deferred when Martin Luther King, Jr. trumpeted its revival in 1963. Over thirty years later, the impact of the civil rights struggle and resultant federal legislation marked a revolution, but many dreams were still on hold.

To understand U.S. successes (and failures) in overcoming racism, it is useful to view societies with comparable experiences. Canada is offered as our example (though one could just as easily look at Mexico or Brazil). The variety of settler societies can be explored in other contexts as well. The settlement of Palestine mainly by European Jews since the Holocaust is one; Indian settlement in China (Hong Kong), similarly under the supervision of the British empire, is another. Nevertheless, the more striking comparison with the United States is South Africa. If Nelson Mandela was South Africa's Martin Luther King, Jr., his imprisonment delayed the realization of racial justice another thirty years. Indeed, the implacability of white South African rule was such that the victory of a black majority government has yielded less economic opportunity than many would have liked and the crimes of the apartheid era have been decriminalized with forgiveness.

What is the meaning of justice, and or racial justice, in a post-racist society? What factors have enabled formerly racist societies to achieve justice? What remains to be done?

I Have a Dream

Martin Luther King, Jr.

This speech, delivered by the Reverend Martin Luther King, Jr. on the steps at the Lincoln Memorial in Washington, D.C., on August 28, 1963 as the keynote address of a civil rights "march on Washington," crystallized the sense of hope denied that was felt broadly by African Americans at the time. What were the grievances he expressed? What were his hopes? How did he believe racism would be overcome in America?

I am happy to join with you today in what will go down in history as the greatest demonstration for freedom in the history of our nation.

Fivescore years ago, a great American, in whose symbolic shadow we stand today, signed the Emancipation Proclamation. This momentous decree came as a great beacon light of hope to millions of Negro slaves, who had been seared in the flames of withering injustice. It came as a joyous daybreak to end the long night of their captivity.

But one hundred years later, we must face the tragic fact that the Negro is still not free. One hundred years later, the life of the Negro is still sadly crippled by the manacles of segregation and the chains of discrimination. One hundred years later, the Negro lives on a lonely island of poverty in the midst of a vast ocean of material prosperity. One hundred years later, the Negro is still languished in the corners of American society and finds himself an exile in his own land. So we've come here today to dramatize a shameful condition.

In a sense we have come to our nation's capitol to cash a check. When the architects of our great republic wrote the magnificent words of the Constitution and the Declaration of Independence, they were signing a promissory note to which every American was to fall heir. This note was a promise that all men, yes, black men as well as white men, would be guaranteed the "inalienable Rights of Life, Liberty, and the pursuit of Happiness." It is obvious today that America has defaulted on this promissory note insofar as her citizens of color are concerned. Instead of honoring this sacred obligation, America has given the Negro people a bad check, a check that has come back marked "insufficient funds."

But we refuse to believe that the bank of justice is bankrupt. We refuse to believe that there are insufficient funds in the great vaults of opportunity of this nation. And so we've come to cash this check, a check that will give us upon demand the riches of freedom and the security of justice.

We have also come to this hallowed spot to remind America of the fierce urgency of now. This is no time to engage in the luxury of cooling off or to take the tranquilizing drug of gradualism. Now is the time to make real the promises of democracy. Now is the time to rise from the dark and desolate valley of segregation to the sunlit path of racial justice. Now is the time to lift our nation from the quicksands of racial injustice to the solid rock of brotherhood. Now is the time to make justice a reality for all of God's children.

It would be fatal for the nation to overlook the urgency of the moment. This sweltering summer of the Negro's legitimate discontent will not pass until there is an invigorating autumn of freedom and equality. Nineteen sixty-three is not an end but a beginning. And those who hope that the Negro needed to blow off steam and will now be content will have a rude awakening if the nation returns to business as usual. There will be neither rest nor tranquility in America until the Negro is granted his citizenship rights. The whirlwinds of revolt will continue to shake the foundations of our nation until the bright day of justice emerges.

But there is something that I must say to my people, who stand on the warm threshold which leads into the palace of justice: In the process of gaining our rightful place, we must not be guilty of wrongful deeds. Let us not seek to satisfy our thirst for freedom by drinking from the cup of bitterness and hatred. We must forever conduct our struggle on the high plane of dignity and discipline. We must not allow our creative protest to degenerate into physical violence. Again and again, we must rise to the majestic heights of meeting physical force with soul force. The marvelous new militancy which has engulfed the Negro community must not lead us to a distrust of all white people, for many of our white brothers, as evidenced by their presence here today, have come to realize that their destiny is tied up with our destiny. And they have come to realize that their freedom is inextricably bound to our freedom. We cannot walk alone.

And as we walk, we must make the pledge that we shall march ahead. We cannot turn back. There are those who are asking the devotees of civil rights, "When will you be satisfied?"

We can never be satisfied as long as the Negro is the victim of the unspeakable horrors of police brutality. We can never be satisfied so long as our bodies, heavy with the fatigue of travel, cannot gain lodging in the motels of the highways and the hotels of the cities. We cannot be satisfied as long as the Negro's basic mobility is from a smaller ghetto to a larger one. We can never be satisfied as long as our children are stripped of their selfhood and robbed of their dignity by signs stating "for whites only." We cannot be satisfied as long as a Negro in Mississippi cannot vote and a colored person in New York believes he has nothing for which to vote. No, no, we are not satisfied, and we will not be satisfied until "justice rolls down like waters and righteousness like a mighty stream."

I am not unmindful that some of you have come here out of great trials and tribulations. Some of you have come fresh from narrow jail cells. Some of you have come from areas where your quest for freedom left you battered by the storms of persecutions and staggered by the winds of police brutality. You have been the veterans of creative suffering. Continue to work with the faith that unearned suffering is redemptive. Go back to Mississippi, go back to Alabama, go back to South Carolina, go back to Georgia, go back to Louisiana, go back to the slums and ghettos of our northern cities, knowing that somehow this situation can and will be changed. Let us not wallow in the valley of despair.

I say to you, my friends, so even though we face the difficulties of today and tomorrow, I still have a dream. It is a dream deeply rooted in the American dream.

I have a dream that one day this nation will rise up and live out the true meaning of its creed: "We hold these truths to be self-evident, that all men are created equal."

I have a dream that one day on the red hills of Georgia, the sons of former slaves and the sons of former slave owners will be able to sit down together at the table of brotherhood.

I have a dream that one day even the state of Mississippi, a state sweltering with the heat of injustice, sweltering with the heat of oppression, will be transformed into an oasis of freedom and justice.

I have a dream that my four little children will one day live in a nation where they will not be judged by the color of their skin but by the content of their character. I have a dream today.

I have a dream that one day down in Alabama, with its vicious racists, with its governor having his lips dripping with the words of "interposition" and "nullification," one day right there in Alabama little black boys and black girls will be able to join hands with little white boys and white girls as sisters and brothers. I have a dream today.

I have a dream that one day "every valley shall be exalted, and every hill and mountain shall be made low; the rough places will be made plain, and the crooked places will be made straight; and the glory of the Lord shall be revealed, and all flesh shall see it together."

This is our hope. This is the faith that I go back to the South with. With this faith we will be able to hew out of the mountain of despair a stone of hope. With this faith we will be able to transform the jangling discords of our nation into a beautiful symphony of brotherhood. With this faith we will be able to work together, to pray together, to struggle together, to go to jail together, to stand up for freedom together, knowing that we will be free one day. This will be the day, this will be the day when all of God's children will be able to sing with new meaning:

> My country 'tis of thee, sweet land of liberty, of thee I sing.
> Land where my fathers died, land of the Pilgrims' pride,
> From every mountainside, let freedom ring!

And if America is to be a great nation, this must become true.
And let freedom ring from the prodigious hilltops of New Hampshire.
Let freedom ring from the mighty mountains of New York.
Let freedom ring from the heightening Alleghenies of Pennsylvania.
Let freedom ring from the snowcapped Rockies of Colorado.
Let freedom ring from the curvaceous slopes of California.
But not only that: Let freedom ring from Stone Mountain of Georgia.
Let freedom ring from Lookout Mountain of Tennessee.
Let freedom ring from every hill and molehill of Mississippi.
From every mountainside, let freedom ring.

And when this happens, when we allow freedom ring, when we let it ring from every village and every hamlet, from every state and every city, we will be able to speed up that day when all of God's children, black men and white men, Jews and Gentiles, Protestants and Catholics, will be able to join hands and sing in the words of the old Negro spiritual:

> Free at last! Free at last!
> Thank God Almighty, we are free at last!

For Many Immigrants, Canada's Racial "Mosaic" Pales at Top

Howard Schneider

This is an article that appeared in a U.S. newspaper about race relations in Canada. In what ways is Canada's history of race relations similar to that of the United States? In what ways is it different? What accounts for these differences? What do these differences tell you about race and racism in the United States?

Surfing the local radio dial, Jamaican native Denham Jolly identified what to him seemed two obvious shortcomings in this most diverse of Canada's cities—the lack of a local rap, jazz and world-beat station that reflected the city's multiracial population and the lack of any black owners in the local broadcasting industry.

He thought he could tackle both issues by developing his own proposal for Toronto's sole remaining FM license, and he entered a recent competition for it with high hopes and a large dose of community backing.

What he discovered, he says now, is that Canada's cherished official ideal of diversity sometimes has its limits.

When the regulators who run Canada's broadcasting authority evaluated Jolly's proposal, they deemed it "interesting." But they decided to let the Canadian Broadcasting Corp. [CBC] have the last FM slot to ensure that it reaches a few central-city blocks where its current AM signal is difficult to pick up amid the skyscrapers.

To the broadcasting regulators, it was important to ensure full coverage for the CBC, an institution considered central to Canada's identity and a reflection of the nation's cultural mainstream.

To Jolly and other Canadians of color, however, placing the CBC's penetration to a few extra blocks above the expansion of the city's racial and cultural broadcasting mix showed a side of Canada that is not extensively discussed—and, he and others feel, not yet well appreciated.

In a nation that prides itself on diversity and visualizes its society as a "mosaic" of equal pieces, the distribution of political, social and economic influence is still largely held by those of European heritage.

"Canadians say they believe in the mosaic, but some of the tiles have never seen a polish from the day they were put on the wall," said Jolly. "There is a lot of lip service, but in matters of race you are never quite sure of your place."

It can be seen in the country's largely white governing institutions—the handful of nonwhite faces, for example, among the 56 recently elected city council members in Toronto, a city some estimate to be more than 40 percent nonwhite—or in the lack of racial diversity in the nation's corporate head offices. In the *Financial Post* magazine's recent survey of Canada's top 200 corporate chief executives, only seven are nonwhite. Of those, five are Japanese or Chinese natives running subsidiaries of Japanese- or Chinese-owned companies; the other two are Asians who built their own businesses in Canada.

It can be seen in poverty, wage and job statistics that in some ways mirror those of the United States, with members of so-called visible minorities—people of color—more likely to be out of work, out of school and living in poverty than white Canadians. "Among men, among the native-born, the ethnic earnings gaps are pretty similar between Canada and the United States," with differences of more than 15 percent in some cases between what white and nonwhite Canadians earn for similar work, said Krishna Pendakur, a professor at Simon Fraser University in Vancouver who recently completed a study of the issue.

It can be seen in the head tables when Canada's elite convene. When Britain's Queen Elizabeth II visited last summer, she spoke approvingly of the Canadian mosaic—a word Canadians use to distinguish their country from an American "melting pot" they think demands too much conformity. But when the queen took her place among 16 head-table guests at a state dinner in her honor, the only nonwhite representatives of that mosaic were jazz pianist Oscar Peterson and his wife.

Growing Nonwhite Population

As much as 13 percent of Canada's population is nonwhite. That is about half the proportion found in the United States, although precise estimates are difficult because Canadian census takers traditionally have tallied individuals by country of origin, not race. Results of the first survey to ask about race will be released early next year.

What is clear, however, is that Canada's multicultural composition is increasingly a multiracial one as well. The fastest growing portion of Canada's population is its native Indian community, and immigration patterns have shifted away from Europe in favor of East Asia, the Indian subcontinent, Africa and the West Indies. In 1996, the number of non-European immigrants living in Canada surpassed the number of European immigrants for the first time.

That is not readily apparent, however, in the country's upper echelons.

When Jamaican-born politician Alvin Curling takes his seat in Ontario's provincial legislature, he is one of only two nonwhites, a fact that makes him envious of the influence and numbers that black U.S. politicians have achieved despite their country's history of more virulent racism.

When Fo Niemi watches the all-white casts of Canada's top political satire shows, scans the all-white audiences at political debates staged by the CBC or looks at the all-white staffs of Quebec's major broadcasters, he said, he sees a Canada much different from the one he experiences on the streets of Montreal.

"It is very glaring," said Niemi, executive director of the Center for Research Action on Race Relations. "When it comes to real inclusion—real integration, real presence in decision-making positions—we still have a fairly long way to go."

The story varies across the country. British Columbia, with a critical mass of Asian and Indian immigrants, has elected three nonwhite members of Parliament who are also junior members of the federal cabinet. There are prominent Asian entrepreneurs and broadcasters, local and provincial politicians, and philanthropists whose names grace academic and other public buildings that they helped fund. According to Pendakur's research, wage differentials are smaller in British Columbia than in the other provinces.

At the other extreme, there is Quebec, where diversity in the upper ranks of society is measured more in terms of who speaks English and who speaks French. The province's political and business elite is all white, and that homogeneity, Niemi said, extends through such institutions as the judiciary, even to local politics in Montreal, despite that city's multi-hued population.

Nor is the country free of the type of institutional issues that the United States has addressed with affirmative action. Over the past year, the federal Health Department was cited for bias in its hiring and promotion and ordered to adopt measures to right the balance. In Toronto recently, the city firefighters' union was accused of discriminating against visible minorities and women.

Ujjal Dosanjh, the attorney general of British Columbia, said his experience shows both Canada's promise as a multicultural and multiracial society and the degree to which its reality still falls short. Personally, he has made it from the Punjab countryside to the second-most-powerful position in British Columbia and feels accepted representing a parliamentary district that is a mix of white, Indian and Chinese Canadians.

On the other hand, he said that British Columbia, as the focus of Asian immigration for many decades, may be more open to the advancement of racial minorities into leadership positions—and thus not reflective of the country as a whole. At meetings with his provincial counterparts and their staff, he said, it is obvious how far Canada needs to go.

The leadership of Canada is "very, very European. . . . At the end of the 20th century, we are still not reflective of the diversity of the country," Dosanjh said. He said he routinely raises the lack of racial minorities in Canada's judicial institutions when he meets with his colleagues. He said his current focus is the prime minister's next appointment to the Supreme Court, a choice typically made with an eye toward regional and French-English linguistic balance.

"The aboriginals have been here for 5,000 years. The Indo-Canadians have been here 100 years. . . . We are now including European diversity on the Supreme Court. That is wonderful," Dosanjh said. "In a very polite but pointed way, I have asked. . . . 'When are you going to include the first visible minority appointment?' "

Different Histories of Slavery

Both Canada and the United States are immigrant nations, but discussions of race and ethnicity in the two countries have proceeded differently.

While much of the dialogue in the United States, for example, deals with the effects of slavery—a discussion that spans 130 years of Jim Crow laws, civil rights protests and affirmative-action debates—Canada has no such legacy to confront. Slavery was in decline here during the early 1800s, and the British government abolished it in 1834. By the time of the American Civil War, Canada was a haven for escaped slaves as the terminus of the Underground Railroad.

Today, there are only a few hundred thousand blacks among Canada's 30 million people, and, because of the countries' differing histories, there is far less of a tendency here to analyze public policy in terms of race.

In addition, the waves of European immigration that transformed many U.S. cities over the last century were not felt as fully in Canada until the 1950s and 1960s, when arrivals from such countries as Italy and Germany began changing Canada's predominantly Anglo-French composition. As recently as the 1930s, it was estimated that 80 percent of Canadians were of either British or French extraction.

It was during that time, as well, that Canada cast itself as a "multicultural" country and confirmed the mosaic as its guiding idea. In large part, that policy derived from the issue that long has governed so much of Canada's politics—competition between the country's English and French founding populations, which have tussled for control of the country since colonial days.

A special commission on biculturalism and bilingualism in the 1960s confirmed the equal status of founding peoples and languages, and the mosaic was a handy device to describe a situation in which two cultures coexisted while maintaining their identities. With immigration from non-English and non-French societies then on the rise, that debate was expanded to endorse multiculturalism and so include other nationalities in the mosaic as well, said political scientist Martin Lubin, a Canada expert at the State University of New York.

"It was a convenient political add-on to the emergent bicultural mythology," Lubin said, and one that was consistent with Canada's sense of itself as a fair and largely classless nation.

However, when researchers started studying the mosaic, they deemed it—as John Porter said in a work considered a classic of Canadian sociology—to be "vertical," with a power structure at the top that was still largely English and French, and people of other origins arrayed in various strata beneath them.

"Segregation in social structure, to which the concept of the mosaic or multiculturalism must ultimately lead, can become an important aspect of social control by the charter group," he wrote in his 1965 book, "The Vertical Mosaic."

"The very small ethnic representation in our elite groups," he wrote, "suggests that the chances of achieving the top positions are few."

Porter's research focused largely on the fate of other European nationalities subordinated to the dominant English and French cultures. Thirty years later, the situation he described has changed. There are many Italians, Germans and other non-English, non-French Europeans in positions of authority. When Canadians speak of the success of their multicultural experiment, it is diversity on this scale—not exclusively multiracialism—that they refer to.

The issue the country confronts today, researchers, politicians and community activists say, is whether people of color will also rise to the upper levels of Canadian society as they come to represent a larger and larger portion of the population.

To political scientist Lubin, the mosaic is still vertical and the chances of its leveling over time are in doubt. "The multicultural mythology enables people to come away with a series of beliefs about what is happening, which is not really happening as rapidly or thoroughly as the official mythology would have us believe," he said.

Avoiding the "American Model"

However, to Canadian officials like Hedy Fry, the secretary of state for multiculturalism and a member of Parliament from British Columbia, there is no reason to think that immigrants of color will not flourish, just as the European immigrant groups did before them.

As Canada's nonwhite groups expand their numbers, with each generation building on the success of the last, she says, she is confident that will happen. Even focusing on race, she contended, is an American habit that is not as relevant to a country without the United States' difficult history of institutionalized racial segregation. Even though blacks, for example, form a small percentage of Canadian society, a leading jurist like Julius Isaac can rise to become the top judge of the country's federal court system.

Fry also pointed to herself as an example, a native of Trinidad elected to the House of Commons and a junior member of the cabinet.

"Twenty-five to 30 years ago, we began to experiment with a different model," she said. "The American model did not work very well. It created people who were angry that they had to give up who they were."

"We have the most successfully integrated country in the world," said Thomas d'Aquino, head of the Business Council on National Issues, an influential coalition of Canada's largest companies. "The politics of color and the politics of race have not played as big a role."

According to a recent membership brochure, only three of the business council's 148 members are nonwhite, and each runs a subsidiary of a Japanese corporation. But d'Aquino said he fully expects the council's membership to diversify over time. Until then, he said, evidence of Canada's multiracial success can be seen in its low levels of racial tension and in the absence of the type of desperate and desperately violent ghettos found in many U.S. cities.

Some analysts, however, are starting to wonder about that issue as well. Tim Rees, a human resources analyst for the metropolitan Toronto government, points out that there are areas of Toronto where immigrants of color cluster and where the foreign- and native-born face the same employment and educational issues—fewer jobs, lower pay and higher dropout rates—that cripple some American neighborhoods. In smaller cities such as Winnipeg, meanwhile, high unemployment and widespread drug use among native-born Canadians has led to the formation of sometimes violent street gangs.

How Canada addresses such issues, Rees said, will determine whether the promise of multiculturalism is realized.

"We've managed to avoid directly confronting that, and we can continue to remain living in this illusion that we are different from south of the border, or different from the United Kingdom, and that is what multicultural policy has allowed us to do," Rees said. "It's a bit of a fool's paradise. . . . What happened in Detroit could happen in Toronto, and it will happen very quickly, and we won't be able to recover after the fact."

Black Power!

Russell Watson with Joseph Contreras and Joshua Hammer

This article from Newsweek *magazine was written shortly after Nelson Mandela was elected President of South Africa in the first election in which South African blacks were able to participate as equals. How does the South African struggle with racism compare with that in the United States? What do the two countries have to learn from each other?*

The crime was sabotage, the sentence was life plus five years. In 1964, Nelson Mandela was locked up in a prison on Robben Island, in the frigid South Atlantic off Cape Town. For years, he broke rocks in a limestone quarry. He was allowed only brief visits with his young wife, Winnie—barely time to talk, no opportunity to touch. He wrote to her that he felt like someone "who has missed life itself." But Nelson Mandela never gave up. He taught himself law, history, economies—and Afrikaans, the better to understand his enemy. He taught the young revolutionaries who were thrown into prison with him; the island became known as "Mandela University." In letters and later in secret meetings, he conducted a long dialogue with officials of the white government, trying to find out if there was a South Africa they could both inhabit. And last week, at 75, Mandela finally had his moment. For the first time, all South Africans could vote in a national election, leaping across the chasm from apartheid to majority rule. "Today is a day like no other before it," Mandela said as the voting began.

For his 30 million fellow Africans, it was the first, exuberant taste of full citizenship after a lifetime in which even second-class status was denied to them. They stood in long lines, stretching across the open African landscape. They marveled at themselves as they waited, patiently and peacefully, sometimes standing amicably right next to whites. They cast their ballots with reverence and glee. "I am about two inches taller than before I arrived," Anglican Archbishop Desmond Tutu joked as he left a polling station. "It's an incredible experience, like falling in love." Julius Molawa, a 48-year-old bricklayer, packed a dozen farm women into his Ford pickup and drove them to the polls. "My heart tells me it's the best day of my life," he said. "I don't have to carry a pass. I can work anywhere in the country I want. I am free."

For whites, too, it was a new day—and a more complicated one. "It's all happening too fast," complained a burly Afrikaner in the farming town of Bothaville. "Most of the blacks aren't ready to vote. The whole place is going to fall apart." But most whites seemed to accept the new reality, grudgingly or otherwise. "I think the blacks are aware that they need us, and we need them," said Gottfried Groebbelaar, a retired psychology lecturer. The generally hard-line Afrikaners, a blend of Dutch, French and German stock, had nowhere else to go—no European homeland to retreat to, no other white colony to take them in. Liberal whites were happy to shed their burden of guilt. "White South Africans should consider themselves one of the luckiest groups of people on the face of the earth," said playwright Athol Fugard. "In spite of our terrible history, we weren't torn apart by the violence disemboweling countries like Yugoslavia."

New regime: The voting was slow and the count even slower. But all signs were that Mandela's African National Congress (ANC) would win a strong majority, and that the new Parliament would elect him president this week. The National Party, the inventor of apartheid, was expected to finish second. Its leader, President F. W. de Klerk, who negotiated the end of apartheid with Mandela, would become one of two deputy presidents. The new government is merely a five-year coalition, full of checks and balances. It will almost certainly lack the means to satisfy the soaring expectations of the blacks who swept the ANC into power. And it may never win the confidence of most foreign investors, whose capital is crucial to the economy.

But even before the votes were counted, Mandela was saying all the right things, preaching reconciliation and promising to govern by consensus. "My full-time occupation is going to be to unite the country," he said in an interview with Newsweek. And senior ANC officials told Newsweek they were strongly inclined to retain several key officials from de Klerk's white government, including Chris Stals, the head of the central bank; Derek Keys, the finance minister; Kobie Coetsee, the defense minister, and the commander of the armed forces, Gen. George Meiring.

Mandela will never win over the lunatic fringe. Before the voting began, bombs apparently set off by white extremists killed 21 people in Johannesburg and Pretoria. "We don't want to fight and maim, but we are preparing," warned Eugene Terre Blanche, leader of the white-supremacist Afrikaner Resistance Movement. Yet, considering that 12,000 people were killed by political violence in the past four years, the polling stations were almost eerily peaceful. "They're the safest places in the country," said de Klerk. There were enormous bureaucratic foul-ups, especially in KwaZulu/Natal, the stronghold of Zulu leader Mangosuthu Buthelezi. The late entry into the race by his Inkatha Freedom Party meant that paper ballots, already crowded by 18 parties, had to be expanded for a 19th. In six rural areas, balloting was extended for a day to accommodate the crowds.

It was the unlikely pairing of Mandela and de Klerk that enabled South Africa to avoid all-out civil war over apartheid, winning the Nobel Peace Prize for the two men. The abandonment of apartheid was forced, in part, by the rest of the world's disapproval, expressed most effectively through economic sanctions. The end of the cold war meant that white hard-liners could no longer hide behind the strategic skirts of the West, denouncing equality as a communist plot. But in the end, peaceful change occurred mainly because de Klerk was willing to negotiate himself out of power—and the cautious, moderate Mandela was determined to win his war of national liberation without soaking the country in blood.

Racial discrimination may be as old as human history, but the system of apartheid—the Word is Afrikaans for "apartness"—was created only in the late 1940s, after the National Party was voted into office by disgruntled Afrikaners. The apartheid era began with the passage in 1949 of the Prohibition of Mixed Marriages Act, which laid the foundation for an elaborate system of discriminatory legislation. Thus, while most other countries were condemning colonialism, white South Africa established a frankly racist regime. Racism alone was not what made apartheid uniquely evil; prejudice and discrimination existed elsewhere, even in some black countries. But by the 1980s, racism was deplored almost everywhere; when other nations succumbed to it, they did so in violation of their own laws and stated principles. Only in South Africa was racism the law of the land.

For years, Frederik Willem de Klerk was an earnest acolyte of apartheid. As a National Party cabinet minister in 1985, he opposed abolition of the Immorality Act, which outlawed interracial sex. "He is too strongly convinced that racial grouping is the only truth," his older brother Willem (Wimpie) de Klerk wrote in a magazine article. But by the mid-1980s, even some of the most fervent defenders of apartheid were beginning to realize that white supremacy was untenable. South Africa had become a pariah nation. The world turned against it after a series of ugly events, including the 1960 Sharpeville Massacre, in which 67 blacks were killed by police, and the 1962 arrest of Nelson Mandela.

In 1968, South Africa's team was barred from the Olympics, beginning an athletic boycott that galled sports-loving white South Africans. In 1977, a year after a bloody uprising began in the black township of Soweto, outside Johannesburg, the United Nations imposed an arms embargo on South Africa. In 1986, the U.S. Congress voted for economic sanctions, overriding President Reagan's veto. American companies and other foreign investors backed away from South Africa, and soon the economy slipped into a long recession.

By then, white officials were holding secret talks with their most famous political prisoner. According to South African journalist Allister Sparks, they also took Mandela for drives in Cape Town and its suburbs to prepare him for freedom. In 1989, de Klerk became president. He had come to realize, he told his brother Wimpie, that apartheid "had landed us in a dead-end street." In an epochal speech on Feb. 2, 1990, de Klerk announced his intention to legalize the ANC and release Mandela.

Black on black: Mandela initially hailed de Klerk as a "man of integrity," but the relationship turned sour under the pressure of black-on-black violence, notably the vicious fighting in Natal between supporters of Inkatha and the ANC. Mandela accused de Klerk of fanning the violence; he called the president a "political criminal." An investigation by a white judge, Richard Goldstone, found that senior police officials had armed Inkatha and organized some of the violence. But despite the ill will between them, Mandela and de Klerk persevered, agreeing last November on an interim constitution and nonracial elections.

Now Mandela must make good on the hopes he has aroused, especially among his black followers. A few blacks talk excitedly about taking over the master's house and swimming pool. Most just want a home of their own, and a job. That task is daunting enough. Caristus Mngwengwe, a 29-year-old shop clerk, lives in the same tiny house he was born in, sharing it now with his wife and three children, his parents and his three brothers. And he is lucky, because he has a job. "Seventy-five percent of my friends don't work," he says. He thinks the ANC will change things. "It won't happen overnight," he says, "but we have to be optimistic."

Mandela has a loosely drawn plan, called the Reconstruction and Development Program, which is the closest thing to an economic blueprint the ANC has yet produced. During his five years in office, the program would build 1 million new homes, electrify 2.5 million dwellings, furnish at least 10 years of free and mandatory education to all children, create 2.5 million jobs through public works and redistribute 30 percent of all arable land. The ANC's opponents deride the program as a populist wish list; one of de Klerk's ministers estimated the cost at $165 billion over five years—roughly equal to the current national budget. ANC officials have estimated the five-year cost of the program at $11 billion.

Social Ills: Although South Africa's economy is beginning to recover, the country faces mountainous problems. Unemployment stands at 46 percent nationally, and, as in other countries, the current economic revival is not producing large numbers of good jobs. Black illiteracy is about 50 percent. A generation of radicalized black schoolchildren has lost critical classroom time to violence and political upheavals. And the time they did manage to spend in shamefully underfunded black schools wasn't necessarily productive.

In his early years as an ANC activist, Mandela pushed an idealistic socialist agenda. His organization's 1955 Freedom Charter called for widespread nationalization. Now, in the post-communist world, Mandela scrupulously avoids the N word. Although he says he is neither a socialist nor a capitalist, at times he sounds almost Reaganite, with talk about keeping taxes low, promoting free markets and encouraging investment. But even some of his admirers wonder whether Mandela is tough enough to control his own followers, including trade unionists clamoring for higher wages and gun-toting "comrades" from the black townships.

"We may still find ourselves with a government trying to pre-empt black demands for bread and circuses by allowing the whites to be delivered as scapegoats," warned author and antiapartheid activist Breyten Breytenbach. Still, if any country on the despoiled African continent can overcome postcolonial problems, it ought to be the South Africa of Mandela and de Klerk. It is a rich country, the world's leading producer of gold and other valuable metals. It has a modern infrastructure and a professional and managerial cadre of First World standards. And for now, at least, it has Nelson Mandela, whose patience, forbearance and largeness of spirit set an example for all South Africans, in captivity and in triumph.

From *No Future Without Forgiveness*

Desmond Mpilo Tutu

Desmond Tutu, recipient of the Nobel Peace Prize in 1984, was Archbishop of Cape Town, South Africa, from 1986 to his retirement in 1996. In this selection from his recent book he reflects on his work on the South African Truth and Reconciliation Commission (TRC), which attempted to enable post-apartheid South Africa to move forward. The principle of the commission was that a full and contrite confession of apartheid-era crimes could be accepted in lieu of punishment. The establishment of the TRC was designed to be a middle-way between the vengeance of war crime tribunals like the punishment of Nazi officials in Nuremberg and the festering sore of neglect. Most of the confessions that the TRC heard concerned gruesome crimes of murder, rape, and torture that were carried out by police and agents of the white South African government. But they also heard stories of retribution committed by members of the African National Congress.

In this selection, Archbishop Tutu looks beyond such overtly criminal acts and asks South Africans to commit themselves to a deeper reconciliation. In South Africa, he says, racism was not only violent; it was also legal, pervasive, and widely accepted. How does he believe South Africans can get beyond that history of accepted racism? Does the United States have anything to learn from this South African experience?

How was it possible for normal, decent, and God-fearing people, as white South Africans considered themselves to be, to have turned a blind eye to a system which impoverished, oppressed, and violated so many of those others with whom they shared the beautiful land that was their common motherland? Apartheid could not have survived for a single day had it not been supported by this enfranchised, privileged minority. If they "did not know," as many claimed, how was it that there were those within the white community who not only knew of the baneful results of official policies but who condemned the vicious policy and worked to end it? And why was this courageous group often vilified and ostracized by the rest of the white community if it was not that those who enjoyed the massive benefits that apartheid assured them at the

very least condoned the evil system and might have made an uneasy peace
with it?

It needs to be noted that many white people grew up knowing no other
system and they acquiesced in it because it was a status quo that brought them
much comfort. The system was not naïve. In fact it was exceedingly sophis-
ticated. The black townships were usually out of sight of whites and it was an
easy step from being out of sight to being out of mind. You had to put yourself
to considerable inconvenience to visit a black township if you were white.
There were those who did, but for most whites it was a great deal more comfortable to remain in your salubrious affluent suburb. We, black and white
South Africans, suffered from an acute form of schizophrenia—we inhabited
two separate and alien worlds physically and psychologically. . . .

The way in which many of our institutions operated under apartheid can be
illustrated with the picture that emerged at our media hearing. In the media,
ownership of newspapers was vested in white hands. News was described from
a white perspective. Even newspapers that might be said to be anti-apartheid,
which saw themselves as liberal, saw nothing wrong in persisting for a very
long time in describing an accident quite normally as one in which "one person
and four natives were injured." It did not seem to occur to the white journalists
and their editors that this was embarrassingly revealing of perhaps their visceral
attitudes—deep down somewhere, unconsciously held, not really articulated
except in this fashion, black people were not quite persons. . . .

Newspapers that claimed to be against apartheid applied it in their news-
rooms with socially segregated facilities such as canteens and toilets. Black
staff got the thin end of the stick in training opportunities and salaries. . . . It
was not unusual for a white reporter's copy to be preferred to that of a black
reporter even if the latter had firsthand experiences of what he or she was
reporting on. When black reporters described the appalling conduct of the
security forces against blacks, their copy was normally toned down as perhaps
maligning these forces. Now we know, of course, that the black reporters were
telling it as it was. The editors would have angrily denied that they were being
racist. No, they wanted "objective" writing. . . .

The South African Broadcasting Corporation was under the thumb of a
secret society, the Afrikaner Broederbond (Brotherhood), an organization
which promoted Afrikaner interests and which had tentacles in every single
sphere of life: in the church, in the schools, in business, culture, the universities, in the professions, in the Defense Force, in sport, in the media, and of
course, politics. Its policies became government policy. . . .

Thus the highest virtue in South Africa came to be conformity, not bucking
the system. The highest value was set on unquestioning loyalty to the dictates
of the Broederbond. That is perhaps why people did not ask awkward ques-

tions. For most, something had to be so because someone in authority had declared it to be so. They found it singularly difficult if not impossible to distinguish between *authoritative* and *authoritarian*. In the end even the most bizarre idea could be accepted because the herd instinct was invoked. Visiting Japanese businessmen, because of the power of the yen, became "honorary whites." A person of Chinese origin born in South Africa would be a non-European; if born in China, he or she was European of course! It would have been utterly ridiculous except that it did have ghastly repercussions. Sometimes people committed suicide because of wrong racial classification, since worth and privileges hinged so much on what racial group one belonged to. It determined where one could live, what schools one could attend, whom one could marry, what job one could do, and even where one could be buried. . . .

In South Africa the whole process of reconciliation has been placed in very considerable jeopardy by the enormous disparities between the rich, mainly the whites, and poor, mainly the lacks. The huge gap between the have and the have-nots, which was largely created and maintained by racism and apartheid, poses the greatest threat to reconciliation and stability in our county. The rich provided the class from which the perpetrators and the beneficiaries of apartheid came and the poor produced the bulk of the victims. That is why I have exhorted whites to support transformation taking place in the lot of blacks.

For unless houses replace the hovels and shacks in which most blacks live, unless blacks gain access to clean water, electricity, affordable health care, decent education, good jobs, and a safe environment—things which the vast majority of whites have taken for granted for so long—we can just as well kiss reconciliation goodbye.

Reconciliation is liable to a long-drawn-out process with ups and downs, not something accomplished overnight and certainly not by a commission, however effective. The Truth and Reconciliation Commission has only been able to make a contribution. Reconciliation is going to have to be the concern of every South African. It has to be a national project to which all earnestly strive to make their particular contribution—by learning the language and culture of others; by being willing to make amends; by refusing to deal in stereotypes by making racial or other jokes that ridicule a particular group; by contributing to a culture of respect for human rights, and seeking to enhance tolerance—with zero tolerance for intolerance; by working for a more inclusive society where most, if not all, can feel they belong—that they are insiders and not aliens and strangers on the outside, relegated to the edges of society. . . .

If we are going to move on and build a new kind of world community there must be a way in which we can deal with a sordid past. The most effective way would be for the perpetrators or their descendants to acknowledge the awfulness of what happened and the descendants of the victims to respond by granting forgiveness, providing something can be done, even symbolically, to compensate for the anguish experienced, whose consequences are still being lived through today. It may be, for instance, that race relations in the United States will not improve significantly until Native Americans and African Americans get the opportunity to tell their stories and reveal the pain that sits in the pit of their stomachs as a baneful legacy of dispossession and slavery. We saw in the Truth and Reconciliation Commission how the act of telling one's story has a cathartic, healing effect.

Israeli in Disguise Learns the Anguish of an Arab

Thomas L. Friedman

One of the ways in which Jews overcame the searing racism of the Nazi era was to seek refuge in the state of Israel; but in some ways their settlement duplicated an old pattern of settler societies. In this newspaper story from The New York Times, *Thomas L. Friedman tells how an Israeli reporter disguised himself as an Arab in order to give his readers in Israel a first-hand account of what it meant to be a Palestinian Arab in Israel. What did the Israeli reporter, Yoram Binur, learn about being an Arab in Israel? In what ways were Israeli attitudes toward Arabs similar to those of settler societies in the Americas and South Africa? Were these attitudes "racist"? What does this story suggest to you about resolving the conflict between Palestinian Arabs and Israeli Jews?*

Jerusalem, May 4—In March a Jerusalem newspaper assigned a Jewish reporter to spend six weeks circulating here and in Tel Aviv disguised as an Arab.

The account by the Arabic-speaking reporter, Yoram Binur, published last month in the newspaper *Kol Hair*, provided sobering insights into the attitudes of some Israeli Jews toward Arabs, and the nature of relations between the two groups. The article has been widely, discussed in Jewish and Arab circles.

To blend in, Mr. Binur, 31 years old, grew a stubbly beard—"about the same length as Yasir Arafat's," he said in an interview. He draped a black-checked Arab headdress around his neck and carried a copy of the Arabic newspaper *Al Fajr* with a picture of Mr. Arafat, chairman of the Palestine Liberation Organization, on the front page. In his pocket he kept a pack of Farid cigarettes, a brand sold only in East Jerusalem, the city's predominantly Arab sector.

I Took a Provocative Walk

Although Jerusalem is a united city, there are certain Jewish areas where Arabs know they do not belong. One, Mr. Binur discovered, is the Ben Yehuda mall in the heart of West Jerusalem.

"I took a provocative walk on Ben Yehuda," Mr. Binur wrote in the opening of his account in *Kol Hair*.

"The passers by stare at me like at a walking bomb, and I feel that the Jews are afraid of the Arab no less than he is afraid of them. Two border policemen call me over and ask for my I.D. card. The Hebrew name doesn't convince them, and I have to support my 'Israeliness' with additional documents, to make them believe the impersonation story.

"After they are convinced, one of them says, 'We said to each other, look at that Arab, how he walks around on Ben Yehuda; let's stop him for a check and then tell him we don't want to ever see him here again.'"

Passengers Avert Their Glances

Mr. Binur found similar reactions in riding the bus in a Jewish neighborhood.

"The passengers on line 15, first bus in the morning, avert their glances," he wrote. "They wonder what an Arab is doing at this hour on a bus leaving Palmach Street. I stare at a pretty woman soldier. We exchange glances for a moment or two. Then two male soldiers sitting next to her join the glance game. Their looks are provocative, threatening, and they caress their Galil rifles. Mv place at the bottom of the ladder is made clear to me without us exchanging even one word, and I lower my stare."

Arab-Jewish dating is rare in Israeli society. Arabs are largely expected to socialize at Arab clubs, Jews at Jewish clubs.

"Friday night, a singles club in Qiryat Hayovel," Mr. Binur wrote. "People move away from me as though I have AIDS, and whenever I move a vacuum is created around me. I sit next to a single woman, offer her in English a Farid

cigarette and express my appreciation of the place. 'Tomorrow, I will recommend this place to the guys in East Jerusalem,' I say. Then I ask her to
dance.

"I didn't get a dance out of her," Mr. Binur wrote. "She went up to the
manager and complained about their letting an Arab enter. The answer she
got, we later learned, was, 'This time we didn't have a choice, but it won't
happen again.' "

He Is Asked for Membership Card

Mr. Binur had a similar experience at another club, at Avalon Tower in Jerusalem. "Everyone in line enters without problem," he wrote. "I am asked to
present a membership card. 'I didn't know I need one,' I said. I present an
Arabic document. They ask me to sit down while they call the manager.

"He takes the document, reads it upside down and asks where I am from.

" 'The West Bank,' I say. The manager asks for my permit to say in Israel.
I explain that I left it at home.

"The manager twists and turns and finally as a last resort says, 'Are you
sure you are single?' I say: 'Of course I'm single. I'm modern. I don't want
two wives.'"

Mr. Binur eventually persuaded the manager to let him in, but the manager
felt the need to explain this to the other guests in the small club. According
to Mr. Binur's account, the manager announced, "Tonight we have here a guest
from Jordan."

"It seems," Mr. Binur wrote, "that 'a guest from Jordan' in the local hierarchy is more respectable than a mere Arab."

Labor Market at Damascus Gate

As part of his reporting, Mr. Binur dressed in grubby work clothes and went
to the morning "labor market" near the Damascus Gate, where Jewish con-
tractors come each day to hire Arab workers.

"At the labor market the workers are pretty relaxed," Mr. Binur wrote. "The
professional workers who will be grabbed for work first enjoy a high status,
expressed by neat clothes and Time cigarettes. They bring tools from home.
Each boss has his 'regulars' who obediently go up to his car. The occasional
workers don't crowd; then, keep their distance.

"A border police jeep gives the market the atmosphere of a South African
township. The workers' way of avoiding conflict with the soldiers is to shrink
in their places, as if they wanted to evaporate, lower their looks to the road,
not to meet the soldiers' eyes.

"The soldiers in the jeep don't seem aware of the terror they cast on a whole street. The jeep moves away, followed by the workers' looks of hatred. There is also a feeling of relief. This time there were no arrests. No work, either."

Tries to Rent an Apartment

One day, Mr. Binur and Rachel Mehager, another reporter for *Kol Hair*, tried to rent an apartment as a Jewish-Arab couple.

"We make an appointment to see an apartment in Qiryat Hayovel," he wrote. "My Arabic doesn't frighten the landlady, and she speaks with me in my language.

"At the end we announce that we like the apartment, and the landlady is happy. Rachel asks if there won't be any problems with the neighbors, because we are a mixed couple. The landlady answers that 'everything will be all right.'

"We tell her that we have had problems in the past. She looks sad and says, 'It is too bad that there are people like that.' But on the way out she remembers a small detail. 'You know, maybe my husband already rented it to someone,' she says.

"We understand and promise to call the next day. Rachel calls. The answer is as expected: 'Very sorry, my husband already rented it.' Later that day a colleague of ours calls about the apartment. It is still available."

The Lessons Drawn

What were the lessons Mr. Binur and his editors drew from his experience as an Arab?

"It only strengthened my view that ruling this huge number of Arabs who live under a different system and laws is more dangerous to Israeli values than it is to the Arabs," Mr. Binur said.

"The racism is definitely there. But at the same time, I found that a lot of it was not really inherent in people. Much of it grows out of their real fear of the Arabs, their stereotypes and the security situation."

Summing up his experience, Mr. Binur said: "I wonder if the average Israeli is aware of the feelings of humiliation, alienation and fear that nestle in the hearts of the Arabs he meets in the market, street or bus? I wonder if the Arab is aware of the fears he arouses in the heart of the Israeli?"

Hong Kong Crusaders Against Racism Gain Little Support, Even from Victims

Keith B. Richburg

Hong Kong was the epitome of the colonial settler society in Asia from the period of the first Opium War in the 1840s until it was turned over by the British to Chinese administration in 1997.

Are the insensitivities to racial prejudice described here to be understood in terms of the dynamics of settler societies, the legacy of British colonialism, or in terms of Chinese or Indian values? Why do not the Indians seem to notice or protest? Is this a problem that should be fixed? If so, how?

HONG KONG—To hear Ravi Gidumal, a locally born businessman, tell of the common trials and petty racial slights experienced by an ethnic Indian in Hong Kong, you might think you were talking to a black man describing life in white America.

There are the taxicab drivers who sometimes refuse to stop to pick him up. There was the time he went to some friends in a popular local bar, only to be told at the front door that Indians were not allowed. There was the time in his late teens when he applied for a job teaching English, only to be told—despite his impeccable British accent—that he was not right for the position because his skin was the wrong color.

"Most Indians who are here will notice it, if not on a daily basis, then quite often," he said. "I wouldn't say it's a major issue—you're talking about such a small minority of people. But it's a niggling problem."

In many advanced societies, such overt displays of racial discrimination might well be illegal, or at least not openly tolerated. But in Hong Kong while a bill of rights prohibits the government from practicing discrimination, there is no similar law prohibiting discrimination based on race or age in the private sector. Members of the territory's tiny ethnic South Asian population are the most frequent victims of deeply rooted racial prejudice from the city's 98 percent Chinese majority.

From *International Herald Tribune*, June 15, 1998, p. 6. Washington Post Foreign Service © 1997, 1998 *The Washington Post*. Reprinted with permission.

"This is a major scandal and something that we've been agitating about for years," said Paul Harris, chairman of the Hong Kong Human Rights Monitor. "You can refuse to hire someone because he is black or white or Oriental."

"Things that in most Western countries would be outrageous or illegal or lead to action for damages, here are not," Mr. Harris said. "You can turn someone down because of their skin color or religion, and the law will not intervene."

There is some disagreement as to exactly how prevalent the problem of racial discrimination is in Hong Kong. Raj Sital, past president of the Indian Chamber of Commerce. said his group once surveyed its members to determine whether there was support for an anti-discrimination law.

"I don't think we even got a handful of replies, so I don't think it's a big problem," he said.

"I was born and raised here," he said. "I really haven't felt it as such."

The Hong Kong government agrees that discrimination is not widespread enough to warrant legislation. Instead, the government published in April a non-binding "code of practice against discrimination," aimed at tackling prejudice through public education and raising awareness.

"We had a consultation last year, and the community at large did not seem to think there was a need for legislation," said Patrick Wong, spokesman for the Home Affairs Bureau, which published the new guidelines. "We don't think it's a very big problem in Hong Kong. We have decided we will support equal opportunity through education."

Even the most outspoken campaigners for equal opportunity laws in Hong Kong agree that in a nonviolent society like this, the effects of petty discrimination are relatively slight—sometimes making the problem seem less urgent.

"People are not violent," Mr. Harris said. "You don't have skinhead attacks like in Germany. That minimizes the effects, but it also makes it less visible."

But Mr. Harris and other advocates still think the government needs to take action. For one thing, they accuse the government of a double standard; there are laws against discriminating by gender or physical disability, but nothing on race or age.

One of the biggest problems, say the supporters of new legislation, is a cultural aversion to conflict in which many victims of racial prejudice suffer the slights in silence.

Mr. Gidumal, who is campaigning for a new anti-discrimination law, conceded that he had found little support for his efforts from the very community he was seeking to protect.

"The Indian community doesn't seem too bothered about it," he said, adding, "There doesn't seem to be a will in the community to do something about it."

Anna Wu, the head of the local consumer council and a former member of the Legislative Council, said, "People in Hong Kong are not open to airing certain types of grievances."

Nevertheless, she pushed for an anti-discrimination law when she was on the Legislative Council.

"Even without a victim coming forward, the government is obliged to legislate to protect," she said. Like others, she cited as the main problem prejudice among the majority Chinese population against people with darker skin.

At the heart of the problem are complex questions of race and identity in a Chinese city that only one year ago rejoined the mainland.

There is also the backdrop of 150 years of British colonialism during which racial discrimination was an entrenched feature of imperial governance. Throughout most of the British rule, top jobs in the civil service were reserved for expatriates—meaning whites—and discrimination in housing, schooling and employment was officially, and strictly, enforced.

Change came only in the 1970s and '80s, and in 1991 a bill of rights was passed, prohibiting the government from discriminating. But after nearly 150 years, Mr. Harris said, "the idea that it's okay to discriminate against people on the grounds of race is deep rooted here."

Given its own history of discrimination, critics say, the former colonial government was loath to introduce an anti-discrimination law.

While Hong Kong is overwhelmingly Chinese, it is home to about 35,000 ethnic Indians. Together with ethnic Pakistanis and Sri Lankans, the total number of Hong Kong people with ancestors in South Asia is more than 50,000. In addition Hong Kong is home to more than 140,000 Filipinos—130,000 of them working as domestic helpers. Many of them also say they suffer from discrimination.

Part 12

Protecting All Others

A crowd of 200,000 gathers at the Lincoln Memorial for the March on Washington in favor of civil rights, August 28, 1963. *(Associated Press Photo)*

Ultimately, the job of ending racism can be reduced to protecting all others. This can be done spontaneously and immediately as it was by those who protected Jews under Nazi occupation during World War II. The villagers of Le Chambon-sur-Lignon, France, who were asked years later what brought them to endanger their own lives by protecting Jews responded almost universally that they never conceived of doing anything else. There simply was no question in their minds; when they were called to account, they could only do the right thing.

Since 1945, we have also devised law and legal principles that enshrine the ethic of human rights and equal protection under the law. The United Nations Declaration of Human Rights (not included here), the United Nations resolution "On the Prevention and Punishment of the Crime of Genocide" (long opposed by the United States), and UNESCO's "Statement on Race and Racial Prejudice" have all helped the international community define what morality means in a postracist age.

We have seen many times in this volume that the existence of racism has often little to do with the existence of race. Nazis needed Jews to wear yellow stars in order to recognize them; Hutus needed family genealogies to recognize Tutsis, despite their supposed physical differences. Racism depended on the belief that the Other was recognizably different—often despite the testimony of eyes and ears. Race may have been superfluous, but the idea of race, and of racial differences, has been a supporting bulwark of racism.

Should we end talk of race? Should we stop classifying each other in races? Is the idea of race the last prop of racial thinking? In the penultimate essay, Jim Sleeper makes a good case for this position. The last piece, and our current antiracist strategy of affirmative action, depends on a contrary judgment. Where do we go from here?

From *The Holocaust, the French, and the Jews*

Susan Zuccotti

When the Nazi army took Paris in 1940, it imposed direct rule on northern France and installed a puppet government, led by French marshal Philippe Petain, on the southern part of the country. Petain governed from the old city of Vichy, about 200 miles south of Paris. After 1941, the Germans began to impose their anti-Semitism on the Vichy regime, as they had done in the north, insisting that Vichy capture and imprison Jews for shipment to concentration camps. Although much of southern France complied with the order, in a high plateau just a few hours south of Vichy, an area of independent French, many of them Protestants who had long resisted Catholic Paris, refused to do the Nazis' work. Zucotti, a modern historian, tells how the inhabitants in one of the towns in this area, Le Chambon-sur-Lignon, risked their lives to save Jewish children in their schools and Jewish families in their homes. How did the people of Le Chambon save Jews? What gave them the courage to resist the orders of their government, and how were they so successful?

"Roughly fifty kilometers from Puy-en-Velay and about forty kilometers from Saint-Etienne, there is a little town, Le Chambon-sur-Lignon, the tiny capital of the plateau of the same name, an ancient Protestant village. There you can still find the caves where the Protestants gathered to practice their religion as well as to escape the king's dragoons." Thus begins Joseph Bass's postwar report on a remote village on a pine-studded plateau, about 960 meters above sea level, in the Massif Central west of Valence and the Rhone River. Leon Poliakov, who helped Bass hide Jews there, later described the department of Haute-Loire where Le Chambon is located as "one of the poorest and wildest regions of the Cevennes." Its Protestant inhabitants, he added, "distrust all authority, listening only to their conscience—or their pastors."

Long before Bass and Poliakov arrived there, hundreds of Jewish and non-Jewish refugees had already found their way to Le Chambon. Some had wandered into town as early as the winter of 1940–41. Most came independently at first, advised by friends or casual acquaintances of an isolated village of about 1,000 people, reputedly sympathetic. Newcomers found shelter with village families or with the roughly 2,000 peasants. most of them also Protestant, in the surrounding countryside. Others took rooms in one of more than a dozen hotels and boardinghouses in this popular summer resort area of pine forests, clear streams, and bracing air. Most were trying to escape internment, and most, needless to say were not legally registered.

During the late spring and early summer of 1942, many foreign Jews and non-Jews released from internment camps to the care of charitable agencies also came to Le Chambon. Local institutions to care for them multiplied, openly and legally. Madeleine Barot and other young Protestant social workers of the CIMADE [a Protestant relief organization] established a family residence at the Hotel Coteau Fleuri, outside of town. Quakers, with the help from Le Chambon's Pastor André Trocmé, funded a boardinghouse for young children. Older students joined two farm-schools operated by the Secours suisse, or moved into residences of the École Cevenol, a private Protestant secondary school slightly north of the village. Still others were welcomed at the École des roches in the village itself.

In August 1942, French police rounding up recent Jewish immigrants in the unoccupied zone did not overlook Le Chambon. They arrived in the village with three empty buses, demanding that Pastor Trocmé provide a list of resident Jews. Trocmé not only claimed ignorance, somewhat truthfully, of names and addresses but promptly sent his Protestant Boy Scouts to even the most distant farms to warn Jews to hide. Other local residents had undoubtedly already seen the approach of the police up the valley, along a road visible for miles from the Plateau. Then and later, that visibility was one secret to security in Le Chambon. Police searched the region for two or three days and returned regularly for several weeks. They apparently netted only one victim, an Austrian who was later released because he was only half-Jewish.

Jews literally poured into Le Chambon after August 1942. By this point, their presence was totally unofficial. They came with the [Jewish resistance network] Service Andre—[its director Joseph] Bass later reported that the pastor never hesitated to help him—and with OSE [children's aid] and other clandestine networks. Some stayed in Le Chambon only long enough to find a guide to Switzerland, but many remained, hidden with families or in boardinghouses or schools. They kept coming, until, as Poliakov observed, "in some hamlets, there was not a single farm which did not shelter a Jewish family." Roughly 5,000 Jews are estimated to have been hidden among the 3,000 native residents, all of whom knew about the refugees.

In his memoirs, Poliakov describes with touching detail his arrival at a local hotel with a group of Jewish children in 1943:

Frightened, they hovered in a corner of the room. The first peasant couple enters: "We will take a little girl between eight and twelve years old," explains the woman. Little Myriam is called: "Will you go with this aunt and uncle?" Shy and frightened, Myriam does not answer. They muffle her up in blankets and carry her to the sleigh; she leaves for the farm where she will live a healthy and simple life with her temporary parents until the end of the war. . . . In a flash, all the children were similarly housed, under the benevolent eye of Pastor Trocmé.

Who was this pastor whose name appears in every account of Le Chambon-sur-Lignon during the war? Born in Saint-Quentin in Picardy in northern France in 1901, André Trocmé studied at the Union Theological Seminary in New York City, where he met his future wife, Italian-born Magda Grilli, in 1925. A pacifist and conscientious objector, Trocmé made no secret of his beliefs after his arrival in Le Chambon in1934. Indeed, he and Pastor Édouard Theis, the director of the École Cévenol, were equally frank after 1940 about their dislike of the Vichy regime and the racial laws. Trocmé often spoke from the pulpit about the evils of racial persecution; Theis taught the same principles at École Cévenol. On August 15, 1942, during a visit to the village by the Vichy youth minister, Georges Lamirand, and the departmental prefect and subprefect, several older students at the school presented the officials with a letter protesting the July 16 roundup [of Jews] in Paris and expressing local support of the Jews.

Trocmé, Theis, and Roger Darcissac, the director of the public school in Le Chambon, were arrested by French police in February 1943 and held for a month. At the end of the year, the two pastors went into hiding. During that period, Theis served as a guide for CIMADE, escorting refugees to Switzerland. Magda Trocmé continued her husband's work during his absence; one scholar has judged that she was at least as important as he in saving lives. Mildred Theis kept the École Cévenol open and continued to shelter refugees. The two women had many aides. Bass remembered pastors named Poivre, Leenhardt, Jeannet, Curtet, Betrix, Vienney, and Besson from surrounding hamlets, as well as the Trocmés' good friend Simone Mairesse. Municipal officials also cooperated, if only by looking the other way. And the people of the plateau, often influenced by their outspoken pastors but guided as well by their own sense of justice, continued to protect their Jewish guests until the Liberation. Of them, Bass wrote after the war, "The conduct of the Protestant pastors and men of action of the plateau of Le Chambon deserves to be told to Jews throughout the entire world."

In considering the rescue of Jews in Le Chambon, two questions arise: why was the local population so sympathetic, and why was it so successful? To answer the first, Madeleine Barot stresses the special status of Protestants in France as a minority persecuted by Catholics. Protestants in Le Chambon still told tales of persecution around their hearths on cold winter nights and visited caves where their ancestors had hidden. The memory of persecution made them suspicious of authority, sympathetic to other minorities, and comfortable with clandestine life. In addition, many French Protestants were skeptical about the Vichy regime, in part because authoritarianism often bodes ill for minorities, but especially because, according to Barot, "Pétain dedicated France to the Virgin, and made it an intensely Catholic state." Finally, Christian anti-Semitism notwithstanding, Bible-reading Protestants of the type living around Le Chambon sometimes articulate a special affinity for the Jews, based on a shared reverence for the Old Testament and a common acceptance of God's special compact with his chosen people.

These various factors certainly did not apply to all French Protestants. Many, especially those of the assimilated and highly educated urban classes who were more removed from their historical and cultural roots, were favorably inclined toward the Vichy regime for the same economic and social reasons as their Catholic neighbors, and held the same variety of attitudes toward Jews. But Protestants around Le Chambon cherished their historic memory. That love, combined with the sturdy individualism and independence of mountain people and the leadership of a group of exceptional pastors, made Le Chambon an equally exceptional place.

But why were the rescuers of Le Chambon so successful? Admittedly, even they had their tragedies and their victims. In the spring of 1943, the Gestapo raided the École des roches, seizing many students along with their dedicated director, Daniel Trocmé, Pastor Trocmé's second cousin. Nearly all, including Daniel, died in deportation. But the Germans did not return and thus failed as miserably as the French police to find most of the Jews they knew were there. Why?

Geographic factors were important. The isolation of the area was made even more extreme by the closing of access roads in winter. Any movement on those same approach roads could be seen from the plateau. Thick forests were good for hiding. The Gestapo and the French Milice [volunteer fascist corps], busy elsewhere, were reluctant or perhaps afraid to enter a hostile area that, however dedicated by its pastor to nonviolence, was surrounded by armed Resistance fighters. Why stir up a sleeping hornets' nest? French police and gendarmes not only shared that reluctance but were also affected by local sympathies for refugees.

Two witnesses tell amusing stories. Madeleine Barot later declared, of her own experience, "When the *gendarmes* in Tence [the nearest town] received an order for an arrest, they made a habit of dragging themselves along the road very visibly, of calling a halt at the cafe before tackling the steep ascent to the Coteau, announcing loudly that they were about to arrest some of those 'dirty Jews.' " Poliakov confirms the description, explaining that when the gendarmes received an arrest order, "they went to the [local] Hotel May and ordered a glass of wine: comfortably seated at their table, they took their papers from their satchels and spelled out 'Goldberg . . . it's about someone named Jacques Goldberg.' Unnecessary to add that when they arrived at Goldberg's domicile half an hour later, the latter was long gone." Poliakov adds that when a more serious danger approached in the form of the Gestapo or the Milice, a telephone call of warning usually preceded them from the valley.

Barot's and Poliakov's accounts both allude to the most important factor in the rescue success rate in Le Chambon—the determination of local residents to protect their guests. The people of Le Chambon lived in a state of constant alertness, with a warning system prepared. Their solidarity also made it difficult for potential informers to act. To whom could they safely leak information? Municipal authorities sympathized with the majority, as did, it appeared, many of the police. Even local censors of mail were likely to prevent a denunciation. In such a situation, a careless informer might even put himself in danger. In addition, it was psychologically more difficult for a solitary anti-Semite or opportunist to express his bile in a region where he was bucking an obvious majority. He could not so easily convince himself that he was acting as a "good and loyal Frenchman." And in any part of France—where so many individual arrests of Jews by preoccupied and understaffed local Gestapo units were prompted by denunciations—the reluctance of informers was decisive.

On the Prevention and Punishment of the Crime of Genocide

United Nations

This United Nations Resolution, adopted by the UN General Assembly on December 9, 1948, was a follow-up to an earlier resolution dated December

Articles 1–8 from 12.2 U.N.T.S. No. 1021, vol. 78 (1951), p. 277.

11, 1946 that made genocide a crime under international law. What do you think of the impact of such UN resolutions? What should be the role of the UN or other international organizations in combating racism or genocide?

Adopted by Resolution 260 (III) A of the United Nations General Assembly on 9 December 1948.

The Contracting Parties,

Having considered the declaration made by the General Assembly of the United Nations in its resolution 96 (I) dated 11 December 1946 that genocide is a crime under international law, contrary to the spirit and aims of the United Nations and condemned by the civilized world;

Recognizing that at all periods of history genocide has inflicted great losses on humanity; and

Being convinced that, in order to liberate mankind from such an odious scourge, international co-operation is required;

Hereby agree as hereinafter provided.

Article 1

The Contracting Parties confirm that genocide, whether committed in time of peace or in time of war, is a crime under international law which they undertake to prevent and to punish.

Article 2

In the present Convention, genocide means any of the following acts committed with intent to destroy, in whole or in part, a national, ethnical, racial or religious group, as such:

(a) Killing members of the group;
(b) Causing serious bodily or mental harm to members of the group;
(c) Deliberately inflicting on the group conditions of life calculated to bring about its physical destruction in whole or in part;
(d) Imposing measures intended to prevent births within the group;
(e) Forcibly transferring children of the group to another group.

Article 3

The following acts shall be punishable:

(a) Genocide;
(b) Conspiracy to commit genocide;
(c) Direct and public incitement to commit genocide;
(d) Attempt to commit genocide;
(e) Complicity in genocide.

Article 4

Persons committing genocide or any of the other acts enumerated in Article 3 shall be punished, whether they are constitutionally responsible rulers, public officials or private individuals.

Article 5

The Contracting Parties undertake to enact, in accordance with their respective Constitutions, the necessary legislation to give effect to the provisions of the present Convention and, in particular, to provide effective penalties for persons guilty of genocide or any of the other acts enumerated in Article 3.

Article 6

Persons charged with genocide or any of the other acts enumerated in Article 3 shall be tried by a competent tribunal of the State in the territory of which the act was committed, or by such international penal tribunal as may have jurisdiction with respect to those Contracting Parties which shall have accepted its jurisdiction.

Article 7

Genocide and the other acts enumerated in Article 3 shall not be considered as political crimes for the purpose of extradition.

The Contracting Parties pledge themselves in such cases to grant extradition in accordance with their laws and treaties in force.

Article 8

Any Contracting Party may call upon the competent organs of the United Nations to take such action under the Charter of the United Nations.

Statement on Race and Racial Prejudice

UNESCO

This, too, is an international declaration—in this case, a statement signed by leading scientists throughout the world. What do you think of its definition and explanation of racism? How do statements like this counter racism? What other international actions might limit racist ideas or practices?

1. "All men are born free and equal both in dignity and in rights." This universally proclaimed democratic principle stands in jeopardy wherever political, economic, social and cultural inequalities affect human group relations. A particularly striking obstacle to the recognition of equal dignity for all is racism. Racism continues to haunt the world. As a major social phenomenon it requires the attention of all of the sciences of man.

2. Racism stultifies the development of those who suffer from it, perverts those who apply it, divides nations within themselves, aggravates international conflict and threatens world peace.

3. Conference of experts meeting in Paris in September 1967 agreed that racist doctrines lack any scientific basis whatsoever. It affirmed the propositions adopted by the international meeting held in Moscow in 1964 which was called to re-examine the biological aspects of the statements on race and racial differences issued in 1950 and 1951. In particular, it draws attention to the following points:

UNESCO, Paris, September 1967.

(a) All men living today belong to the same species and descend from the same stock.

(b) The division of the human species into "races" is partly conventional and partly arbitrary and does not imply any hierarchy whatsoever. Many anthropologists stress the importance of human variation, but believe that "racial" divisions have limited scientific interest and may even carry the risk of inviting abusive generalization.

(c) Current biological knowledge does not permit us to impute cultural achievements to differences in genetic potential. Differences in the achievements of different peoples should be attributed solely to their cultural history. The peoples of the world today appear to possess equal biological potentialities for attaining any level of civilization.

Racism grossly falsifies the knowledge of human biology.

4. The human problems arising from so-called "race" relations are social in origin rather than biological. A basic problem is racism, namely, antisocial beliefs and acts which are based on the fallacy that discriminatory intergroup relations are justifiable on biological grounds.

5. Groups commonly evaluate their characteristics in comparison with others. Racism falsely claims that there is a scientific basis for arranging groups hierarchically in terms of psychological and cultural characteristics that are immutable and innate. In this way it seeks to make existing differences appear inviolable as a means of permanently maintaining current relations between groups.

6. Faced with the exposure of the falsity of its biological doctrines, racism finds ever new stratagems for justifying the inequality of groups. It points to the fact that groups do not intermarry, a fact which follows, in part, from the divisions created by racism. It uses this fact to argue the thesis that this absence of intermarriage derives from differences of a biological order. Whenever it fails in its attempts to prove that the source of group differences lies in the biological field, it falls back upon justifications in terms of divine purpose, cultural differences, disparity of educational standards or some other doctrine which would serve to mask its continued racist beliefs. Thus, many of the problems which racism presents in the world today do not arise merely from its open manifestations, but from the activities of those who discriminate on racial grounds but are unwilling to acknowledge it.

7. Racism has historical roots. It has not been a universal phenomenon. Many contemporary societies and cultures show little trace of it. It was not evident for long periods in world history. Many forms of racism have arisen out of the conditions of conquest, out of the justification of Negro slavery and its aftermath of racial inequality in the West, and out of the colonial relation-

ship. Among other examples is that of antisemitism, which has played a particular role in history, with Jews being the chosen scapegoat to take the blame for problems and crises met by many societies.

8. The anti-colonial revolution of the twentieth century has opened up new possibilities for eliminating the scourge of racism. In some formerly dependent countries, people formerly classified as inferior have for the first time obtained full political rights. Moreover, the participation of formerly dependent nations in international organizations in terms of equality has done much to undermine racism.

9. There are, however, some instances in certain societies in which groups, victims of racialistic practices, have themselves applied doctrines with racist implications in their struggle for freedom. Such an attitude is a secondary phenomenon, a reaction stemming from men's search for an identity which prior racist theory and racialistic practices denied them. None the less, the new forms of racist ideology, resulting from this prior exploitation, have no justification in biology. They are a product of a political struggle and have no scientific foundation.

10. In order to undermine racism it is not sufficient that biologists should expose its fallacies. It is also necessary that psychologists and sociologists should demonstrate its causes. The social structure is always an important factor. However, within the same social structure, there may be great individual variation in racialistic behaviour, associated with the personality of the individuals and their personal circumstances.

11. The committee of experts agreed on the following conclusions about the social causes of race prejudice.

(a) Social and economic causes of racial prejudice are particularly observed in settler societies wherein are found conditions of great disparity of power and property, in certain urban areas where there have emerged ghettoes in which individuals are deprived of equal access to employment, housing, political participation, education, and the administration of justice, and in many societies where social and economic tasks which are deemed to be contrary to the ethics or beneath the dignity of its members are assigned to a group of different origins who are derided, blamed, and punished for taking on these tasks

(b) Individuals with certain personality troubles may be particularly inclined to adopt and manifest racial prejudices. Small groups, associations, and social movements of a certain kind sometimes preserve and transmit racial prejudices. The foundations of the prejudices lie, however, in the economic and social system of a society.

(c) Racism tends to be cumulative. Discrimination deprives a group of equal treatment and presents that group as a problem. The group then tends to be blamed for its own condition, leading to further elaboration of racist theory.

12. The major techniques for coping with racism involve changing those social situations which give rise to prejudice, preventing the prejudiced from acting in accordance with their beliefs, and combating the false beliefs themselves.

13. It is recognized that the basically important changes in the social structure that may lead to the elimination of racial prejudice may require decisions of a political nature. It is also recognized, however, that certain agencies of enlightenment, such as education and other means of social and economic advancement, mass media, and law can be immediately and effectively mobilized for the elimination of racial prejudice.

14. The school and other instruments for social and economic progress can be one of the most effective agents for the achievement of broadened understanding and the fulfilment of the potentialities of man. They can equally much be used for the perpetuation of discrimination and inequality. It is therefore essential that the resources for education and for social and economic action of all nations be employed in two ways:

(a) The schools should ensure that their curricula contain scientific understandings about race and human unity, and that invidious distinctions about peoples are not made in texts and classrooms.

(b) (i) Because of the skills to be gained in formal and vocational education become increasingly important with the processes of technological development, the resources of the schools and other resources should be fully available to all parts of the population with neither restriction nor discrimination.

(ii) Furthermore, in cases where, for historical reasons, certain groups have a lower average education and economic standing, it is the responsibility of the society to take corrective measures. These measures should ensure, so far as possible, that the limitations of poor environments are not passed on to the children.

In view of the importance of teachers in any educational program, teachers should be made conscious of the degree to which they reflect the prejudices which may be current in their society. They should be encouraged to avoid these prejudices.

15. Governmental units and other organizations concerned should give special attention to improving the housing situations and work opportunities available to victims of racism. This will not only counteract the effects of racism, but in itself can be a positive way of modifying racist attitudes and behavior.

16. The media of mass communication are increasingly important in promoting knowledge and understanding, but their exact potentiality is not fully known. Continuing research into the social utilization of the media is needed in order to assess their influence in relation to formation of attitudes and behavioural patterns in the field of race prejudice and race discrimination. Because the mass media reach vast numbers of people at different educational and social levels, their role in encouraging or combating race prejudice can be crucial. Those who work in these media should maintain a positive approach to the promotion of understanding between groups and populations. Representation of peoples in stereotypes and holding them up to ridicule should be avoided. Attachment to news reports of racial designations which are not germane to the accounts should also be avoided.

17. Law is among the most important means of ensuring equality between individuals and one of the most effective means of fighting racism.

The Universal Declaration of Human Rights of 9 December 1948 and the related international agreements and conventions which have taken effect subsequently can contribute effectively, on both the national and international level, to the fight against any injustice of racist origin.

National legislation is a means of effectively outlawing racist propaganda and acts based upon racial discrimination. Moreover, the policy expressed in such legislation must bind not only the courts and judges charged with its enforcement, but also all agencies of government of whatever level or whatever character.

It is not claimed that legislation can immediately eliminate prejudice. Nevertheless, by being a means of protecting the victims of acts based upon prejudice, and by setting a moral example backed by the dignity of the courts, it can, in the long run, even change attitudes.

18. Ethnic groups which represent the object of some form of discrimination are sometimes accepted and tolerated by dominating groups at the cost of their having to abandon completely their cultural identity. It should be stressed that the effort of these ethnic groups to preserve their cultural values should be encouraged. They will thus be better able to contribute to the enrichment of the total culture of humanity.

19. Racial prejudice and discrimination in the world today arise from historical and social phenomena and falsely claim the sanction of science. It is, therefore, the responsibility of all biological and social scientists, philosophers,

and others working in related disciplines, to ensure that the results of their research are not misused by those who wish to propagate racial prejudice and encourage discrimination.

This statement was prepared by a committee of experts on race and racial prejudice which met at Unesco House, Paris, from 18 to 26 September 1967.

Toward an End of Blackness: An Argument for the Surrender of Race Consciousness

Jim Sleeper

What does the author mean by "an end of blackness"? Is he in favor of it? What would replace it? Do you think that would be a good thing? Would that mean an end to racism?

What, according to Sleeper, were the appeals and the failures of Alex Haley's Roots? Has America become a nation of ethnics?

Is Sleeper's answer to racism American civic identity, the American ideal of freedom and justice, or is it nationalism?

What do you think of his suggestion that the greater challenge today is the collective amnesia of the global market?

Are blacks further along on the journey out of blackness than whites are on the journey out of whiteness? Why? Will we all be better off when we get there?

Last January, not long after the national furor over the decision by an Oakland school board to recognize "Ebonics," I happened upon a C-SPAN telecast of the awarding of seven Congressional Medals of Honor to black World War II veterans, each of whose "gallantry and intrepidity at the risk of his life" had been ignored for more than fifty years. President Clinton strode across the East Room of the White House to present the medals to Vernon Joseph Baker, seventy-seven, the only recipient still living, and to the others' families. "History has been made whole today," the President told the assembly. The honorees, he said, had "helped us find a way to become a more just, more free nation . . . more worthy of them and more true to its ideals."

History has not been made whole for American blacks, of course, and yet something almost archaic in the recipients' bearing and in the ceremony itself reminded me that none of us in the younger generations can say with certainty what an American wholeness might be or, within any such presumed wholeness, what blackness and whiteness might mean. If we have trouble thinking about race, possibly it's because we no longer know how to think about America itself.

At least Second Lieutenant Baker seemed to have less trouble fifty-two years ago than we do now. In April 1945, he single-handedly wiped out two German machine-gun nests in Viareggio, Italy, drew fire on himself to permit the evacuation of wounded comrades, and led his segregated battalion's advance through enemy minefields. Asked by reporters after the East Room ceremony whether he had ever given up hope of winning the medal, he "sounded surprised . . . as if the question presumed arrogance," said one report. "I never thought about getting it," Baker said. Asked why he had joined the army in the first place, Baker responded, "I was a young black man without a job." Ah, yes, that. Prodded to comment on having risked his life for his country while in a segregated unit, he answered, "I was an angry young man. We were all angry. But we had a job to do, and we did it. . . . My personal thoughts were that I knew things would get better, and I'm happy I'm here to see it."

Asked what the ceremony meant to her, Arlene Fox, widow of First Lieutenant John Fox, who died in Italy in 1944, said, "I think it's more than just what it means to this family. I think it sends a message . . . that when a man does his duty, his color isn't important."

Even in the prime of their anger, Baker and Fox, as well as the black leaders and writers of their generation, such as A. Philip Randolph, Bayard Rustin, Richard Wright, and Ralph Ellison, did not urge the importance of color as much as they found color imposed on them in ways that affronted something in them that wasn't "of color" at all. Proud though they were of what blacks had endured and would overcome (as Baker "knew" they would), they believed, before most of the rest of us, that after a long dalliance with a white manifest destiny the American republic would recognize no black or white sanction from God. In Baker's black 92nd Infantry Division, in Randolph's Brotherhood of Sleeping Car Porters, and in countless churches, blacks found it within themselves to treat a society torn by racism not as inherently, eternally damned but as nevertheless worth joining and redeeming. Blacks who thought and acted that way shared with whites an important belief: not, alas, a consensus that racism was wrong but a deep certainty that, despite it, they were all bound passionately to the promise of the nation.

But what was that promise? It seems a long time now since the Smothers Brothers crooned "The Lord is color-blind" to what CBS must have assumed was a reasonably receptive national audience in the late 1960s. Today many of us would think such an audience naive or hypocritical, if not racist; it is almost as if any assertion that color isn't important insults what has come to be known as black pride. It is almost as if we fear that if race lost all weight in our social equations or disappeared entirely through interracial marriages and offspring, we would have nothing of value to say or give to one another. The problem is not that racism has grown stronger; it is that American civic life has become weaker—and not primarily because of racism. If we find it difficult to say that a black person's color isn't important, that is because we no longer know how to say that being an "American" is important—important enough to transcend racial identity in a classroom, in a jury room, or at the polls.

"An individual's moral character is formed by narrative and culture," writes the sociologist Alan Wolfe. "Contracts between us are not enforced by laws or economic incentives; people adhere to social contracts when they feel that behind the contract lies a credible story of who they are and why their fates are linked to those of others." But what is America's story, when Vernon Baker's and Arlene Fox's descendants can climb to the very summit of the American Mt. Parnassus only to find there Dick Morris, *Vanity Fair*, Dennis Rodman, Time Warner Inc., and a retinue of dancing pollsters? The old American story of white manifest destiny, thankfully gone, was coherent enough to give blacks enough moral footing and traction to undo its moral affronts. By comparison, our new stories (the space shuttle *Challenger*? *Forrest Gump*? curricular gardens of multicultural delight?) are incoherent—much like Bill Clinton, truly a man of our time. In 1963, James Baldwin wondered aloud why any black American would want "to be integrated into a burning house." Obviously, he was not proposing resegregation. What, then? How were black Americans to think about themselves? Baldwin's emigration to France left the question open. And so have we all.

For a short while twenty years ago, Alex Haley's *Roots* seemed to offer an answer. Turning on an intrepid black American's report of an astonishing encounter with his African past, it promised to weave a recovered, emblematic black story into the American national narrative, whose promise, whatever it was, would become more coherent for resolving the contradictions in its black story line. The story of Haley's story is worth retracing, because *Roots* wound up demonstrating both that blackness has no reliable myth of its own and that the summit of the American Parnassus is bare.

Published late in 1976, *Roots* became the next year's top nonfiction best-seller (selling some 1.5 million copies in one year) after a record 130 million Americans saw the twelve-hour ABC miniseries it inspired. At least 250 colleges began offering credit courses based significantly on *Roots*. Travel agencies packaged back-to-Africa "Roots" tours. Even before TV had anointed Haley, I watched him tell a rapt audience of Harvard undergraduates, many of them black, of his meeting with the griot, or oral historian, of a village in Gambia from which, Haley said, his ancestor Kunta Kinte had been abducted to America in 1767. When he noted, as he had in the book, that the griot "had no way in the world to know that [his story's particulars] had just echoed what I had heard all through my boyhood years on my grandma's front porch in Henning, Tennessee," there were gasps, and then the packed Quincy House dining hall was awash in tears.

With this unprecedented return by a black American to the scene of the primal crime against his West African forebears—"an astonishing feat of genealogical detective work," Doubleday's original dust jacket had called it—the long, tortuous arc of black dispossession and yearning for a historic reckoning seemed, at last, to come home. *Roots* wasn't just Haley's own story; it was "a symbolic history of a people," he told a British reporter who raised doubts about its accuracy. "I, we, need a place called Eden. My people need a Pilgrim's Rock."

Indeed they did. The sudden lurch toward integration in the 1960s had disrupted old black coping strategies, scrambling the coordinates of an uneasy racial coexistence and confounding pious hopes for a smooth transition to the integration envisioned by so many of Baker and Fox's generation. Some white-ethnic Roman Catholics and Jews, who had resisted their own assimilation into Anglo-Saxon norms, now intensified the subcultural revivals of "unmeltable ethnics." Responding to these assertions and, at the same time, to the equally unsettling prospect of black dissolution into whiteness through integration, a retaliatory black parochialism surfaced in public life for the first time in decades, assailing blacks whom it deemed too accommodating and forcing even assimilationist whites to acknowledge their own hyphenated Americanism.

Appearing amid the confusion, *Roots* at first startled, then relieved, pessimists on both sides of the color line. By the grace of Haley's pilgrimage, it seemed, blacks could recover and share the true story of their dispossession. His mythopoetic triumph tugged at people's hearts, strengthening hopes for a decorous pluralism of peoples and a decent integration of persons. Americans of all colors were transfixed, even as charges emerged that Haley had taken too many folkloric and fictional liberties with material he'd claimed was historically true. (He settled out of court for $650,000 with author Harold Courlander, passages of whose novel *The African* Haley had pretty much copied.) Yet while *Roots* was denounced as a scholarly "fraud" by the historian Oscar Handlin, it was defended as an irresistible historical novel and pedagogical tool by other historians, including David Brion Davis, who told the *New York Times*, "We all need certain myths about the past, and one must remember how much in the myths about the Pilgrims or the immigrants coming here has been reversed." Haley received a "special" Pulitzer Prize and a rare "Citation of Merit" from a National Book Awards panel. ABC produced a second miniseries, *Roots: The Next Generations*, based on his new book *Search*, which chronicled his family's later tribulations and triumphs, including Haley's own work on *The Autobiography of Malcolm X*. "Now, as before," wrote Frank Rich in *Time*, "*Roots* occupies a special place in the history of our mass culture: it has the singular power to reunite all Americans, black and white, with their separate and collective pasts."

Today *Roots* is seldom mentioned. The History Channel's twentieth anniversary broadcast in February was little remarked by viewers or print commentators. The book is still in stores—Doubleday calls it "an important title on the Dell backlist"—but it's not much read in college or high school courses. Few books on American racial matters mention Haley (who died in 1992). "*Roots*?" laughs the black religion scholar C. Eric Lincoln. "It's disappeared! Alex Haley was my friend, and I can tell you, he was a journeyman freelance writer, not a political writer or historian. He was given a status he didn't expect."

Roots's virtual disappearance can't be explained with the observation that it accomplished its mission by transforming the consciousness of a generation. Nor is it enough to say that *Roots* shortchanged women by portraying them as passive helpmates; Haley's misconstruals have been redressed by Alice Walker, Toni Morrison, Maya Angelou, and others. What drained *Roots* of its power with blacks as well as whites was a disillusionment in at least three dimensions. First, Haley idealized an Africa and a blackness that had been so overwhelmed (indeed, defined) by European invasion that they flourished only as negations of whiteness. Second, so complete was this submergence that Haley himself idealized American blacks' white abductors, if only implicitly, by telling blacks' own story in Western terms. In doing so he met his third pitfall: he tried to skirt Western mythology's tragic sense of life by telling an upbeat story for the mass market. *Roots* became the next "myth for a day," turning immense historical pain into immense profit. That was what slavery had done, and it was what *Roots* was meant to counter. But Haley's TV-friendly, docudramatic tale of black dispossession subtly reinforced the moral neutrality of classical liberalism, where markets are stronger than myths and history is not so much falsified as tamed.

In Africa, Haley depicted a precolonial Eden that hadn't existed, created his account of Kunta Kinte's youth there more out of current anthropology than history, paired all of this with the tale of his own communion with village elders in postcolonial Gambia, and inflated black Americans' expectations of sub-Saharan Africa, past and present. For American blacks, there was no there there: "Whatever Africans share," writes the Ghanaian intellectual Kwame Anthony Appiah, "we do not have a common traditional culture, common languages, a common religious or conceptual vocabulary. . . . [W]e do not even belong to a common race . . ." When Americans making visits inspired by Haley's epiphanies got past their African hosts, they found strangers as indifferent or hostile to them as "fellow whites" in my grandparents' native Lithuania might be to me were I to visit there now—strangers who may resemble me racially but whose religion, myths, and current interests have little in common with those of my Jewish "tribe," which they drove out or exterminated in the 1940s. American Afrocentrists (and liberal whites) seeking a romantic, Pan-African foil to a racist America found the same "ethnic cleansing" furiously under way in Nigeria, Rwanda, Zaire, and the Sudan. The very designation "black" was no more useful a moral, political, or cultural identification than is "white" in Lithuania or the Balkans.

"Blackness" did have one use: as a foil to whiteness. It is hard to exaggerate—yet hard for some blacks to acknowledge—how overwhelming was the European presence in Africa. Even the work of such celebrated Pan-African writers as Wole Soyinka and Chinua Achebe presupposes what Appiah calls "the recognition that a specifically African identity began as the product of a European gaze." They write and are read almost exclusively in English and French.

Some apparently indigenous African traditions were concocted in response to, and sometimes with the tactical support of, white colonizers, and in order to construct so-called national liberation movements. Africans had to devise "national" identities with European military, economic, philosophical, and linguistic tools.

For Americans, especially, the tie to Africa proved, in the words of the black economist and social critic Glenn Loury, "an empty hope, all remnants and echoes." American black luminaries who pursued those echoes only to fall for African dictators' charms might do well to heed the black writer Albert Murray's comment last year on C-SPAN that the Jeffersonian idea that all are equal didn't come from Africa, where others were also enslaved. The blacks on the Underground Railroad "weren't trying to get back to the tribal life in Africa . . . they have no birthrights anywhere in the world except in America."

Black Americans' only coherent memories and myths begin in the holds of the slave ships to which other Africans had consigned them—a point that haunted Maya Angelou on a visit to Ghana, as she wondered whether some of her hosts' ancestors had arranged to sell her own.

By assigning two white men to kidnap Kunta Kinte, Haley wasn't just distorting African history (in which the majority of slaves were captured and sold to whites by blacks); he was juggling European archetypes, borrowing Western literary themes meant to appeal to whites as well as blacks. He formulated sub-Saharan Africa's diffuse cultural attitudes into a Western myth of "exile" or "pilgrimage" for a black American audience that had internalized such notions from the Old Testament and for other Americans who needed to understand, in both Christian and Enlightenment terms, what their own forebears had perpetrated or suborned. But the African slaves had no signs that an African god was punishing them for their sins with an exile like that of the Jews, or blessing their "errand into the wilderness" like that of the Puritans. *Roots* wasn't a product of its protagonists' own mother culture; it was the work of a thoroughly Western, Christian, American writer who took as much from Hebrews and Puritans as from Africans. The novel is a Western account of a monstrous Western crime—a crime only according to Western religious and political standards—that triumphed later to abolish slavery, as no African authority had done and as the Sudan hasn't done yet.

The irony, of course, is that the Western Enlightenment principles that supported African colonial liberation failed to prevent colonialism in the first place. And the ghastly, bloody misadventures in Europe since 1914 remind us that Western "values" often only ratchet up the human struggle with evil into unprecedented levels of barbarity. Even the notion that skin color is destiny derives from the ignorant scientific and cultural prejudices that draped nineteenth-century European imperialist states in all their clanking, blundering glory.

If there is any glory for the West in all this, it lies not in Western power but in Western thought, which projects triumphs out of tragedies and which, for all its misuses, nourishes the capacity for rational self-contradiction that alone has put such words as "democracy," "liberation," and "human rights" into the minds and hearts of peoples on all five continents. The West's true Eden is not Haley's bucolic African village but the garden in which a serpent corrupted two human beings with the apple of knowledge. Haley's distortions—like those of countless Western writers before him—misrepresented the West as much as they did Africa. When people of any color imagine their origins as racially pure and their heroes as morally infallible, they shrink from the tragic Western truth rooted in the story of The Fall.

They also misunderstand that if the West has any hope of improving on its work, that hope is in America. *Roots* showed, yet could not quite proclaim, that blacks brought as slaves into the American national experiment were so thoroughly uprooted from African sources that they were obliged to accept— for lack of anything else—the transcending liberal and Christian promises of their newfound land. Blacks internalized those promises and rehearsed their implementation long before Vernon Baker joined the 92nd Infantry Division in Italy. Precisely because they had not chosen to join this society, could not dominate it, and could not leave it, they had the highest possible stakes in redeeming its oft-stated, oft-violated ideal.

In that sense, surely, blacks became, for better or worse, the most "American" of us all. In a nation born of fraught departures, clean breaks, and fresh starts on new frontiers, they had to construct their moral universe, again in the words of Glenn Loury, "almost out of nothing, almost heroically, in the cauldron of slavery. Or, as my friend Nathan Huggins puts it, 'We're not an alien population, we're the alienated population. We're after getting our birthright. We're the son who hasn't been acknowledged.' See, that binds you. You can't turn back from it. Part of what I want is an acknowledgment of my place, my legitimacy, my belonging." The special depth of this need is what makes blacks "America's metaphor," as Richard Wright called them—moral witnesses to a selfcreating America, as well as the country's harshest, sometimes most nihilist, assailants.

No wonder whites at first felt relieved by the *Roots* story: it had an ending happy enough to make whites as well as blacks feel better about themselves. Although Haley didn't make much of the point in the book, white Americans had responded to black fortitude and resistance not only with cross burnings and guns but with the Abolitionist crusade, the great pedagogical project that sent W.E.B. Du Bois and hundreds of New England schoolteachers South during and after Reconstruction to "uplift" freed slaves. Despite all of their cruelties, condescensions, and overweening moral self-regard, white Americans participated in a civil-rights movement that combined black Baptist communalism with a race-transcendent, New England Calvinist theology of personal responsibility and justification by a faith beyond color.

So, if there was any real nobility in Haley's effort to weave blacks more vividly into the American tapestry—to make Kunta Kinte a mythic American like Paul Revere—it consisted of the tragic but potentially redemptive fact that the author had to use the abductors' language and metaphysical looms. If *Roots* hasn't helped a new generation of American blacks to fit itself into the national tapestry, we must find something else that can, for separating the black thread would harm all of us even more than hiding it deep in the weave, as we've done in the past. Even Louis Farrakhan knows this, no matter how strenuously he insists on the separatist claims of the Nation of Islam. Not for nothing did he hold his march on the Washington Mall, amid all those white monuments, rather than in the part of the Mississippi Delta that the enthusiasts of his predecessor, Elijah Muhammad, once designated as the provisional seat of the Republic of New Africa. Had Farrakhan gone there, many fewer black men would have followed.

Yet *Roots* failed to forestall the ascendancy of Farrakhan not only because Haley dissembled about Africa and juggled tragic Western myths to tell a black story but also because those myths are losing their traction against the forces of a global market that employs the techniques of mass marketing to guarantee the liquidity of collective amnesia. The relentless logic of the market overwhelms not only the worst racist pretensions, white as well as black, but also the best American civic cultural traditions. Commitments to reason, individual rights, and freedom of contract aren't "Eurocentric" ruses meant to co-opt and subordinate nonwhites; they embody historic human gains, and it would be folly to abandon them for fantasies of racial destiny.

When Vernon Baker said, "I knew things would get better," surely he did not think they would get "blacker" in the sense that blacks would become so protective of blackness that whites' enthusiasm at the prospect of Colin Powell's running for president would engender marked black ambivalence about it. Nor, surely, did Baker's "better" characterize extenuated rationalizations of Ebonics, gangsta-rap celebrations of black self-immolation, or widespread black support for O.J. Simpson's acquittal and the "black" jurisprudence and epistemology invoked to excuse it.

Similarly, when Arlene Fox said, "When a man does his duty, his color isn't important," she was not applauding some recent efforts to redefine "duty" in ways that make one's skin color one's destiny all over again. Three years ago, while defending race-norming in college admissions and a dizzying array of campus "diversity" programs that transform everyone with a dark skin into a walking placard for disadvantage, Rutgers University president Francis Lawrence slid, infamously, into lingo about blacks' "genetic hereditary background." It was an all too emblematically liberal Freudian slip, born of believing that the best way to overcome racism's legacies is to create separate, remedial tracks for blacks while denying that one is doing anything of the sort by enshrining and embellishing disparities as cultural "differences."

On the other hand: Colin Powell could yet become president, and Oprah Winfrey could own a movie studio; black candidates keep winning in white-majority districts, and more blacks and nonblacks are marrying, which explains why many of the novels in black bookstores are about multiracial relationships. Many blacks, in fact, have anticipated and met a challenge now facing everyone else in the country; we are all being "abducted" from our ancient ethnic moorings by powerful currents we no longer control or fully comprehend. Thanks significantly to blacks, who started from "nothingness" here, other

Americans have a better start on what now has become a more general problem. Europeans sometimes say that white Americans walk and talk "black."
The observation fits neatly with the feeling among some Africans that black
Americans are not "black" at all. America needs blacks not because it needs
blackness but because it needs what they've learned on their long way out of
blackness—what others of us have yet to learn on the journeys we need to
take out of whiteness.

For all its wrong turns and dead ends, the quest by black Americans or
acknowledgment and belonging in our national life is the most powerful epic
of unrequited love in the history of the world. "Afrocentrism," Gerald Early
has written, "is a historiography of decline, like the mythic epic of the [lost,
antebellum] South. The tragedy is that black people fail to see their 'Ameri-
canization' as one of the greatest human triumphs of the past 500 years." Even
if every broken heart could be mended and every theft of opportunity be redressed, there would remain a black community of memory, loss, and endurance. Yet the country's special debt to blacks cannot be paid by anything less
than an inclusion that brings the implosion of the identity of blackness—and,
with it, of whiteness. The most that blacks can expect of the rest of us (and
the most that Vernon Baker and Arlene Fox have expected) is that we will
embrace and judge blacks—and let ourselves in turn be embraced and judged
by them—as individual fellow participants in our common national experiment. As brothers, some used to say.

Aversive Racism and the Need for Affirmative Action

John Dovidio

*Affirmative action has become a hotly debated tool to counter racism. What
are the arguments for and against affirmative action? Does affirmative action require a deepening awareness of racial identity? Is this the opposite
of the "end of blackness" (and whiteness) proposed by the previous author?*

From *The Chronicle of Higher Education,* July 25, 1997, p. A30. Reprinted with permission of Jack Dovidio. All rights reserved.

What does awareness of "race" have to do with racism? What is to be done?

It is clear that court decisions and other moves against affirmative action in Texas and California have discouraged minority-group students from applying and being admitted to college, particularly to professional schools. Certainly we should re-examine preferential-treatment programs critically and carefully to determine their benefits and harms. But we also need to ask whether, as many critics of such programs suggest, the United States now can afford to pursue a color-blind approach to equal opportunity.

Over the past three decades, nationwide surveys have documented significant declines in whites' overt racism toward blacks, including expressions of prejudice, negative stereotyping, and resistance to racial equality. Nevertheless, substantial differences in the social, economic, and physical well-being of blacks and whites persist; the gaps in their income levels and unemployment rates are growing. Blacks continue to report greater distrust of government and other people than do whites. In one survey, for example, only 16 per cent of blacks, but 44 per cent of whites, felt that "most people can be trusted." These data, and similar empirical evidence for other minority groups, challenge the assumption that racial differences no longer are a critical issue for our society.

My own research on whites' prejudice against blacks calls into question whether racism has really declined as much as surveys indicate. Over the past 20 years, I have conducted research with Samuel L. Gaertner, a professor of psychology at the University of Delaware, that explores how overt racism has evolved into more subtle and perhaps more-insidious forms.

In contrast to traditional forms of prejudice, the emotional reaction of what I call today's "aversive" racists to minorities is not one of overt dislike or hostility, but rather one of anxiety or discomfort. As a consequence, aversive racists attempt to avoid interracial interaction whenever possible. And although they try not to behave in overtly negative ways toward blacks (which would threaten their self-image as unbiased), they frequently express their bias indirectly, by favoring whites rather than discriminating against blacks and members of other minority groups.

For instance, an employer influenced by feelings of aversive racism might subtly re-evaluate the most important qualifications for a job, depending on the race of different applicants. If, say, a white applicant had broader experience and a black applicant had more up-to-date training, the employer would decide that experience was more important; if the white applicant had more-recent training and the black more experience, the employer would decide that experience was less important. Thus, the aversive racist would find a way to hire the white applicant without admitting to himself or herself that racial bias played a role in the choice.

Because aversive racists consciously endorse egalitarian values, they do not show prejudice in situations in which discrimination would be obvious to others or to themselves. However, aversive racists do discriminate, usually unintentionally, when they can rationalize their actions in ways that apparently have nothing to do with race. Thus, as in the example I cited above, they will justify favoring one person on the basis of some factor other than race—for example, a particular educational background—or they will say the criteria involved are ambiguous, allowing them to favor a white person with, perhaps, better grades over a black person with better recommendations.

Another way in which aversive racists often unconsciously discriminate is by providing special favors or support—such as mentoring or special opportunities for promotions—to people with backgrounds similar to their own. This allows them to avoid thinking of the actions in racial terms.

Whites are most likely to manifest aversive racism by failing to help blacks or other members of minority groups, without any overt intention to cause them harm. In one study, for example, Samuel Gaertner and I found that when whites thought they were witnessing an emergency, they were just as likely to help a black victim as a white victim—if the whites believed that they were the only witnesses and that their personal responsibility was clear. But if whites believed that there were other witnesses to the emergency, and they could justify not helping by believing that someone else would intervene, only half as many of them helped a black victim as helped a white victim. The presence of other witnesses gave aversive racists the chance to justify not helping black victims without invoking race: They could let someone else help the blacks.

The subtlety and unintentionality of aversive racism can contribute to distrust and tension among racial and ethnic groups. Because aversive racists are unaware of their own prejudice and discriminate only when they can justify their behavior on grounds other than race, they tend to underestimate the continuing impact of race. They certainly dismiss racism as a motive for their own behavior, and they think blacks or members of other minority groups see prejudice where it doesn't really exist. Members of minority groups, in contrast, see aversive racists denying their own bias and yet sometimes acting in a biased fashion. As a result, it is not surprising that members of minority groups suspect that prejudice exists everywhere.

Critics of affirmative action frequently argue that "reverse discrimination"—in which members of minority groups are favored over whites who are equally or even more qualified—is now a greater problem than racism. Empirical research, including some of my own work, demonstrates that reverse discrimination does occur. However, it occurs primarily when the bias carries few personal consequences for the individual favoring minority groups. In more personally significant situations, discrimination against minority groups is still more likely to occur. For instance, we have found that white students favored the admission of qualified black students to colleges as a general principle, but were biased against qualified black applicants who sought admission to their own college or university.

Approaches to dealing with traditional, overt racism—such as passing laws that require desegregation—generally are not effective in combating the aversive racism that we see today. Simply providing color-blind equal opportunity is not enough, because aversive racists are not color blind. A growing body of research demonstrates that, upon meeting black people, whites immediately think first about the individuals' race rather than about other characteristics, such as sex, age, or socio-economic status. Thus, any negative stereotypes and attitudes that whites have about blacks are automatically activated. My colleagues and I recently have found that when whites see a black person, they experience negative thoughts and feelings even if the whites report—and often truly believe—that they are not racially prejudiced.

Three key elements of affirmative-action programs make them more effective against aversive racism than equal-opportunity policies are. First, affirmative-action programs are designed to assemble, in a self-conscious way that can counteract the effects of subtle bias, a diverse pool of fully qualified candidates for admission to educational programs or for employment or promotion.

Second, affirmative-action programs produce statistics that allow organizations to gauge their progress toward diversity. Systematic monitoring of racial disparities—for instance, in student or faculty attrition, or in the number of employees promoted above a certain level—can reveal the cumulative effects of aversive racism that might go unnoticed, even by the victims, on a case-by-case basis.

Third, affirmative-action programs focus on outcomes, not intentions. Demonstrating intent to discriminate is difficult in cases of aversive racism, where bias typically is not intended.

It is important for us to understand that although aversive racism may be unconscious, unintentional, and subtle, it is neither inevitable nor immutable. Significant changes can occur in individuals and society. Expressed racial attitudes have changed dramatically since Congress enacted civil-rights legislation 30 years ago. The personal, social, and economic well-being of blacks, women, and other traditionally disadvantaged groups has improved since the advent of affirmative action.

We should not delude ourselves, however, into thinking that equality has been achieved, that equity is now guaranteed, or that our society is beyond bias regardless of court rulings and other actions hostile to affirmative action. Racism is not a problem that will go away on its own if we ignore it, as more than 200 years of history prove. Proponents of affirmative action must work aggressively to find ways to get scholars' research data before the courts, because it is clear that we still need to combat racism actively and self-consciously. Good intentions alone are not sufficient to guarantee equality. Affirmative action is not a perfect solution, but it is still needed.

Index

About the Editors

Kevin Reilly is Professor of History at Raritan Valley College. He has also taught at Rutgers, Columbia, and Princeton Universities. He is the founding president of the World History Association and the author of numerous college texts and readers in world history, including *The West and the World* (1980), *Readings in World Civilization* (1995), and *Worlds of History* (2000).

Stephen Kaufman, Ph.D., is Professor of Anthropology at Raritan Valley College. He has taught at Queens and York Colleges at the City University of New York before coming to Raritan Valley. He is the founding director of the college's Holocaust and Genocide Studies Institute and still serves as a member of its advisory board. On a recent sabbatical, Dr. Kaufman studied at Yad Vashem in Israel and completed his work on the fate of blacks under the Nazi regime. A frequent traveler around the world, he has had ample opportunity to witness the consequences of racism as well as the positive changes in diverse cultures.

Angela Bodino is a professor of English with a background in literature and composition. She is an adjunct instructor at the Rutgers University Graduate School of Education, and a codirector of the National Writing Project site at Rutgers University. In 1998, she was named the New Jersey Professor of the Year by the Carnegie Foundation for the Advancement of Teaching and Learning, an award given by the national organization of the Council for the Advancement and Support of Education.